Madison Avenue in Asia

Madison Avenue
in Asia

Politics and Transnational Advertising

Michael H. Anderson

Rutherford ● *Madison* ● *Teaneck*
Fairleigh Dickinson University Press
London and Toronto: Associated University Presses

Associated University Presses
440 Forsgate Drive
Cranbury, N.J. 08512

Associated University Presses
25 Sicilian Avenue
London WC1A 2QH, England

Associated University Presses
2133 Royal Windsor Drive
Unit 1
Mississauga, Ontario,
Canada L5J 1K5

338.887
AN2m
133450
Sept.1985

Library of Congress Cataloging in Publication Data

Anderson, Michael H., 1945–
    Madison Avenue in Asia.

    Bibliography: p.
    Includes index.
    1. Advertising agencies—Asia.   2. Advertising
agencies—United States.   3. International business
enterprises.   I. Title.
HF6182.A78A5   1983   338.8'87   81-69878
ISBN 0-8386-3101-0

Contents

List of Tables

List of Figures

List of Illustrations

Preface

How has the rapid internationalization of advertising affected Asian developing nations bedeviled with chronic political instability and economic problems? Do the globally active, foreign advertising agencies help or hinder genuine national development in Third World Asia?

To address these questions, this book perceives the transnational advertising agency (TNAA) as a subset of the ubiquitous transnational corporation (TNC) and as an important nonterritorial actor in contemporary political and communication relations. The analysis focuses on the theoretical and political significance of the rapidly expanding TNAA as it functions transnationally and within three postcolonial free-market economies—Malaysia, Singapore, and Indonesia—and in relation to one centrally planned economy, the People's Republic of China.

The purpose of this book is to stimulate debate about advertising power relationships within and between these Asian nations and a few relatively strong, rich, industrially advanced nations, led by the United States—the home of Madison Avenue. The book was prompted by growing Third World self-questioning and concern that external influences, including advertising, constrain indigenous development and contribute to rising tensions and conflicts over political sovereignty, national policies and plans, and sociocultural issues. Through politically charged debates within UNESCO and in other ways, developing nations have spoken out about advertising imbalances and other communication inequities and the need for "a new, more just and more efficient world information and communication order."

This book is a recognition that advertisers, media practitioners, policymakers, and consumers cannot and do not live isolated from today's increasingly interdependent world and from different value systems. Also, it is a recognition of the "new order" controversies and processes and the necessity for greater international public and private attention to the policies and practices that guide how advertising and other aspects of sophisticated mass communication, including news, are defined, disseminated, and used.

To help encourage such debate and move advertising problems from the back burner of communication policy concerns, this book applies Johan Galtung's structural theory of imperialism to advertising, which is conceived of as a component of a larger, Western "development package" through which nations may influence others. The controversial concept of "advertising imperialism" is introduced as a particular type of communication exchange that fosters a general structural relationship that keeps some nations and some groups in harmony and others in conflict. Also, the present and changing character of the TNAAs is examined as a means to understanding advertising power and its political and nonpolitical implications for Third World nation building.

The heart of this analysis describes the contemporary transnational advertising structure within the global and Asian marketplaces. Because of Asia's vast size and diverse geography, languages, and cultures, generalizations are risky at best. Therefore, this book only skims the surface of Asian advertising and development concerns before presenting case studies of Indonesia, Malaysia, Singapore, and the increasingly outward-looking post-Mao China. Comparisons between TNAAs and indigenous advertising agencies are based on 1977–78 field research in Asia, including more than two hundred interviews with indigenous and expatriate advertising experts, and contact through 1981 with leading advertising industry representatives in New York and elsewhere. The more than a dozen TNAAs that operate in at least one of the four nations are examined for their global and regional patterns of growth.

Particular attention is given to America's dominant position over the massive, uneven flow of advertising internationally; the TNAAs' historically intimate ties to a few major TNC advertisers from the West or Japan; the evolution of modern advertising as a spin-off from past colonial patterns; Britain's role as America's closest advertising ally; the "go-between" function of predominantly Chinese Singapore and Hong Kong in advertising and other relations between the Asian hinterlands and the TNAAs and their home nations; and the inability of Japan—despite its burgeoning economic power—to exert much foreign influence through its few giant advertising agencies.

These findings suggest that the TNAAs do exercise power over value forming institutions and that advertising—at least in major parts of Asia, if not in the developing world generally—does exhibit the general interaction structure that Galtung's model hypothesized.

Finally, this book suggests the "real world," strategic implications that advertising dependency has for structural change. Policy prescriptions leading toward an integrated national advertising policy within a framework of the UNESCO initiated debates over the "new order" are suggested. The analysis concludes, however, that American hegemony over advertising is unlikely to change very quickly since those holding advertising power in both the industrialized and developing nations are generally content with existing development strategies and structures, which—for the advertising agencies—began emerging around the turn of the century when J. Walter Thompson of New York established a branch office in London. Progress toward more national, self-reliant advertising in these Asian developing countries (with China as a possible exception) at the least must await change toward people-oriented development theory and practice, which in turn must await greater mass awareness within and cooperation among developing nations themselves.

In the interim, the "Madison Avenue connection" in Asia will continue to characterize relations between a few industrialized and the many developing societies, and the debate will continue over whether foreign-influenced advertising obstructs or facilitates alteration of the various imbalances in communications and other relations today.

Credits

Acknowledgments

My interest in the advertising agency, that private organization which operates so actively outside its home territory, and in the important national and international political and communication issues raised by its existence was sparked by my association with several organizations.

The U.S. Peace Corps first got me interested in developing societies in Asia and thrust me headfirst into the realities faced by people trying to live a better life. My three years of experience (1968–70) with my Malaysian students, coworkers, and neighbors—first in a kampong in northern Peninsular Malaysia and later in Kuala Lumpur—helped immeasurably to reduce my ignorance of the causes of underdevelopment and to shape my ideas about "development" as something more than simply "economic growth" or "Westernization."

In Honolulu, the East-West Center's Communication Institute has provided a supportive atmosphere indispensable to the creation of this book. Besides providing a very generous grant allowing me to study at the University of Hawaii and conduct field research in Asia in 1977–78, and to participate in its communication policy and planning project, the Institute has given me a priceless opportunity to learn about the role of mass communications within diverse Asian cultures and diverse concepts of development. Dr. Syed A. Rahim, Dr. Jim Richstad and other researchers and students have helped make my Center experience meaningful and this work possible.

The Political Science department at the University of Hawaii has inspired me to question the basic institutions, including mass media and political institutions, that influence how people both live and how nation-states "develop." A special thank-you must go to Professor Robert B. Stauffer, who introduced me to the transnational corporation as a political actor and encouraged me to examine its Third World implications.

My appreciation also must be extended to those in Malaysia, Singapore, Indonesia, and elsewhere in Asia and in the United States who facilitated the work that led up to this book. In Kuala Lumpur, Mr. R. Balakrishnan and the important regional training institute he directs, the Asian-Pacific Institute for Broadcasting Development, made my time in Malaysia very rewarding. In Singapore, Dr. Kernial Sandhu, director of the Institute of Southeast Asian Studies, made me a research associate and provided first-rate support facilities. In Jakarta, the Indonesian Institute of Sciences (LIPI) and Dr. Astrid S. Susanto (of both the University of Indonesia and the Indonesian National Planning Agency) were helpful.

Thanks, too, must go to the institutions and individuals that provided information, and particularly to some two hundred advertising and other specialists who allowed themselves to be interviewed in person or to be questioned by mail. The Malaysian and Singapore Advertisers Associations and the Association of Accredited Advertising Agents (4 As) in both of these countries were particularly cooperative. Among the dozens of advertising agencies contacted in preparing this volume, Dentsu, McCann-Erickson, and Ogilvy & Mather were especially cooperative. The International Advertising Association, Starch INRA Hooper, and *Advertising Age* also warrant a special word of appreciation.

I deeply value my contacts with these organizations and, more generally, with communication practitioners, policymakers, and others interested in social marketing and advertising. Of course, I assume sole responsibility for all material in this book, which I hope will stimulate a new awareness of the power, problems, and possibilities of advertising for the developing nations of contemporary Asia. Also, I hope this volume will suggest that an adversary relationship between transnational corporations, like foreign-operated ad agencies, and their host countries does not have to be inevitable.

New York City

Introduction:
The Crisis in the Wide, Wide World of Advertising

> Advertising must be counted on as one of the more impor-
> tant forces in our present world. It is becoming a factor to
> be reckoned with on the international level, since those few
> countries producing the major part of advertising in the
> world can have a strong commercial/cultural impact on the
> large majority of other countries. American advertising
> stamps its imprint all over the world and continues to in-
> crease steadily.
>
> —The International Commission for the
> Study of Communication Problems[1]

These are hardly the proverbial best of times for the United States and the
mammoth industry of advertising in today's uncertain international communication and political environment, where nationalism and instability
are on the rise.

Despite the unmistakable fact that advertising has become a lucrative
growth industry in most countries and that the United States in the 1980s
continues to dominate advertising globally, change is in the air. Advertising's critics have never been more vocal, and the days of the free flow of
American-influenced advertising and trade could well be numbered if
public support for commercial communication continues to decline.

The fact that an antiadvertising climate is developing globally was dramatically illustrated during the early months of the Reagan administration.
In May of 1981, the United States stood alone against 118 other nations at
the World Health Assembly in Geneva when it opposed a resolution banning the public advertising and promotion of infant formula products.
Approved to protect children from the abuse or misuse of infant formula,
the international code of marketing of breast-milk substitutes pertained to
the dissemination of promotional material to the general public and was in
the form of a recommendation to be adopted by member nations.

Even before the controversial code vote was taken, two advertising experts in the United States had made a prediction:

The professional international advertising man, as we know him today, may soon be listed among the world's endangered species. The advertising profession is now in the process of losing its dynamic proportions, its sense of exciting creative exploration . . . and, if you will, its strength and ability to perform the very marketing functions which made it the driving force in so many developed and developing economies.[2]

The serious problems confronting transnational advertising run deeper than the obvious inflationary and other economic instability problems that plague virtually all societies today. The challenges extend beyond the rise of aggressive consumerism, or the trend toward smaller families, or the arrival of some sharply different and enticing life-styles that are being widely promoted through Western media. American scholar John Kochevar grasped the very real political problems facing the industry when he wrote:

Advertising is mass communication designed to inform people about products and encourage their consumption. It is intended to return short-term comparative advantages to its sponsors. If it also leads to hatred of the system, of advertisers and of the United States, then it portends its own demise. The contradiction is apparent. If people believe transnational advertising has an effect, it may be very important indeed.[3]

At the heart of the transnational advertising industry's disquieting future, then, are its increasingly uneasy relations with the governments of the "have not" societies over the possibility of change and over what constitutes national mass culture and the good life. The developing nations are in flux, to say the least, and governments have become increasingly assertive about their national interests and what is socially—and politically—acceptable as a form of commercial communication. To a growing number of governments in Asia (and elsewhere), the negative features of advertising seem to outweigh the positive (although it must be emphasized that social marketing and "noncommercial" uses of advertising by governments are increasing rapidly everywhere).

The crisis surrounding the influence and role of foreign influenced advertising—and news and entertainment—has resulted from an unmistakable exacerbation of tensions over political and cultural identity and over transnational corporate power. Much of the trouble has been reflected in the rise of complicated social legislation and communication policies and plans as explosive issues on the world's political agenda and in the serious questioning to which the traditional materialist definition of development has been subjected.

By the early 1980s, Western-based advertising agencies—like the international news agencies throughout the 1970s—had been drawn into the widening debate over the relationship of communication to power. Third World politicians, for example, were increasingly talking about the need for an international advertising code to reduce misleading or false advertising and about the need to find alternative sources of revenue for media so as to reduce dependence on private advertising. Concurrently, the advertising industry itself was only waking up to the magnitude of its political problems. Gradually, advertising practitioners from the West were becoming more sophisticated about arguing that their service industry was being undermined by dangerous bureaucratic and authoritarian forces at international, as well as national, levels.

Within many developing and industrialized societies, of course, advertising has long been subjected to harsh criticisms, but only very recently have these attacks become international and grown highly political and intensely threatening to "free press" and "free trade" concepts. Eugene H. Kummel, chairman of the giant New York–based advertising agency McCann-Erickson Worldwide, has recognized the industry's serious image problems in the 1980s:

> The problem of advertising's image has existed for many years. It is due in part, I suspect, to the apprehension people feel about any kind of persuasive activity. Also the fictional advertising characters of novels and of Hollywood movies haven't helped. But the attacks that have originated in the intellectual community are almost wholly based on ideology.[4]

Not unexpectedly, transnational communicators and businessmen argue that the industry is not comprised of power-hungry charlatans. They also maintain that advertising is very much a necessity rather than a luxury and that it encourages people to expect something better and helps cure economic ills. C. R. Devine, an executive of *Reader's Digest* and chairman of the International Advertising Association, has said that:

> Advertising is the cheapest and most effective method yet devised to achieve maximum distribution and sale of the world's goods and services. During the 1980s, it will do more to raise living standards in Asia than all the Stalin-type five-year plans governmental bureaucrats and economic theorists can devise.[5]

Advertising in the Global Village

Today, the stakes in the debate over communication resources and change are high. In fact, few international concerns are as frustratingly complex and politically and socially sensitive as the question of why advertising constitutes such a big problem between developed and developing nations and in international forums such as UNESCO or the UNESCO-appointed International Commission for the Study of Communication Problems (better known as the MacBride Commission).[6]

One basic reason is that the contemporary, postcolonial world order is in anything but perfect harmony. Despite the high ideals of cooperation and the symbols of global harmony expressed by various internationalists and in highly visible international advertising campaigns, the real world continues to exhibit dominance relations, great disparities of wealth, and sharply contrasting consumption patterns and life-styles. These are found both within and between societies. In international relations as in domestic affairs, long-standing patterns of power and of old-fashioned nationalism have not changed much since the end of World War II.

At the same time, however, the world seems to be moving uneasily toward transformation into one global system under a transnational power structure and one world economy. In this "global village," transnational politics appears to be replacing traditional nation-state politics, and governments of so-called sovereign polities clearly no longer have a monopoly over political and communication issues.

The trend toward greater solidification of dependent relationships has not gone unnoticed in the Third World, where demands for structural changes can no longer easily be discounted as mere rhetoric. Progress toward a "global shopping center" has increasingly been perceived with profound concern and frustration as evidence of further perpetuation of conflict producing forms of dependency and corporate dominance at the expense of the nation-state. It has helped give rise to Third World demands for the establishment of a new order in advertising and other communication areas, as well as in economic and political relations between nations.

What many in Asia and elsewhere in the Third World want today is not, for example, America's heavily promoted Coca-Cola. Many disadvantaged nations and individuals want something other than a continued reliance on foreign assistance, life-styles, entertainment, ideas, and goods—which Coca-Cola seems to symbolize almost everywhere—at the expense of mutual respect, social justice, cultural integrity, and sovereignty. Instead of emphasizing Western messages of materialism and economic growth, some developing nations are assigning greater importance to indigenous goods and services and media and messages; to change in the deeper, structural sense; and to self-reliance and problem solving as objectives of national development.

Third World dissatisfaction over a lack of power to decide its own development processes may be more strident and widespread than ever, but it certainly is not new. Complex interwoven forms of domination have historically characterized rich-poor relations and have evolved from a development model that reflects a predominantly one-way flow of Western industrial (predominantly American) values, beliefs, information, and institutions.

The transnational corporations (TNCs) and messages such as "Things Go Better with Coca-Cola" are strongly endorsed in such a model and are given a particularly important role within the transnational power structure that determines how both individuals and nations develop. In practice, the TNCs are major, nonterritorial actors in the global system, in which trade and capital flows are largely market-determined, and few issues are of greater controversy than the influence these giant entities have on host nations' development and on the workings of contemporary capitalism.[7] The term *transnational corporation* is used rather than *multinational corporation* to describe a private organization that conducts business in two or more nations and is controlled to a significant extent by a parent organization that pursues a more or less common, coordinated strategy wherever it operates. *Transnational* does *not* imply that either management or ownership is in the hands of several nations, and most TNCs certainly would not fit such a definition. The term does imply influence extending beyond conventional nation-state political boundaries.

An essential question that this book raises within the Asian context is exactly what effects these *external* influences have on *internal* aspects of a poor nation's political processes and overall national development policies and plans. This basic, inherently political question was posed by Richard J. Barnet and Ronald E. Muller in *Global Reach:*

> The colossal power of the global corporation to shape the societies of the underdeveloped world is not a matter for debate. The evidence comes largely from the corporations' own annual reports. But the burning political issue concerns the use of that power. Is the global corporation in the business of exploitation or development?[8]

The emergence of the "corporate village" concurrently with the late Marshall McLuhan's "global village" undoubtedly has made it possible for a few more people in poor nations to pursue consumption and affluence and gain access to foreign goods, mass media, and alternative life-styles, most of which originate in high production/high consumption societies in the industrialized West.[9] But the impact of the TNCs on the needs and aspirations of Third World masses living amidst scarcity and poverty is not always encouraging. The consumption gap between the few rich and the many poor continues. Progress toward reducing cultural shock, eliminating poverty and other forms of inequality, ensuring citizens' full participation in their nations' decision making processes, or fostering national, self-reliant action has been slow at best.

The debate generated by this book should help contribute to a better understanding of some of these consequences of today's world order and of Third World efforts to redress what are to them unjust situations.

Transnational Advertising Agencies

Any effort to understand why Third World nations are comparatively weak in a number of dimensions and why they behave as they do must take into account external forces, including the TNCs, which have vast economic and technological resources and function within a dynamic international market system based on unequal power relationships. Most of these transnational forces emanate from a handful of relatively strong, rich, industrially advanced nations and have various degrees of influence on weak, poor, nonindustrial nations.

This book focuses on the significance of one group of these private, internationally active entities, the transnational advertising agencies (TNAAs). As a powerful, particularly glamorous subset of the TNCs, the TNAAs operate within and between many developing societies to support and serve various components of the larger, transnational power structure. Inevitably, the TNAAs affect—and are affected by—the political, economic, and social environment within their host nations. The TNAAs' participation in the internal affairs of these societies seems sometimes to give rise to tensions over national development policies and plans.

Except perhaps for J. Walter Thompson (JWT), the large prestigious American ad agency, and Dentsu, the giant Japanese agency, the names of the TNAAs are not well known to the people in poor or rich nations in Asia (or anywhere else) that come into daily contact with their commercial messages. In 1981, for example, few outside the advertising industry itself paid any attention to the makings of a super-giant worldwide network affiliation begun when the world's first and second largest agencies—Dentsu and Young & Rubicam (Y & R)—established in Tokyo the first of what could be a number of joint ventures around the world.

The names and activities of other large advertising factories such as McCann-Erickson, Ogilvy & Mather International (O & M), Leo Burnett, Ted Bates & Company, and SSC&B:Lintas, are even less well known than the Big Three—Dentsu, Young & Rubicam, and J. Walter Thompson.

Despite the faceless nature of the TNAAs, they are immensely relevant subjects for careful attention. This is because advertisements are perceived as influential and are widely disseminated within and between societies, and their creation, production, and distribution has become a large and growing business. By 1980, total advertising expenditure worldwide had reached approximately $110 billion. The world's biggest advertising power, clearly the United States, controlled $55 billion—about half of this sum.[10] Also, the United States controlled most of the TNAAs, whose far-flung operations in advertising, public relations, and other communication and marketing fields could be found in many Third World, as well as First World, societies. To many of the TNAAs (and, obviously, to their TNC clients), the vast Asian region has become an increasingly important growth area.

Much of the massive "free" flow of advertising is created and monopolized by a few transnationals rather than by indigenous local or national advertising agencies.[11] The vast majority of the TNAAs are American owned or affiliated, and most have their global headquarters on or near

Madison Avenue in New York City or in one of only a few other business/communications/cultural/political centers—London, Paris, Tokyo, and Chicago.

Taken together, these TNAAs comprise an important, mobile, colorful, fast-growing, multi-billion-dollar segment of the global mass communications industry, and they have a significant overall impact on the international flow of communications in terms of who gets what.

Some suggest that with the rapid growth of these TNAAs and the international sprawl of advertising generally, the transnational power structure has acquired additional powerful weapons to bolster its position of dominance. The TNAAs are sometimes accused of reinforcing the transnational power structure by serving as instruments by which Third World nations can be penetrated and the status quo preserved to the continued detriment of the poor. However, little research has been done on this specific hypothesis of the hegemonic nature of transnational corporations in the advertising business or, even more generally, on the advertising/communication/cultural dimensions of the transnational power structure in Asia, or anywhere else.

A Theoretical Framework

This book will provide insight into these issues and concerns in Asia by using dependency theory, a framework that offers basic conceptual tools to analyze advertising or any other transnational exchanges between the "have" and the "have not" nations. It will present a critical analysis of the structure of transnational advertising, first globally, and then within three postcolonial, developing Asian nations: Indonesia, Malaysia, and Singapore. It then will examine how transnational advertising influences are beginning to be felt in the important Asian socialist nation of the People's Republic of China.

To accomplish these objectives, parts of Norwegian peace researcher Johan Galtung's structural theory of imperialism—with its intra- and international dominance/dependency relationships—will be applied to advertising in each of these nations.[12] Using his model as a means of trying to understand how advertising functions across national boundaries, each of these nation-state cases will be treated as a *Periphery* nation or subunit of a larger, transnational industrial system controlled by *Center* nations, particularly the United States, Britain, and Japan. With the exception of China, each of these Periphery nations is a former Western colony that gained political independence after World War II, and basically pursues the conventional Western growth model of development that encourages, or at least permits, TNAAs and other TNCs to do business and allows free market forces, like advertising, to play a major role in indigenous life.

China, of course, is very different from most other Asian developing nations, and it will be treated apart from the three Southeast Asian case studies.

The dominance of American advertising is fairly well known, or at least intuited, even among laymen. Far more important to this book, then, is the question of how particular TNAAs operate, especially over time, in different Asian settings, each of which presumably shares the "tensions" described in the Galtung model: the "harmonies of interest" and the "disharmonies." The case study technique was chosen as the most appropriate comparative method by which to study TNAA-related dynamics across several national contexts. Field research was conducted in Indonesia, Malaysia, and Singapore in 1977–78. The final analysis and updating was done in mid-1981 in New York City, where many of the world's advertising policies and trends are determined along that famous stretch called Madison Avenue.

Findings will be used to analyze transnational advertising patterns in the interactions between rich and poor, Center and Periphery nations. Consideration will be given to whether TNAAs in these Asian nations are agents of development and/or agents of foreign penetration working through local elites, as "bridgeheads," to constrain Third World development by maintaining superordinate-subordinate relationships.[13]

To systematically bring together these interrelated aspects of the TNAAs' activities outside their home nations, this plan will be pursued:

Chapter 1 will present the basic conceptual framework. Galtung's work will provide the suggestive model for the case studies. To date, the literature on imperialism has given little explicit attention to advertising or to transnational advertising agencies as parts of the apparatus through which the transnational power structure manifests itself and gives rise to tensions and conflicts in Asia or elsewhere. Chapter 2 will introduce some of the concerns that developing nations—and sometimes even industrialized nations—have about advertising and transnational corporations. Chapter 3 will explain on what basis Galtung's model is applied to contemporary advertising structures, processes, and mechanisms.

The next two chapters will describe the TNAAs—their structure, size, geographical distribution, clients, resources, and ideologies. Chapter 4 will sketch a global overview of the spread of advertising and specify exactly which corporations among the TNAAs are worthy of particular attention because of their sheer size or their presumed influence on the Third World. Chapter 5 will present an overview of the contemporary advertising scene in the vast, highly diverse, and politically important Asian region.

Chapters 6 through 9 will present a detailed discussion of transnational advertising in the three Southeast Asian nations of Indonesia, Malaysia, and Singapore, and in post-Mao China. Expanding upon the salient political and social issues that consistently seem to arise relating to TNAAs in the Third World, each case study on a particular nation will offer an overview of the unique setting within which advertising and the TNAAs must function and will discuss them in terms of sovereignty, national development objectives, and sociocultural considerations—each of which seems to be a major source of TNC-related tensions and conflicts in host nations.

Chapter 10 will discuss the First World and Third World advertising interaction suggested by Galtung's model and applied to these four Asian societies. Overall, this chapter will examine whether their advertising exhibits the general interaction structure that Galtung hypothesized. It evolves from the premise that the TNAAs play such a special role in Third World development that they deserve continuous, vigorous attention from scholars and policymakers, as well as from advertisers and professional communicators. The dominance/dependency relationships, particularly when applied to transnational communications and to the Southeast Asian context, are virtually unexplored, and their research and public policy implications pose exciting challenges for anyone interested in development issues.

Chapter 11 will offer some thoughts on what the nature of political change and the future of transnational advertising in Asia could be. Despite obvious external and internal obstacles, alternative development options exist in terms of organizations, structures, and corporate, national, and international policies. Some of these center around UNESCO's initiatives toward implementing the still-evolving concept of the "new world information order." Attention will also be give to examining why Periphery-nation governments—alone or in concert—might need to, or would want to, reduce dependence on the TNAAs.

Finally, a word needs to be said about the very real problems that researchers must confront in studying an institution such as advertising and its public consequences. Leo Bogart, writing about advertising, was correct when he observed:

> Research on a great social institution can never be conducted from the position of the Establishment. The only useful inquiry is an objective one. But to be objective, the researcher can hardly fail to be critical in spirit, to question all articles of faith, and therefore to risk appearing heretical to the high priests of the institutions which are the objects of his research as well as its patrons.[14]

Conducting a useful, objective inquiry into a transnational institution is an especially risky and challenging task. Getting "inside" private organizations like the TNAAs and collecting data about advertising relationships and interactions within and between Third World nations is particularly troublesome. There is little hard data about TNAAs generally and far less about their specific involvement in Asia, particularly in China where their

presence is a very recent phenomenon. The fact that the TNAAs are profit
making organizations that routinely pursue policies of corporate and client
secrecy creates enormous difficulties for intruding researchers or journalists who are most comfortable with a full range of neatly quantifiable data
and facts, as well as a firsthand feel for what happens in each unique host
nation.

Other factors also work against efforts to systematically get an insider's
view and to obtain very much cooperation from either the TNAAs themselves or the Third World centers of political and advertising power. The
"Establishments" of both Center and Periphery nations are understandably
on the defensive due to an increasingly hostile Third World environment.
All the problems that scholars have in systematically studying the management, structure, and organization of *any* TNC or *any* communications enterprise in a host nation apply fully to the TNAAs.[15]

Doing field work in Indonesia, Malaysia, and Singapore, then, required
resourcefulness and diplomacy in dealing with the various "high priests"
and with different political and cultural settings.[16] Several less than perfect
approaches to gathering data had to be used. In addition to the important
tool of direct observation, a combination of three methods—the "unobtrusive" approach[17] and the more traditional interview and questionnaire—
were used. For material on China, secondary sources had to be used.

Notes

1. International Commission for the Study of Communication Problems (MacBride Commission), "Interim Report on Communication Problems in Modern Society" (Paris: UNESCO,
September 1978), p. 37.

2. Dean M. Peebles and John K. Ryans, Jr., "Advertising as a Positive Force: Changing the
Advertiser's Role in the Consumer/Advertising Abuse Controversy." (Article prepared for
Columbia Journal of World Business, n.d.), p. 1.

3. John J. Kochevar, "The Effects of Advertising in the Developing Nations" (Paper presented at the International Communication Association Conference, Acapulco, Mexico, May
1980), p. 1.

4. Eugene H. Kummel, "A Time for Education" (Speech before the Central Region Annual
Meeting of the American Association of Advertising Agencies, Chicago, 13 November 1980),
p. 6.

5. C. R. Devine, "Imperative for Advertising in the New Asia" (Speech at the 11th Asian
Advertising Congress, Manila, 15 November 1978), p. 4.

6. In addition to formal debate within UNESCO and other UN forums, controversy
around matters of international communication in recent years has centered around the work
of the UNESCO-appointed MacBride Commission. Established in 1977 and chaired by Nobel
and Lenin Prize winner Sean MacBride of Ireland, the commission analyzed the totality of
"communication problems, in their different aspects, within the perspective of the establishment of a new international economic order and of the measures to be taken to foster the
institution of a 'new world information order.'" The commission's final report has been
published as *Many Voices, One World*. (Paris: UNESCO, 1980).

7. The work on transnational corporations is vast and continues to flourish. Perhaps the
best introduction to the numerous issues and complex questions surrounding TNC activity in
the Third World is found in Richard J. Barnet and Ronald E. Muller, *Global Reach: The Power*

of the Multinational Corporations (New York: Simon and Schuster, 1974). Other overviews are: Jack N. Behrman, *National Interests and the Multinational Enterprises* (Englewood Cliffs, N.J.: Prentice-Hall, 1970); Courtney C. Brown, ed., *World Business: Promise and Problems* (New York: Free Press, 1970); and Charles P. Kindleberger, *The International Corporation: A Symposium* (Cambridge, Mass.: M.I.T Press, 1970); Mira Wilkins, *The Emergence of Multinational Corporations and World Order, Sage Contemporary Social Science Issues* 2 (Beverly Hills: Sage Publications, 1972); entire issue of *The Annals of the American Academy of Political and Social Science* 403 (September 1972); entire issue of *International Studies Quarterly*, 16, no. 4 (December 1972); Department of Economic and Social Affairs, *Multinational Corporations in World Development* (New York: United Nations, 1973); Mira Wilkins, *The Maturing of Multinational Enterprise: American Business Abroad from 1914 to 1970* (Cambridge, Mass.: Harvard University Press, 1974); George W. Ball, ed., *Global Companies: The Political Economy of World Business* (Englewood Cliffs, N.J.: Prentice-Hall, 1975); Robert Gilpin, *U. S. Power and the Multinational Corporation* (New York: Basic Books, 1975); Jon P. Gunneman, ed., *The Nation-State and Transnational Corporations in Conflict, with Special Reference to Latin America* (New York: Praeger, 1975); Abdul A. Said and Luiz R. Simmons, eds., *The New Sovereigns: Multinational Corporations as World Powers* (Englewood Cliffs, N.J.: Prentice-Hall, 1975); Paul Streeten, "Policies towards Multinationals" *World Development*, 3, no. 6 (June 1975); pp. 393–97; Karl P. Sauvant and F. G. Lavipour, eds., *Controlling MNEs: Problems Strategies, Counterstrategies* (Boulder, Colo.: Westview, 1976); David Apter and L. W. Goodman, eds., *The MNC and Social Change* (New York: Praeger, 1976); and Lawrence C. Franko, *The European Multinationals, A Renewed Challenge to American and British Big Business* (Stamford, Conn.: Greylock Publishers, 1976).

Many of the TNC studies have had a business management slant, and researchers have been interested in such issues as their structure, their business strategies, and their problems with governments and unions. Typical examples are available in such business trade publications as *Fortune, Harvard Business Review,* and *Columbia Journal of World Business* and in the projects of such business schools as Wharton and Harvard. The latter, for example, has been conducting the "Multinational Enterprise Project" for more than a decade under Raymond Vernon. Several of his works deserve reading: *Sovereignty at Bay: The Multinational Spread of U. S. Enterprises* (New York: Basic Books, 1971); *The Economic and Political Consequences of Multinational Enterprise: An Anthology* (Cambridge, Mass.: Harvard University Press, 1972); and *Storm over the Multinationals: The Real Issues* (Cambridge, Mass: Harvard University Press, 1977).

For a more critical perspective, see: Stephen Hymer, "The Multinational Corporation and the Law of Uneven Development," in Jagdish N. Bhagwati, ed., *Economics and World Order from the 1970s to the 1990s* (New York: Macmillan Co., 1972); Robert B. Stauffer, *Nation-Building in a Global Economy: The Role of the Multinational Corporation,* Sage Professional Paper in Comparative Politics 01-039 (Beverly Hills, Calif.: Sage Publications, 1973), and "Transnational Corporations and Host Nations: Attitudes, Ideologies, and Behaviors" (Paper prepared for a conference on Transnational Corporations, sponsored by the Asian and Pacific Development Administration Centre (APDAC), Kuala Lumpur, Malaysia, July 1978); Harry Magdoff and Paul M. Sweezy, "Notes on the Multinational Corporation," in K. T. Fann and Donald C. Hodges, eds., *Readings in U. S. Imperialism* (Boston: Porter Sargent Publisher, 1971), pp. 93–115; Pierre Jalee, *Pillage of the Third World* (New York: Monthly Review Press, 1968); and Louis Turner, *Invisible Empires*(New York: Harcourt Brace & Jovanovich, Inc., 1971). For journalistic critiques of the TNCs, a periodical like the London based *The New Internationalist* is useful.

Numerous studies have been undertaken on specific TNCs or nation-states. Examples from these areas of the literature would include: Edwin M. Epstein, *The Corporation in American Politics* (Englewood Cliffs, N.J.: Prentice-Hall, 1969); Richard J. Barber, *The American Corporation: Its Power, Its Politics* (New York: E. P. Dutton, 1970); Kari Levitt, *Silent Surrender: The Multinational Corporation in Canada* (New York: St. Martin's Press, 1970); Anthony Sampson, *The Sovereign State of ITT* (New York: Fawcett Publications, 1972); Ralph Nader and Mark J. Green, eds., *Corporate Power in America* (New York: Grossman Publishers, 1973); R. A. Jackson, ed., *The Multinational Corporation and Social Policy: Special Reference to General Motors in South Africa* (New York: Praeger, 1974); Theodore H. Moran, *Multinational Corporations and the Politics of Dependence: Copper in Chile* (Princeton, N.J.: Princeton University Press, 1974); Charles T. Goodsell, *American Corporations and Peruvian Politics* (Cambridge, Mass.: Harvard University Press, 1974); J. D. Richardson, "Foreign Investment and Artful Nationalism; Some Political-Economic Generalizations and Interpretations of Philippine Experience" (Paper prepared for a conference on "The Political Economy of Development," Manila, December 17–18, 1974); Thomas P. McCann, *The Tragedy of United Fruit* (New York: Crown Publishers, 1976); and Robert Shaplen, "Annals of Crime: The Lockheed Incident" *New Yorker*, 23 January and 30 January 1978.

8. Barnet and Muller, *Global Reach*, p. 147.

9. *Global village* refers to the trend toward a shrinking world due to new technology, which has resulted in virtually instant global mass communications. *Corporate village* stresses the role played by transnational corporations in influencing development worldwide. The phrase is explained in Cees Hamelink, *The Corporate Village: The Role of Transnational Corporations in International Communication* (Rome: IDOC Europe Dossier Four, 1977).

10. Robert J. Coen, "Vast U.S. and Worldwide Ad Expenditures Expected," *Advertising Age*, 13 November 1980, p. 10. Coen, a senior vice president of McCann-Erickson, is a respected expert on international and United States advertising trends.

11. For an introduction to the structure of transnational advertising, see Michael H. Anderson, "Transnational Advertising Agencies: A Global Overview" (Paper presented at the East-West Communication Institute Advanced Summer Seminar on Transnational Communication Enterprises and National Communication Policies, Honolulu, August 6–19 1978); Karl P. Sauvant, "Multinational Enterprises and the Transmission of Culture: The International Supply of Advertising Services and Business Education," *Journal of Peace Research* 13, no. 1 (1976), pp. 49–65; and Herbert I. Schiller, "Transnational Advertising," in Thomas H. Guback and Tapio Varis, *Transnational Communication: Film and Television* (Paris: UNESCO, January 20, 1977), pp. 85–89.

12. Galtung is a highly prolific writer in the discipline known as peace research. A number of his papers appear in *Essays in Peace Research* and *Essays in Methodology*, published in 1975 and 1976 by Christian Ejlers, Copenhagen. Basic to Galtung's work on imperialism and "structural violence" is his "A Structural Theory of Imperialism," *Journal of Peace Research* no. 2 (1971), pp. 81–117. For a critique of Galtung's work, see Kenneth E. Boulding, "Twelve Friendly Arguments with Johan Galtung," *Journal of Peace Research* 14, no. 1, pp. 75–86.

13. The concept of "bridgehead" is used by Galtung and others in the dependency or structural school to refer to those Periphery nation elites who strongly identify with, and assist, Center elites and their organizations, including transnational corporations like the TNAAs, as they secure new markets and expand their Center-dominated activities in the Third World.

14. Leo Bogart, "Where Does Advertising Research Go from Here?" *Journal of Advertising Research*, March 1969, p. 12.

15. For examples of efforts by outsiders to study advertising agencies, see Joseph Bensman, "The Advertising Agency Man in New York," in Tunstall, *Media Sociology: A Reader* (London: Constable, 1970), pp. 202–17; David G. Lyon, *Off Madison Avenue* (New York: G. P. Putnam's Sons, 1966); Martin Mayer, *Madison Avenue, U.S.A.* (New York: Harper Brothers, 1958); John Pearson and Graham Turner, *The Persuasion Industry* (London: Eyre and Spottiswoode, 1965); and Tunstall, *The Advertising Man in London Advertising Agencies* (London: Chapman and Hall Ltd., 1964). For an insider's view, see David Ogilvy's *Blood, Brains & Beer: The Autobiography of David Ogilvy* (New York: Atheneum, 1978), and *Confessions of an Advertising Man* (New York: Ballantine, 1972).

16. Field research was conducted in Kuala Lumpur from March to June of 1977; in Jakarta from July to October; and in Singapore from November to January of 1978. In each nation I had an institutional affiliation: The Asian Institute for Broadcasting Development, Kuala Lumpur; the Indonesian Institute of Sciences (LIPI), Jakarta; and the Institute of Southeast Asian Studies, Singapore. En route to Malaysia, I visited Dentsu headquarters in Tokyo. Since 1980, I have lived in New York City and have had personal contact with major Madison Avenue ad agencies. I use "field work" in a broad, almost traditional anthropological sense to refer to my efforts as a researcher in Malaysia, Singapore, and Indonesia to systematically observe and participate in a setting as a means to better understand advertising and its relation to politics. My use equates understanding with intense and intimate direct observation since I feel that the transnational corporations are not a particularly favorable subject for researchers who wish to learn about a society through only surveys or interviews. The TNCs are too complex and too politically sensitive a research topic for traditional social science based on questionnaires and interviews.

Communication is another difficult research area. For a useful discussion of the problems of doing a study on the place of communication in politics, see Jay G. Blumer and Michael Gurevitch, "Towards a Comparative Framework for Political Communication Research," in Steven H. Chaffee, *"Political Communication: Issues and Strategies for Research,"* Sage Annual *Reviews of Communication Research* 4 (Beverly Hills: Sage Publications, 1975), pp. 165–93.

17. For a thorough discussion of "unobtrusive measures" as a creative alternative route to data collection, see Eugene J. Webb, Donald T. Campbell, Richard D. Schwartz, and Lee Sechrest, *Unobtrusive Measures: Nonreactive Research in the Social Sciences* (Chicago, Rand McNally & Company, 1966).

Madison Avenue
in Asia

Part I

Advertising's Transnational Dimensions

1
Advertising and Development

The study of the use of power in the past must be comple-
mented by an analysis of the distribution of power in the
present. The opportunities for development are conditioned by the functioning of the world economy in which
the underdeveloped countries find themselves. There are
some international economic forces which obviously tend to
stimulate development, but there are many other forces
which perpetuate inequalities and tend to retard development.

—Keith Griffin[1]

Broadly speaking, anyone studying advertising, transnational corporations, or other forces affecting power relationships and how nations develop can choose to analyze theoretical and practical questions within one
of several conceptual perspectives—the so-called traditional or mainstream
development perspective, or an alternative one. Galtung's research falls
within the latter evolving category of development work and offers a structural approach to the politics of making nations more equal to one another
and more immune to the impact of others' power.

One major perspective is the internationalist-modernization approach. It
is also widely known as the conventional, establishment, liberal-diffusionist,
Western, free world, or, simply, the American perspective. This approach
is based on the bipolar nature of societies: traditional-modern, preindust-
rial-industrial, noncapitalist-capitalist, backward-advanced, enclave-
hinterland, underdeveloped-developed, north-south, east-west, and so
forth. The modernization approach originated among structural-
functionalist American social scientists during the 1950s and early 1960s,
and its influence on scholarship (in the form of "nation-building" literature
based on universal theories and a linear view of development) and on
Third World development plans (largely in the form of transplanted Western institutions and economic growth policies) continues to be substantial.[2]

An alternative to this dominant intellectual package is the "dependency"
perspective.[3] It stresses the historic uses of power and other factors that

have created an interconnectedness between powerful rich and powerless poor nations and conceives of development in inclusive political, cultural, and social terms, as well as in narrow economic terms. Still emerging, this "dependencia" perspective has its origins in Latin America with the work of such critics as Andre Gunder Frank and has been a distinct approach only since about the mid-1960s.[4]

Originally economically based, Marxist inspired, and dogmatic, dependency theorists have gradually moved closer to mainstream liberal policy-making and academic thinking. Increasingly, this perspective is being used by United Nations and others international organizations, as well as by serious scholars and others from diverse developing and developed societies. Much of this research advocates alternative interpretations and responses—often in nationalistic and humanistic terms—to postcolonial global realities. Those working within such a world view maintain that the predominance of international structures and external influences has helped foster "underdevelopment," rich-poor nation and class gaps, the phenomenon of foreign dependence called neocolonialism, and the status quo.[5] In short, this dependency work on new perceptions and indicators of development looks outside as well as inside the nation-state for the causes of inequality within and between societies.

The modernization approach discusses the trends toward integration into a cosmopolitan, homogeneous "one world" and focuses its attention on the nation-state.[6] The latter is assumed to be an autonomous, independent, sovereign entity, since formal political colonialism has all but disappeared. This approach tends to blame internal constraints—traditional values, beliefs, and institutions—for keeping societies backward, irrational, low-achieving, or in other ways "inferior" to the rich industrialized nations. It argues that unless these barriers are removed through a uniform process of gradual change and diffusion of innovations, these latecomers will never catch up and become modern. Underdevelopment, then, is understood as an original state and as something every nation has to outgrow.

This framework presumes that Western industrial values, institutions, capital, technology, life-styles, communications, and planning can positively and, at best, painlessly help a poor nation to "take off," mature, and develop into a society more like the already modernized world of the United States, Western Europe, and Japan.

Both perspectives are controversial, greatly oversimplified, and—whether explicitly or implicitly, consciously or unconsciously—ideological. By the latter, I mean value-laden in that the scholar's or policymaker's approach is based on one political map, chosen from among many, which is used both to define the present and to provide a guide to a qualitatively different future.

Great controversies about explanations *and* remedies rage not only between but also within these largely incompatible ideological camps of development thinking and practice. Major factors separating the two perspectives are the different theoretical assumptions about basic units and levels of analysis, particularly the nation-state, and also different emphases on internal versus external variables influencing development.

The dominant paradigm has always emphasized the special importance of the "demonstration effect" of mass communications as a way of changing societies. Ithiel de Sola Pool, for example, has included advertising as an effective carrier of modern ideas:

> Advertising itself may also be a powerful instrument of development. It is a way of facilitating the distribution of commodities, broadening the market, and making people aware of possibilities with which they would not otherwise be familiar.[8]

The commercial media and the market, then, have been linked with other "modern" sector factors, including urbanization, literacy, GNP growth, TNCs and Western political institutions, as facilitating the benefits that will eventually trickle down to those who "play the game."[9] The assumption is that people who work hard will prosper and the leaders who accept the conventional development model and who maintain law and order will get ahead.

Since the early 1970s, scholars operating within this perspective have certainly become less glaringly ethnocentric and far more sensitive to Third World "new order" movements. This shift has been reflected in greater attention to the ideals of global interdependence and the need for both rich and poor nations to develop mutually advantageous partnerships and cooperation.[10] But the basic assumptions about development as an end rather than a means have not changed, and the emphasis on Western-style economic growth, industrialization, foreign investment through TNCs, foreign-influenced communications, and capital-intensive technology continues. The perspective assumes that any trend toward greater interdependence is good for a finite world's development because the basic rules of the game under which a few nations maintain control have not changed. While the dependency perspective concludes that basic structural changes are needed in the global order, the modernization approach understandably presumes that the basic system will and should remain intact and that pressures for change should be resisted or channeled toward greater internationalization or denationalization. Such an interdependency stance is disconcerting to nations that are still trying to define their unique national identity and that value goals such as self-determination, independence, and affirmation of their national personality.

Compared to the dominant modernization paradigm, the dependency perspective is less well established, but it is growing in scientific respectability and in political influence. The latter development has occurred as increasingly vocal, politically conscious Third World nations—individually and collectively—have sought alternative explanations for the existing pat-terns of power that make them relatively weak. They also want policy and strategy options that would help put them in a position to function other than as "dependent partners," "docile clients," or, very occasionally, "disci-plined rebels."[11]

Analytically, proponents of the dependency perspective concentrate on the global system, which is interpreted as a dynamic unit under which nation-states function as nominally independent subunits. External factors have contributed to contemporary imperialism, which is responsible for a situation in which poor nations are conditioned by rich nations.[12] Depen-dency theorists maintain that nations cannot achieve autonomy or self-development until deep-rooted structures in the unequal total global system are fundamentally changed, and equality of distribution is empha-sized over economic growth. They conclude that development is not simply an easily quantified evolutionary transformation that all societies pass through en route to a predefined end.[13] According to these theorists, heterogeneity exists among nations, and the experiences of Europe and the United States are fundamentaly different from, but intimately connected with, those confronting the developing nations.

The dependency perspective explains that, over time, complex patterns have combined to make—and keep—Third World nations (the Per-ipheries) relatively weak vis-à-vis industrial societies (the Centers or "met-ropoles"). The actions of both territorial and nonterritorial actors, including the TNCs, foster an asymmetrical situation based on inequalities both between and within nations. Poor societies have been penetrated by, and subjected to, various dynamic processes and pressures that mix to-gether and reinforce one another to form a cohesive transnational power structure that controls patterns of interaction and exchange and affects how nations develop.[14]

The theories of the dependency perspective certainly differ from, and pose a challenge to, those of the dominant, ahistorical, diffusionist ap-proach that I have called "internationalist-modernization." The latter approach places great importance upon the need for strong linkages and increased integration as a means of preserving the status quo. The depen-dency approach, on the other hand, questions the assumption that the free flow of outside, modern forces is the route to solving the problems of a weak, industrially poor society. It generally concludes that imported West-ern institutions and values intentionally or unintentionally generate depen-dency and function as a hindrance to the development of genuinely independent nations. The perspective maintains that unless the complex structural obstacles created through a historical process of foreign penetra-tion are overcome, nations will never be autonomous or self-reliant.

The major reason for choosing to examine TNAAs from the depen-dency perspective is a belief that the dominant paradigm simply has not worked very well to explain why some nations today are more successful than others at achieving development. The modernization perspective has given insufficient attention to the "costs" of external influences such as the TNCs or advertising. Nor does the modernization paradigm explain why mass poverty, unemployment, and other forms of inequality and socio-political tension continue despite economic growth in many poor nations.[15]

By the end of the Development Decade of the 1960s, the dominant paradigm, with its traditional emphasis on a growth model and on high levels of private consumption (stimulated by Western-style advertising and other free market practices), was under heavy attack from both skeptical scholars and frustrated policymakers. These critics, including a growing number of those who had helped pioneer the perspective, increasingly discovered that it is vulnerable because it is elite-oriented, culture-specific, superficial, ahistorical, and ethnocentric in favor of copying Western institutions, technology, consumerism, reliance on foreign luxury goods and expertise, and so forth. In particular, the role of mass communications and advertising has come under attack as people have belatedly realized that the media are not the great positive change agents or the magic multipliers that many experts thought and that many people were led to believe.[16]

Throughout the 1970s and into the 1980s, a growing number of scholars and policymakers began to perceive the conventional development perspective as supporting essentially conservative models of development that placed too much emphasis on *things* and *stability* rather than on *people* and *change*. The thrust of much of the criticism was that the modernization perspective had taken the human dimension to much for granted and had failed to give sufficient consideration to the fact that every nation had its own needs and operated within a unique cultural and historical environment, while at the same time existing in a larger international setting that was heavily influenced, if not dominated, by Western values and institutions.

Robert B. Stauffer's observation about the continued influence of the American model in Southeast Asia and elsewhere in the Third World is fitting:

> There elites who have been richly rewarded for their steadfastness to the model continue to advance its themes of gradual change, openness to private foreign investment, political stability, protection of established distributive patterns, acceptance of dependence on the industrial nations for their technology and their pace of industrialization, etc. Many of these true believers in Southeast Asia energetically compete with one another in proving their continuing adherence to the model. In so doing they merely duplicate behavior patterns common elsewhere in the Third World.[17]

The world's thinking about development continues to be heavily influenced by the traditional model despite significant empirical evidence that American-style development has not produced the expected benefits, and regardless of the torrent of contemporary work attacking the dominant paradigm and "growth without development," and significant post-Vietnam War and post-OPEC political and economic factors that have stimulated new multiple development models as well as some institutional reforms.

Advertising, private foreign investment in the form of transnational corporations, and mass media are important influences enmeshed in the global system and directly related to national development in rich and poor societies. Each of these influences is assigned an important role within the Western development model and is a factor in the consumption oriented patterns and life-styles emerging in the Third World under the control of communications and marketing processes.[18]

Galtung's Theory

In the power game of nations, some stronger players have always controlled others, and dominance, not equality, has been the rule.

In contemporary world politics, the many Third World nations are weak, poor, and vulnerable compared to the few affluent, economically advanced, highly industrialized First World nations. This relative lack of power is not merely the result of dependent nations having fewer political, military, economic, cultural, and communications resources. It also has very much to do with the quality of the alternatives a nation faces. The result of poor nations being placed in such a structural relationship is their dependency on the First World. Through complex mechanisms that can erode autonomy, poor nations are at a disadvantage in their interactions with rich nations and in their domestic efforts to implement long-term development strategies.

The major reason for postcolonial politics being this way is that these underdog Third World societies historically have systematically been subjected to dynamic processes and pressures. These reinforce one another, and the result is a cohesive transnational power system that controls the world economy as a totality. Increasingly, nonterritorial actors such as the transnational corporations have been prime mechanisms through which dominance is maintained. Under such a system, Third World nations' development patterns and policy options are limited, and the existing structure tends to be reinforced in subtle ways and on a daily basis.

Galtung has theorized that a complex structure of dominance, more than anything else, has resulted in asymmetrical relationships of exploitation and penetration in which some nations—socialist, as well as capitalist—have more "power-over-others" and more "power-over-themselves" than other nations. This latter distinction is particularly important because it has to do with the way nations may counteract power from stronger nations. Galtung has explained:

> balance of power is not the only approach to countervailing power. There is also "autonomy," which can be seen as power-over-oneself, the ability to set goals that are one's own, not goals one has been brainwashed into by others, *and* to pursue them. A person, or a nation, may be lacking in power-over-itself not only because it is the object of power-over-others—but also for lack of internal development, of maturation into autonomy.[19]

According to Galtung's theoretical perspective of power, imperialism is "a sophisticated type of dominance relation which cuts across nations, basing itself on a bridgehead which the center in the Center nation establishes in the center of the Periphery nation, for the joint benefit of both."[20] Inherent in the theory is the notion that imperialism does not just happen. There are reasons, not unconnected to the old "divide and rule" principles, why Center nations have imposed certain structures on Periphery nations, why such a situation has existed historically, and why it continues to be self-maintaining today even though actual direct occupation by Center nations is old-fashioned and has all but disappeared. Galtung has argued:

> Obviously, the more perfectly the mechanisms of imperialism within and between nations are put to work, the less overt machinery of oppression is needed and the smaller can the center groups be, relative to the total population involved. *Only imperfect, amateurish imperialism needs weapons; professional imperialism is based on structural rather than direct violence.*[21]

For this study, I will use Galtung's definition of imperialism as a relation between a Center nation—an obviously strong, big power nation like the United States—and a Periphery nation—an obviously weak nation like Indonesia—in which "the Center nation has power over the Periphery nation, so as to bring about a condition of disharmony of interest between them." More specifically, Galtung has maintained that:

> Imperialism is a relation between a Center and a Periphery nation so that (1) there is a harmony of interest between the center in the Center nation and the center in the Periphery nation, (2) there is more disharmony of interest within the Periphery nation than within the Center nations, (3) there is disharmony of interest between the periphery in the Center nation and the periphery in the Periphery nation.[22]

Galtung's structure of imperialism is illustrated as a two-nation construct in figure 1. The idea of this model is the linkage of inter- and intra-national relations with master-servant inequalities and alliance formations at several levels. The Periphery nation serves the interests of the Center nation; the Periphery's center, as a local elite bridgehead, serves the interests of the

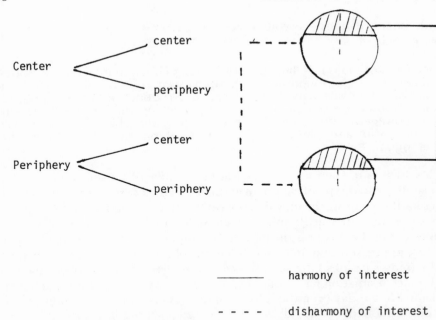

Center <   center
                periphery

Periphery <   center
                 periphery

—————— harmony of interest

- - - - disharmony of interest

Fig. 1. The Structure of Imperialism in Galtung's Theory. (SOURCE: Galtung, *A Structural Theory of Imperialism*, p. 84.) Reprinted with permission of *Journal of Peace Research*, International Peace Research Institute, Oslo, Norway.

Center nation; and the periphery in the Periphery are used to mutual advantage of both the elites in the Periphery and the Center as a whole. This arrangement means there is more conflict, or disharmony, of interest in the Periphery than in the Center. In short, the elites of both types of nations are tied together in one system, and they use various interactions to enrich themselves at the expense of other nations and groups. The centers in the Center and in the Periphery are partners and have an alliance, as privileged "top dogs" in their respective societies, that keeps their standards of living closely interrelated. At the same time, the periphery in the Periphery is always kept in its place in the lower strata.

Also, inequality is maintained by a feudal interaction structure that basically reinforces the status quo by keeping the periphery from interacting easily with other peripheries *or* with more than one Center. The gaps of inequality, the minimal amount of multilateralism, and other interaction-induced differences between rich and poor nations, then, cannot be eliminated very easily because of these general structural relationships, which are based on a combination of fragmentation and exploitation.[23] In such a situation of structural violence, the Periphery nations, and particularly the common people within these nations, are obviously at a disadvantage and have great difficulties organizing themselves to change anything.

The importance of Galtung's basic framework is that it stimulates both conceptual and practical questions about inequality within and between nations and about the dynamic processes introduced into the Third World from the outside. His theory offers a flexible, comprehensive explanation of how relations and consequences evolve from various influences external to a Periphery nation. It suggests that a more subtle dominance system than formal colonialism is in evidence and continues to exercise various degrees of power over Periphery nations, many of which are ex-colonies that have a history of close association and cooperation—not dissociation—with "their" Centers.

Military imperialism is the most obvious type of domination by a Center nation, but it is only one form of domination. Galtung cites four other types of imperialism and exchange that occur between Center and Periphery nations. Economic systems, political systems, culture, and communications mutually reinforce one another and generate vertical interaction relations. In such relations, there is often an imbalance in the flow of exchange between two nations. More important, there also is a difference in the far-reaching effects such a flow has *within* each nation. Both the Center and the Periphery may benefit from an exchange, but the enriching effects within the Periphery are distributed unequally. Bridgeheads in the Periphery gain at the expense of their masses, and the Center gains at the expense of the Periphery because it imposes its standards of processing on the less sophisticated nation that provides raw materials. Table 1 shows the vertical nature of interaction between the Center and the Periphery. Not only do these two types of unequal nations exchange different things, but they also play very different processing roles, with the Center giving the commands and the Periphery reacting.

The multidimensionality of Galtung's model is important because it emphasizes the pervasiveness and the complexities of Center nation power and its constantly changing nature. No one type of domination is more

Table 1

The Five Types of Imperialism

Type	Economic	Political	Military	Communication	Cultural
Center nation provides	processing, means of production	decisions, models	protection, means of destruction	news, means of communication	teaching, means of creation - - autonomy
Periphery nation provides	raw materials, markets	obedience, imitators	discipline, traditional hardware	events, passengers, goods	learning, validation - - dependence

SOURCE: Johan Galtung, "A Structural Theory of Imperialism," p. 92. Reprinted with permission of *Journal of Peace Research*, International Peace Research Institute, Oslo, Norway.

important than the others, but Galtung has stressed the importance of communication in enabling a Center nation to transfer its "ideas, goods, and bads" to the Periphery.[24]

In the context of this study, Galtung's framework is particularly appropriate since it recognizes the growing importance of communication and the transnational corporations as links between the centers in the Center and in the Periphery. For example, Galtung has contended that communication—whether in the form of "hardware," such as satellites, or "software," such as mass media messages—and the TNCs (presumably including strategically located service organizations like the TNAAs) are major weapons in emerging patterns of "professional imperialism." Such tools seem ideally suited to maintain less direct and concrete types of contemporary imperialism and relations of deep dependence.

Galtung's scenario of world order must be seen *structurally,* not as a "devil theory" that interprets reality in terms of a few rich capitalistic nations of the West that are motivated to conquer the world through brutal, punitive, or any other kind of power.[25] Galtung has maintained that the present global structure is "very similar to the colonial pattern" of the past, but he also has rejected impugning Center motives by carefully cautioning:

> The whole conception underlying nonterritoriality will have a northwest color or imprint. Dominant personnel will be taken from that region, sources of finance will have to be found there, and so on. But this should not be seen as a deliberate, Machiavellian plot to engulf the rest of the world, using nonterritoriality as the machinery of neocolonialism just as territoriality was used for colonialism, with a chain of bases and supply points reaching out to the colonized periphery. One should rather see it structurally, in terms of the post-industrial Northwest having to expand to make the neo-modern socioeconomic system meaningful at all.[26]

Galtung's concept of imperialism, then, is not only rich and complex in terms of relations and structures, but it is also general. It rejects the simple notion that the elimination of one important element, such as private capitalism, would eliminate *the* cause of imperialism.[27] Instead, it stresses the idea that the end of one type of imperialism, say political, will *not* bring about the end of other types.[28]

Also, Galtung's imperialism is not solely limited to the industrial capitalist world. Galtung and other structural theorists have borrowed from Marxist thought and included the traditionally important economic dimension. But Galtung's concept of inequality and structural violence through military, political, economic, communication, and cultural control certainly also applies to Communist and socialist nations, where Center nations such as the Soviet Union and elite groups use socialist imperialism to exercise power over the weak and the poor.[29] Just as mass media, classes, and industries exist as part of the distribution system in the centrally planned societies, so, too, can "imperialism." The Soviet Union, for example, has a state owned advertising agency that functions somewhat along the same lines as privately owned agencies within the individualistic, capitalistic, free-market economies.[30] In any society, advertising can be structured to address certain practical problems related to creating demand and to providing information. It can also serve special interest groups and foster intranational inequality.

In addition to theoretical importance, Galtung's model has obvious policy implications for Third World policymakers and transnational corporate practitioners interested in taking (or preventing) actions to make nations more equal to one another. "Dissociative" and "associative" policies have the potential to move nations away from conflict, and the options for action range from total isolation to total integration. But regardless of the policies pursued, nations must pay various costs and run various risks as they struggle with development strategies within the limitations of the existing world order.

Advertising Imperialism

In communication, as in many other areas of relations between nations, today's world consists of rich and poor nations. Recognition of this fact and of the general importance of information as a critical source of power within the dynamics of the global system has been underscored by Juan Somavia:

> It is only recently that the *communications-advertising-culture dimension* has begun to make itself evident as an integral part of the transnational instrumentality. It is becoming increasingly clear that the transnational communications system has developed with the support and at the service of the transnational power structure. It is an integral part of the system which affords the control of that key instrument of contemporary society: information.[31]

This book is concerned with the advertising dimension of the transnational power structure, and *advertising imperialism* is used to mean the way in which advertising exchange between nations is structured internationally with the effect that some nations may dominate other nations and create a disharmony of interest between them. It is one way in which advertising-rich Center nations penetrate into, and maintain a hold over, weaker Periphery nations whose indigenous communications resources are less sophisticated. Through local advertising and local elites tied to foreign interests, the transnational power structure is able to use information and persuasion to maintain influence over the Third World. The concept implies great, as well as unequal, power over advertising in and between nations. It also implies that the development goals of Center and Periphery nations are incompatible, even though these societies are closely coupled.

Advertising imperialism, then, is a relation between a Center and a Periphery nation in which:

1. The Center exercises domination by imposing a certain advertising structure on the Periphery, and
2. The Center penetrates the Periphery by creating a center of local, internationalized elites to serve as a bridgehead for the Center in its advertising spillover into economics, politics, culture, and other areas within the Periphery society.

In Galtungian terms, advertising imperialism is a subtype of communication imperialism, one of the five types of exchange between Center and Periphery nations. Like the transnational political, military, economic, and cultural dimensions of imperialism, advertising generates interaction patterns that use two mechanisms of imperialism:

1. The principle of *vertical interaction relation,* which is the major source of inequality within and between nations. Periphery nations are integrated into an asymmetrically structured world in which advertising decision making and processing occur based on an unequal division of labor in which some nations make the major, most complex decisions and other nations carry them out. The repercussions of advertising exchange are unequal for elites and peripheries because of their differential access to advertising resources. The peripheries are at the bottom of the pyramid, with their interactions mediated from above.
2. The principle of *feudal interaction structure,* which reinforces inequality within and between nations through "divide and conquer" activities that prevent Periphery nations from organizing themselves effectively to overcome their advertising underdevelopment. Such a structure fosters dependency of the Periphery on the Center for advertising through a concentration of advertising trade partners and a commodity concentration. This means that a Periphery nation will have most of its advertising interaction with "its" Center and that its trading commodities, the raw materials that it exchanges with the Center, will be few in number. Through such a structure, the Center is protected from the Periphery, and long-established colonial interaction patterns are maintained.[32]

Historically, then, advertising imperialism is related to a general structural relationship of colonialism between rich and poor nations and to different forms of imperialism that have contributed to great inequalities of advertising power deriving from what a nation is, something a nation has, and the nation's position in the transnational advertising power structure. Just as they can influence weaker nations' governmental, mass media, and business structures, Center nations also can influence Periphery nations' advertising. The TNAA, as a subset of the TNC, functions mainly as a conveyor of advertising influences from the Center to the Periphery through which various centers can be tied together.[33]

Compared to other types of imperialism, advertising imperialism arrived relatively late on the global scene since it has had to rely so heavily on relatively modern communications technology and mass media channels, particularly television. In many Third World nations, the TNAAs have only been present since about the 1960s, although foreign influence on advertising through other organizations goes back much further. Advertising as an institution and the TNAA as a type of international business organization have been integral parts of the Western development package that has been widely disseminated in the post–World War II period. Transnational advertising thrives on the practice of "free flow"—the idea that nations must keep their borders reasonably open to foreign ideas, whether in the form of advertisements, news, entertainment, products, education, personnel, technology, and so forth.

The overall result of such massive flows is that Periphery nations view reality largely through the eyes of the Center. Galtung has emphasized this important point with reference to the flow of news:

> The Periphery nations do not write or read much about each other, especially not across bloc borders, and they read more about "their" Center than about other Centers—because the press is written and read by the center in the Periphery, who want to know more about that most "relevant" part of the world—for them.[34]

In the case of advertising, similar exchange and perception patterns seem likely. Galtung's framework suggests that advertising materials from a few Center nations are seen as most relevant by Periphery nations' advertising industries. Consumers in such societies have frequent contact with imported and TNAA-produced materials. Even if such advertising materials are entirely locally produced, they tend to be created by local branches of the TNAAs and, therefore, have a degree of processing through Center expatriate eyes or Center-trained local eyes.

In short, the consequences of advertising imperialism would seem to be that a few produce advertisements, while many consume them; interaction generally is one-way (Center to Periphery, West to East, North to South, rich to poor, urban to rural, etc.); and the substance of the messages is often a standardized commercial product that can be packaged and widely syndicated by the TNAAs.

If Galtung's theory accurately reflects advertising reality, the Center penetrates Third World nations through the active presence of TNAAs. In turn, these foreign business organizations have bridgeheads in the Periphery that they have recruited to work on their behalf as "transmission belts" for value (such as profits, services, market data, creative ideas, etc.) forwarded to a few Center nations, where the TNAAs' headquarters are concentrated.[35] Such bridgeheads are integrated into a division of labor, and they share a harmony of interest with their metropoles. Their consumption patterns, high education, personality traits, advertising skills, and relatively high incomes make these internationalized elites much closer to Center elites than to their own nations' masses. As the TNAAs prosper in a given host nation, so, too, do the bridgeheads in their capacity as local agents for the Center. Enclaves of these elites consist of specialists who sell their services to the TNAAs, politicians and government officers who make it possible for the TNAAs to operate as official guests in a Periphery nation, and media owners who provide channels through which the TNAAs may disseminate their commercial messages.

Advertising bridgeheads, if they function like Galtung's ideal, should operate as denationalized subcenters and should see themselves "more as partners of the center in the Center than as partners of the periphery in the Periphery."[36] The result should be intra-Periphery conflict in which local elites linked to the TNAAs have goals different from those of other citizens, including those local elites *not* directly benefiting from the TNAAs' presence and the masses in the more traditional sectors. Obviously, those who are privileged and included in any alliance of Center center and Periphery center groups do not want to give up their power and relatively high living standards, and they strive to maintain the status quo by supporting continued policies of integration and association with the Center. They resist efforts to pursue alternative development policies and goals that would mean dissociating with the Center and thinking of development in terms of "autonomous" or "auto-centered" processes whose objectives emphasize improving the quality of life of the masses.[37] Also, they support law-and-order policies that work to foster structural violence by containing those forces advocating changes in the Periphery's internal power structure.

Strong nations might be gaining from their dominant relationships with poor nations, but without these bridgeheads personally associated with the TNAAs, advertising imperialism cannot exist. These local advertising elites, as a species of bridgehead, are indispensable to the model. They help maintain a relationship in which there is disharmony of interest within both Center and Periphery nations, and in which "there is more disharmony in the Periphery nation than in the Center nation." This means that the Center nation as a whole gains more, over time, from advertising relations than does the Periphery as a whole, and also that a constant—or growing—inequality exists between the center in the Periphery and the periphery in the Periphery. The total relationship, then, is built on both external and internal dominance relations, with the Third World masses—the periphery in the Periphery—losing at the combined hands of center and periphery from the Center and the center from their own advertising-dependent societies. Through "divide and conquer" actions, potential antielite trouble in the form of countervailing advertising power from the masses in the Periphery or from the Periphery as a mobilized whole can be avoided by the Center, and the transnational power structure can be maintained.

Advertising imperialism, then, can be analyzed as but one piece of a modern, more general dominance system supported actively by the TNAAs, other TNCs, and a host of other nonterritorial actors that are adjuncts of the communication industry and of business generally.[36] Under this system, advertising-strong nations exercise power over advertising-weak nations, and the Periphery's advertising industry is conditioned by the needs of the Center rather than the needs of the Periphery's majority.

Advertising is but one of many instruments used by the Center to control information and in other ways influence the type of society necessary to the global system as a whole. The TNAAs, compared to the larger world of TNCs, are relatively small in number of employees, volume of sales (called "billings" by an ad agency), and number of Third World offices. In general, however, it seems reasonable to hypothesize that the TNAAs operate along the lines of other service TNCs and the transnational media that operate within a Center-controlled system. Herbert Schiller and others have emphasized the symbiotic relationship between transnational media and this larger, incalculably complicated system:

> The transnational media are inseparable elements in a worldwide system of resource allocation generally regarded as capitalistic. They function as private profitmaking enterprises seeking markets, which they term audiences. They provide in their imagery and messagery the beliefs and perspectives that create and reinforce their audiences' attachment to the way things are in the system overall. It is pointless, therefore, to attempt to measure the impact of any individual medium or message. Each is a contributor in its own way to a systemic process. All are mutually reinforcing and capable as well of absorbing occasional discordant messages and influences. The consequences of the transnational media's heavy outputs are not measurable either. They are observable as typifying a way of life.[39]

The TNAAs, globally or in a particular host nation, then, must be understood as functioning within a much larger totality operating within and between nations. Advertising is a highly visible, important component of this transnational structural package, but scholars and policymakers have given it relatively little systematic, critical attention.[40]

Notes

1. Keith Griffin, "Underdevelopment in Theory," in Charles K. Wilbur, ed., *The Political Economy of Development and Underdevelopment* (New York: Random House, 1973), pp. 68–81.

2. The conventional development literature is vast and has been heavily influenced by the Social Science Research Council and its Comparative Politics Committee. Classics from the American dominant paradigm include: Gabriel A. Almond and James S. Coleman, eds., *The Politics of the Developing Areas* (Princeton, N.J.: Princeton University Press, 1960); Almond and Bingham Powell, *Comparative Politics* (Boston: Little, Brown, 1966); David Apter, *The Politics of*

Modernization (Chicago: University of Chicago Press, 1965); E. E. Hagen, *On the Theory of Social Change* (Homewood, Ill.: Dorsey, 1962); A. O. Hirschman, *The Strategy of Economic Development* (New Haven, Conn.: Yale University Press, 1959); Daniel Lerner, *The Passing of Traditional Society: Modernizing the Middle East* (Glencoe, Ill.: The Free Press, 1958); David McClelland, *The Achieving Society* (New York: Van Nostrand, 1961); Lucian Pye, *Politics, Personality and Nation Building* (New Haven, Conn.: Yale University Press, 1962); Everett Rogers, *Diffusion of Innovation* (New York: The Free Press of Glencoe, 1962); and W. W. Rostow, *The Stages of Economic Growth* (Cambridge: Cambridge University Press, 1960).

For an overview of this mainstream literature, see Robert B. Stauffer, "Development American Style: Hidden Agendas for the Third World" (Paper prepared for presentation at an East-West Technology and Development Institute Graduate Student Workshop, February 17–18, 1975, Honolulu).

 · 3. An introduction to dependency is available in Susanne Bodenheimer, "Dependency and Imperialism: The Roots of Latin American Underdevelopment," in K. T. Fann and Donald C. Hodges, eds., *Readings in U. S. Imperialism*, Boston: Porter Sargent Publisher, 1971, pp. 155–81; Bodenheimer, *The Ideology of Developmentalism: The American Paradigm-Surrogate for Latin American Studies*, Sage Professional Paper in Comparative Politics 01-015 (Beverly Hills, Calif.: Sage Publications, 1971); Frank Bonilla and Robert Girling, eds., *Structures of Dependency* (Stanford, Calif.: Bonilla and Girling, 1972); J. D. Cockcroft, Andre Gunder Frank, and Dale L. Johnson, *Dependency and Underdevelopment: Latin America's Political Economy* (Garden City, N. Y.: Doubleday, 1972); Robert R. Kaufman, Harry I. Chernotsky, and Daniel S. Geller, "A Preliminary Test of the Theory of Dependency," *Comparative Politics* 7, no. 3 (April 1975), pp. 303–30; Sanyaya Lall, "Is Dependence a Useful Concept in Analyzing Underdevelopment?" *World Development* 3, nos. 11 and 12 (1975), pp. 799–810; and Harry R. Targ, "Global Dominance and Dependence, Post-Industrialism, and International Relations Theory," *International Studies Quarterly* 20, no. 3 (September 1976), pp. 461–82.

For a critique of dependency, see Robert A. Packenham, "The New Utopianism: Political Development Ideas in the Dependency Literature" (Paper prepared for a colloquium in the Latin American Program, The Wilson Center, Washington, D.C., 29 September 1978); and David Ray, "The Dependency Model of Latin American Underdevelopment: Three Basic Fallacies," *Journal of Inter-American Studies and World Affairs* 15, no. 1 (February 1973), pp. 4–20.

4. For an introduction to Frank's writing, see his "Sociology of Development and Underdevelopment of Sociology," in *Latin America: Underdevelopment or Revolution?* (New York: Monthly Review Press, 1969), pp. 21–94. For an application of his work to a particular nation, see "On the Mechanisms of Imperialism: The Case of Brazil," in Fann and Hodges, *Readings in U. S. Imperialism*, pp. 237–48. For other important dependency work on Latin America, see F. H. Cardoso, "Dependency and Development in Latin America," *New Left Review*, no. 74 (July–August 1972), pp. 83–95; Theotonio Dos Santos, "The Structure of Dependence," in Wilbur, *The Political Economy of Development and Underdevelopment*, pp. 109–17; Celso Furtado, *Development and Underdevelopment* (Berkeley: University of California Press, 1964); and Osvaldo Sunkel, "Big Business and 'Dependencia'," *Foreign Affairs*, April 1972, pp. 517–31, and "National Development Policy and External Dependence in Latin America," *Journal of Development Studies* 6, no. 1 (October 1969), pp. 23–48. For additional critical work from this perspective, see Paul A. Baran, *The Political Economy of Growth* (New York: Monthly Review Press, 1957). For a critique of Frank, see Alec Nove, "On Reading Andre Gunder Frank," *Journal of Development Studies* 10, nos. 3 and 4 (April/July 1974), pp. 445–55.

5. For an insightful discussion of underdevelopment theory, see Lawrence R. Alschuler, "A Sociological Theory of Latin American Underdevelopment," *Comparative Political Studies* 6, no. 1 (April 1973), pp. 41–61.

Much of the new direction in theories of dominance and dependency has come from the European peace researchers. For an introduction to this perspective, see issues of the *Journal of Peace Research* or work by Galtung. Also, see H. Hveem, "Global Dominance System," *Journal of Peace Research* 10, no. 4 (1973), pp. 319–40; Dieter Senghaas, "Conflict Formations in Contemporary International Society," *Journal of Peace Research* 10, no. 3 (1973), pp. 163–84; and Senghaas, "Peace Research and the Third World," *Bulletin of Peace Proposals* 5 (1974), pp. 158–72.

6. Pye has written about a "world" or "cosmopolitan" culture as "a nearly uniform pattern

of the Western industrial world imposing its practices, standards, techniques, and values upon the non-Western world." See his discussion in *Aspects of Political Development* (Boston: Little, Brown, 1966), pp. 9–11. See also Ernest Dichter, "The World Customer," *Harvard Business Review*, July/August 1962, pp. 113–22.

7. This viewpoint is implicit in the dominant paradigm literature. For an example of an explicit statement of this position, see Ithiel de Sola Pool, "The Influence of International Communication on Development" (Paper prepared for the International Conference on Communication Policy and Planning for Development, Communication Institute, East-West Center, Honolulu, April 5–10, 1976), pp. 15–16. Pool concluded: "Developing countries should insist on the freest possible access by telecommunications to the best available information resources from anywhere in the world. It is in their interest to oppose all restrictions on the free flow of information. Copyright, security restrictions, and commercial restrictions on the transfer of technical information, all check the progress of developing countries. Rapid transfer of technology is facilitated by the maximum possible flow of travel, messages, literature, and on line interaction across the world's borders. Dependence occurs whenever advanced countries possess know-how and techniques which developing countries are not able to acquire for themselves at will. Independence is therefore promoted by unrestricted free flow of information between countries so that the developing country can acquire for itself whatever intellectual and cultural products it desires at the lowest possible price. The freer the flow of information, the wider the developing country's range of choice and the sooner it can acquire for itself the ability to produce the same sort of information or programming at home."

Jerome Slater takes a similar stance in "Is United States Foreign Policy 'Imperialist' or 'Imperial'?" *Political Science Quarterly*, 91, no. 1 (Spring 1976), p. 81: "What the Third World needs from the United States and the rest of the developed countries is not less but more aid, trade, and private investment, though undoubtedly on better terms than in the past."

8. Pool, "Communications and Development," in Myron Weiner, ed., *Modernization: Dynamics of Growth*, (New York: Basic Books, 1966), p. 108.

9. For examples of influential communication research within the dominant paradigm, see: Lerner and Wilbur Schramm, *Communication and Change in the Developing Countries* (Honolulu: University of Hawaii/East-West Center Press, 1967); Pye, *Communications and Political Development* (Princeton, N.J.: Princeton University Press, 1963); Schramm, *Mass Media and National Development* (Stanford, Calif.: Stanford University Press, 1964); Schramm and Lerner, eds. *Communication and Change: Ten Years After* (Honolulu: University of Hawaii/East-West Center Press), 1976.

10. These points are discussed in Denis Goulet, "World Interdependence: Verbal Smokescreen or New Ethic?" Development Paper no. 21 (Washington: Overseas Development Council, March 1976), and Ali A. Mazrui, "The New Interdependence," in Guy F. Erb and Valeriana Kallab, *Beyond Dependency: The Developing World Speaks Out* (Washington, D.C.: Overseas Development Council), September 1975, pp. 38–54.

11. These major Third World options are considered in Tibor Mende, *From Aid to Recolonization: Lessons of a Failure* (New York: Pantheon Books, 1973), pp. 218–27. For other discussion of alternatives, see Paulo Freire, *Pedagogy of the Oppressed* (New York: Herder and Herder, 1972); Mahbub ul Haq, "Negotiating a Bargain with the Rich Countries," in Erb and Kallab, *Beyond Dependency: The Developing World Speaks Out*, pp. 157–62; Haq, *The Poverty Curtain: Choices for the Third World* (New York: Columbia University Press, 1976); Ivan Illich, "Outwitting the Developed Countries," *New York Review of Books*, 6 Nov. 1969, pp. 20–24; T. Nulty and L. Nulty, "Pakistan: The Busy Bee Route to Development," *TransAction* 8 (February 1971), pp. 18–26; E. F. Schumacher, *Small is Beautiful: Economics as if People Mattered*, (New York: Harper and Row, 1973); Thomas E. Weisskopf, "Capitalism, Underdevelopment, and the Future of the Poor Countries," in Jagdish Bhagwati, *Economics and World Order* (New York: Macmillan, 1972), pp. 43–77; and Edward J. Woodhouse, "Revisioning the Future of the Third World: An Ecological Perspective on Development," *World Politics*, October 1972, pp. 1–33. For examples of country case studies of alternative routes to development, see Wilbur, *The Political Economy of Development and Underdevelopment*, particularly part six: "Comparative Models of Development," pp. 273–319.

12. For a useful discussion of several distinct types of imperialism, see Karl W. Deutsch, "Imperialism and Neo-Colonialism," *The Paper of the Peace Science Society (International)* 23

(1973). See also Deutsch, "Theories of Economic Imperialism," in Steven J. Rosen and James R. Kurth, *Testing Theories of Economic Imperialism* (Lexington, Mass.: Lexington Books, D. C. Heath and Co., 1974), pp. 15–33. For an introduction to imperialism also see Harry Magdoff, *The Age of Imperialism: The Economics of U. S. Foreign Policy* (New York: Monthly Review Press, 1973), or collected essays in Roger Owen and Bob Sutcliffe, eds., *Studies in the Theory of Imperialism* (London: Longman, 1972); and E. L. Wheelwright, *Radical Political Economy* (Sydney: Australia and New Zealand Book Co., 1974).

13. Quantification of development has long posed a problem for scholars and policymakers. For a discussion of indicators reflecting basic changes in development theory and practice, see Galtung, "Towards New Indicators of Development," *Futures*, June 1976, pp. 261–5. For a conventional approach to indicators and their use in mass communication development, see Schramm and W. Lee Ruggels, "How Mass Media Systems Grow," in Lerner and Schramm, *Communication and Change in the Developing Countries*, pp. 57–75.

14. "Penetrated" political systems in the context of "linkage politics" are discussed in James N. Rosenau, *Linkage Politics: Essays in the Convergence of National and International Systems* (New York: Free Press, 1969). The transnational power structure as it relates to communications is analyzed in Juan Somavia, "The Transnational Power Structure and International Information," *Development Dialogue* 2 (1976), pp. 15–28. For a discussion of proposals for a "new order" for communications, see Chakravarti Raghavan, "A New World Communication and Information Structure," *Development Dialogue* 2 (1976), pp. 43–50. For a more comprehensive summary of the key issues in efforts to create a new international economic order, see "Towards Third World Collective Self-Reliance," *What Now: The 1975 Dag Hammarskjold Report on Development and International Cooperation* (Uppsala, Sweden: Dag Hammarskjold Foundation, 1975).

15. For an excellent discussion of the ties between TNCs, media, and development, see Richard Worthington, "The Cultural Connection: MNCs and the Mass Media." (Paper presented at the annual meeting, Western Political Science Association, San Francisco, April 1976). Barnet and Muller, *Global Reach: The Power of the Multinational Corporations*, (New York: Simon and Schuster, 1974), especially chapter 6, "The Global Corporations and the Underdeveloped World," pp. 123–47, also emphasizes these connections and the costs of TNCs to national development.

16. The literature questioning the dominant paradigm is rapidly increasing in the area of communication. For example, see Everett Rogers's edited issue of *Communication Research* 3, no. 1 (April 1976), for an excellent concise collection of articles on "Communication and Development: Critical Perspectives." See also S. N. Eisenstadt, "The Changing Vision of Modernization" (Paper distributed at Communication and Change in the Developing Countries Conference, Communication Institute, East-West Center, Honolulu, January 12–17, 1975); Philip Elliott and Peter Golding, "Mass Communication and Social Change: The Imagery of Development and the Development of Imagery," in Emanul de Kadt and Gavin Williams, *Sociology and Development* (London: Tavistock, 1974), pp. 229–54; Peter Golding, "Media Role in National Development: Critique of a Theoretical and Orthodoxy," *Journal of Communication*, Summer 1974, pp. 39–53; and Jim Richstad, ed., *New Perspectives in International Communication* (Honolulu: East-West Communication Institute, 1976). For a discussion of some of the troublesome problems created by foreign communication forces, see Y. V. L. Rao, "Information Imbalance in Asia," (A Working paper prepared for presentation at the Regional Conference on Information Imbalance in Asia, Kandy, April 21–25, 1975). For an interesting argument for why national communication output should actually be decreased to help bring about stability and order in some societies, see Huntington, "Political Development and Political Decay," *World Politics* 17, no. 3 (April 1965), pp. 386–430. For a discussion of communicators' concerns over their "dependence" on the West, see "Statement by the Participants in the 1975 Dag Hammarsjkold Third World Journalists' Seminar," *Development Dialogue* 1 (1976), pp. 104–9. Also, see Galtung and Mari Holmboe Ruge, "The Structure of Foreign News," in Jeremy Tunstall, *Media Sociology* (London: Constable and Co. 1970), pp. 259–98.

17. Stauffer, "Development American Style: Hidden Agendas for the Third World," p. 2. For an interesting presentation of the argument that, in general, America (as well as the Soviet Union and Japan) is declining in terms of *both* its power and its influence as a model, see

Galtung, *The European Community: A Superpower in the Making* (London: Allen & Unwin Ltd., 1973); and Galtung, "Conflict on a Global Scale: Social Imperialism and Sub-Imperialism—Continuities in the Structural Theory of Imperialism," *World Development* 4, no. 3 (March 1976), pp. 153–65.

18. For the argument that the acceptance of Western values and consumption patterns constitutes "self-colonization," see Sauvant, "His Master's Voice," *Ceres*, September-October 1976, pp. 27–32. For an excellent discussion of the power of TNCs to influence the values that determine how people in the Third World and elsewhere live, see Barnet and Muller, *Global Reach*, particularly pp. 172–84. For an overview of the literature on the social and cultural impact of TNCs in less developed nations, see Krishna Kumar, "A Working Paper on the Social and Cultural Impacts of Transnational Enterprises" (Honolulu: Culture Learning Institute, East-West Center, August 1978).

19. Galtung, *The European Community*, p. 33.

20. Johan Galtung, "A Structural Theory of Imperialism," *Journal of Peace Research* 8, no. 2, 1971, p. 81.

21. Ibid., p. 91.

22. Ibid., pp. 83–4.

23. This point is emphasized in Galtung, *The European Community*, p. 40. He concluded: "The problem is not just that one happens to be strong and the other weak; one rich, the other poor; one full of initiative, the other apathetic. Such differences may always arise, and may or may not be exploited as resource power. But in structural power these differences arise from the way the structure, more particularly the division of labor in the economic cycle itself, is set up. *For this reason one cannot fight against exploitation simply by redistributing resources.* The fight against exploitation is a fight for the change of the total structure, and particularly of those economic cycles that induce exploitation. This can take two forms: restructuring them so that the costs and benefits are more equally distributed, or simply cutting them."

24. Ibid., p. 34.

25. For a stronger critical view, see Senghaas, "Peace Research and the Third World," p. 167. He concluded: "Beginning with the end of the first wave of penetration into the societies of the third world by the metropoles of the day in the phase of pillage colonialism up to the current massive penetration by mighty social forces such as the multinational corporations, the dominance structure of center-periphery relations between the dominating capitalist metropoles and the dominated peripheries as well as the societal formation of periphery capitalism in their respective characteristic forms constituted the political and socio-economic basis for the open and disguised plundering of the third world."

26. Galtung, "Nonterritorial Actors and the Problem of Peace," in Saul H. Mendlevitz, ed., *On the Creation of a Just World Order* (New York: Free Press, 1975), p. 164.

27. This point is emphasized in Galtung, "A Structural Theory of Imperialism," pp. 99–100.

28. Ibid., p. 81.

29. See, for example, his discussion of the Soviet Union's particular form of imperialism over its periphery nations in Galtung, "Conflict on a Global Scale".

30. For a discussion of how the Soviet Union is using mass advertising, see Lyman E. Ostlund, "Russian Advertising: A New Concept," *Journal of Advertising Research*, February 1973, pp. 11–19. One major TNAA, Marsteller, Inc., New York City, actually has had an office in Moscow since 1973. Under an agreement with Vneshtorgreklama, the state advertising agency, Marsteller helps American corporations market their products in the Soviet Union. Marsteller's Hong Kong office has done work for the Canton trade fair. Other TNAAs are at least thinking about activities in the centrally planned nations. For example, see Alexander Brody, "It's the People that Count," *Madison Avenue*, March 1973, p. 5 (reprint). As executive vice president of Young & Rubicam International, Brody concluded: "Whether or not Young & Rubicam can have a fully owned, profit-making agency in a socialist country is, I think, beside the point. What is more important is that long-term, all of us have responsibilities as citizens of the world in addition to the countries we work in. Using ourselves as the example, the people who work for Young & Rubicam internationally move about, and as they move, they see more. As they see more, they recognize that their obligation is not just to the people in their own village, but beyond. In this same way, I think we have some responsibility

for helping to develop, demonstrate, and perhaps teach these methods to people in socialist countries, as well as to others. This does not, as I said, necessarily mean setting up shop in the middle of Moscow. Time will help us evolve the proper method."

31. Somavia, "The Transnational Power Structure and International Information," p. 17.

32. For a general discussion of these two mechanisms, see Galtung, "A Structural Theory of Imperialism," pp. 89–91.

33. See Galtung's general discussion of private and governmental transnational corporations as conveyor mechanisms in his "A Structural Theory of Imperialism," p. 95.

34. Ibid., p. 93. For an example of a study testing Galtung's model with reference to news flow, see Jim Richstad, "News Flow in the Pacific Islands: Selected Cases," *Communications and Development* 2, no. 2 (Summer 1978), pp. 7–11.

35. Galtung and other writers on dominance relations emphasize that the flow between Center and Periphery nations is uneven and that periphery alliance formation to change inequalities from the pure type of imperialistic relationship is difficult to achieve.

36. Galtung, "A Structural Theory of Imperialism," p. 84.

37. Senghaas, "Peace Research and the Third World," p. 167, has concluded: "On the basis of dependent reproduction, *autonomous* or *auto-centered* development processes (the goals and results of which are *structurally homogeneous societal formations*) remain not only somewhat improbable without a previous break with the metropoles and thus with a capitalistic dominated world economic system; they are completely improbable. *Growth* processes are naturally possible and probable; but experience, above all since the end of World War II, has clearly shown that in particular in those periphery countries with an advanced level of development *there can be growth without development*—insofar as development is understood not only and not primarily as the further growth of the privileged dynamic poles.

38. Herbert Schiller has probably given more attention to cultural and communications related "imperialism" than anyone else. See, for example, his "Advertising and International Communications," *Instant Research on Peace and Violence*, 4 (1976), pp. 175–82; "The Appearance of National Communications Policies: A New Arena for Social Struggle," *Gazette* 21 no. 2 (1975), pp. 82–94; *Communication and Cultural Domination*, White Plains, N.Y.: International Arts and Sciences Press, 1976; "Madison Avenue Imperialism," *TransAction* 81, nos. 5 and 6 (March/April 1971), pp. 52–64; *Mass Communications and American Empire* (Boston: Beacon Press, 1969; and *The Mind Managers* (Boston: Beacon Press, 1973).

By the mid-1970s, transnational communications corporations had become a popular area of research. For example, see William H. Read, *America's Mass Media Merchants* (Baltimore: The Johns Hopkins University Press, 1976); Jeremy Tunstall, *The Media Are America: Anglo-American Media in the World* (New York: Columbia Unviersity Press, 1977); and Tapio Varis, "Aspects of the Impact of Transnational Corporations on Communication," *International Social Sciences Journal* no. 4 (November 1976), pp. 807–29.

39. Schiller, "Transnational Media and National Development" (Paper presented to the Fair Communication Policy Conference, East-West Communication Institute, Honolulu, March 28–April 3, 1976), p. 16.

40. Much of the work on transnational advertising, for example, is from the perspective of the headquarters nation of the TNAA rather than the host nation. Also, much of the writing takes an American business school approach. See, for example, Arnold K. Weinstein, "Foreign Investment by Service Firms: The Case of the Multinational Advertising Agencies," *Journal of International Business Studies*, Spring/Summer 1977, pp. 83–89, or Weinstein, "The International Expansion of U. S. Multinational Advertising Agencies," *MSU Business Topics* 22, no. 3 (1974), pp. 29–35. Some business school research, however, has begun thinking in "trans-national" rather than "foreign-and-domestic" terms. See, for example, James Killough, "Improved Payoffs from Transnational Advertising," *Harvard Business Review* 56, no. 4 (July-August 1978), pp. 102–10. He concluded that labels such as "domestic" or "international" are no longer relevant since "there is increasingly just one global market."

2
Third World Concerns

The transnationalization of commerce and mass communications has provoked great controversy within developing countries and international forums. A United Nations report on transnational corporations in world development observed:

> In a certain sense, the manifold operations of foreign-based multinational corporations and their pervasive influence on the host country may be regarded as a challenge to national sovereignty. The challenge has, moreover, economic, social, political, and cultural dimensions which are frequently inseparable from one another. The tensions and conflicts thus generated are, likewise, the result of complex interaction between many agents in many areas.[1]

Another United Nations report, which examined the structure of transnational advertising, noted:

> Advertising, which in its present form began as a United States phenomenon, has by now spread across national frontiers, its functions having evolved from information to persuasion through stimulating and channeling consumption, often contributing to a homogeneity of consumption patterns. The arguments in favor of and against advertising are well known. They refer to its economic and social impact and center around the question of the appropriate size of advertising expenditures, given scarce economic resources, especially in developing countries, whether they stimulate demand for goods that are not appropriate, given the income and demand structure in developing countries, and whether they contribute to a cultural standardization among countries. Given the role of advertising in the economic, social, and cultural life of a country, and its potential for exercising a cultural impact through links with the media, it is important to examine the role of transnational advertising agencies in this context.[2]

By the early 1980s, an unmistakable antitransnational advertising climate was being created. The transnational advertising industry was facing very serious challenges, and advertising policy and planning was becoming an international political issue. A major stimulus for some of the controversy was a report by the UNESCO appointed International Commission for the

Study of Communication Problems under chairman Sean MacBride.[3] Its goal was "to study the totality of communication problems in modern societies" and a number of its recommendations had great implications for transnational advertising's future. According to the advertising industry's interpretations of the report's "potentially damaging proposals," the Mac-Bride Commission proposed "a preference for non-commercial types of communications; a tax on advertising; guidelines for advertising content; and greater state control over the activities of transnational companies."[4]

In addition to the MacBride report and other UNESCO efforts in the area of international communication policy and planning, other factors have given rise to consumer advocacy and antiadvertising feelings. Questionable infant formula and tobacco advertising are but two of a growing number of controversial advertising-related issues that have attracted global attention and that have particular relevance to developing nations.

The Swiss-based Nestlé and other transnational manufacturers of baby food products have been under intense pressure from both consumer groups and some governments over alleged aggressive promotion of powdered milk products for babies. In 1981, the World Health Organization (WHO) and the United Nations Children's Fund (UNICEF) supported an international marketing code designed to curb unjustified sales and promotional practices. Only the United States opposed the code, which recommended the end of direct advertising and sales of infant formulas and stressed the value of breast milk. The industry's critics maintained that unethical advertising and promotional practices have been key factors in the decline of breastfeeding in many societies.

Another significant public health related controversy concerns tobacco manufacturers, who account for a large percentage of advertising expenditures in a number of societies. In many developing and industrialized countries, they have come under strong pressure for aggressively disseminating messages that link a glamorous life-style with cigarette smoking. Governments are launching antismoking campaigns and passing legislation that regulates tobacco sales or bans advertising, including tobacco company sponsorship of sports events and use of influential media, especially television, that appeal to young people.

Costs and Benefits of Transnational Advertising

The TNAAs, like other TNCs, participate in—and have an effect on—the internal political and social affairs of so-called sovereign nations. Their penetration into a host society through foreign ownership and control can have both positive and negative impact on particular groups and on overall national development efforts. Private and public institutions, development policies and plans, life-styles and consumption patterns, and culture can be affected by the reach of the TNAAs with the support, and in the service of, the transnational power structure.

In Galtungian language, these private entities have "power-over-others." Their position in the Center controlled global system and their vast resources enable the TNAAs to exert various pressures that influence a nation's ability to control its own development. In simple language, the TNAAs have the ability to dominate advertising in ways that small, local advertising agencies in weak, poor nations cannot. They clearly can influence a nation's efforts to build its own autonomous institutions.

Generalizations about the precise costs and benefits that the TNAAs bring to their host (and home) nations are difficult to make. This is because nations and their development policies and patterns, problems and pressures are in a constant state of flux and are products of various interwoven factors operating within and between nations. What can be said with certainty, however, is that the presence of the TNAAs in any Third World society *does* generate some tensions and conflicts.

Unlike the TNCs in extractive industries, which tend to be isolated from the mainstream of a host nation's life, the TNAAs and other urban-centered transnational service enterprises do not have any raw materials to extract from a nation. And, unlike transnational manufacturing enterprises that require input such as heavy capital investment and large numbers of local workers, the TNAAs operate relatively inconspicuously. They work out of private offices rather than large factories, deal in white-collar skills, and employ comparatively small numbers of local and expatriate staff. But still the TNAAs are subject to charges that they are affiliated with an externally controlled, elitist, transnational power structure and that they dominate the local advertising scene and exploit the weaknesses of host nations.

The thrust of much of the criticism has been summarized by three Asians writing about advertising. An Indian has concluded:

> For a complete understanding of the problem, a certain historical perspective becomes necessary. The roots of the present situation must be traced back to the fact that advertising—like all other modern commercial activity—was a gift of the white man. In advertising agencies, as in branches of civil administration, the white man tended to select and favor such people whose lifestyles were most like his own.[5]

A Filipino has argued:

> because of centuries of Western domination, advertising in Asia has in the past been used mostly to sell Western goods and ideas. Western in approach and orientation, it is often a manifestation of the vestiges of colonialism that still have to be shaken off. That advertising has become a very influential force in society all the more underscores the need to de-

Westernize it, to reshape it to conform more closely to Asian needs rather than over-simplistically condemn it as a Western aberration.[6]

And a Pakistani adman has been critical of local Asian advertising agencies for copying the TNAAs and overly emphasizing economic growth:

> Like the ad agencies of Madison Avenue and ad agencies from other parts of the industrialized north, Asian ad agencies have assumed that their health and happiness lie in growth alone, in watching the curve of the billings graph climb up, up and away. Perhaps the truth is that in Asia growth alone is not enough. In Asia, above all, economic activity— and therefore advertising activity too—must be guided by the concept of development which incorporates the element of growth but does not exclusively consist of growth alone.[7]

In general, then, the TNAAs are often perceived within the Third World as being too strong, antinational, monopolistic, and uncontrollable because of three issues: political sovereignty, national development goals, and socio-cultural considerations. These will be analyzed in detail in the cases of China, Indonesia, Malaysia, and Singapore later in this book, but a few general remarks are appropriate here.

The TNAAs' mere presence—especially in ex-colonial societies—is often felt to have an adverse effect, psychologically and in other ways, on the politically independent nation's communications choices and its overall efforts to manage and determine its own affairs. Schiller, for example, has argued:

> one measure of a nation's loss of control of its own mass media (apart from the obvious loss through foreign ownership), is the degree of penetration of foreign advertising agencies in the mechanics of national marketing. Such a penetration signals also fundamental changes in the country's cultural ecology, as a changed communications structure increasingly transmits and reinforces attitudes that fit nicely with the requirements of the multinational corporate goods producers that are financing the new system.[8]

Host nations sometimes feel that foreign based corporations contribute to a dilemma in which governments have problems relating to their people's authentic aspirations and everyday needs because of undue and unwanted external interference and influence. In the case of the TNAAs, any government that allows them to operate also is accepting bits and pieces of a much larger development "package" that gives legitimacy to Western institutions, commercialized mass media, industrialization, consumerism, foreign investment, foreign life-styles, etc. Intimately linked to the transnational power structure, these external influences are very often beyond the means of any individual nation to effectively control.

The TNAAs are also perceived as pursuing private goals and undertaking activities that somehow are inconsistent with the host nation's explicit national objectives and plans or its implicit development patterns. Although they certainly do have the ability to rapidly inject outside technology, capital, and managerial and communications expertise into a society, the TNAAs have a very different concept of "development" and interpretation of not only what is "good" advertising but also what national policies and plans mean.

One reason both advertising (indigenous sometimes as well as foreign) and the transnational advertising agencies are suspect in the eyes of a government may have to do with their support of change that would challenge the existing institutional structures. A senior TNAA executive has stressed that advertising "creates rising economic and social expectations" and "teaches the possibility of change, encourages people to seek change, to challenge, and to expect and demand something better."[9] To the TNAAs, then, advertising does not produce a "commercial mentality" but tends to encourage a more pleasant and improved life, which in most developing societies could come about only through major changes in the status quo.

It is relatively easy to see how powerful foreign businesses like the TNAAs can get themselves involved in political and other matters that raise all sorts of interrelated tensions and problems over a host nation's sovereignty and its national development objectives and processes. A TNAA like J. Walter Thompson, for example, gets directly involved in local politics when it does advertising or public relations campaigns for governments such as Greece, Chile, and the Philippines, or when it is suspected of having links with American intelligence operations dating back to World War II.[10] TNAAs can also influence local decision making when they engage in questionable practices such as making political contributions or giving bribes and kickbacks.[11]

Less tangible than these actions, however, is the TNAAs' ability to affect a society's sociocultural domain.[12] More research into this controversial third issue of concern is certainly needed, but most TNC supporters and critics would agree that foreign-operated enterprises are highly culture-bound and have a powerful influence on some nations' indigenous culture. As Karl Sauvant has concluded:

> The values and patterns of behavior acquired during the colonial era and especially the consumption patterns created, maintained, or reinforced by transnational advertising agencies do not reflect the conditions of developing countries. Rather, they reflect the wants and the abundance of developed countries. At least for the time being, these wants can only be satisfied through continued inputs from abroad. Consequently, economic dependence on countries and institutions that can help to fulfill these foreign-oriented wants continues and is reinforced.[13]

Are the culture and values reflected by TNAAs and their advertising favorable to national development? The TNAAs generally argue that their commercial messages are ideologically neutral; that their advertisements merely reflect—not manipulate—the host nation's current but constantly changing values, and that their presence does not have any dysfunctional impacts such as imposing an alien culture on a defenseless public.[14] A statement by an Ogilvy & Mather International executive summarizes the general TNAA position that advertising is only salesmanship:

> We believe that advertising is neither an art form, nor a cultural trend setter. We recognize that we must always try to work within the rigid confines of good taste, social acceptance, honesty, and professional ethics. At the same time our experience teaches us that people are people all over the world. Their wants and preferences have suprising similarities. It is our job to find the most appealing and most suitable persuasive arguments to consumers in each country.[15]

Despite such a TNAA stance, the Third World has experienced a sharp rise in nationalism, especially since the 1960s,[16] and critics have attacked the TNAAs, and sometimes advertising generally, for producing messages that are intrusive, banal, offensive, undesirable, and irrelevant.[17] Some have seen the TNAAs as having the ideological power—especially over the long term through informal daily education via the mass media—to debase traditional local cultural standards, import unwanted values and life-styles, and threaten national identity.[18] Some also have seen the TNAAs as having the power to surmount petty national and cultural differences and bring people together toward a world culture and greater interdependence among consumers and their global village. They have been credited with having the ability to inform people about the outside world and to introduce potentially useful ideas, alternatives, and behavior—especially about the consumer way of life—that can help a society change for the better.[19] Critics have attacked such a way of life because of the alien values and patterns that it is perceived to support.[20] The sheer volume and effectiveness of the TNAAs' advertisements have been said to introduce or condone aggressiveness, materialism, romanticism, elitism, racism, conformism, and so forth, and such beliefs have been said to gradually contribute to the creation of a new, elite-oriented culture that has nothing to do with the indigenous one it is rapidly replacing.

The TNAAs are frequently assumed to be a prime contributor to a weakening of the indigenous culture in Third World nations because they often have a near monopoly over the local advertising industry and their advertisements are felt to reflect their home nation values. Much of the criticism of transnational advertising asserts that advertisements produced by the TNAAs will project disruptive, nonindigenous values and beliefs. The TNAAs are commonly perceived by host nations as working closely with their TNC clients to influence various local, value forming institutions, particularly the mass media. Together, the TNAAs and their client TNCs are seen as avid internationalists trying to reach large audiences with messages that enforce universal standards of "good" advertising and of the "good life" as a way of inexpensively surmounting very real and significant differences between nations and within nations.

Rather than a homogeneous world culture—often felt to be American culture in disguise, some host nations argue for advertising that is exclusively created and implemented by and for their own local people. Rather than be inundated by imported or at least heavily foreign influenced advertisements, some nations say they want indigenous advertising designed to preserve and strengthen their own culture.

To those who feel their cultural identity and national development aspirations are threatened by the global trend toward TNAA advertisements based on universal themes, TNAA supporters generally respond by saying that concepts of "cultural identity," "authentic local culture," and "nationalism" are often old-fashioned and murky at best.[21] Defending the Western model of development, the TNAAs—like their TNC clients and their home governments in Washington, London, Tokyo, etc.—argue that it is not realistic or very pragmatic for a host nation in today's increasingly interdependent world to cut itself off from the benefits that the TNAAs, acting honestly and professionally, can help bring to a poor nation through various structures, techniques, and personnel. Implicitly, the TNAAs make the argument that everyone ultimately will benefit from a free flow of advertising ideas and from the physical presence of TNAA "intruders" in the Third World. A comment by a J. Walter Thompson executive typifies how the transnational adman sees his role in Third World markets:

> Besides taking business, the multinationals have brought it and developed it. They can play a part in making it a larger garden for all. Besides taking people, they have brought some and developed others. There are many successful advertising professionals working in national agencies all over the world today who owe their training to the intruders. In many countries, indeed, these intruders have been instrumental in building a professional agency industry. And as for profits—yes, hopefully, good work and success has been rewarded. However, the net outflow of money has been minimal for there have been losses as well as profits; and there are the direct and indirect investments.[22]

Host nations obviously realize that the TNAAs can and do make contributions to some sectors of their society, and that is the reason the TNAAs are allowed into the poor nations' "gardens" in the first place. At the same time, however, some groups within poor nations resent the sizable presence of the TNAAs inside their borders and mistrust them because at times they seem insensitive to genuine nationalism and cultural differences. Also, the TNAAs sometimes are feared because they seem adept at using a number of tricks—ranging from subtle use of subliminal communication in their messages to not-so-subtle use of money to buy favor with various interest groups—to maintain their dominant role in local advertising and to continue to profit from widespread syndication of relatively homogeneous advertising campaigns and structures.

These and other concerns suggest that the TNAAs are widely perceived as "transmission belts" for nonindigenous influences that can both help and hinder a nation's efforts to gain power over itself. Regardless of the nature of the host nation environment and government, however, the TNAAs *must* work with sets of local ruling elites, including media, business, and political leaders, who encourage (or at the very least allow) nonindigenous advertising and other influences to operate.[23] Therefore, the TNAAs' general impact on a society is a conservative one that reinforces existing structures. New resources—personnel, technology, equipment, management organization, or capital—may be introduced by the TNAAs, but they tend to reinforce the transnational *and* domestic powers that be and, therefore, may be impeding genuine national development.[24]

My argument is not that the TNAAs act deliberately to exacerbate Third World nations' problems of underdevelopment. But it does seem likely that the TNAAs—acting in alliances with host nation partners who share their interests—might well make these problems highly visible and accentuate them with the overall effect of contributing to a weakening of the nation-state. In short, the TNAAs, like other strong, flexible, growing TNCs, pose a challenge to a nation's sovereignty and overall development processes. This challenge is especially irritating to some Third World nations who are troubled because advertising is so highly visible and seemingly wasteful and because it is so often perceived—correctly so—as American influenced. The chairman of Young & Rubicam has suggested the reason for American domination when he spoke about Madison Avenue's "invasion" since the early 1960s: "Cadres of experts in every phase of agency function were flung overseas to teach, inspire, and raise the international standards from the relative to the absolute."[25]

As American-style advertising influences were being exported abroad, American expatriates and other Western admen brought along not only their marketing and persuasive communications skills, but also their personal, professional, *and* home nation values and life-styles. The transplantation process involving these culture-bound elements has not always gone smoothly. Separating skills from values is impossible, and tensions have inevitably developed when host societies have wanted some kind of know-how but not the full package of personal and professional values—not to mention some traditions and institutions—that accompany transnational admen when they move abroad.

In effect, the TNAAs do far more than provide mere advertising services. They also on a daily basis—mostly during a person's leisure time—

transmit consumerism and other values, communicate information, influence behavior both of individuals and of institutions, and affect development policies and plans. In a word, they exercise *power*. By exercising such power, they can create advertising *dependency*, which means that Third World societies think that advertising resources supplied by the Center are indispensable and simply cannot be obtained elsewhere.

Transnational advertising, then, can be perceived as a salient political problem, as well as a theoretical concern, because it is widely perceived as having to do with influence. A Filipino adman with SSC&B:Lintas summarized the problem from the Third World perspective when he said:

> Indeed, advertising has to play a complex role in developing economies, very unlike its role in economies such as that of the U.S.A., where it is woven into the fabric of American democratic life. Careless practice in a developing economy, particularly in moving ideas, even good ones, across national boundaries can make the advertising institution fit like a square peg in a round hole.[26]

Notes

1. United Nations, Department of Economic and Social Affairs, *Multinational Corporations in World Development,* p. 47.

2. Centre on Transnational Corporations, "Transnational Corporations in Advertising" (Technical Paper), (New York: United Nations, 1979), p. 2.

3. For an analysis of the controversial work of the MacBride Commission, see Michael H. Anderson, "A Primer on the MacBride Commission and Communication Policies for Tomorrow" (Paper prepared for the Communication Policy and Planning Project, East-West Communication Institute, Honolulu, June 1980).

4. Eugene H. Kummel, "A Time for Education" (Speech before the Central Region Annual Meeting of the American Association of Advertising Agencies, Chicago, November 13, 1980), p. 10.

5. Deepak S. Raja, "Advertising Without Alienation," *Media Asia* 2, no. 4 (1975), p. 229.

6. Norma Olizon, "Asia's Growing Ad Power Will Be Exhibited In Manila," *Advoice,* September 1978, p. 2.

7. Javed Jabbar, "The Great Betrayal," *Media,* August 1980.

8. Schiller, "Madison Avenue Imperialism," *TransAction* 81, nos. 5 and 6 (March/April 1971), p. 53.

9. Kummel, "A Time for Education," p. 9. He is chairman of McCann-Erickson Worldwide and chairman of the Board of Directors of the 4As (the American Association of Advertising Agencies).

10. A number of TNAAs accept both local and foreign governments as clients. For a discussion of JWT's work for the Philippines government, see Vergel O. Santos, "Masagana 99: A Lesson in Salesmanship," *Media,* December 1974, pp. 13–17. For a report on JWT's work as a communications counselor to the Chilean military government, see "JWT's Dialog Drops Chile, Citing Ideology Conflict," *Advertising Age* 18 November 1972, p. 1. For background on allegations of close ties between the CIA and JWT dating back to World War II and the Office of Strategic Services, predecessor of the CIA, see Ramona Bechtos, "Undercover Admen: JWT Linked to CIA Front," *Advertising Age,* 3 February 1975, pp. 1, 50. For JWT President Don Johnston's denial, see "JWT Denies CIA Link-up," *Advertising Age,* 10 February 1975, p. 57. He said that JWT "does not have now, will not have, nor do I have knowledge of the company ever having had any relationship, officially or unofficially, with the CIA." According to Johnston, "To become involved in any covert activity on behalf of any

68 MADISON AVENUE IN ASIA

government would not only be totally contradictory to our company philosophy, but would seriously jeopardize the solid reputation which we have worked over 100 years to build."

11. In 1976–77, for example, two publicly owned TNAAs—Ogilvy & Mather International and the Interpublic Group of Companies—admitted to the U.S. Securities & Exchange Commission, under its voluntary disclosure program, that questionable foreign payments had been made. For details of each TNAA's payments investigation, see Interpublic Group of Companies, Form 8-K, filed with the Securities & Exchange Commission, Washington, D.C., 22 October 1976, and Ogilvy & Mather International Inc., Form 8-K, filed with the Securities & Exchange Commission, Washington, D.C., March 25, 1977. O & M's payments totalled nearly $800,000 and IPG's about $500,000. These TNAAs' sums are relatively small compared to payments made by other major American TNCs.

12. For an overview of how the TNAAs can influence cultural systems as well as consumption patterns and social and political institutions, see Kumar, "A Working Paper on the Social and Cultural Impacts of Transnational Enterprises," (Honolulu: Culture Learning Institute, East-West Center, August 1978), especially pp. 35–42. He noted: "As the largest and most efficient enterprises, they (the TNAA's) are able to institutionalize their own norms on the entire industry, at least, during its early phase of development. Thus they help to determine the nature, forms and styles of advertising. Advertising TNEs (transnational enterprises) also create and diffuse relevant skills and expertise in the host LDCs (less developed countries). On the negative side, advertising TNEs can discourage the growth of indigenous firms. By practically monopolizing the advertising revenues of the TNEs in LDCs, they deprive local firms (wherever they exist) of the most lucrative business." (p. 37)

13. Sauvant, "His Master's Voice," *Ceres,* September-October 1976, p. 31.

14. This point is made in Jeremy Bullmore, "Advertising: What Is It and What Is It For? Part One: What Is It?" no. 1 in a series of J. Walter Thompson Papers (London: J. Walter Thompson, February 1976), pp. 1–3. He noted: "*Advertising,* as such, can do absolutely nothing. It's simply there, waiting to be used. *Advertisements,* in theory, can do practically everything: introduce the new, confirm the old, congratulate the existing buyer/user/consumer/employee, or attempt to convert him. Advertisements can, and do, encourage consumption and encourage thrift; and advocate a vote for any number of competing brands, companies or political parties." (p. 3)

15. Andrew Kershaw, "Select Committee on Economic and Cultural Nationalism: A Brief" (Toronto: Ogilvy & Mather (Canada) Ltd., 2 January 1973), p. 32.

16. For a discussion of rising Third World nationalism and its impact on the transnationals generally, see S. Watson Dunn, "Rising Nationalism vs. the International Language of Advertising" (Paper presented at the annual meeting of the Association for Education in Journalism, Ottawa, 18 August 1975). He concludes: "the trend toward national markets and the search for national identity do not, as it might seem at first glance, represent a reversion to old-fashioned nationalism either culturally or politically. Instead, they seem to represent a search for symbols, including products, services and the ads that promote them, which reflect that identity. This does not mean that all international campaigns need to be discarded. For example, some corporations, such as Coca-Cola, have been successful at coming up with themes that lend themselves to internationalization with only minor adaptations. Multinational marketers who can figure out how to reflect national identity in their ads will make out the best in the next decade." (p. 17)

17. Luis Ramiro Beltran and Elizabeth Fox de Cardona raise some of these issues in "Latin American Mass Communication as Influenced by the United States: The Myth of the Free Flow of Information" (paper prepared for the Meeting on Fair Communication Policy for the International Exchange of Information, East-West Communication Institute, Honolulu, Hawaii, 29 March–3 April 1976) especially pp. 4–5 and 18–20. For a case study of one Third World nation in which the indigenous culture was not reflected in its print-media advertising, see T. T. Marquez, "The Relationship of Advertising and Culture in the Philippines," *Journalism Quarterly* 52, no. 3 (1975), pp. 436–42.

18. Concern about the negative impact of TNAAs has not been limited to the Third World. For a discussion of similar concerns in a developed nation, see "Foreign Ownership and the Advertising Industry," prepared as part of the study, "Foreign Ownership: Corporate Behavior and Public Attitudes" for the Select Committee on Economic and Cultural Nationalism of the Legislative Assembly, Province of Ontario, Canada (Toronto: Kates, Peat, Marwick & Co.,

June 1973). In response to the Ontario provincial government's interest in advertising, the leading TNAAs in Canada defended their contributions to Canada in a document submitted to the committee. See "Viewpoint on the Canadian Advertising Industry as Submitted to the Select Committee on Economic and Cultural Nationalism of the Ontario Provincial Government by the Leaders of Ten Canadian Advertising Agencies" (Toronto, December 1972). The government's findings are reported in Legislative Assembly of the Province of Ontario, "Interim Report of the Select Committee on Economic and Cultural Nationalism: Advertising and the Advertising Industry" (Toronto, 7 October 1974).

19. For a concise summary of this dominant paradigm view, see, for example, E. Lloyd Sommerlad, *The Press in Developing Countries* (Sydney, Australia: Sydney University Press, 1966), p. 64. He stresses advertising's role in economic change: "Advertising is sometimes frowned on as culturally objectionable, as at best a necessary evil; but it is, surely, of positive value in stimulating economic and social development. Economic growth involves a change from subsistence economy to a market economy. This is a new concept for traditional villagers who . . . need some motivation to produce more than their own needs and to make a market system work. A function of advertising is to 'create a want in the consumer.' Thus it can be a motivating factor to produce for a cash sale. This is part of the 'raising aspirations' role for the mass media."

20. For a critical analysis of TNAAs and TNCs within a broad cultural context, see Mattelart, "Cultural Imperialism in the Multinationals' Age." For a discussion of research on advertising as a "negative force," see Beltran, "Communication Research in Latin America: The Blindfolded Inquiry?" *Der Anteil der Massenmedien bei der Herausbildung des Bewusstseins in der sich wandelnden Welt, Konferenzprotokoll II* (Internationale wissenschaftliche Kenferenz, Leipzig, DDR, September 17–21, 1974), p. 376–77.

21. Dunn, "Rising Nationalism vs. the International Language of Advertising," pp. 17–18, argues that the concepts of "national identity" and "nationalism" are fuzzy.

22. Sutton, "All Advertising Is Local; So Why are the Multinational Agencies Peeing in Our Garden? (Paper prepared for Tenth Asian Advertising Congress, Sydney, Australia, 3 November 1976), p. 11.

23. For a discussion of the transnationals' having to come to terms with dominant groups in the local political system to gain access to a country, see Huntington, "Transnational Organizations in World Politics," p. 358.

24. Huntington, loc. cit., argues that the immediate impact of the transnational will probably be conservative but that over the longer-run it may also redistribute power. Galtung does not make such a distinction. Rather, he argues that external forces like the TNCs reinforce the status quo through close ties between Center elites and Periphery elites, or bridgeheads.

25. Edward N. Ney, "The World of Advertising is Not One World" (Paper delivered at the American Association of Advertising Agencies, Chicago, 10 November 1977), pp. 10–11. In his talk, Ney rejects "a sort of American conceit that 'one world' would be an American sort of place" and adds that "despite numerous attempts to bury it, nationalism does not die easily" and today's transnationals have "run hard into strong countervailing forces." (p. 5)

26. Sergio Salas, "Boon or Bane?" *Pentad*, no. 4 (1979), p. 7.

3
Advertising: An Application of Power

Nations, according to Galtung, can have two kinds of power: resource, or difference, power, and structural, or relation, power.[1]

A world power like the United States is also an advertising power, or Center nation, because it has more and better advertising and related communications resources than do other nations. When these resources are combined with others (culture, technology, language, GNP, military, population, land area, capital, and so forth) possessed by the Center and exercised in relation to the Periphery, a Center's influence over others is considerable.

Apart from the power nations obtain from what they *have,* nations also gain some of their power from their *place* in a structure. The United States, for example, is a structurally powerful, advertising Center nation because of the commanding position it occupies in the near-global advertising industry relative to Periphery nations. A Center nation has advertising self-respect and self-sufficiency and, as Galtung has emphasized, "structural power really becomes operational when one nation gets under the skin of the other so that it is able to form and shape the inside of that nation."[2] This book examines whether the TNAAs, controlled by Center nations, are important vehicles through which advertising penetration occurs in China, Indonesia, Malaysia, and Singapore.

Center and Periphery are considered as those nations having transnational advertising agencies operating within their borders and distinguished by these criteria:

1. *Absolute properties suggesting resource power.* I shall use conventional "development indicators" as regularly compiled by international organizations like the World Bank and the United Nations, and "advertising indicators" as compiled or reported by individual advertising agencies or their professional organizations and by the International Advertising Association (IAA) in New York City, and *Advertising Age.* The latter two are the most authoritative sources of information on transnational advertising. A "Center" nation is high on rank dimensions, while a "Periphery" nation is low.
2. *Interaction relation and interaction structure suggesting structural power.* I

70

shall use data on advertising partner and commodity concentration to examine the kind of direct contact that the Peripheries have with the outside world. I shall want to determine whether the center is "more centrally located in the interaction network than the periphery—the periphery being higher on the concentration indices." I shall also consider advertising exchange relations to determine whether the "center enriches itself more than the periphery."[3]

These major measures of concern vary considerably with time and place, and any one by itself is far from perfect as a basis for empirical research. In combination, however, they are useful in providing some insight into the complexities of advertising imperialism as a particular subtype of dominance and power relationships. The absolute property measure, for example, does illustrate that some nations are richer than others, as well as being stronger, healthier, better educated, more literate, more knowledgeable about advertising, more accessible to mass media and advertising, and so forth. Relative to a great number of other nations, the industrially advanced and advertising-rich nations like the United States, Britain, and Japan qualify as Center nations and stand in an asymmetric relation of exploitation and penetration. None of these Centers, however, is equally dominant in all five of Galtung's types of imperialism or in advertising imperialism. Japan, for example, is comparatively strong in economics, weak in military and culture, but increasingly strong in advertising. On the other hand, the United States is relatively strong in economics, politics, culture, and communications, but its military or "policing" power, as demonstrated by the Vietnam war or the Iranian hostage crisis, has declined since the end of World War II. In advertising, the United States is a particularly powerful Center because it hosts the central offices of many large TNAAs with numerous offices around the globe, and its advertising is attractive to Periphery elite. No other nation is even close to the United States in either absolute resources or relative structural power.

The interaction relation and interaction structure aspects of Center-Periphery relations are crude at best. They are particularly difficult to measure in a formal testing sense because of the problems getting reliable data about the quantity and quality of advertising interaction. Galtung's notions of "raw materials," "processed goods," and "degree of processing" are especially difficult to apply to something as imprecise as advertising exchange. For example, print media advertising is particularly difficult to pin down since it can so easily enter a society and since most governments do not require specific permission to import Center-made newspaper and magazine advertising materials.

Governments do not systematically keep statistics on something as imprecise as "advertising trade," and advertising agencies and mass media—whether local or transnational—are reluctant to give anyone access to their internal records that might provide the basis for some quantification of advertising production, exchange, and actual use. Agencies like to boast that much of their work is "original" and "locally produced," but anyone outside of the system would have great difficulty determining what and how much local and how much foreign input—whether of expertise, ideas, symbols, language, technology, graphics, and so forth—went into the creation of a particular advertisement. This is especially a problem with TNAA materials since so many different hands are involved in the different stages of creation, processing, and distribution of any advertising campaign. Frequently, a TNAA-created ad will have so many nonindigenous elements in it that the "localness" and any spin-off effects from production are impossible to define. For example, a former Asia-Pacific creative director for McCann-Erickson has described the multinational input that went into a commercial film he made for that American TNAA to launch a famous American cigarette in the Philippines:

> Conceived in Manila, geared in Singapore, shot in Malaysia by a cameraman from Vietnam featuring a model from Australia (and four ladies from Indonesia, Edinburgh, Melbourne, and South Africa), processed in Tokyo, music arranged and recorded in Sydney along with voice-over and editing in Hong Kong.[4]

Sometimes a particular advertisement may appear very "local" to the average Third World consumer, but a close examination of the actual creation and production would show that the creative concept, the research developments, and other key ingredients going into the advertisement—not to mention the budget and the media placement plan—were external to the host nation. Separating the Periphery from the Center mix of skill and education, and quantifying the precise contribution that various individuals, organizations, and nations make to the division of labor and the overall advertising process is a serious problem.

Both resource and structural power are important, but the former expressed in absolute properties—such as the nation's total annual advertising expenditures, its per capita advertising expenditures, and its volume of TNAA billings and gross income—will take on greater prominence simply because more cross-national data is available in this area. Greater reliance on the more abstract interaction structure and relation aspects of the Center-Periphery distinction must await the development of more precise concepts and indices and, more important, the availability of additional kinds of data about the TNAAs and other agencies. Increasing the quality and quantity of information about transnational advertising will require considerable TNAA cooperation, which is highly unlikely given the current general state of confrontation between TNCs and the Third World.

Without advocating a formal, rigid testing of advertising imperialism, I will be exploring the structure within and between nations to see whether advertising exchange can provide any confirmation of the validity of Galtung's work. Data will be collected in three areas:

1. *Partner concentration.* I shall want to see if and how China, Indonesia, Malaysia, and Singapore are involved in feudal patterns of advertising transactions and, more specifically, what Center nation(s)—if any—they are dependent on for advertising. I will be interested in learning what nations these diverse Asian societies have as advertising exchange partners, with whom they exchange advertisements, training, ideas, personnel, and technology. If Galtung's theory holds true, China, Indonesia, Malaysia, and Singapore will have few advertising trading partners, and those they have will tend to be concentrated in the advertising-rich, Center nations. I expect to show that one Center nation—the United States—tends to dominate advertising in each of these nations, just as it generally does elsewhere in transnational communications exchange. Other Western or industrial nations such as Britain, Australia, and Japan, which have such strong historic ties in the Asian region also may function as Center nations vis-à-vis advertising in China, Indonesia, Malaysia, and Singapore but their role probably is as an intermediary between the super-Center nation, the United States, and the Periphery nations.

Galtung's concept of *go-between* is particularly significant because it realistically recognizes that the world is not neatly divided into Center and Periphery. There are several Centers, for example, and important subtle distinctions need to be made between nations regardless of whether they are analyzed in terms of political, military, economic, cultural, or communication (including advertising) interaction. Just as there are extreme super-Centers and extreme super-Peripheries so, too, are there nations that are interspersed somewhere between Center and Periphery on a continuum. These go-between nations are part of the same transnational network that the Center and the Periphery are tied into, but their degree of processing is ahead of the Periphery and behind the Center.[5] Go-between nations can often be distinguished from the rich and poor nations they interact with through what Galtung calls "highly visible and consensual racial, ethnic, or geographical distinctions."[6]

An important consequence of Center-Periphery relations with go-betweens can be subimperialism. This is a situation in which a Center nation builds on already existing structures and makes use of another nation's imperialism or aspiration in that direction.[7] Under such a partnership arrangement, the Center makes use of bilateral ties with a "favorite country" to maintain the status quo and particular types of development patterns and processes.

2. *Commodity concentration.* Galtung maintains that Center nations trade in a highly diversified range of commodities, including knowledge, communications skills, technology, and techniques. Periphery nations, on the

other hand, are under great pressure to concentrate on a very narrow range of commodities and services. These nations tend to be pushed into monoculture—the production of a few particular agricultural products such as rubber, palm oil, and rice in Malaysia, or of highly profitable, exportable natural resources such as oil and timber in Indonesia and tin in Malaysia. Singapore, because of its small size and its lack of raw materials other than labor, has historically specialized in a narrow range of transportation and small-scale entrepot trading activities. China is a special case because—until recently—it has stressed foreign trade conducted without modern advertising and prided itself on self-reliance. For each case study, I shall examine which aspects of this commodity called advertising are already produced locally, which can or should be produced locally, and which are being produced abroad and imported—particularly from the TNAAs' headquarters but also from their other offices in both Center and Periphery nations.

3. *Vertical trading.* Galtung argues that vertical interaction between Center and Periphery is a significant factor in maintaining inequality, and I shall examine this vertical interaction relation as it specifically pertains to advertising. According to my theory, dependent peripheral nations are involved primarily in productive activities that are comparatively primitive, standardized, labor intensive, and low in skill and capital equipment. Center nations, on the other hand, are involved in activities that generally require expensive skills and capital. A highly specialized service industry like advertising seems to have aspects of both. It is highly labor intensive and makes frequent use of standardized techniques and concepts, but it is also intimately linked with the transnational corporations, which spend large sums of money on advertising and have relatively sophisticated, highly individualized marketing needs.[8] A strategically located industry like advertising appears to fall into the category of activities that have relatively high spin-off effects, even in Periphery nations. Galtung has maintained that the Center nations gain proportionally more from their trading with Periphery nations than vice versa, and the result is that the gap between the rich and the poor nations is perpetuated, even though local Periphery elites identify with Center elites and profit from them. In this context, I shall consider the importance of the TNAAs relative to the strictly local agencies. My assumption is that the TNAAs will have the upper hand in each nation's advertising industry but that tensions and state pressures on advertising and TNCs will vary somewhat depending on internal political and other conditions.

Presumably, by changing or breaking down these different forms of dependency having special relevance to advertising, Third World nations would be in a stronger position to free themselves from Center domination and achieve self-development.[9] In general, such developments would complement other Periphery efforts designed to implement a new global economic and communication order. In particular, they would help create a "new advertising order" in which *nondependent* advertising agencies might play a major role.

Advertising per se is not "bad" or "unjust" for any society. Advertising dominance relations (rather than relations of equality), however, are harmful and unfair to a society because they contribute to advertising dependency and to an unequal distribution of benefits within and between nations. Like other dynamic forces that can influence a Periphery nation, advertising cannot contribute to genuine, autocentered development unless it is autonomous and is able to withstand foreign pressures. In other words, nondependent advertising is necessary (but not sufficient) for advertising equality, including greater participation from non-elites.

An advertising agency—whether it is a TNAA or a local entity—is autonomous if it meets two criteria for local participation:

1. A majority of its *ownership* is in the hands of citizens of the host Periphery nation.
2. Its administrative and creative *decision making processes* are in the hands of managers who are citizens of the host Periphery nation.

Together, these criteria ensure that, formally at least, the agency's power is explicitly controlled by indigenous rather than by foreign interests.[10] Majority local ownership and management control by citizens holding senior agency positions such as general manager and creative director help ensure that the locus of decision making and ultimate legal responsibility physically rests within the Periphery nation itself. Such an intra-agency organizational structure ideally should increase an agency's social responsibility and accountability to Periphery governments *and* to the people and should help make certain that the senior management and creative personnel of any agency are aware of local conditions and needs and are personally familiar with national development policies and plans. Without such consciousness, the possibility of a redistribution of global advertising power or of a Periphery nation ever modifying its advertising industry to better serve indigenous rather than foreign needs is slight, and advertising sovereignty cannot be achieved.

As a pure type, then, nondependent advertising would foster autonomous advertising agencies that function without reliance on substantial foreign inputs of any kind. The nondependent agency would be a creative national rather than a reactive foreign entity. It would be in a position to counteract external pressure from the TNAAs and other components of the transnational power structure. It would have more than pro forma control over its own operations—it would hire local staff and managers; it would control its own finances and planning; it would rely on local clients rather than TNC clients; it would actively use indigenous ideas (advertising concepts, visuals, music, copy, packaging, etc.); and it would be highly conscious of its social responsibilities to serve national development goals defined in terms of satisfying the fundamental needs of the majority. These goals would emphasize decreasing the gap between rich and poor through policies and plans that solve urgent social problems such as poverty, illiteracy, and malnutrition, which afflict the poor in what Galtung calls the periphery of the Periphery.

Nondependent agencies do not need to be totally independent or self-sufficient. They do not have to be entirely cut off from the dealings with the Center, but any exchange would be carefully controlled so that agencies would be involved only in voluntary, mutually beneficial exchange with other nations. In other words, Third World agencies would not be passive recipients and mere customers of the Center. Instead, they would have sufficient power to actively maintain contacts with a *variety* of nations—both rich and poor (North and South, East and West)—but particularly with fellow poor nations and regional neighbors. These nondependent agencies would have sufficient power-over-themselves to be able to make themselves immune to the destructive impact of advertising power exerted from the outside.[11]

Third World advertising agencies currently meeting my two criteria of majority local ownership and senior administrative and creative control are not necessarily conducive to autonomous development and the elimination of exploitation. Obviously, even a wholly indigenously owned and operated agency can have negative consequences on the host nation depending on how those in power decide to use it. Such an agency, for example, may voice unhappiness with the existing advertising order, but its actions might indicate it is content with overall dependent relations, whether exhibited through the TNAAs or other forces, that maintain the transnational power structure. This will be the situation if those running an agency are serving as TNAA fronts, or in other ways functioning as bridgeheads for the Center, and are content with highly formal equality and nothing more.[12]

Static Propositions

Given Galtung's theory, rich with implications, my own nearly four years' experience living, working, and studying in Asia, and personal knowledge about the way advertising, transnational corporations, and political systems function, some tentative statements can be made about what one can expect to find in the TNAAs and their operations in Periphery Asian nations.

The following selection of propositions are divided into those that describe how things are (relying on static data), and those that describe how things are changing over time. This latter "dynamics" category is particularly important since any diagnosis of dependence relationships requires the observation of trends over time.[13] Advocates of the TNAAs, and more generally of the dominant paradigm of development, suggest that penetration of the periphery is necessary to serve as a stimulating mechanism, but that over time the operations serve the ends of the Third World nation. Critics of this argument maintain that continued penetration by the TNAAs and other sources of external power basically reinforces a feudal structure and persists in keeping nations weak and dependent.

I shall concentrate on describing the presence or absence of advertising dependency in the four Asian host nations. I make no claim for the completeness of this list of propositions, and it will not be possible to present data—except of the impressionistic variety—from *each* nation for *each* proposition. But even limited findings based on a systematic consideration of these propositions should serve as a means to better understand advertising power and Third World politics at a concrete level.

Static Propositions

1. *Major decisions in advertising agencies in the Periphery are controlled more by foreigners than by local citizens.*

To assess the validity of this assertion, I will need to apply Galtung's thinking on "vertical trading" to the production of advertisements. I will need to understand the influence that the TNAAs have on the national advertising industry in each of the nations, and I will need to understand agencies' decision making processes and division of labor, and to determine what skills—local or foreign—are necessary to "process" advertising. If Galtung's theory is valid, I should find that relatively unsophisticated types of advertising and managerial activities are conducted locally by indigenous personnel, but activities requiring costly capital, major transnational corporate clients, and a high degree of skill, sophistication, and creativity are conducted in, or heavily influenced by, the Center's TNAAs. In addition, I should find that the Center trains Periphery advertising personnel to filter and process their work with Center eyes.

2. *In the Periphery, indigenous advertising personnel and government policymakers concerned about the regulation of advertising have little interaction with their counterparts in other periphery nations.*

In a feudal Center-Periphery structure, interaction with the outside world is monopolized by Center nations, with the result that Periphery-Periphery interaction is missing or minimal. This means that in advertising interaction between a Center and "its" Periphery, the Periphery interacts relatively little with other Peripheries and has great problems organizing to balance the power pressures imposed by the Center. Figure 2 illustrates this possible relationship, assuming that the United States is the world's

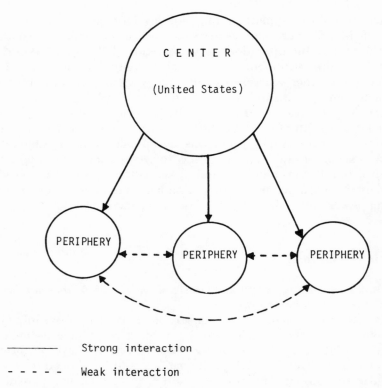

Fig. 2. Hypothesized advertising relations between Center and its Peripheries.

most powerful advertising Center nation and that it has a multi-Periphery empire. The significance of such a structure is that the TNAAs operating in Periphery nations maintain close contact with their sister agencies, particularly in neighboring nations that share similar market and other characteristics and also, of course, with the parent TNAA headquarters in the Center. Advertising elites in the Periphery have a heavy professional and social reliance on the Center, but not on their fellow Periphery nations, even if geographically close.

3. *For its advertising, the Periphery nation depends on only one advertising Center nation.*

This proposition is based on Galtung's contention that in the feudal interaction structure, "Periphery interaction with other Center nations is missing."[14] Advertising exchange patterns, like those for other types of exchange, are vertical, and Periphery interaction is monopolized with the implication that interaction with other Center and Periphery nations is missing. Center nations, however, interact freely with a variety of Center and Periphery nations as their advertising partners.

4. *Advertising subimperialism is maintained in the Periphery through a bilateral arrangement in which the Center nation builds on already existing structures and uses another nation as a go-between partner to maintain the status quo in a region.*

In this multi-empire world, imperialist systems can exist globally and regionally. Particularly powerful Centers might use ties with less powerful go-between nations to exercise control over advertising within a particular Periphery region. This proposition is based on Figure 3, which shows Galtung's model of how the United States might interact. Galtung has explained:

> The formula is simple: establish a bilateral relation between the U. S. on one hand and a region on the other, select a "favorite country" which can

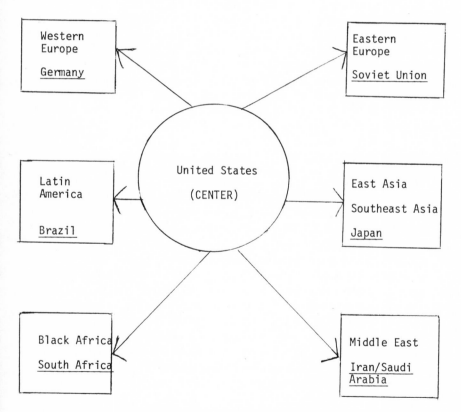

Fig. 3. Hypothesized bilateral advertising relations between the United States and Periphery regions through "Favorite Countries." (SOURCE: Galtung, *Conflict on a Global Scale: Social Imperialism and Sub-Imperialism—Continuities in the Structural Theory of Imperialism,*" p. 163.)

support local forces in exercising control so as to maintain a status quo, a law and order pattern compatible with capitalist types of "development."[15]

Nations qualifying as the Center's "favorite country" probably are more interested in their own self-interest than in helping any Center, but they also probably recognize that a coordinated Center is in the best interests of all existing Centers. A head-on confrontation with a super-Center like the United States would not be in the best interests of the centers within the go-between nations. Therefore, a favorite country or a go-between might allow advertising subimperialism by a more powerful Center so that it, in turn, could continue to benefit from other types of imperialism, particularly economic, that it may deem more significant than advertising over the long-term.

In practical advertising terms, this proposition is particularly important. It suggests that Periphery nations may have different complex sets of links to the outside world and that the higher the level of dependency on external factors, the fewer the policy options available to Periphery government officials interested in nondependent advertising. Some Periphery nations are more fully "internationalized" and better integrated into this structure of dominance and, therefore, they have fewer policy alternatives open to them vis-à-vis the TNAAs, as well as the TNCs generally. In Karl W. Deutsch's terms, these nations are likely to have fewer "emancipatory capabilities" by which they could overcome neocolonialism.[16] Other Peripheries have greater capabilities because they are less tightly intertwined with the transnational power structure generally.

5. *Periphery nations that had to struggle and even use direct violence to gain their political independence from a "mother" Center nation are more likely to pursue dissociative policies toward TNAAs than are those nations which gained independence more peacefully.*[17]

Galtung generally has emphasized the problems that ex-colonial nations have in bringing about structural changes in their societies. Since advertising in many of these Periphery nations was imported as part of a larger Western development package, it is easy to understand how an organization like the TNAA could become firmly embedded in the Periphery and why the status quo is so difficult to change. Those nations which amicably gained their independence from their ex-colonial rulers are more accommodating to foreigners, including advertising specialists. Those nations, on the other hand, which had to struggle to win their political freedom tend to resist foreigners. It seems reasonable to expect that some of the anticolonial, anti-Western feelings of confrontation from the preindependence periods have carried over into contemporary policies through which the Periphery nations consciously strive to decouple themselves from their former political rulers.

Dynamic Propositions

1. *In advertising there is growing Center coordination, particularly among the capitalist powers.*

Galtung has argued that despite a degree of economic competition, Center capitalist nations—particularly the United States, Japan, and members of the European Community—are moving closer together as partners.[18] Concerted elite action by these friendly Centers is designed to preserve the status quo and maintain existing development patterns. Such Centers are not interested in escalating their differences into genuine confrontation. In advertising, as in many other areas, the world has more than one Center, but because of changing global realities, including oil crises and Periphery elites' desires for greater autonomy, these Centers are increasingly motivated to coordinate their efforts. This has become necessary so that the basic system that supports advertising and fosters economic growth can be maintained to the advantage of the Centers and the centers in the Peripheries. Galtung has hypothesized that a socialist Center like superpower Soviet Union also is involved in increased "collusion" with other Centers as a means of stopping a total power decline.[19] Such an evolving cooperative arrangement between capitalist and socialist Centers, however, is of little significance to transnational advertising. This is because socialist Centers are not particularly interested in exporting the services of a socialist-style TNAA into the Periphery.

2. *The TNAAs' power in Periphery nations is changing in form but not decreasing relative to the indigenous non-TNAA enterprises.*

The Periphery nations are giving more formal attention to the pursuit of strategies designed to make themselves less susceptible—more "immune," in Galtung's terms—to any destructive impact from foreign influences, including advertising. There have been notable positive spin-offs from the presence of the TNAAs, and these are helping Periphery nations develop an indigenous advertising producing capability. But despite joint ventures, TNAA-funded training, the formation of local agencies by former TNAA employees, and other benefits, the TNAAs continue to maintain a dominant position in Periphery nation advertising. Strictly indigenous agencies in the Periphery are still not a serious threat to the status quo, and the TNAAs are able to continue to exhibit great flexibility by adjusting to changing conditions and maintaining great power over dominated societies. In Galtung's terms, power relations change, but the power level of Periphery parties remains relatively low. Advertising imperialism, like other forms, goes through various phases, but the Center is resilient enough to maintain a decisive edge over the Periphery. Galtung has emphasized that in this type of changing interaction "the control is less concrete: it is not a physical presence, but a link; and this link takes the shape of international organizations."[20] As one of these organizations, the TNAAs link the center in the Center with the center in the Periphery in a harmony of interest.

3. *In plural Periphery nations, the presence of the TNAAs has a destabilizing effect on ethnic relationships and is exacerbating social and political tensions between different ethnic groups through influences on negative, intra-actor effects.*

Ex-colonial periphery societies often qualify as *plural societies* because of their people's ties to highly visible race, language, religious, and other divisions rather than to the political nation-state.[21] As plural societies, they seem prone to conflict and exernal domination.[22] In such divided societies, the TNAAs contribute to existing intra-Periphery problems by their hiring and other practices that tend to benefit one particular dominant ethnic group. Such practices create intra-elite conflict over Center relations.[23] In Periphery nations, the TNAAs need local contacts or partners, and they tend to use the more urban, affluent, economically active groups rather than others as their bridgeheads.[24] This alliance between a particular group or class of elites and the TNAAs aggravates existing deep-rooted intrasociety cleavages and also places the Periphery group under great cross-pressure.[25] On one hand, the bridgeheads function as the pawn, or minor partners, of the Center. On the other hand, they operate as the exploiters of the periphery in their own society. Galtung's theory predicts that such a vulnerable position eventually requires the group of bridgeheads to take sides: "Either it will have to relocate and join the center in the Center, or it will have to stand in solidarity with the periphery in the Periphery."[26]

Given an unstable, complex situation in the Periphery plural society, disharmony between particular ethnic groups' centers and the center of the Center is likely, and tensions arise that create hostility against a minority group—elite and nonelite. Galtung has suggested that a result could be that populist or nationalist forces—either of counter-elites in the Periphery or of the majority groups' centers *and* the periphery of the Periphery—unite and take actions that are contrary to what the components of the transnational power structure or their bridgeheads would want. In opposition to an allegedly racist, or at least an unfair, society, the victimized group—as "a pariah minority"—would support the Center by lobbying for the status quo (or "refeudalization"), through corruption or other means, to buy off periphery political elites.[27] Political instability and changes in the status quo generally tend to produce losses for both the Center and their bridgeheads in the Periphery. On the other hand, members of the plural nation's minority group (both elites and nonelites) could possibly interpret such a situation as a threat to their survival as loyal citizens of the Periphery, and set their ethnic differences aside to join with other groups in the threatened Periphery nation to oppose continued Center domination of advertising or other aspects of Periphery life.

In such a defeudalization process, all people, including the nonelites of all ethnic groups, might have their living conditions improved. A more likely outcome would be that the Center elites and their bridgeheads would be eliminated from power and replaced by a new set of elites, this time from indigenous groups. The new "top dogs" in the Periphery may or may not be interested in achieving an equitable distribution of income and other aspects of living conditions or in altering national development policies and plans.

Notes

1. See Galtung, *The European Community: A Superpower in the Making* (London: Allen & Unwin Ltd., 1973), pp. 35–37, for his important discussion of the various sources of power.

2. Ibid, pp. 43–44.

3. Galtung, "A Structural Theory of Imperialism," *Journal of Peace Research* 8, no. 2., 1971, p. 103.

4. Geoff Pike, "The Real-Life Adventure of Low-Budget Films," *Media*, October 1975, p. 10.

5. For Galtung's analysis of a third nation interspersed between Center and Periphery, see his "A Structural Theory of Imperialism," pp. 104–5.

6. Ibid., p. 104.

7. See Galtung, "Conflict on a Global Scale: Social Imperialism and Sub-Imperialism— Continuities in the Structural Theory of Imperialism," *World Development* 4, no. 3 (March 1976), especially pp. 160–64.

8. This point is elaborated upon in G. K. Helleiner, "The Role of Multinational Corporations in the Less Developed Countries' Trade in Technology," *World Development* 3, no. 4 (April 1975), pp. 173–74.

9. Karl W. Deutsch has written about "emancipatory capabilities—the abilities of countries to make their way by loosening or modifying their involvement in whatever is left of the imperialistic system." See his discussion of how nations might overcome neocolonialism in "Imperialism and Neocolonialism," *The Paper of The Peace Science Society (International)* 23 (1973), especially p. 24.

10. Reliance on control only through majority shareholding by local nationals is risky since there are many ways that foreigners can continue to exercise control over a business. For a discussion of some of these, see Franklin B. Weinstein, "Multi-National Corporations and the Third World: The Case of Japan and Southeast Asia" (Paper prepared for the 1975 annual meeting of the American Political Science Association, San Francisco, September 2–5, 1975), pp. 10–12.

11. Galtung has compared a nation's developing more power-over-itself to "immunization against bacteria." See *The European Community*, pp. 34–35.

12. For an excellent discussion of the role that international organizations, incuding the TNCs, play as the "great equalifiers" of elites, see Galtung, *The European Community*, p. 44. He notes that bridgeheads in the Periphery are often satisfied with highly formal equality and never demand anything more from elites in the Center.

13. For a testing of Galtung's theory, with special emphasis on trends over time, see Herb Addo, "Trends in International Value-Inequality 1969–1970: An Empirical Study," *Journal of Peace Research*, 13, no. 1 (1976), pp. 13–34.

14. Galtung, "A Structural Theory of Imperialism," p. 89.

15. Galtung, "Conflict on a Global Scale", p. 163.

16. Deutsch, "Imperialism and Neocolonialism," p. 24.

17. Vernon has made this same point in emphasizing that "the circumstances—often accidental and idiosyncratic in character—under which the country received its independence" have much to do with how a society reacts to transnational corporations. See "Problems and Policies Regarding Multinational Enterprises," in his *The Economic and Political Consequences of Multinational Enterprise: An Anthology*, (Cambridge, Mass.: Harvard University Press, 1972), pp. 166–68.

18. Galtung, "Conflict on a Global Scale," p. 163.

19. Ibid., p. 164.

20. Galtung, "A Structural Theory of Imperialism," p. 95.

21. One of the oldest—but still very useful—models of "plural societies" was developed by J. S. Furnivall, an economist and colonial administrator. He noted that in tropical colonial settings such as Burma and Indonesia, the rulers and the ruled were of different ethnic backgrounds and lived side by side and yet apart from one another within the same political unit. The theory maintains that racial divisions within former colonial societies are the result of a deliberate "divide and rule" policy of the colonial rulers and that such societies are inherently prone to conflict. For an introduction to Furnivall's ideas, see his *Colonial Policy and Practice* (New York: New York University Press, 1956).

22. For analyses of "plural societies," see such works as Malcolm Cross, "On Conflict, Race Relations, and the Theory of the Plural Society," *Race* 12, no. 4 (April 1971), pp. 477–94; Leo Kuper and M. G. Smith, *Pluralism in Africa* (Berkeley: University of California Press, 1969); Alvin Rabushka and Kenneth Shepsle, *Politics in Plural Societies: A Theory of Democratic Instability* (Columbus, Ohio: Charles E. Merrill Co., 1972); and Katherine West, "Stratification and Ethnicity in 'Plural' New States," *Race* 13, no. 4 (April 1972), pp. 487–95.

23. For a case study of intra-elite conflict caused by demands for what Galtung calls "refeudalization," see Robert B. Stauffer, "The Political Economy of a Coup: Transnational Linkages and Philippine Political Response," *Journal of Peace Research* 9, no. 3 (1974), pp. 161–77.

24. The more urban, affluent, economically active groups in ex-colonial societies frequently are immigrants that the colonial master imported to carry out specific economic functions. In many of these nations, Chinese and Indians arrived during the colonial period under "open door" immigration policies designed to attract laborers and traders.

25. This is a critically important point within the context of the plural societies of this study. Galtung makes no reference to the ethnicity of any bridgehead in his theory, but see his "A Structural Theory of Imperialism," p. 108, for a discussion of this basic point within the context of defeudalization.

26. Ibid.

27. Weinstein, "Multinational Corporations and the Third World," p. 20. He discusses how the overseas Chinese generally control the region's economic structure, perpetuate corruption, and contribute to social tensions that impede national integration.

Part II

Transnational Advertising Structure

4
The Global Scene

Advertising is becoming internationalized rather than Americanized—the only trouble is in telling the two adjectives apart.

—David S. Nicholl[1]

A central problem facing anyone undertaking a study of contemporary advertising power in Asia or anywhere else is determining exactly how national and transnational forces are linked.

Part I addressed this problem theoretically by contending that the TNAAs are significant vehicles through which advertising and other influences of the transnational power structure can flow within and between nations. It presented an abstract framework as a foundation upon which to analyze the ability of the TNAAs to create tensions and exercise corporate power over their hosts. Also, it broadly argued that these giant advertising businesses are feared because they possess certain power resources and are organized to perpetuate dominance over weak nations and weak indigenous advertising organizations.

Some nations are, indeed, advertising Center nations because of power-over-others and power-over-themselves. Such power, however, seems contextual, and it does not lend itself to anything but gross generalizations about its consequences on national development. Therefore, case studies of particular nation-states and particular TNAAs, at particular times, are essential if advertising power in Asia is to be placed in perspective.

Succeeding chapters will now progress from this conceptual framework to deal concretely with the present-day transnationalization of the advertising industry. This chapter will describe the evolution of the TNAAs as commercial entities exercising their influence on a near-global basis.

The TNAAs' Evolution

The United States invented modern advertising and controls most of the TNAAs that use their corporate power to transmit capital, personnel, ad-

87

vertising accounts, and ideas around the world without much attention to political boundaries. As *Fortune* concluded: "The problems and solutions are much the same in London, Paris, or Bombay, since modern advertising, an American export, is essentially the same everywhere."[2]

The first American advertising agency to "go international" was J. Walter Thompson (JWT). In 1899, the New York agency established an office in London. The subsequent twentieth century spread of the transnational advertising agency beyond its national home base—particularly New York's Madison Avenue—is a reflection of major changes that have taken place in world capitalism's market system. Many of these changes, especially those related to the emergence of near-global consumerism and to how business is organized and controlled transnationally, have occurred rapidly since World War II and have affected both rich and poor societies. Developments in the creation and dissemination of mass messages that have helped give rise to the TNCs' global operations are obvious in most corners of the "shrinking" globe.

Less apparent, however, are the striking changes that have occurred within the service industry as opposed to the manufacturing or extractive industries, which make their profits more from material rather than human resources. The most significant change taking place in contemporary business has not been simply the trend towards bigness. Theodore Levitt has argued that the biggest revolution is: "the industrialization of service, in which the same kind of managerial rationality (*how* we think) is being applied in the non-goods-producing sector. The most visible way this is being done today is in mass merchandising of consumer goods and services."[3]

As part of an intensely competitive service industry, advertising agencies play a glamorous and an especially important management role, as well as a creative role, in helping to sell goods, services, and ideas to the masses. Especially since the 1960s and continuing into the 1980s, advertising agencies, predominantly headquartered in the United States, were going transnational.[4] Like the transnational manufacturers, the transnational ad agencies first went to Europe, usually Britain, and then later to less affluent, non-Western parts of the world.[5] Wherever they went, they took with them their home-office structures, creative and managerial skills, personal and professional values, corporate ideologies, and various technologies. The spread of the TNAAs coincided with the general demise of face-to-face contact as a means of selling and promoting goods and services. As the cost of personal selling increased almost everywhere, the relative efficiency and effectiveness of advertising as a sales communications tool gained in importance everywhere.[6]

Today, transnational advertising organizations are powerful members of a distinct subset of TNCs that continue to expand and profit from transnational activities, linking consumer and seller, rich and poor, First World and Third World. The TNAAs' enormous size relative to indigenous agencies and the quantity of resources at the disposition of themselves and their TNC clients worldwide inevitably contribute to influencing development policies and patterns. Most directly, the TNAAs have an impact on nations' mass media, especially television, through the steady stream of advertisements they create and distribute. These agencies also have a more subtle impact on economic, cultural and political policies and actions within and between societies.

In 1975, for example, Philip Morris, Inc., America's fastest growing cigarette manufacturer, ordered Leo Burnett, one of its TNAAs, to prepare an advertisement which proudly announced:

Marlboro. Now the number one selling cigaret around the world.
Not so long ago, Marlboro was just another brand. And Marlboro Country was somewhere west of the Mississippi. Then the ideas of a full-flavored cigaret caught on. Soon Marlboro Country was in Chicago, New York and a lot of towns along the way. Today Marlboro Country stretches from New York to Berlin to Sydney. Now Marlboro Country is everywhere.[7]

This "Marlboro Country" advertisement with its basic western American cowboy approach is but one illustration of two revolutionary phenomena that have greatly affected the world's consumers.[8] One phenomenon has been the march of the TNCs, large global businesses like Philip Morris of New York City, into almost every corner of the world. These TNCs, more often than not based in the United States or at least the industrially advanced societies of Western Europe and Japan, have rapidly spread branches, subsidiaries, and joint ventures around the world to tap new consumer markets and maximize profits for the parent corporation.[9] United States direct foreign investment, for example, increased from an estimated $12 billion in 1950 to $50 billion in 1960 to $140 or more billion by 1977.[10]

Today, major advertisers no longer limit their base of operations to the domestic market. An elite group of near-global advertisers would include such American TNCs as Procter & Gamble, Coca-Cola, Ford, IBM, General Foods, Gillette, Exxon, Colgate-Palmolive, and ITT; such European giants as Beecham, Bayer, Nestlé, Unilever, Philips, Shell, and British-American Tobacco; and such Japanese big names as Toyota, Sony, Matsushita, Honda, Sharp, Kao, Hitachi, and Shiseido.[11]

The lure of untapped markets has motivated these corporations, as "World Managers," to move their commercial activities abroad in hopes of realizing the dream of "One Great Market."[12] The result has been that Marlboro Country, the Pepsi Generation, McDonald's Big Mac, and other advertising campaigns have become household words to millions in more— and less—developed societies.

Philip Morris, then, is but one TNC that has acquired a vast array of manufacturing and marketing skills and other advantages from its very large transnational activities. Like other TNCs, Philip Morris has profited as frontiers around the world have been abolished and as mass media advertising has been effectively used to help in that process. In the United States, Philip Morris is but one of more than twenty thousand national and regional advertisers today, but it is also one of perhaps two hundred extremely large and aggressive TNCs that also are active far beyond their traditional home marketplace.[13]

The obsession of TNCs with growth and expansion has led to the rise of a second phenomenon that is as much a part of the American development package as the TNC manufacturers themselves. It was only natural that as the TNCs expanded abroad they would bring with them the need for effective, Madison Avenue-style advertising expertise. To sell "everywhere," the TNCs hired advertising agencies. At first, these agencies only handled the manufacturer's local, regional, and national advertising campaigns. Later, these agencies handled overseas advertising as marketing and production expanded, usually first to Britain and then from Europe elsewhere. The result of such developments was an almost frantic rush by major American agencies to get a foothold in markets around the globe.[14] These agencies' basic motivations can be summarized as:

1. To grow and make profits in an orderly manner.
2. To serve the transnational advertising needs of major domestic clients who were now operating overseas.[15]

As manufacturers like Philip Morris and Coca-Cola or service enterprises like Pan American Airlines and American Express were expanding into the global market, they naturally wanted the same standard of advertising counsel abroad that they had been used to getting from their home agencies. Philip Morris, therefore, turned to Leo Burnett, the Chicago agency that produced the first famous Marlboro cowboy-with-tattoo ad in 1955. The Coca-Cola Company turned to McCann-Erickson, the New York agency that is one of four agencies within the agency conglomerate called the Interpublic Group of Companies (IPG) and that first gained part of the Coca-Cola account in 1942 in Brazil and won the American domestic Coke business in 1955.[16] Pan Am turned to JWT, which created the airline's memorable phrase, "the world's most experienced," and had been affiliated with the giant American international carrier since the 1940s.[17] American Express increasingly used Ogilvy & Mather.

The close alliance between TNCs and their TNAAs has been explained by the head of McCann's international operations:

In general, McCann-Erickson has grown internationally in parallel to key international clients. Some of these (e.g., Esso, General Motors) we have served for over 50 years in various international markets. It has not been our strategy to open an office in a new country and then look for clients. We generally open offices to serve existing clients who have become active in these markets.[18]

This pattern seems to hold for TNAAs' entrances into poor and rich nations. For example, in 1960 McCann-Erickson became the first American agency to gain entrance into the affluent, but traditionally closed Japanese market. It established a unique 51 percent joint venture arrangement with Hakuhodo, Japan's second largest agency, which itself later moved abroad.[19] The partnership has resulted in a successful foreign-affiliated agency in Japan. The clients of McCann-Erickson-Hakuhodo, Tokyo, were old-line McCann clients—Coca-Cola, Nestlé, Exxon, and Gillette. Exxon, as Standard Oil Company of New Jersey, was the agency's first client in the United States, and the two corporations have grown together internationally. McCann works for Exxon in about thirty-four nations, Coca-Cola in forty-one, Nestlé in twenty-seven, and Gillette in thirty-three.[20]

To serve such increasingly transnational advertisers, the American agencies themselves had to become transnational enterprises by expanding abroad in great numbers. Before the 1960s, three American agencies— JWT, McCann, and Young & Rubicam (Y&R)—represented almost all of the international advertising agency activity outside the United States. In 1937, for example, only four American agencies were operating abroad and they had twenty-one offices. By 1957, eight agencies were active in fifty-eight overseas offices. A decade later, twenty-seven American agencies were operating 159 offices overseas.[21] Such dramatic TNAA expansion usually took one of three major forms:

1. *Branch agency,* in which the overseas office is a local office or subsidiary of the parent TNAA. The branch may have been started from scratch, or it may have been an existing agency that the TNAA bought out.
2. *Affiliate,* in which the parent TNAA has substantial, but not 100 percent, control of the overseas agency. The parent TNAA might have majority or minority interest in a "joint venture" with indigenous interests.
3. *Associate,* in which the parent TNAA is loosely or tightly connected to a local advertising agency, but has no official equity. This form can vary considerably from a very informal gentleman's agreement in which the two parties agree to assist one another when the need arises to a more formal agreement in which the TNAA, for a fee, actually manages the agency under a management contract or technical assistance agreement.

Obviously, the first option is the most desirable from the TNAA's perspective, and well-established giants like JWT, Y&R, and McCann have been extremely successful in arranging wholly-owned subsidiaries. TNAAs that have been expanding in recent years generally have not been able to pursue option 1 in light of rising nationalism in many nations and a growing desire on the part of host governments to have greater control (pro forma, at least) over foreigners doing business within their borders. The TNAAs, however, have gone along with affiliate and associate relationships and have used them to their advantage through mutually beneficial arrangements with local partners—Galtung's "bridgeheads."

Regardless of the formal arrangement through which the TNAAs initially establish shop, they are able to successfully pursue a strategic middleman role between the advertiser, on one hand, and the consumer—through the mass media—on the other. Such an arrangement ensures that the advertisers' messages are created and disseminated efficiently within a local marketing environment. Figure 4 illustrates this very important "com-

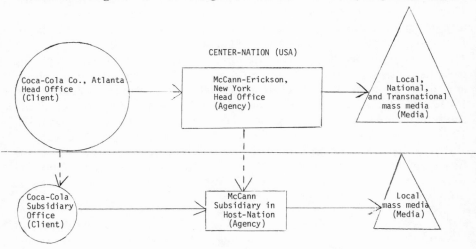

Fig. 4. "Common Account" interaction between transnational advertiser (Coca-Cola) and transnational advertising agency (McCann-Erickson) and mass media in Center and Periphery nations. Note that the example of Coca-Cola and its agency is virtually an "ideal" type of "common account" arrangement. At home and abroad, Coca-Cola uses McCann-Erickson. Media materials created jointly by Coca-Cola and McCann in the Center nation of the United States are transferred via their subsidiaries in the Periphery nations. Broken lines indicate transnational interaction.

mon account" arrangement using the example of Coca-Cola and its agency, McCann-Erickson. The arrangement, in Galtungian terms, is an interaction pattern in which the TNC subsidiary in the Periphery nations uses the same TNAA that its parent head office uses in the Center.

The Coca-Cola/McCann relationship is more intimate than the average TNC/TNAA partnership, but unless any client and its agency work in close harmony at home and abroad, their chances of producing successful advertising—especially across more than one society—are slim. With few, if any, exceptions, the most successful transnational advertisers hire equally successful TNAAs, and the two transnational entities grow and prosper together, as do their local business partners. If a TNC's sales or image is slipping, chances are good that the delicate relationship with its agency has become strained, and the TNC will probably take the initiative to find a different TNAA partner with whom it is more comfortable. Advertising agencies are always in a vulnerable position because clients can easily fire them on short notice. But unlike many small or local agencies, the TNAAs are financially strong enough to withstand the loss of any one client, even if its annual billings total millions of dollars.

In addition to serving domestic clients better and making more profits, another significant reason for the TNAAs' intense overseas expansion should be mentioned. Tom Sutton, a JWT vice president, has emphasized it:

> They [TNAAs] found that the whole is stronger than the sum of its parts. The interaction of different types of talent in different countries started to contribute everywhere. The cross fertilization of ideas, the exchange of people, the exposure to new situations all helped to build a stronger whole. Thus, while at times the financial return may have been disappointing, the intangible gains were such that they themselves became a motivating force for multinational agency operations.[22]

Today, this phenomenon of largely American-based TNAAs that, in effect, are more powerful than the sum of their individual offices scattered around the globe is an accepted part of the industrial world's market economy system. Overall, such a system assigns the institution of advertising a critical role in stimulating economic growth and the consumers' pursuit of abundance. Historian David M. Potter has argued:

> If we seek an institution that was brought into being by abundance, without previous existence in any form, and moreover, an institution which is peculiarly identified with American abundance rather than with the abundance throughout Western civilization, we will find it, I believe, in modern American advertising.[23]

Modern American advertising has been virtually created by a group consisting of large mass media, consumer-goods manufacturers, and advertising agencies headquartered in industrial urban centers (particularly New York, Chicago, and Detroit). As an institution of commercial information and persuasion, advertising has evolved to serve an economy that is based on plenty and that strives to create and satisfy new wants and new needs. As an American institution, advertising—and the agencies that create its messages and the corporations that sponsor them—clearly contribute to a propensity to consume and are an integral, synchronizing part of America's mass consumption society.

With the spread of the TNCs and the rise of more efficient, cheaper means of mass communication, American advertising has gone transnational. By the mid-1970s, for example, an American giant agency like JWT was describing its global development in this manner:

> JWT has evolved, both politically and philosophically. The term "branch office" is no longer relevant. Each office *is* the J. Walter Thompson Company in its local market. Each office is capable of making an intellectual or professional contribution to the whole. And each one offers, to an enormous number of clients around the world, a full range of creative, marketing, media and research services.[24]

By 1974—the TNAA's 110th year in business, JWT was calling itself "a total communications company," and, like other TNAAs, had diversified into other fields of communications and even into areas far beyond. It had moved from being primarily an American advertising agency serving American corporations at home and abroad into an American transnational persuasive communications corporation serving diverse host-society, American, and other transnational public and private clients.[25] By 1980, JWT had acquired the prestigious Hill and Knowlton, the world's largest public relations company, and was developing a second worldwide advertising network around its Euro-Advertising network.

Because of the agency's great profitability and size and lengthy history of intensive transnational activity, JWT today does symbolize the oligopolistic nature of transnational advertising.[26] Like a few other supergiant TNAAs, JWT is a well-established, large, aggressive, flexible, profitable, Center-based corporation that excels at selling its diverse communications skills to many buyers around the world. The JWT pattern of expansion, its strong commitments to on-the-ground operations in a variety of foreign markets, its full range of services and resources, and its philosophy of not only how to make successful advertising but also how to make foreign profits, has become a model for younger transnationals to emulate and to try to improve upon.

Galtung's predictions that international organizations will be exposed to increasing criticism and that they increasingly will grow "much more in depth and breadth than in number" seem to fit the case of contemporary TNAAs.[27] Throughout the 1970s and into the 1980s, rising costs, increased world economic instability, consumerism, and growing nationalistic pressures, especially within—but not limited to—Periphery nations, were combining to make transnational expansion difficult under the old ground rules. Younger TNAAs trying to establish a worldwide network along the lines of a JWT or a McCann-Erickson were confronted with a different set of challenges. Pioneer TNAAs had the option of opening a brand new agency and developing it along headquarters office lines, but the younger TNAAs interested in extensive foreign activities in rich and in poor societies found themselves having to give up hopes of totally controlling and owning their own offices in some societies. As a price for participating in domestic business in some foreign nations, the TNAAs increasingly found themselves having to work out ad hoc arrangements with local elites and having to increase contact with host governments who formally gave permission to the TNAAs to operate within their boundaries.

While the TNAAs were able to expand their global networks under these somewhat different rules, local agencies in many of these host nations were springing up and trying to gain sufficient strength—not only creative and financial, but also political—to make it more difficult for nonindigenous businesses to dominate their local industry. Such indigenous developments would tax the TNAAs' flexibility and resources to a greater extent than anyone would have felt possible back in the days when an agency like JWT would feel the urge to establish an office somewhere and could simply go ahead and do it using its own direct agent and without much input from local authorities or the local advertising industry, if such a thing even existed.[28]

Before taking a closer look at the characteristics of the major TNAAs, let us briefly consider the general character of contemporary international advertising.

Global Expenditures

Dollar expenditures are an important measuring stick of the size and importance of advertising in both rich and poor nations. Extreme caution must be exercised, however, with any data on advertising expenditures, particularly within the Third World.

With the exception of statistics for the United States, Japan, and Western Europe, much of the data on global advertising is based on "guesstimates" compiled by advertising industry representatives who have a vested interest in documenting the rapid growth of advertising. Statistics on Third World nations are especially imprecise and unreliable. Many nations simply do not have advertising organizations capable of gathering facts and figures systematically, and many governments have little awareness of, or interest in, the advertising industry and cannot afford the time and effort required to carefully monitor the quantity *or* quality of advertisements. In addition, many media and many advertising agencies—big and small, transnational or local—are reluctant to make public much information about their operations.

Getting a grip on the full extent of transnational, or even national, advertising is also difficult because some advertising (often called "promotions")

bypasses the media. Also, a large volume of advertising bypasses advertising agencies completely. Numerous local and regional advertisers, especially retail businesses, in most nations handle their own advertising
through internal advertising departments that do almost everything the
outside or independent agencies do. These data collection and reporting
problems are serious, but a general global picture of advertising expenditures can be pieced together.

One generalization that can be made without qualification is that the
United States is—and always had been—*the* world's advertising power, or
undisputed Center. By 1980, for example, about half of the estimated
world advertising expenditure total of some $110 billion a year was ac-
counted for by the United States. America's share of world advertising has
declined somewhat as Japan and other parts of the world gradually increase their advertising expenditures and develop their domestic
economies and mass media, but the United States clearly continues to
dominate. In 1950, for example, about 78 percent of the total world advertising expenditures of an estimated $7.4 billion was spent in the United
States. In 1960, about two-thirds of the world advertising total of $18.1
billion was American. By 1970, the American percentage had dipped to 57
percent but the total expenditures had nearly doubled to $35 billion.[29]
Estimates are that by the year 2000 advertising worldwide will approach
the trillon-dollar mark and the United States should account for more than
40 percent of this total, as figure 5 shows.

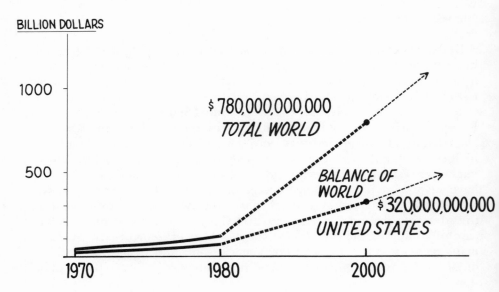

Fig. 5. Advertising projected into the twenty-first century. (SOURCE: Reprinted with
permission of Robert J. Coen, Senior Vice President, McCann-Erickson, Inc., New
York, 1980.)

As domestic America's share of the global advertising pie has decreased slightly, the outlook for the growth of advertising worldwide has continued good. For example, the share held by Japan and the rest of the world has been increasing, as table 2 shows. In absolute terms, advertising expenditures outside of the United States for the decade 1965–75 rose by 172 percent—from $10.1 billion to $27.5 billion. Throughout this decade and beyond, many nations were implementing American-oriented mass media, particularly television, and were allowing commercial broadcasting channels to compete with government owned and operated stations. Throughout these and later years, TNAAs were expanding into new Third World and actively soliciting TNC and local clients.

The drop in America's percentage of the global advertising expenditure pie is hardly surprising since the advertising industry was virtually created in the United States and only in the last decade or so have many developing nations had truly "mass" media facilities, the government policies, and the basic infrastructure that would support Westernized, fast-growing economies and modern advertising.

While America's percentage share has diminished somewhat, its absolute super-Center position continues unchallenged. Its resources—in terms of advertising expenditures—continue to grow absolutely. Structurally, America sits firmly atop the world's advertising pyramid as table 3 illustrates.

A useful indicator of how advertising generally is doing globally is information on expenditures for particular regions and nations.[30] Despite the problems in making region-to-region or nation-to-nation, year-to-year comparisons, some advertising industry survey data are available to suggest how advertising is emerging in different settings.[31] Table 4 presents data on these national indicators:

1. Total reported advertising expenditures (in $ millions)
2. Gross national product (in $ billions)
3. Advertising as a percent of gross national product.

The 1970 data covered seventy-five nations—a group that accounted for more that 96 percent of the total gross national product, more than 98 percent of the energy consumption, and more than 93 percent of all exports of noncommunist nations. The 1974 figures were for 86 nations—a group that accounted for more than 95 percent of both the total gross national product and energy consumption, and more than 90 percent of the non-Communist nations' exports.

The two surveys' data on "percent of world's expenditures made in each region" support earlier statements about the phenomenal growth of advertising in nations like Japan and the resulting gradual redistribution of the world's advertising expenditures. But in terms of an absolute indicator

Table 2

Regions' Share in Percent of World Advertising, 1970 - 1976

Region	1970	1971	1972	1973	1974	1975	1
United States	61%	57%	53%	53%	51%	52%	
Japan	6	7	7	7	7	7.5	
Canada	3	3	3	3	3	3	
Western Europe	24	26	29	29	30	28.5	
Rest	6	7	8	8	9	9	

NOTE: Percentage by year

SOURCE: Jurgen Schrader, "Advertising in Europe," Campaign, 16 December 1977, p. 21.

Table 3

Comparison of Advertising Expenditure by Major Regions in 1974

	Advertising Expenditure (in millions of dollars)	Population (million)	GNP (in billions of dollars)	Per Capita Advertising	Advertising as percent of GNP
Japan	4,163.4	109.7	413.1	37.95	1.01
ASEAN	241.1	224.0	65.8	1.08	0.37
European Community	9,115.6	259.0	1,057.6	35.20	0.86
United States	26,780.0	212.0	1,294.9	126.32	2.07

NOTE: ASEAN is the Association of Southeast Asian Nations. Members include Malaysia, Singapore, Indonesia, Philippines, and Thailand.

SOURCE: Original data compiled by International Advertising Association, but published in Toshio Yamaki, "Ad Business Makes Big Progress," The Japan Economic Journal, 13 December 1977, p. 1.

Table 4

Worldwide Advertising Expenditures by Region, 1970 and 1974

Region	Total Advertising Expenditures (In Millions of U.S. Dollars)		Per Capita Expenditures in Reporting Nation (In Millions of U.S. Dollars)		Percent of World's Expenditures Made in Each Region	
	1970	1974	1970	1974	1970	1974
United States & Canada	$20,637.2	$28,483.7	$91.25	$121.51	62	58
Europe	8,016.9	12,003.9	23.93	35.06	24	24
Asia	2,447.5	4,765.4	2.28	4.18	7	10
Latin America	1,141.1	2,077.4	4.46	7.00	4	4
Australia & New Zealand	543.7	983.7	34.92	60.35	2	2
Middle East & Africa	333.2	854.1	1.27	2.60	1	2
Total World	$33,119.6	$49,168.2	15.27	20.86	100%	100%

NOTE: The 1970 data covered 75 nations, and the 1974 data 86 nations.

SOURCE: Tenth IAA Survey of Advertising Expenditures Around the World, New York: International Research Associates, 1970, p. 7; and World Advertising Expenditures 1976 Edition, Mamaroneck, New York: Starch INRA Hooper and International Advertising Association, 1976, p. 10. Reprinted with permission of Starch INRA Hooper.

Table 5

Population, Advertising Expenditures, and Per Capita Advertising Expenditures

For a Group of Rich and Poor Nations in 1970 and 1974

Nations	Total Population (In Thousands)		Total Reported Ad Expenditures (In Millions of U.S. Dollars)		Per Capita Advertising Expenditures (In U.S. Dollars)	
	1970	1974	1970	1974	1970	1974
Australia	12,713	13,300	456.5	864.3	35.91	64.99
Bangladesh	n.a.	71,300	n.a.	8.9	n.a.	0.13
Brazil	92,237	105,100	350.0	941.9	3.79	8.96
Ethiopia	. . .	27,200	. . .	0.7	. . .	0.03
France	50,775	52,500	996.6	1,981.7	19.63	37.75
Ghana	9,030	9,600	3.2	2.4	0.35	0.25
Guatemala	5,189	5,600	3.8	7.2	0.73	1.29
India	550.376	586,300	73.4	96.4	0.13	0.16
Iran	28,662	32,000	20.0	47.6	0.70	1.49
Italy	53,670	55,600	489.0	942.8	9.11	16.96
Japan	103,540	109,700	2,115.3	4,163.4	20.43	37.95
Kuwait	733	900	2.7	9.7	3.68	10.78
Mexico	48,313	58,100	214.7	353.4	4.44	6.08
Nepal	10,900	12,300	0.7	0.6	0.06	0.05
Philippines	38,493	41,500	35.1	50.3	0.91	1.21
South Africa	21,314	24,900	99.1	356.2	4.65	14.31
South Korea	31,739	33,500	40.1	85.9	1.26	2.56
Sri Lanka	12,514	13,700	3.3	2.2	0.41	0.16
Switzerland	6,280	6,500	428.0	744.2	68.15	114.49
United States	204,765	212,000	19,600.0	26,780.0	95.72	126.32

SOURCE: Extracted from Tenth IAA Survey of Advertising Expenditures Around the World, New York: International Research Associates, 1970, pp. 10-11; and World Advertising Expenditures 1976 Edition, Mamaroneck, New York: Starch INRA Hooper and International Advertising Association, 1976, pp. 15-16. Reprinted with permission of Starch INRA Hooper.

such as advertising dollar expenditures or per capita expenditures, the affluent industrial nations of North America and Europe far outdistance the poorer, less industrialized nations of Asia, Latin America, Africa, and the Middle East.

Just as the world's regions differ in the volume of advertising and in how advertising expenditures are placed in the different media, individual societies also show extreme variance.[32] In 1974, for example, the prosperous United States was spending $126.32 per person on advertising and Switzerland $114.49 while Third World nations were spending only pennies. In that year, for example, Ethiopia spent three cents per capita, Nepal five cents, Bangladesh thirteen cents, Sri Lanka sixteen cents, India sixteen cents, Pakistan twenty cents, and Ghana twenty-five cents.

Table 5 presents data comparing these and other rich and poor nations by population, advertising expenditures, and per capita advertising expenditures in 1970 and 1974. The data suggest that while nearly all nations are spending more every year on advertising and on per capita advertising expenditure, the gap between the advertising-rich and the advertising-poor nations remains substantial.

Nations also differ tremendously according to advertising as a percent of gross national product. For example, in 1974 affluent societies like the United States and Switzerland spent 2.07 percent and 1.82 percent of their GNP, respectively, on advertising. But in poor nations, the percentage is minuscule. Advertising in Ethiopia is .03 percent of the GNP, in Nepal .06

Table 6

Advertising Expenditures, Gross National Product, and Advertising as a Percentage

of Gross National Product for a Group of Rich and Poor Nations in 1970 and 1974

Nation	Total Reported Expenditures (In Millions of U.S. Dollars) 1970	1974	Gross National Product (In Billions of U.S. Dollars) 1970	1974	Advertising as a Percent of GNP 1970	1974
Australia	456.5	864.3	31.6	52.2	1.44%	1.66
Bangladesh	.....	.8.9	...	7.7	...	0.12
Brazil	350.0	941.9	38.0	77.2	0.92	1.22
Ethiopia	...	0.7	...	1.3	...	0.03
France	996.6	1,981.7	138.0	255.1	0.72	0.78
Ghana	3.2	2.4	2.3	2.9	0.14	0.08
Guatemala	3.8	7.2	1.7	2.5	0.22	0.29
India	73.4	96.4	50.0	71.0	0.15	0.14
Iran	20.0	47.6	9.9	25.6	0.20	0.19
Italy	489.0	942.8	87.3	138.3	0.56	0.68
Japan	2,115.3	4,163.4	185.6	413.1	1.14	1.01
Kuwait	2.7	9.7	2.9	7.2	0.09	0.14
Mexico	214.7	353.4	31.5	48.7	0.68	0.72
Nepal	0.7	0.6	0.8	1.1	0.09	0.06
Philippines	35.1	50.3	8.5	10.3	0.41	0.49
South Africa	99.1	356.2	16.8	26.1	0.59	1.37
South Korea	40.1	85.9	7.0	12.4	0.57	0.69
Sri Lanka	5.1	2.2	1.6	2.6	0.32	0.08
Switzerland	428.0	744.2	19.6	40.9	2.18	1.82
United States	19,600.0	26,780.0	927.6	1,294.9	2.11	2.07

SOURCE: Extracted from Tenth IAA Survey of Advertising Expenditures Around the World. New York: International Research Associates, 1970, pp. 10-11, and World Advertising Expenditures 1976 Edition. Mamaroneck, New York: Starch INRA Hooper and International Advertising Association, 1976, pp. 20-21. Reprinted with permission of Starch INRA Hooper.

percent, in Ghana and Sri Lanka .08 percent, in Bangladesh .12 percent, and in Kuwait .14 percent. Table 6 compares 1970 and 1974 data on advertising as a percent of GNP for a group of these rich and poor societies.

Together, these data indicate clearly that the distribution of advertising throughout the world—between regions and nations—is anything but equal, and that the highly developed, industrialized nations in terms of GNP tend to also rank highest in advertising as a percent of GNP. With the notable exception of Japan, these economically advanced and advertising- and media-rich societies tend to be from North America and western Europe. This situation is hardly surprising since these were the same societies that pioneered mass-consumer manufacturing that depended on mass advertising to create demand for goods. They also defined the rules and structures under which commercial private mass media, and support services such as advertising, public relations, and market research, would operate at home and abroad.[33]

Because of America's unique combination of political and economic strength, its market size, and its commercial and ideological success at creating and then selling to other nations such modern organizations as commercial television and the advertising agency, it is understandable why the influence of America on other nations' advertising (*and* media, *and* economies, *and* politics, *and* culture) has been substantial.[34] As one Latin American columnist wrote: "The U.S. is a neurotic Midas who homogenizes everything he touches. Americans, indeed, have a mania for uniformity. Which wouldn't be a serious matter if America were a satellite nation. But since she is a leader it has grave implications."[35]

Also, given the fact that many "satellite" nations are obviously trailing America and a few other advertising-rich nations in advertising and other consumption levels, it is understandable why the TNAAs, the TNCs, and other components of the transnational power structure are eager to gain access to what SSC&B:Lintas called the "2 billion consumers most companies ignore" who live in the "emerging" or "growth" markets of the Third World.[36] Through penetration of these societies, the Center nations are able to maintain both resource and structural power over weaker nations and actively support continuation of Western-style development patterns. Third World nations may be expanding (*very* rapidly in such cases as Brazil, Kuwait, and South Korea) in terms of advertising expenditures, but these indicators tell nothing about non-economic conditions within these societies. The advertising dependent nation may be rapidly growing, but the intranational benefits of "the good life" might be flowing more to a few elites than to the masses. Through bridgeheads in the Periphery, the TNAAs and the TNCs are able to enter some markets and contribute to dominance rather than equality and to continuation of economic growth rather than genuine national development. The Western development model obviously benefits the rich nations and a small elite in the poor nations, but at the same time it leaves the Periphery's majority far behind on any number of indicators of human needs and satisfaction, including such conventional development indicators as access to modern urban-based mass media.

Given that advertising is rapidly growing around the world and that advertising and the TNCs are so intertwined with the notion of development as essentially economic growth, it is easy to see why advertising-rich Center nations see the world as their oyster.

Aggregate Size and Profitability

Leo Burnett, founder in 1935 of the TNAA bearing his name, was once asked about his Chicago-based agency's very rapid growth. His reply: "Look, I'm just a kind of ink-stained wretch. I don't know much about these financial matters. I do know, however, that if you make enough good ads, inevitably you grow and make some money."[37]

TNAAs like Leo Burnett, of course, have not merely "grown and made some money"—they have boomed and become highly profitable, global communications enterprises.[38] Their operations are sizable indeed—in terms of their billings, income, number of offices in different nations, employee strength, and influence on their hosts. Like other subsets of the TNCs, the TNAAs are relatively powerful compared to the indigenous businesses that compete with them and that do not operate beyond their own national borders.

Among the biggest and the richest of the thousands of advertising agencies in the nonsocialist societies competing aggressively for the consumers' attention are an elite group of giant TNAAs, including Leo Burnett, that are the subject of this study. These TNAAs tend to have similar corporate methods of operation and attitudes about globalism wherever they extend their reach. As Young & Rubicam's executive vice president in charge of Europe, Middle East, Canada, Latin America, Asia/Pacific has emphasized: "The disciplines and standards are the same in Hong Kong and in Sao Paulo, in London and in Adelaide, because we approach the problems in the same professional way and have access to all the tools everywhere."[39]

Table 7 suggests the great success that the TNAAs have had at using their tools in many different political and cultural settings. It lists the world's fifty largest agencies by gross income and billings at the start of 1980. The United States dominates the list with thirty one agencies—most of which have very extensive operations beyond the domestic American market. Thirteen of the top fifteen agencies were American. Of the non-American agencies in the top fifty, eleven were Japanese; four French; two Brazilian; one West German; and one Swiss.[40] Of the top ten agencies outside the United States, eight (nos. 1, 12, 20, 22, 31, 33, 34, and 38) were

Japanese and two (nos. 18 and 36) French. Each nation represented on the list is a mini-Center of advertising compared to the United States. Compared to Third World societies, however, each is affluent, industrialized, media-rich, and transnationally active in terms of business. With the exception of Brazil (which many do not consider a developing or non-industrialized nation), no Third World advertising agency was listed.

The world's largest ad agency was non-American, Dentsu of Tokyo.[41] Founded in 1901, this Japanese corporate giant employs more than fifty-three hundred and had billings of $2,437 million and gross income of $352.8 million in 1979. Dentsu created modern Japanese advertising, and it has always dominated the rapidly expanding ad industry there, but its influence outside of Japan is insignificant compared to the major American TNAAs. Of Dentsu's worldwide billings, only about 3 percent comes from foreign activity. Despite this very limited transnational involvement, Dentsu deserves consideration because of its potential as a powerful TNAA, especially in those areas where Japanese investment is large.[42] Also, it obviously deserves attention because of its large direct influence on Japanese business and media generally.[43]

Dentsu has long dominated the domestic Japanese advertising scene, but the agency's influence outside Japan has been minor.[44] Its foreign branches and offices—except for Hong Kong, Thailand, and the United States—are relatively small, and serve more as information collection and liaison offices than as full-service agencies. The other large Japanese agencies, including Dentsu's major competitor, Hakuhodo, and the major European agencies also are relatively unimportant transnationally. Some of these, such as France's Eurocom and Publicis Conseil, are important in their home markets and to a limited extent regionally, but they cannot compare with the American TNAAs in geographic spread, resources, and extent of influence internationally. Also it must be noted that many large national agencies have found that they must have formal association with an American TNAA to remain competitive. Advertisers, too, often want American ties.

The United States, then, as the world's super-Center advertising nation has almost a monopoly on advertising. In the occasional individual market, of course, a non-American TNAA might be more important than an American agency, but overall no other Center nation even comes close to America's firm domination of international advertising. British agencies, for example, are conspicuously missing from the world's biggest lists, even though advertising is well-developed in Britain. This is because major British agencies have been purchased by or directly founded by American TNAAs, including JWT, Young & Rubicam, and McCann-Erickson, which used London as a base from which to expand into the rest of Europe.

In 1973, Dentsu surpassed JWT as the world's largest single advertising agency (see Table 7). By 1981, however, Young & Rubicam—through its

Table 7

World's Top Fifty Ad Agencies at the Start of the 1980s

Rank	Agency	Gross Income	Billings
1	Dentsu	$ 352.8	$2,437
2	J. Walter Thompson	253.9	1,693
3	McCann-Erickson	252.3	1,687
4	Young & Rubicam	247.6	1,921
5	Ogilvy & Mather	206.2	1,393
6	Ted Bates	181.0	1,177
7	SSC&B	153.2	1,021.6
8	BBDO	144.8	985.5
9	Leo Burnett	141.1	950.7
10	Foote, Cone & Belding	137.6	918.1
11	D'Arcy-MacManus & Masius	128.0	853.6
12	Hakuhodo	127.4	896.3
13	Grey Advertising	106.3	710.0
14	Doyle Dane Bernbach	104.0	701.0
15	Benton & Bowles	95.4	640.4
16	Campbell-Ewald	84.2	561.9
17	Compton	77.7	524.6
18	Eurocom	77.2	519.7
19	Dancer Fitzgerald Sample	68.4	469.9
20	Naito Issui Sha	65.0	370.3
21	N W Ayer	63.9	428.4
22	Daiko Advertising	62.5	491.8
23	Wells, Rich, Greene	56.6	377.6
24	Marsteller	54.3	362.5
25	Needham, Harper & Steers	50.4	336.2
26	Kenyon & Eckhardt	49.2	328.3
27	Norman, Craig & Kummel	48.0	323.1

28	William Esty Co.	45.6	304.0
29	Bozell & Jacobs Int'l.	45.2	304.0
30	Intermarco-Farner	43.5	291.6
31	Dai-Ichi Kikaku	38.4	272.6
32	KM&G Int'l.	37.7	245.1
33	Tokyu	34.4	239.9
34	Yomiko	30.7	172.9
35	Cunningham & Walsh	29.3	225.2
36	Publicis Conseil	29.2	201.2
37	Ross Roy	26.9	179.0
38	Asahi Kokoku Sha	26.0	165.4
39	Campbell-Mithun	23.8	158.4
40	MPM/Casabranca	23.1	86.7
41	Wunderman, Ricotta & Kline	22.7	151.2
42	TBWA	22.6	150.8
43	Dai-Ichi	22.2	158.1
44	Alcantara Machado Periscinoto	20.8	83.1
45	Asahi Tsushin	20.8	143.9
46	Groupe Roux Seguela Cayzac & Goudard	18.9	97.3
47	William Wilkens & Co.	18.6	93.7
48	Nationwide Ad Service	18.2	69.8
49	Orikomi	18.1	134.6
50	GGK	17.8	118.4

NOTE: Figures shown are in millions and are based on total equity interest in foreign shops. Advertising Age, the source of this information, emphasizes that this table represents only estimates because reporting procedures of a few agencies varied slightly from those requested. This list is used only to suggest the relative influence of American agencies. Figures for several agencies need qualification, and readers should consult the original table entitled "World's Top Fifty Ad Agencies in 1979."

SOURCE: Reprinted with permission from the April 30, 1980 issue of Advertising Age. Copyright 1980 by Crain Communications, Inc.

1979 acquisition of Marsteller—topped JWT, and McCann-Erickson was larger in income outside of the United States. But by almost any criteria, JWT continues to be very large, influential, and successful. By 1980, the agency was a unified worldwide federation of some sixty-seven offices in thirty-two nations, with people and physical resources that included more than sixty-three hundred employees producing advertising in about twenty languages, for more than four thousand brands. Many of its nearly fifteen hundred clients were world market leaders, and included such prestigious TNCs as Ford, DeBeers, Gillette, Warner Lambert, Kodak, Kraft, and Lever. The agency's global billings surpassed $1,690 million and its income was almost $254 million. Operations outside the United States accounted for about half of JWT's business.

Five other American TNAAs—Y&R, McCann-Erickson, Ogilvy & Mather, Ted Bates, and SSC&B also had billings of more than $1 billion by the start of the 1980s. Like JWT, each of these agencies was headquartered in New York City and served numerous American and other TNC clients, as well as local advertisers, through extensive near-global networks. For example, McCann-Erickson is the largest American TNAA in income outside the United States. Founded in 1902, the agency has nine offices in the United States plus some sixty offices in forty-six other nations, including even the People's Republic of China. The agency is the flagship of the supergiant Interpublic Group of Companies, Inc., New York. McCann's largest clients are General Motors and Coca-Cola.

Historically, JWT, Y&R, and McCann-Erickson have been the leaders of both the domestic American and the world advertising industries. Before the 1960s, when most large American agencies had foreign offices only in nearby Canada or a few select European or Latin American markets, these three pioneers represented almost all of the significant transnational advertising agency activity outside of the United States.

The greatest period of transnational advertising expansion has come since the 1960s, when the three veteran giant agencies found themselves having to face—for the first time in some markets—a number of young American TNAA competitors, especially in the lucrative European market, but elsewhere in the developing economies as well. For example, a relatively young agency like Ogilvy & Mather demonstrated rapid growth both in the United States and foreign markets. In the early 1970s, its chairman told a meeting of the agency's heads of offices gathered in London:

> I think that the moment has come to say for the first time that our aim is to be Number One. Number One in *quality*. Number One in *reputation*. Number One in *profitability*. And, yes, even Number One in *size*. In fact, I really don't see any acceptable alternative to this objective. We either grow in quality, reputation, profitability, and size. Or we stagnate and eventually wither. We *must* grow. Partly, of course, because we are a public company with constant pressures for growth. But more impor-

tantly, I really think, because those of us in this room, whose careers on the average are only half to two-thirds over, don't want to stagnate and wither at the end.[45]

By 1980, the thirty-three year old agency was anything but stagnant. It was in fourth place on the list of America's biggest agencies by both world billings and income and by income outside the United States. It had a staff of about six thousand people in one hundred nine offices in thirty-four countries. Its seventeen hundred clients included numerous major transnational advertisers. Virtually all the American TNAAs were experiencing rapid, profitable growth, but Ogilvy & Mather claimed to be the fastest growing agency in the world, and it was pursuing a policy of doubling its international billings every five years. And, like other advertising agencies operating internationally, it was actively developing public relations, direct response advertising, and specialty agencies.[46]

Despite an apparent general increase in nationalism and increased attention to Third World concerns over "a new international information order," the TNAAs did not seem particularly troubled or adversely affected profitwise. O&M's chairman, John Elliott, Jr., seemed to speak for all TNAAs in the 1970s when he reported to his stockholders: "We are not unmindful of the problems of nationalism, consumerism, and regulation that we face along with other multinational companies. But they have not seriously affected the profitable conduct of our business, nor do we expect them to in the foreseeable future.[47]

The sprawl of their foreign operations made the American TNAAs particularly well-suited to take advantage of the rapid expansion of advertising outside the United States. Between 1961 and 1975, world advertising expenditures increased 140 percent in the United States but 580 percent outside the United States, and the American agencies have been able to take good advantage of such increases.[48] Since the 1960s, the nondomestic portion of these agencies' business has become extremely important to their growth and stability. Non-United States billings have been providing more than half of the business for such TNAAs as JWT, McCann-Erickson, Ted Bates, and SSC&B:Lintas.

Many TNAAs are basically organized as one large agency, but there are several agency groups or conglomerates that influence transnational advertising, and the trend is clearly toward big world agency groups.

The largest group by far is the mammoth Interpublic Group of Companies, the holding corporation established around McCann-Erickson in 1961 by Madison Avenue management wizard Marion Harper. Organized along the lines of General Motors, the publicly owned IPG has a variety of diversified marketing and communications organizations and three large groups of worldwide advertising agencies, which operate separately and compete with one another. In 1981, they were:

1. McCann-Erickson Worldwide
2. Marschalk Campbell-Ewald Worldwide
3. SSC&B:Lintas Worldwide (including 49 percent interest in the SSC&B:Lintas International agency system)

As separate advertising agencies, McCann-Erickson by 1980 was the world's third largest; SSC&B was number 7; and Campbell-Ewald number 16. Combined, all the various IPG units employ some eighty-eight hundred people and probably account for about 2 percent of the total worldwide advertising expenditure.

By either billings or income, IPG's size was staggering. Its 1979 world gross income, for example, was nearly $374 million—up 20.5 percent in a year.[49] When considered in the aggregate as a single corporate entity, IPG certainly surpassed *both* Dentsu and JWT in size. Transnationally, IPG is certainly the most active of any agency group. It has wholly-owned agencies from A to Z—from Australia to Zambia and from Argentina to Zimbabwe. In places where it is not profitable and/or politically possible to have IPG-owned operations, it has associate agencies. IPG-affiliated agencies in Bahrain, Egypt, Nigeria, Turkey, South Korea, Ghana, Pakistan, and United Arab Emirates fall into the latter category. Overall, IPG operates in some eighty-four offices in fifty-eight nations, and it modestly has described itself:

> In many areas of the world, advertising agencies within the Interpublic Group constitute the largest or close to the largest local advertising agency or group of advertising agencies. The Interpublic Group believes it is the largest advertising agency business in the world, measured by its income from commissions and fees.[50]

The worldwide influence of IPG grew considerably in the late 1970s when it acquired SSC&B and SSC&B:Lintas International—the latter a London-based TNAA that was founded and fifty-one percent owned by Unilever, the giant British-Dutch consumer goods manufacturer. Through this acquisition, IPG is acquiring a network of some sixty-eight agencies in thirty-three countries.

Compared to IPG, the other major world agency groups tend to be small, loosely organized networks. Some, like the French Univas network or Group Publicis-Intermarco-Farner, have their transnational activities limited primarily to Europe.

Throughout the hectic 1960s and 1970s, some of the relatively small multinational agency groupings were being organized—often with a regional emphasis and not always successfully. Meanwhile, the major American TNAAs were aggressively acquiring existing agencies in foreign markets, entering into various types of joint ventures (sometimes with other TNAAs, as in Japan, sometimes with promising national agencies, as in Australia), starting new agencies entirely from scratch (although by the 1980s this had become an extremely expensive and politically unwise undertaking), or at least establishing various working relationships with foreign agencies far away from North America or Europe.

Concentration Patterns

Few individual nations or regions have been forgotten by the American TNAAs. While several of them have concentrated their foreign activities in only a handful of relatively affluent societies or in only one region, virtually all of the world's biggest agencies consider their nondomestic activities important, and it is reasonable to anticipate that continued global expansion will be the rule rather than the exception. Increasingly, agencies were talking about "super-growth," and SSC&B:Lintas emphasized why it was vital:

> If major multinational clients are to be properly serviced, there must be strong central coordination, financial control and discipline, and cost comparisons on a global scale. Information systems, international training, regional contact and centralised technical development are vital to super-growth. In all these areas economy of scale is of essence: their cost must not double when billings double. There is a premium on growth. Agencies which have not understood this have fallen by the wayside. Those which have, like SSC&B:Lintas, have flourished.[51]

Despite worldwide inflation and other economic and political crises of the 1980s, the TNAAs are not in any sense retreating from efforts to extend their global reach. Despite the many problems of operating outside their home bases, the TNAAs feel the risks of failure are well worth taking, and there is every reason to believe that transnational expansion will continue. As political and economic conditions in the developing economies of Africa, Asia, the Middle East, and South American grow (but not necessarily with a corresponding growth in social justice), the TNAAs surely will be looking for additional offices, even if they cannot be 100 percent owned by their home office in a Center nation.

In addition to operating in various ways in many different nations, the TNAAs also operate in a big way in most of these host nations. Their office facilities (increasingly linked to computers and telecommunications systems), professional standards, client list, growth, and international reputation combine to give the TNAAs an important advantage in most of the places they are allowed to enter. They tend to rank high among the top ten agencies in many markets—rich or poor—and they inevitably provide stiff competition to the indigenous advertising agencies in these various host societies.

Analysis of *Advertising Age* data on agencies operating outside the United States in 1972 indicates that out of seventy-five nations, a TNAA was the top agency in billings in about thirty-two of the reporting nations. In 1974, out of sixty-nine nations, a TNAA was number one in about thirty-two of the reporting nations. In 1976, out of sixty-four nations, a TNAA was the top agency in forty-three nations. These rough figures indicate that the TNAAs are a dominant force in many societies, and such a pattern surely will continue beyond the 1980s. In 1972, approximately forty-three percent of those nations reporting had a TNAA in the top position. By 1974, this had increased to fifty-five percent, and two years later, about sixty-seven percent of those nations reporting had a TNAA in the number one position.[52]

In many nations, not only the single top, but most—or occasionally all—of the top positions were held by TNAAs. In some nations the only agency reporting billings figures was a transnational agency. The one reported TNAA in such nations may have had local or even other TNAA competition, but it probably was minimal. In general, the TNAAs are proud of their size and want the rest of the advertising industry within a nation to know their strength. Weaker, smaller, less "professional" agencies are less likely to want anyone to know how relatively poor they are compared to "the big boys," and they may not make public their figures. Those they do release might well be greatly inflated since clients shy away from agencies that are losing business.

Table 8 suggests how ten major American TNAAs were ranked in a major group of rich and poor markets according to 1977 data on gross income. The data, while not always complete, show how each of these TNAAs ranked within the advertising industry in particular host societies. The data say nothing about the precise nature of the ownership/management arrangement under which each of these TNAAs operated in a nation, but many—if not most—of these overseas TNAA offices were 100 percent foreign-owned. In some cases, other arrangements—including majority, or occasionally minority, ownership—may have existed, but the largest TNAAs prefer to have firm control over their domestic and foreign offices, even in those situations where they are not allowed to legally own the operation.[53] Few TNAAs would risk damaging their international reputation by entering into an arrangement in which their management control and input were not substantial.

Flexibility seems important to the TNAAs, as this statement from JWT's executive vice president for Canada, Latin America, Asia/Pacific Region, suggests:

> We do not have a policy in the sense of a cut and dry company formula that can be used for every situation. Obviously, there are considerable differences in local legislation and in other factors which affect such issues. We certainly prefer 100% ownership, whether immediate or

Table 8

Ten Major American Transnational Advertising Agencies and Their Ranking

by Gross Income in 1977, in Major Rich and Poor Host Nations

Host Nation	JWT	Y&R	McCann	O&M	Burnett	Bates	BBDO	SSC&B	FCB	D'Arcy
Argentina	1							6		
Australia	8	11	3	9	7	1		10	15	6
Austria	2	4	3	5				1		7
Brazil	3	14	4	9	15			8		
Britain	1	5	2	4	11	9	19	8	12	3
Canada	1	11	6	7	10			26	13	
Chile	1									
Colombia			3		1					
Dominican Republic		1								
Ecuador			1							
El Salvador			1							
France	21	3	11	22	30	9	24	5		27
Ghana								1		
Guatemala	1		2							
Honduras			1							
India	1			3				2		
Iran			1							
Italy	2	3	1	28	12	21	15	6	7	17
Jamaica			2							
Kenya		1	2							
Mexico	6	5	2		7		13	12	15	4
Netherlands	4	6	5	14	26	24	1	2	18	23
Norway		6	14	7		2		5		10
Pakistan								1		
Peru	2		1							
Philippines	2		4							
Puerto Rico	5	1	4		8				10	
Sierra Leone								1		
South Africa	3		5			8	2	6	7	
Spain	1	6	3		16		7	4	11	
Sweden	20	7	16			3	15	13	22	10
Switzerland	11	9	6		25			7		10
Thailand			4	2		3		1		
Trinidad			2							
Venezuela	3	2	8		4					
Uruguay			2							
West Germany	4	6	1	8	24	12	3	2	14	19

NOTE: This table makes no distinction between a wholly-owned TNAA subsidiary, a joint venture, or any other legal arrangement that a TNAA may have with a host nation. It merely illustrates the approximate position of the TNAA's operation within the national advertising industry of some important First and Third World nations. Also, it says nothing about the size of the TNAA's local activity. In some nations, the top two or three agencies are TNAAs, and they maintain a substantial income or billings lead over all other agencies.

SOURCE: Compiled from "Gross Income of 722 International Agencies," Advertising Age, 17 April 1978, pp. 26-38 .

worked out over a prearranged schedule. This is a valid general statement, but in some specific cases we were involved in minority equity
situations where we do not really wish to go further, either because we've
gotten what we wanted (i.e. a strong representation in that market), or
because we do not wish to increase our local exposure. So, we have
various arrangements, each tailored to local circumstances, with of
course by far the preponderance of 100% owned subsidiaries.[54]

Analysis of the advertising industry within many rich *and* poor nations
supports the widely held assumption that advertising is essentially Ameri-
can-dominated. American-owned (or at least affiliated) agencies generally
are *very* strong compared to either strictly local agencies—for which reliable
comparative data is sketchy—or the small group of non-American agencies, limited mainly to a few Japanese and European agencies.[55] Data from
1977, for example, show that:

> In West Germany, nine of the top ten agencies are American-linked.
> In Australia, the top twelve agencies are American-linked.
> In Britain, too, the leading twelve agencies are American-linked.
> In Venezuela, four of the leading five agencies are American.
> In Italy, seven of the top eight agencies are TNAAs (Univas is one).
> In Norway, five of the top seven are American.
> In Denmark, six of the top ten agencies are American.
> In Austria, the leading five agencies are American, and the Interpublic
>   Group of Companies has two agencies, McCann-Erickson (no. 3) and
>   Troost Campbell-Ewald Werbeagentur (no. 15).
> In Trinidad, all three agencies are American, and in Jamaica all four
>   agencies reporting are American.
> In Kenya, two of the three agenices reporting are American.
> In Spain, six of the leading seven agencies are American.
> In the Netherlands, five of the top six agencies are American.
> The only agency reporting in the Dominican Republic, Ecuador,
>   Nigeria, Sierra Leone, and Sri Lanka was American-affiliated. The
>   only agency in Morocco was connected to Univas.
> In Mexico, five of the top seven agencies were American.[56]

American TNAAs are without direct representation in only a handful of
the major nations outside the Communist world. According to 1977 information, American TNAAs did not operate in such places as Curacao,
Egypt, Malta, Morocco, Paraguay, and Turkey. In some of these markets,
of course, local agencies represented the TNAAs' interests informally, but
the TNAAs themselves did not have formal operations. The reasons for
the absence of American TNAAs varies with the nation. In most cases,
American TNAAs felt a particular market was too small to risk investment
in, while in some cases local political conditions made it difficult for a
foreign agency to operate. In either event, a nearby TNAA branch office
or even world headquarters could monitor those places in which the agency
was not personally represented.

American agencies do *not* dominate the local advertising industry in every nation in which they happen to operate. For example, the leading agency in such markets as Brazil, France, Greece, Japan, Portugal, Norway, Switzerland, Sweden, and Uruguay is a non-American agency, but American agencies are present in all these nations and are not unimportant, even in nations known for their cultural pride and economic or political independence.[57]

In less affluent industrialized nations, the TNAAs seem to have even greater influence, since advertising is such a relatively new industry. The TNAAs' indigenous competitors, despite their presumably better understanding of local cultural and economic conditions, generally are second to the foreign agencies in "performance," "productivity," and "professionalism."

Overall, this chapter has presented data to show that transnational advertising is a profitable, growing, and pervasive business worldwide and also that many nations' advertising is heavily influenced by a relatively small number of American-owned or affiliated corporations. Such patterns of advertising power indicate clearly that, structurally, the world is predominantly organized into a few advertising Centers and many advertising Peripheries. The number of Center nations can be counted on one hand, and the United States is the leader among them.

Let us now turn our attention to Asia. Particular attention will be given to Southeast Asia, where economic, political, and communication—as well as historical—factors have made it possible for advertising and transnational corporations to prosper. Outside of Japan, Southeast Asia has the liveliest advertising and mass consumption and media scene in all of Asia, and the TNAAs are probably as active there as they are anywhere else in the so-called developing world.

Notes

1. David S. Nicholl, *Advertising—Its Purposes, Principles, and Practice* (London: MacDonald and Evans Ltd., 1973), p. 18.
2. Irwin Ross, "J. W. Thompson is Alive and Well in 30 Countries," *Fortune*, October 1970, p. 105.
3. Theodore Levitt, "The Services Revolution," *Transamerica Corporation 1977 Annual Report* (San Francisco: Transamerica Corporation, 1978), p. 4.
4. TNAAs' overseas expansion is discussed, for example, in "Madison Avenue Goes Multinational," *Business Week*, September 12, 1970, pp. 48–58; Tunstall, *The Media Are America: Anglo-American Media in the World* (New York: Columbia Univ. Press, 1977), especially pp. 54–57; and Arthur L. Grimes, "International Marketing: Opportunities and Problems," *Financial Executive* 33 (November 1965), pp. 58–63.
5. See, for example, Daniel Seligman, "The Belated Use of Advertising," in Michael J. Thomas, *International Marketing Management* (Boston: Houghton Mifflin Co., 1969), pp. 366–79, and R. R. Walker, *Communicators: People, Practice, Philosophies in Australian Advertising, Media, Marketing* (Melbourne, Australia: Landsdowne Press, 1967).
6. The Interpublic Group of Companies, Inc. felt so strongly about this point that it de-

voted the cover of its 1975 Annual Report to this quotation: "The importance of advertising to the consumer is accelerating as personal selling continues its general decline. Today, more than ever before, advertising is the basic communications link between the consumer and the marketer."

7. This Marlboro advertisement featured a globe and appeared in numerous publications, including *More*, March 1975, p. 19.

8. Leo Burnett's Marlboro campaigns are widely regarded as among the best cigarette advertisements in American advertising history because of their very distinctive brand theme and their strength of continuity.

9. See Barnet and Muller, *Global Reach: The Power of the Multinational Corporations* (New York: Simon and Schuster, 1974) for an overview of TNC global expansion. For a discussion of the American business challenge in the European context, see Jean-Jacques Servan-Schreiber, *The American Challenge* (New York: Atheneum, 1968). For an interesting argument that there has been a dramatic gain in the competitive position of non-American, particularly European, corporations, see Franko, *The European Multinationals, a Renewed Challenge to American and British Big Business.* (Stanford, Conn.: Greylock Publishers, 1976) For an overview of Japan's economic status, see such works as Frank Gibney, *Japan, the Fragile Superpower* (New York: W. W. Norton, 1975), and Herman Kahn, *The Emerging Japanese Superstate* (Englewood Cliffs, N.J.: Prentice-Hall), 1970.

10. Sanford Rose, "Why the Multinational Tide is Ebbing," *Fortune,* August 1977, p. 112.

11. Lawrence G. Franko has made the pertinent observation that American corporations have a different image than corporations of other nations. See his *The European Multinationals, A Renewed Challenge to American and British Big Business* (Stamford, Conn.: Greylock Publishers, 1976).

12. See Barnet and Muller, *Global Reach,* pp. 18–19, for the argument that these "World Managers," in their push to achieve "One Great Market," pose "a direct challenge to traditional nationalism."

13. According to *Philip Morris, Inc. Annual Report 1977* (New York: Philip Morris Inc., 1978), it is the second largest cigarette company in the United States and the largest "U.S.-based international cigarette company, selling its 160 brands in more than 170 countries and territories." Philip Morris is typical of other corporations who increasingly stress international operations: "Geographic diversity is a continuing strength of our international operations. It enables us to maintain overall stability and growth in times of fluctuating currencies and at diverse levels of economic activity" (p. 5).

14. For data supporting this widely perceived trend, see Weinstein, "The International Expansion of U.S. Multinational Advertising Agencies," *MSU Business Topics* 22, no. 3 (1974), pp. 30–33.

15. See Weinstein, "Foreign Investments by Service Firms: The Case of Multinational Advertising Agencies," *Journal of International Business Studies,* Spring/Summer 1977, p. 84, for the major "executive interest, offensive, defensive, and client service" motivations for American TNAAs' overseas investments.

16. The ties between Coca-Cola and McCann-Erickson are among the most intimate of any TNC and TNAA. For insight into the agency's relations with Coca-Cola, see Claude D. Marlatt, Jr., "How the Coca-Cola Export Corporation Coordinates International Advertising Programs" (Paper presented at the A.N.A. Advertising Management Workshop, Callaway Gardens, Pine Mountain, Georgia, April 23–26, 1978), and Grimes, "International Marketing: Opportunities and Problems." For discussion of the importance of advertising to Coca-Cola's success, see Hunter Bell, "Fifty Fabulous Years of Overseas Growth for Cola-Cola, 1926–1976," *Refresher USA* 3 (1976); The Coca-Cola Company, "A New Look for Coca-Cola: A Synopsis of the '70s;" and "Advertising Concepts Develop," *The Chronicle of Coca-Cola Since 1886* (Atlanta: The Coca-Cola Company, 1974), pp. 14–15.

17. *1977 Annual Report J. Walter Thompson Company* (New York: J. Walter Thompson Co., 1978), pp. 14–15 (special insert).

18. Theodore D. O'Hearn executive vice president international operations, McCann-Erickson Worldwide, New York City. Personal communication to author, 23 May 1978.

19. For an introduction to this joint venture, see McCann-Erickson-Hakuhodo, "Agency Credentials" (Tokyo: McCann-Erickson-Hakuhodo, 1 November 1976). For an overview of contemporary advertising, see "Supplement on Japan's Market and Advertising," *The Japan*

Economic Journal, 13 December 1977, pp. 21–31; Hiroshi Nakajima, "Import Advertising in Japan," *The International Advertiser* 10, no. 5 (1969), pp. 17–21; George E. Olcott, "Export Advertising in Japan: When Tsukiji Replaces Madison Avenue," *The International Advertiser* 10, no. 5 (1969), pp. 21–22; and Sutton, "The Japanese Advertising Enigma," *PHP* 9, no. 8, August 1978, pp. 72–79. For current information about Japanese advertising from the advertising industry's perspective, see the annual two-volume marketing, advertising, and media analysis produced by Dentsu called *Dentsu's Japan Marketing/Advertising.*

20. These figures, suggesting the diversity of products and the different nations in which McCann operates, are from *1975 Annual Report* (New York: The Interpublic Group of Companies, Inc., 1976), pp. 10–21.

21. Sutton, "A Profits' Prophet," *The International Advertiser* 10, no. 2 (1969), p. 6.

22. Sutton, "All Advertising Is Local; So Why Are The Multinational Agencies Peeing in Our Garden?" (Paper prepared for Tenth Asian Advertising Congress, Sydney, 3 November 1976), pp. 7–8.

23. David M. Potter, "The Institution of Abundance: Advertising," in C. H. Sandage and Vernon Fryburger, *The Role of Advertising* (Homewood, Illinois: Richard D. Irwin, Inc., 1960), p. 18.

24. *JWT 1975 Annual Report* (New York: J. Walter Thompson Co., 1976), inside front cover.

25. The TNAAs generally are actively pushing the notion that an advertising agency, to be most effective, must coordinate all aspects of a client's communications. This "total communications" concept has moved the TNAAs into a diverse range of persuasive communications and marketing-related activities, including research, public relations, and sales promotions, designed to serve the needs of diverse clients in local, national, regional, and international markets.

26. By "oligopoly," I refer to a market situation in which a very few giant firms sell to many buyers and there is little difference in the products and services offered. Airlines, auto makers, steel makers, and communications corporations are generally considered to function in an oligopoly. As an industry, advertising frequently claims to be highly competitive. In the United States, for example, there are about six thousand advertising agencies. Transnationally, however, only a few agencies are highly active, and only a handful of TNAAs get most of the business. By 1978, for example, four TNAAs—Dentsu, JWT, Young & Rubicam, and McCann-Erickson—had passed the $1 billion billings figure, and only the three American agencies among the four were operating full-service operations on a truly worldwide basis. Dentsu is a supergiant that dominates the domestic Japanese market, but transnationally it is unimportant compared to the American TNAAs.

27. Galtung discusses the increasing criticism of international organizations in "A Structural Theory of Imperialism," *Journal of Peace Research* 8, no. 2 (1971), p. 95 and in "Nonterritorial Actors and the Problem of Peace," in Saul H. Mendlevitz, ed., *On the Creation of a Just World Order* (New York: Free Press, 1975), pp. 162–63, Galtung examines the probable future growth of TNCs.

28. Founded in 1864, JWT truly pioneered the idea of an advertising agency actively seeking business outside its home nation. By 1900, the agency had a London office, and in the 1920s it followed General Motors abroad into such distant markets as Bombay, Sao Paulo, Warsaw, Johannesburg, and Alexandria. In 1925, the agency acquired Unilever's Lux Toilet Soap account and carefully created and exported an international advertising campaign. This famous "9 out of 10 screen stars care for their skin with Lux" made the product the best selling soap brand in the world. Some of JWT's early foreign branches were adversely affected by war and depression, but the agency's head, Stanley B. Resor, gained experience and persisted in developing an international network of primarily wholly-owned agencies. Through the foresight of Resor and veteran associates like Sam Meek, JWT was able to get a substantial head start over other TNAAs in foreign markets.

29. Personal correspondence with Robert Coen, Senior Vice President, McCann-Erickson, New York, 17 March 1978, and 24 January 1979.

30. The most reliable ongoing source of data on transnational advertising agencies is found annually in *Advertising Age,* the Chicago-based trade publication that is virtually the bible of the advertising industry, at least in the United States. For years the weekly called itself "the national newspaper of marketing," but by 1977, responding to transnational trends, decided

to rename itself "the international newspaper of marketing" and to greatly expand its coverage of nondomestic U.S. advertising, particularly European. In addition to *Advertising Age*'s annual compilation of advertising data by nation and by major agencies, the International Advertising Association (IAA) and Starch INRA Hooper, a research organization, have conducted a series of worldwide surveys of advertising expenditures. Twelve such surveys have been conducted, the latest published in 1976, but the problems of making region-to-region, or nation-to-nation, year-to-year comparisons are difficult because of incomplete information, somewhat different data collection procedures, and constantly fluctuating currency exchange rates. Also, most advertising figures are self-reported statistics from media or agencies themselves. In some cases, this means figures are inflated to give the impression that business is booming. In other cases, this means figures are lower than reality. A TNAA in a particular nation, for example, may release figures smaller than reality to avoid the possibility of stimulating nationalistic pressures.

31. Advertising, of course, varies not only by nation and region but also by media. In general, print media are the most important advertising channel everywhere, but significant differences do exist by region, nation, and local setting. The most important difference is the urban-rural dichotomy. Advertising needs mass media, and in most nations broadcasting, newspapers, cinema, and so forth are concentrated in the cities and towns where the standard of living is higher and people are more consumer oriented. Also, governmental and advertising industry policies and preferences and consumer needs and tastes also are factors that contribute to differences in advertising.

32. For example, Latin America has a well-developed, highly competitive radio industry, while some European nations do not have commercial radio and, therefore, radio advertising is relatively weak. In Japan, television is an extremely important medium, but in some parts of Europe it has relatively low importance because governments do not encourage the use of TV as an advertising channel. For an overview of the broader issue of how mass media tend to grow along with other traditional indicators of social and economic development, see Schramm and Ruggels, "How Mass Media Systems Grow," in Lerner and Schramm, *Communication and Change in the Developing Countries* (Honolulu: East-West Center Press, 1967). They conclude: "If regional differences do indeed exist they must be based on underlying geographical, historical, social, or cultural differences (p. 73)." For these same reasons, generalizations about advertising are risky without a careful look at a particular setting.

33. These ancillary services generally work together to support the transnational communications and business structure. This study is concentrating on the TNAAs, which sometimes provide marketing and communications skills beyond the traditional confines of an advertising agency. As the TNCs expanded abroad, they found they needed the same set of consultants and specialists in public relations, market research, investment, management, legal affairs, and so forth that they depended upon at home. Advertising services are emphasized in this research, but other services are also important. Their development patterns and their overseas impacts in many ways parallel those of the TNAAs.

34. Tunstall, *The Media Are America*, p. 201, makes the important observation that both British and American media operate on "an 'as if' basis—as if it were possible to be value neutral" with the result that: "In these transactions many small forms of deception are common. Nevertheless, the Anglo-American media are in general more open, more capable of being selected from and altered, than are most other media. Their enormous world presence alone makes them highly visible; and the conventions of neutrality upon which they operate are more-or-less well understood."

35. Carlos Alberto Montaner, "The Americanization of the Planet," *Atlas, World Press Review*, November 1976, p. 39.

36. This reference is from a full-page ad showing a large globe and the headline, "There are 2 billion consumers most companies ignore". The ad was placed by SSC&B:Lintas Overseas and appeared in *Advertising Age*, 18 April 1977, p. 23.

37. Leo Burnett, "Leo Burnett Discusses the Agency and the Ad Business," *Advertising Age*, 23 October 1967 (reprint supplied by Leo Burnett Co., Chicago).

38. Many of the TNAAs were founded by dynamic individuals who ran their agencies as highly personalized businesses under their direct control. Such an old-fashioned business style has all but disappeared as the TNAAs' founders died, as Burnett did in 1972, or retired from active management. With the passing of such dominant individuals, the TNAAs have become

more like other large corporations and seem to be run by committee or a core of generally faceless executives. One of the few old-style advertising executives still greatly influencing a TNAA is David Ogilvy. He is retired from active management of Ogilvy & Mather International but continues to wield great influence as head of the agency's International Creative Council and a prolific writer.

39. Alexander Brody, "Letter from Alex Brody," *Y&R International: Canada, Puerto Rico, Dominican Republic, Brazil, Mexico, Venezuela* (New York: Young & Rubicam, 1976), p. 3.

40. Craig Endicott, "Foreign Ad Shops Earn Stripes during 1979," *Advertising Age,* 14 April 1980, p. S-8.

41. For an introduction to Dentsu, see: Ramona Bechtos, "Dentsu Gives Itself a Broader Label: Consultants on Life Styles and Society," *Advertising Age,* 23 August 1976, p. 22; Eduardo Lachia, "Japan's Dentsu Leads the Advertising World in Billings and Profits," *The Asian Wall Street Journal,* 3 May 1977, pp. 1, 10; and Luther Link, "Dentsu Critic Calls it 'Public Menace'," *Advertising Age,* 21 January 1974, pp. 69–70. For a self-description by the agency, see *This is Dentsu* (Tokyo: Dentsu Incorporated, 1978).

42. Dentsu has cautiously been expanding its international activities, particularly in terms of developing what the agency calls "a global marketing research network to serve the needs arising from efforts of Japanese corporations to develop overseas markets." For insight into the agency's expansion plans, see John R. Thomson, "Int'l Growth a Main Priority for No. 1 Dentsu," *Advertising Age,* 10 October 1977, p. 26.

43. Unlike American advertising agencies in their home nation, Dentsu is widely known within Japan. Its involvement in such special promotions as the 1964 Tokyo Olympics, the 1970 Osaka World Exposition, and the 1972 Sapporo Winter Olympics brought it attention outside the advertising industry. Unlike American ad agencies, Dentsu maintains an active public relations campaign for itself and it actively seeks close ties with the Japanese government. Its influence on the media has always been substantial. For example, more than a quarter of all Japanese media billings is handled by Dentsu; Dentsu's late president, Hideo Yoshida, actively lobbied both advertisers and the government for support of commercial broadcasting in Japan; and the agency introduced the use of computers into advertising and also the function of account servicing, modern market research, and public relations. Dentsu also approached American TNAAs, especially Young & Rubicam, and borrowed American-style organization and technology to modernize the Japanese advertising industry.

44. An explanation of why Japanese agencies have not been more active in foreign markets has been offered in "Overseas Subsidiaries Begin to Turn Profit," *The Japan Economic Journal,* 13 December 1977, pp. 22 and 29 (supplement): "Although Japan's exports now total $70 billion a year, international accounts—mainly comprising export ads placed by Japanese companies—still occupy only a small portion of Japanese ad agencies' total billing. In fact, export ads, which are paid for here [in Japan] in foreign currencies by Japanese firms, totaled only $100 million in 1976. The total volume of export ads is much larger because Japanese firms also advertise overseas through their subsidiaries and affiliates. But it is difficult to arrive at an exact figure. Most Japanese enterprises operating overseas choose local ad agencies, rather than Japanese-affiliated ones. The tendency is the opposite for foreign firms here. It can be said that capable local ad agencies are helping Japanese firms expand sales of their products in many foreign countries. Because of Japanese firms' preference for foreign ad agencies for export ads, Dentsu and Hakuhodo Inc., the leading agencies here, have not expanded very much overseas."

Several other reasons for the lack of deep foreign involvement by Japanese agencies seem important. One is simply that the domestic advertising business has been expanding so rapidly since the 1960s that agencies have been so preoccupied with home market growth that they haven't had time to plan foreign activities. Another reason is cultural. Since international advertising is so heavily Western influenced and English-based, the Japanese are at a great disadvantage outside Japan because their foreign language abilities are poor. Finally, Dentsu in particular is a very conservative corporation and it has moved cautiously into overseas markets. This perhaps has been wise given the strong anti-Japanese investment sentiments in some nations where Japanese corporations are highly visible. Domestically, Dentsu is close to virtually all of Japan's big TNCs.

45. John Elliott, Jr., "Our Priorities As We Look to the Future," *Viewpoint,* Winter 1978, p. 5.

46. For basic information about Ogilvy & Mather, see *Ogilvy & Mather International Inc., Advertising Annual Report 1980* (New York: Ogilvy & Mather, 1981). This agency is by far the most open of any of the TNAAs. Its founder, David Ogilvy, has published widely, and the agency produces excellent materials about its operations and its advertising and management philosophy. See, for example, Ogilvy's *Principles of Management* (New York: Ogilvy & Mather, 1970). Also, see the agency's quarterly employee publication, *Viewpoint: By, For, and About Ogilvy & Mather.* In contrast with the publicly owned Ogilvy & Mather, the privately owned Ted Bates & Co. makes no annual report public nor does it prepare any promotional materials on its worldwide activities. Ogilvy & Mather has cited these figures as a basis for its claim as the fastest growing agency in the world:

Worldwide Billings Growth of Top Ten Agencies—1966 through 1976

Ogilvy & Mather	329.9%
Leo Burnett	227.9
Grey	171.6
Ted Bates	164.2
Y&R	119.7
McManus & Masius	119.2
BBDO	93.6
McCann-Erickson	91.2
J. W. Thompson	78.8
Foote, Cone & Belding	73.7

These figures are reported by O&M executive Dieter Karp, "Is Our Belief Going to Kill Us?" *Viewpoint,* Winter 1978, p. 3.

47. For this statement and an overview of one corporation's success in a growth business like advertising, see Elliott's comments in "Report to Stockholders," Ogilvy & Mather International Inc. 1976 Annual Meeting, May 6, 1976, New York City, p. 5.

48. Ogilvy & Mather has said that world advertising expenditures between 1961 and 1975 increased 140 percent in the United States and 580 percent outside the United States. See the agency's "Report to Stockholders," pp. 4–5.

49. The Interpublic Group of Companies, Inc. *Annual Report 1979* (New York: The Interpublic Group of Companies, 1980), p. 2.

50. See the 1978 copy of IPG's "Annual Report on Form 10-K," p. 2. The report is required by the Securities and Exchange Commission.

51. In 1977, SSC&B:Lintas held its world conference in Rio de Janeiro, and its theme was "Super-growth." This quote is from *SSC&B:Lintas World Review 1977* (London: SSC&B:Lintas International, 1978), p. 5.

52. These figures compiled from "International Agency Section," published annually in *Advertising Age.* The figures are not complete since some agencies (TNAAs and local) failed to report their billings or income.

53. This has been the situation, for example, in Nigeria since 1974. Foreigners are not allowed to own agencies, but this has not prevented TNAAs like O&M and SSC&B:Lintas from continuing to exert a major influence. Under a management agreement, O&M runs the independently owned Ogilvy Benson & Mather (Nigeria) Ltd. The former SSC&B:Lintas agency in Lagos retains "very strong links with the SSC&B:Lintas network" and "the unit has an office in Lintas House in London, and makes use of many of the technical and creative facilities of SSC&B:Lintas Overseas." See *SSC&B:Lintas World Review,* pp. 26–27. Both of these agencies in Nigeria historically evolved from close colonial ties to the British. The former SSC&B:Lintas agency remains the most influential and the biggest in the nation.

54. E. G. A. Bathon, personal correspondence with the author, March 28, 1978.

55. The precise details of TNAA ownership arrangements are difficult to determine, and they frequently change. Therefore, I use "American agency" or "American-linked agency" broadly to refer to those operations in a host nation that somehow publicly and formally associate with an American TNAA. Such association might mean complete TNAA ownership and management, but it could also mean only minority holding or management service assistance by the TNAA. Some TNAAs actually seem to prefer less than full ownership. Several

TNAA executives told me that the actual percentage of their ownership in a given agency is not that important. Far more important are the understandings worked out between the TNAA and its local partners on how things actually are to work within the agency rather than how they might look on paper.

56. These examples are compiled from agency profiles in "International Agency Section," *Advertising Age,* 17 April 1978, pp. 27–120. Each year the section gives a comprehensive overview of foreign agencies, their income, billings, new accounts, and total employees.

57. Japan may be a notable exception to this statement. While most American TNAAs (Ogilvy & Mather excluded) have offices in Japan, they tend to be small operations compared to major Japanese agencies. In 1977, for example, the largest wholly-owned, foreign agency in Japan was JWT. It was number 14, and Y&R was a distant number 24.

THE FREEDOM TO CHOOSE

The free marketplace—whether for products or ideas—is, like freedom itself, an ideal. In truth, the very thought that each individual man or woman should one day be free to make up his or her own mind about those things which affect his or her life is a controversial idea.

It is opposed by some who fear that too much freedom breeds anarchy, by others who feel that people lack the wisdom to make their own decisions, and that they require someone else to think for them. The ideal of freedom is also opposed by those who would substitute popular opinion for individual conscience and force conformity with every viewpoint held by the majority.

We believe in the ideal of individual choice, and we work each day in pursuit of this ideal.

It seems to us a measure of human progress that there are indeed so many places in the world where people have gained the freedom to choose between competing products, services, and ideas.

The challenge of our future will be to help them use that freedom in a well-informed fashion, in ways that encourage and hasten its extension to all people.

The Interpublic Group of Companies, Inc.
Worldwide Advertising and Marketing Communications
1271 Avenue of the Americas, New York, New York 10020
(212) 399-8000

INTERPUBLIC GROUP'S AD

Transnational ad agencies do far more than merely promote goods and services for their transnational clients or irritate local ad agencies that resent foreign competition. As part of a larger transnational system, the TNAAs work to maintain the affluent way of life of the industrialized West. The United States, where most of the TNAAs are headquartered, epitomizes this way of life with its emphasis on economic growth, consumption, individual and corporate freedom, and the need for strong, privately owned media. In this 1979 ad, the giant Interpublic Group of agencies seems to speak for all transnationals with its "Freedom to Choose" philosophy. (Courtesy of Interpublic Group of Companies, Inc.)

Venga al sabor
Venga al mundo Marlboro

MARLBORO CIGARETTE AD

For years, the famous, distinctive "Marlboro Man" and "Marlboro Country" campaigns have been classic examples of how uniformity in advertising can establish a clear, high quality, internationally recognized image for a product. This ad in Spanish was used in Chile. Marlboro, the best-selling cigarette in the world, is owned by Philip Morris Inc., New York. Leo Burnett, Chicago, has been the ad agency since 1955 when the brand in its present packaging was first launched. In 1979, *Advertising Age* named Marlboro the "second greatest advertising and marketing success of the past half-century." First place went to Volkswagen. (Courtesy of Philip Morris, Inc.)

COKE'S COMMERCIAL IN THAILAND

Wherever it is sold, Coca-Cola—like Marlboro cigarettes—uses a high degree of uniformity in its trend-setting marketing methods. Uniformity is achieved through close coordination by and between the headquarters of Coca-Cola and its TNAA, McCann-Erickson. In Thai, for example, the "refreshing" message of Coca-Cola is the same as it is in any language. This still from a Coke film in Bangkok illustrates how McCann-Erickson took the concepts it used in its CLIO award winning "Mean Joe Greene" TV commercial in the United States and adapted them for use in Thailand. Instead of an American football player endorsing the product, a soccer player who would appeal more to an Asian audience was featured. (Courtesy of the Coca-Cola Company)

COKE BILLBOARD IN CHINA

Coca-Cola is probably the best known single product on earth. It is consumed more than 200 million times a year in more than 135 countries, including the People's Republic of China. Coke's distinctive, familiar advertising—created by McCann-Erickson and in more than eighty languages—has been a major factor in the drink's global success. Coca-Cola was one of the first American consumer products to be advertised in post-Mao China. This scene shows the first Coke billboard, erected in July 1979 at a railway station in Guangdong (Canton). For Chinese New Year in 1981, Coke sponsored a documentary on the Olympics on nationwide television in China. (Courtesy of the Coca-Cola Company)

Asia is incredibly diverse. India alone, for example, has more than 600 million people and a wide range of social, economic, religious, linguistic, and regional differences. Such a complex society requires great sensitivity on the part of admen. As this case of Lux soap illustrates, advertising needs to be carefully adapted to local audiences. Lux, the largest selling soap in India and the entire world, is made by Hindustan Lever Ltd., a Unilever subsidiary. Hindustan Thompson, the J. Walter Thompson associate in India, is the Lux ad agency, and it follows the transnational advertising guidelines formalized by Unilever and JWT headquarters decades ago. In India, as elsewhere, Lux is sold with the film star endorsement theme, and Hindustan Thompson uses at least thirty stars to reach various regional audiences. In addition to English, any Lux ad must be implemented in at least ten different major Indian languages. The stars have to be carefully chosen to conform with regional popularity. For example, a star who is popular in Kerala State by virtue of her work in Malayalam-language cinema might not be known in neighboring Tamil Nadu where Tamil is spoken. These sample ads show two actresses in different Indian language adaptations of the same basic ad stressing "pure, mild Lux—beauty soap of the film stars." One star is endorsing in Hindi and the other in Malayalam. (Courtesy of Hindustan Thompson)

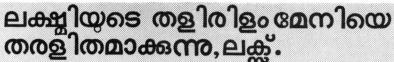

Even if you don't read the label, you know it's ICI paint.

- Take off the lid and stir the paint. Sniff. No harsh smell. Smooth consistency. And you see the colour you bought. That's ICI.
- Paint it on. See how smoothly it goes on, how bright and clean the colour is. That's ICI.
- Now leave a spot unpainted. Then after the rest of the paint dries, paint on the unpainted spot. If the colour doesn't match well, it's not ICI.

The Better Paint

L-9/747-ICI

ICI PAINT AD

Transnational ad agencies get most of their business from transnational corporations. For example, the London-based SSC&B:Lintas International, which in the early 1980s became part of the giant Interpublic Group of Companies, New York, advertises for the British-based ICI in such diverse markets as Finland, Pakistan, Singapore, and Malaysia. This ad, prepared by the agency's office in Kuala Lumpur, makes the point that despite economic, geographic, and cultural differences, do-it-yourself painters are pretty much the same worldwide and are willing to pay a high price for ICI paints to get a high quality product. This ad is not culture-specific and it would likely work anywhere that people have need for paint. For other products, such as foods, cigarettes, and beauty aids, different market conditions require very different approaches to advertising. (Courtesy of SSC&B:Lintas International Ltd.)

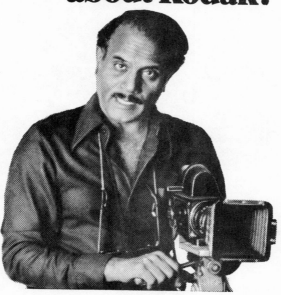
KODAK AD IN INDIA

Transnational advertisers have a great advantage over local advertisers because of economies of scale and the fact that their products and trademarks are household words in many countries. Some governments and indigenous businessmen have become increasingly sensitive about the presence of wholly-owned foreign businesses. In India, for example, the government has forced foreign businesses to reduce their holdings to 40 percent and to become public corporations. Transnationals like Kodak, Philips, and Firestone have all had to take on new names for their Indian operations. This corporate ad was developed by Hindustan Thompson, JWT's Bombay associate, to tell consumers that Kodak is now operating under a new name. A prominent Indian producer is used to reassure people that—regardless of the name change—the same high quality international Kodak products that have been in India since at least 1913 would continue to be sold. JWT's first office in Asia was established in Bombay in 1929, but the American agency no longer has equity in the office because of Indian nationalism. (Courtesy of Hindustan Thompson)

Asia. We wrap it up over 30 different ways.

TIME is the most flexible international media in Asia—or the world. We can give you all of Asia. Or one discrete local market. Or your choice of over 30 local, national, or regional editions. Surprisingly the cost for a full-color page can be as little as US $825. And, in every market, TIME delivers Asia's leaders; its decision makers. The people with the purchasing power.

TIME
for multinational marketing.

TIME MAGAZINE REGIONAL AD

Transnational media like *Time, Reader's Digest, Newsweek, Asian Wall Street Journal,* and the *International Herald Tribune* consider Asia an important area of expansion. These successful Western-based publications use sophisticated marketing and production techniques and work closely with the TNAAs to meet their clients' needs. Transnational publications are too expensive for the average Asian to buy or the average indigenous businessman to advertise in. Both the editorial and advertising contents tend to be directed to urban, prosperous, well-educated consumers. This *Time* ad stresses that advertisers can reach these Asian elites through some thirty different editions. (Courtesy of *Time* magazine)

ASIAN RADIO LISTENERS

Transnational publications, television, and cinema are more glamorous media, but radio continues to be the most efficient way of reaching the masses. Many Asians are poor, illiterate, and isolated from urban Westernized living, but they usually have access to a transistor radio. The estimated number of radio receivers in Asia increased from 17 million in 1963 to 76 million in 1973. Advertisers like radio because its ad rates are cheap and messages can easily be produced to meet local needs. Most radio and television operations in Asia are run directly by the government or by public corporations, and accept commercials. (Courtesy of Kay Muldoon for World Bank and IDA)

5
The Asian Scene

... one beneficial aspect of the U.S. involvement in Vietnam
is that it drew attention of American businessmen to Southeast Asia and its scope as a market—a Coca-Cola invasion is,
I think you will agree, infinitely more welcome than a visita-
tion of B-52s. It is, in fact, this new awakening of interest in
the area, from Americans, Europeans, or even other Asian
nations that has contributed to the rapid real growth in
Southeast Asia as a world market. The competition is
tough, severe even in some markets, but the rewards can be
great.
        —Michael J. Ball, Executive Director
        International, Ogilvy & Mather International Inc.[1]

New York's sophisticated Madison Avenue—long a symbol of a power-
fully persuasive, Center-based industry that plays a highly visible role in
affluent Western societies—seems a long way from Southeast Asia or anywhere else in the vast Asian region.

Indeed it is—physically. The metropolis of New York is many thousands
of miles from the exotic sounding, diverse peoples and problems of Southeast Asia. To Kuala Lumpur's multiracial bazaars, Jakarta's teeming slums,
Singapore's bustling Change Alley,[2] and the region's vast hinterlands containing oil, tin, rubber, timber, rice, and other valuable materials and rich
human resources, foreign advertising influences might not seem terribly
relevant. Unlike the industrially advanced nations, the Southeast Asian
nations are comparatively poor, rural, agrarian societies that seem anything but homogeneous in terms of class, race, life-styles, languages, and
institutions such as government or mass media. Incomes are often at subsistence level, and many people have little money for savings or for expenditures on heavily advertised luxury items like cars, cameras,
appliances, liquor, or travel. The masses in these nations struggle even for
the basic necessities of food, clothing and housing.

It is in these relatively poor societies that one might hardly expect to find
very many TNAAs because advertising budgets are relatively small and

129

media and general economic development have not "progressed" to the stage where foreign advertising agencies would find it highly profitable to invest directly. And yet, despite being half-way around the world from one another, Madison Avenue—and everything it represents in the life of consumer oriented, industrial societies—and the Asian region *are* closely interrelated. The TNAAs and dependent advertising are booming due to the structural power of the United States over some of the countries and to their general acceptance of Western economic development policies. The latter stress association and integration, and assign the TNCs, including the TNAAs, an important role in stimulating economic growth processes. In short, Galtung's model fits past and present advertising relations between the Center (led by the United States) and the Peripheries of at least some parts of Asia, particularly Southeast Asia.

The TNAAs' Presence in Asia

The TNAAs—like the institutions of commercial communication, including advertising—prosper in environments that are politically stable and where economic conditions foster Western-style growth and standards of living and where transnational trade and mass communications thrive.

Although local, national, and international advertising and commercial influences can be found to one degree or another in virtually every Asian society, transnational advertising tends to do best in affluent, industrialized, media-rich, and aggressive societies like Japan, Hong Kong, or Singapore. To a lesser degree, it also is active in those developing societies—such as Malaysia, Philippines, Indonesia, and Thailand—where the population is still mainly rural (but a Western-oriented capital city is booming), political stability exists, and the government's policy fosters development primarily through foreign investment and close commercial and cultural ties to the West. With the exception of Thailand, each of the societies mentioned above experienced colonial rule, and all of them experienced great hardships during World War II. Table 9 shows how these and other Asian developing countries compare with a group of major industrialized countries on a series of key development indicators, including advertising expenditures.

Occasionally, transnational advertising will enter a high-risk/high-gain situation and do business in a country with a potentially enormous population of consumers. China in its current post-Mao period is an example of a country which foreign admen and investors generally are willing to enter even though the political risks are great and the short-term possibility of profits is slight.

Advertisers and their advertising agencies like profits, but they do not like on-again, off-again government regulations and other factors that limit

Table 9

Key Indicators for Selected Asian Developing Countries and Major

Industrialized Countries

try	Population (Millions)	GNP Per Capita	Adult Literacy Rate Percent	Life Expectancy at Birth (yrs) 1978	Urban Pop. as Percentage of Total Pop. 1980	Daily Caloric Supply Per Capita as Percentage of requirement 1977	Total Measured Media Advertising Expenditures, 1977 (in Millions of U.S. Dollars)
loping							
anistan	14.6	240	12	42	15	110	. . .
adesh	84.7	90	26	47	11	78	. . .
a	32.2	150	67	53	27	106	. . .
a	952.2	230	. . .	70	25	105	. . .
Kong	4.6	3,040	90	72	90	126	. . .
a	643.9	180	36	51	22	91	143.8
nesia	136.0	360	62	47	20	105	63.3
	35.8	2,160	50	52	50	130	. . .
a, Rep. of	36.6	1,160	93	61	55	119	189.0
ysia	13.3	1,090	60	67	29	117	45.6
l	13.6	120	19	43	5	91	.5
stan	77.3	230	21	52	28	99	16.9
a New Guinea	2.9	560	32	50	17	85	. . .
ppines	45.6	510	87	60	36	97	81.4
apore	2.3	3,290	75	70	100	134	53.7
_anka	14.3	190	78	69	27	96	5.1
an	17.1	1,400	82	72	77	120	118.4
land	44.5	490	84	61	14	105	99.2
nam	51.7	170	36	51	23	83	. . .

strialized Countries

alia	14.2	7,990	100	73	89	129	1,186.4
e	53.3	8,260	99	73	78	136	1,720.0
ny, Fed. . of	61.3	9,580	99	75	85	127	3,148.9
	114.9	7,280	99	76	78	126	4,779.0
d Kingdom	55.8	5,030	99	73	91	132	2,568.9
d States	221.9	9,590	99	73	73	135	25,269.0

Figures should be used cautiously since data are sometimes only estimates and are not always strictly rable for all countries. The data are used only to suggest major differences between countries and en the developing and the industrialized groups of countries.

E: All figures except advertising expenditures are from The World Bank, World Development Report, 1980. ngton: The World Bank, August 1980. Advertising figures are from World Advertising Expenditures, a 1977 by the International Advertising Association and Starch INRA Hooper. Permission to reproduce has been ed by Starch INRA Hooper, Mamaroneck, N.Y. The entire list of 1977 ad expenditures in the study was shed in "1977 Ad Expenditures in 50 Countries," Advertising Age, 24 March 1980, p. 266.

business activities or create substantial risks such as the recent upsurge of Islamic fundamentalism in some Third World societies. This is why TNAAs (and foreign investors and media generally) are not active and/or would not be welcome in some Asian societies. Political ideology, for example, is a major reason why transnational advertising is not a force in Afghanistan, Vietnam, or Iran. In the latter case, a few TNAAs trying to do business in Teheran had to stop after the fall of the Shah of Iran. Government regulations discouraging foreign investment are the reason TNAAs no longer have wholly-owned offices in India. (India had been about the first Asian nation to attract TNAA attention—in 1929 JWT established an office in Bombay. Its first Southeast Asian office was opened in Manila in 1956, about a year after Grant Advertising opened an agency in Singapore).

Widespread poverty and limited availability of media in low-income countries like Bangladesh, Burma, Pakistan, and Sri Lanka discourage the growth of both industry and advertising. The TNAAs generally are not very interested in South Asian and other developing societies where per capita advertising investment is relatively low and where trained personnel and media facilities are scarce. Also, the TNAAs are uninterested in small or isolated markets, such as the Pacific Island nations of Western Samoa, Fiji, Papua New Guinea, etc.

Southeast Asia generally stands in contrast to the relatively poorer, less politically stable developed nations of the rest of Asia. Except for industrialized Japan, advertising thrives best of all in the Association of Southeast Asian Nations (ASEAN) states—Indonesia, Malaysia, Philippines, Singapore, and Thailand—and in Hong Kong.[3] Let's take a closer look at several of those nations which have fascinated the TNAAs.

The TNAAs' Presence in Southeast Asia

Indonesia, Malaysia, and Singapore—individually and as ASEAN participants—are very much integrated into a larger world economic order. This statement by a transnational survey research organization active through Southeast Asia reflects the nature of the market within which these nations and the TNAAs function:

> At a time when the world balance of natural resources is changing, Southeast Asia is in a singularly strong position. This wealth is providing the basis for booming economies in which local production and manufacturing is flourishing. Many international companies have established highly successful manufacturing and marketing organizations in the region, and are selling brands which are household words in the West. We brew millions of gallons of beer and stout. In every town in Southeast Asia you will find international brands of everything . . . cigarettes, toothpaste, hair-dressings, deodorants, shampoos, razor blades, sanitary

towels, analgesics, contraceptives, detergents, and tomato ketchup. . . . In addition to local manufacture, we import large quantities of industrial and consumer goods. Telecommunications have kept pace with this development. Satellites bring global events "live" to our televison screens.[4]

The region's importance as part of a Global Shopping Center is less well-known than its importance as a source of raw materials for "old" Center nations (ex-colonial powers like Britain and Holland), and increasingly for "new" Center nations (particularly the United States, Japan, and Australia). By 1978, for example, the ASEAN region was supporting a marketplace with a population of about 245 million people—greater than that of South America, and generating foreign trade amounting to more than $52 billion annually. Japan and the United States were the most important trading partners. Together, they accounted for about half of the region's exports and almost 40 percent of its imports.[5]

Given the sheer economic (not to mention the accompanying political, military, and communication) importance of Southeast Asia and its potential relative to other developing regions, it is not hard to understand why the TNAAs would be fascinated by the business potential in such dynamic economies. Also, it is not hard to understand the important role that advertising would generally play in stimulating economic growth and introducing Western-style consumer patterns. The executive in charge of international operations for Ogilvy & Mather, the biggest agency in Southeast Asia, has explained:

> One of the reasons developed countries have such high advertising expenditures is that years ago marketers discovered social problems and used advertising to make consumers aware of them. We discovered, or invented, for instance, B.O., night starvation, vitamin deficiencies, stringy hair, bad breath, and, latterly, smelly crotches. These problems give birth to Horlicks, Ribena, Lifebuoy, Stripe, Clearasil, and a hundred forms of after-shave. These products have, in turn, given employment to manufacturers of oils, fats, packaging, fragrances, bottlers, canners, and so on. They nurture wholesalers, retailers, salesmen. And, of course, they keep advertising people well stocked with Mercedes-Benz.[6]

TNAAs have played a leading role in communicating these problems and in introducing these products to Indonesia, Malaysia, Singapore, and other markets within Asia. By 1980, for example, Ogilvy & Mather could boast that its income had increased 284 percent over the previous five years and add:

> We have offices in Bangkok, Hong Kong, Kuala Lumpur, Singapore, associate companies in Jakarta, Manila, Seoul, Taipei and Tokyo and contractual agreements with four agencies in China. In addition to this we have a further 85 offices in 23 countries around the rest of the world.
> Our communication with them is fast and efficient. It enables us to get

market information from overseas, often faster than our clients. It makes it easy for us to coordinate the complexities of a regional or international campaign.[7]

As tables 10 and 11 show, Ogilvy & Mather is not alone in its interest in Southeast Asia. Many of the major TNAAs consider the so-called developing markets of this region and elsewhere in the vast Asia/Pacific region extremely important.[8]

In 1978, for example, fourteen TNAAs—ten American, three Japanese, and one Australian—had offices in at least one of the three neighboring Southeast Asian nations in this analysis.[9] Of Indonesia, Malaysia, and Singapore, the latter clearly is the most hospitable to the TNAAs. It hosted thirteen, while Malaysia hosted nine and Indonesia eight. As latter chapters in this book report, these numbers were increasing in the 1980s. For example, Ogilvy & Mather had established a second agency network under the name of Meridian. Its first Meridian agency was opened in Singapore in 1979, and in less than two years the network had expanded to Thailand, Malaysia, Indonesia, and Hong Kong. Significantly, each office was staffed and managed by nationals. SSC&B:Lintas, too, was establishing a second unit under the name Sprint. The growth of these major TNAAs' subsidiaries was understandably of great concern to local agencies, which feared these second TNAA units would attract smaller accounts that usually had gone to indigenous agencies.[10]

The largest TNAAs tend to be especially active in Southeast Asia, Australia, New Zealand, and Japan. For example, of the TNAAs in Indonesia, Malaysia, and Singapore, each is among the world's largest twenty-five agencies. Seven of the world's ten biggest agencies had operations in one form or another in at least two of these three nations. By the early 1980s, even conspicuously missing TNAAs like Y&R and BBDO International had opened offices in Singapore. This was about the same time that JWT began to give greater attention to the region by establishing a regional headquarters in Singapore and that Dentsu and Y&R, together, began joint ventures worldwide.

As elsewhere, the American TNAAs dominate transnational advertising. The two major French TNAAs are not active in Southeast Asia, and the direct Japanese agency presence is surprisingly minimal. For example, although it is the world's biggest single agency, Dentsu maintains a full-service agency only in Singapore. This situation exists despite the fact that the Japanese economic presence throughout the ASEAN region is substantial.[11]

Any transnational advertising in the region, then, tends very much to be in the hands of American-owned or associated agencies, which consider this particular region or grouping of nations important to their global patterns of growth and profitability. Leo Burnett agency, for example, talks about the area in these terms:

Extremely important both in terms of current contribution to our regional turnover and profit; and in terms of growth. Indeed the growth pattern of the last few years has been greater than our international average growth rate. We confidently expect this to continue in line with the growth of the Southeast Asian economy.[12]

Ogilvy & Mather has noted:

Southeast Asia is a relatively small part of O & M in terms of billings— less than 5 percent of our total worldwide business in fact. But what makes the region so attractive to us is that it is growing rapidly and that it is very profitable. Please note that I believe our agency is uniquely profitable in Southeast Asia. I don't mean we are the only profitable agency in the region but we are the most profitable international or regional agency by far and often more profitable than local agencies country by country.[13]

As table 11 indicates, a TNAA like SSC&B:Lintas is very active in diverse societies all the way from India east to Thailand, south to Malaysia, Singapore, and Indonesia, and still further south and east to Australia and New Zealand. General results from this vast region were excellent. In 1978, for example, the TNAA summarized its previous year in such different markets:

A region containing sharper economic, political, and cultural contrasts than any other in the SSC&B:Lintas world, and rarely have these contrasts been more marked than in 1977. While the economies of Malaysia and Singapore grew rapidly, Mrs. Gandhi's defeat in India reduced growth, and in Thailand inflation doubled. Pakistan had a year of political upheaval and New Zealand suffered a disastrous year economically.

Despite these tortuous conditions, SSC&B:Lintas achieved results well beyond estimates in the region as a whole. Billings increased by more than 20 percent in total, an impressive achievement in light of the fact that the rate of inflation in most of the countries in the region has been below a double digit figure.

The trading position has been strengthened by the acquisitions of business in all fields of activity, including corporate and government advertising.

Continuous cross-fertilisation between the International Centre and agencies, and within the regional network as well, has helped the most remote units to continue updating their skills and upgrading their standards, and numerous opportunities have been given to demonstrate to international clients that regional cooperation is a reality.

The SSC&B:Lintas long-term programme for personnel development has been intensified and significant investments have been made in training executive staff and in giving senior managers international exposure, in the U.S. or in Europe.[14]

This statement reveals a great deal about the operations and values of the TNAAs generally. Like the other TNAAs, SSC&B:Lintas "likes" the region, but it wants political stability so that economic growth can be

Table 10

Transnational Advertising Agencies in Malaysia, Singapore, and Indonesia, 1977-78

Agency	Global Headquarters	Asian/Pacific Regional Headquarters	Asian/Pacific Offices
Ted Bates & Co.	New York, U.S.A.	Sydney, Australia	Australia, Hong Kong, Malaysia, Singapore, Thailand
Leo Burnett	Chicago, U.S.A.	Sydney, Australia	Australia, New Zealand, Hong Kong, Malaysia, Singapore, Thailand
Chuo Senko	Tokyo, Japan	Tokyo, Japan	Hong Kong, Indonesia, Thailand
Compton	New York, U.S.A.	Sydney, Australia	Australia, Hong Kong, Singapore, Philippines, Japan,[a]/New Zealand
DFS Dorland Fortune	London, Great Britain	Sydney, Australia[b]/	Australia, Hong Kong, Singapore, Indonesia, Japan
Dentsu	Tokyo, Japan	Tokyo, Japan	, Hong Kong, Singapore,[c]/ Indonesia, Thailand, Taiwan
Kenyon & Eckhardt	New York, U.S.A.	London[d]/	Australia, New Zealand, Hong Kong, Malaysia, Singapore, Indonesia,[e]/ Philippines, Thailand, Taiwan, Japan, India, Sri Lanka
Hakuhodo, Inc.	Tokyo, Japan	Tokyo, Japan	Malaysia, Singapore, Indonesia, Thailand
Marsteller, Inc.[f]/	New York, U.S.A.	Hong Kong	Malaysia, Singapore, Hong Kong, Japan
McCann-Erickson	New York, U.S.A.	Tokyo, Japan	Australia, New Zealand, Hong Kong, Malaysia, Singapore, Indonesia, Philippines, Thailand, Japan[g]/
Needham, Harper & Steers	Chicago, U.S.A.	Sydney, Australia	Australia, Singapore, New Zealand, Hong Kong
Ogilvy & Mather	New York, U.S.A.	Sydney, Australia	Australia, New Zealand, Hong Kong, Malaysia, Singapore, Indonesia, Thailand, India
SSC&B:Lintas	New York, U.S.A.	London, Great Britain	Australia, New Zealand, Malaysia, Singapore, Indonesia[h]/ Thailand, India, Pakistan, Hong Kong, Philippines[i]/
J. Walter Thompson	New York, U.S.A.	Sydney, Australia	Australia, New Zealand, Hong Kong, Malaysia, Singapore[j]/ Philippines, Japan, India[k]/

NOTE: The offices listed include only those that have formal affiliations, or some form of special agreement, with a TNAA listed on the world's biggest agencies list for 1977. By the early 1980s, many of these agencies had added one or more offices to their Asian/Pacific networks. For example, Dentsu and McCann-Erickson both had offices in Beijing, China; both Compton and Needham, Harper & Steers had started Malaysian operations; JWT had established a wholly-owned agency in Singapore; and O&M had established a second network, Meridian, with offices in Singapore, Thailand, Malaysia, Indonesia, and Hong Kong. In addition, major TNAAs entered the region. For example, both Y&R and BBDO established offices in Singapore in the early 1980s.

a/
    Compton in Tokyo is associated with Dai-Ichi Kikaku, a major Japanese agency.

b/
    DDF in Australia and Southeast Asia are under the Fortune Group, Sydney. Fortune is one of the four major partners in a worldwide consortium called DDF International, incorporated in Switzerland but based in London.

c/
    Dentsu's Singapore office is only a liaison office, not a full-service agency. In Jakarta, Dentsu is employed by an Indonesian agency and under contract for services.

d/
    In Asia, Kenyon & Eckhardt operate under the name Grant, Kenyon & Eckhardt. K&E bought the Grant International Asian operations in 1975. In Hong Kong, K&E is affiliated with two agencies. K&E's area director for Asia is based in London and also serves as chairman of the Singapore agency. Until 1978, his office was in Singapore.

e/
    K&E has no personnel or equity in Indonesia, but it maintains close relations with Matari Advertising, Jakarta. K&E documents say the TNAA operates in Indonesia through a "special agreement office."

f/
    Asian operations stress "public affairs/governmental services" rather than advertising. They do business as Burson-Marsteller-Marsteller's public relations unit and the world's second largest public relations firm. The world's largest public relations agency is Hill & Knowlton, Inc., New York, with Asian operations in Japan, Hong Kong, Singapore, Malaysia, Australia, and New Zealand. In Malaysia, its offices in Kuala Lumpur and Penang operate under the name of Eric White Associates Pty. Ltd. In 1974, Hill & Knowlton acquired Eric White Associates, Sydney, which was the largest public relations firm outside the United States and had offices in Australia, New Zealand, Hong Kong, Malaysia, and Singapore.

g/
    In Tokyo, McCann-Erickson has a joint venture with Hakuhodo. It also maintains its Pacific regional office in Tokyo.

h/
    Since 1978, the SSC&B:Lintas office in Jakarta has had to operate solely as an in-house agency for its biggest client, Unilever.

i/
    In 1978, SSC&B:Lintas expanded into both Philippines and Hong Kong.

j/
    JWT's Singapore office was a branch of PTM Thompson, the Malaysian agency that is twenty-five percent owned by JWT, New York. Later, JWT established a wholly-owned operation in Singapore.

k/
    JWT's Bombay office opened in 1929, but the agency no longer has an equity interest in the Indian operation, which it regards as an affiliate rather than a "full JWT operation." The Manila and Tokyo offices were both opened in 1956.

SOURCES: This table is compiled from a variety of sources, including TNAAs' annual reports and other documents and interviews with advertising industry representatives.

Table 11

Five Major Transnational Agencies and Their 1977 Gross Income in the Asia-Pacific Region

(In Thousands of Dollars)

	Lintas	Burnett	O&M	JWT	McCann	Bates
Australia	3,740	6,000	4,630	5,500	7,690	12,500
New Zealand	560		750			
Thailand	1,270		700		380	600
Malaysia	670	910	1,150	490	340	650
Singapore	310	650	800		220	210
Philippines				980	520	
Indonesia	1,350					
SubTotal	3,600	1,560	2,650	1,470	1,460	1,460
Hong Kong		1,075	820		100	790
India	740		530	1,110		
Japan		400		7,300	1,360	
Total	8,640	9,035	10,350	15,380	10,510	14,750
Total Excluding Japan	8,640	8,635	10,350	8,080	9,150	14,750

NOTE: The above information for 1977 only does not reflect the full extent of these major agencies' activities in the region. For example, Burnett in Thailand was affiliated with Diethelm Advertising Ltd., Bangkok; both O&M and McCann had personnel in Indonesia operating through special arrangements with local Indonesian agencies; and JWT's Malaysian operation, PTM Thompson, maintained an office in Singapore. In cases where the TNAAs did not maintain their own offices in a nation, they usually had formal or informal associations with an established agency which could represent them in the local market.

SOURCE: _Advertising Age_ figures compiled by SSC&B:Lintas International, June 26, 1978.

translated into continued corporate growth and profits. It also wants to define professionalism and control staff development so that the ideas of "the International Centre" can be efficiently transmitted to different markets for smooth implementation in the service of TNC clients. Such implementation, coordinated by TNAA executives in the Center, can be carried out by local elites serving as their bridgeheads in Malaysia, Singapore, and Indonesia. An O&M executive has emphasized the importance of these nationals working for the TNAAs:

> I think an agency in a developing country must aim to be staffed by nationals, must learn from the experience of those countries which have employed advertising on a wide scale for decades, and must be acutely conscious of the social, racial, and political environment. I think nationals are vital as the backbone to an agency because:
>
> 1. They are the people who will remain in a country. They are not ships passing in the night.
> 2. They understand intuitively and can appreciate more quickly objective evidence relating to socio-economic factors.
>
> I think many agencies have been slow in the past to develop nationals in key positions and it is our objective to accelerate this process as fast as we can.[15]

More than other TNAAs, O&M was practising what it was preaching. In 1980, for example, it named a Thai woman as managing director of its Bangkok agency. She became the first woman to head an O&M office in the region and also the first national to run an office owned by the TNAA in Asia. The TNAA was also openly talking about the day when all of its offices would probably be run by local personnel.[16]

The TNAA admen in the Center nation headquarters; the "modernizing elite" employed by the TNAA in Kuala Lumpur, Singapore, or Jakarta; and the consumers (rich or poor, urban or rural) *are* structurally part of one capitalist world order. Its various political, military, economic, cultural, and communication components combine to create increasing interdependence among seemingly diverse, unconnected nations and groups and to maintain the overall system with cooperation from nationals.

The TNAA executives and staff from New York, London, Chicago, or Tokyo may not speak the same language, worship the same way, or eat the same foods as a poor or rich periphery nation consumer, but through various direct and indirect associations, facilitated by bridgeheads and other resources, they *know* the periphery market. Through experiences in other societies, they know how to protect their interests by encouraging greater interaction and communication between TNAAs and the local advertising industry and between Center and Periphery nations. The subtle result of such integration with advertising-weak nations is advertising dominance, which maintains the existing structure.

Advertising in Indonesia, Malaysia, and Singapore

An obvious characteristic of the way in which nations are structured is the great inequality between Center and Periphery nations. Chapter 4 suggested the great gaps between Center advertising-rich nations like the United States and Japan, and Periphery advertising-poor nations like those discussed in this book. The structure also exhibits striking differences between Peripheries. Tables 12 and 13, for example, emphasize the relative affluence of Singapore compared to its two neighbors according to several basic social, economic, and communications indicators. Together, the tables show that the benefits of a "good" society—whether interpreted in terms of the conventional economic indicators like per capita income, or access to media, or ownership of certain heavily advertised products—are distributed very unequally within and between rich and poor nations. Advertising plays an important role in bringing these differences out in the open and intensifying competitions and frustration over how human needs can be satisfied.

In any advertising comparison of Southeast Asia, the nation of Malaysia seems to be an important benchmark since it is situated midway on a Periphery nation continuum with large, poor, rural, sprawling Indonesia at one extreme, and small, rich, urban, compact Singapore at the other. Historically and culturally, too, Malaysia with its large numbers of indigenous Malay and immigrant Chinese groups stands in between predominantly Chinese Singapore and predominantly Malay (and Muslim) Indonesia. From 1963 to 1965, Singapore was part of the Federation of Malaysia, and both ethnically and linguistically the Malays of Malaysia and Indonesia are related and have comprised the area's largest indigenous (*bumiputra* or *asli*) group. In both Malaysia and Indonesia, Bahasa Melayu (the Malay language) is the sole national language, and even in Singapore that language is considered official. Issues of ethnicity, language, and cultural identity have contributed to sensitive communal and political problems in all three societies.

Despite significant differences, however, the three nations are part of one geographical and political region, Southeast Asia, and all host a number of TNAAs that influence local advertising and the society at large. More significantly, all three independent nations pursue a Western-style development strategy that generally encourages economic growth, advertising supported mass media, and foreign investment. Table 14 uses media penetration figures to indicate how Malaysia, Singapore, and Indonesia compare within a Southeast Asian framework. Similar general growth patterns, particularly rapid for television, seem to be showing up elsewhere in Asia and in the Third World generally and are contributing to rapid advertising growth. Table 15 uses the case of rural Malaysia to suggest that

Table 12

Key Social, Economic, and Communications Indicators

for Indonesia, Malaysia, and Singapore

Indicator	Indonesia	Nation Malaysia	Singapore
GNP per capita (U.S. dollars) 1976	240.0	860.0	2,700.0
Population (millions) mid-1976	135.2	12.7	2.3
Urban population (percent of total) 1975	19.0	30.0	90.0
Labor force in agriculture (percent) 1970	66.0	50.0	3.0
Income distribution (percent of private income received by)			
Highest 5% of households	33.7	28.3	. . .
Highest 20% of households	52.0	56.0	. . .
Lowest 20% of households	6.8	3.5	. . .
Lowest 40% of households	17.3	11.2	. . .
Distribution of land ownership (percent owned by) 1962			
Top 10% of owners	48.0	. . .	. . .
Smallest 10% of Owners	3.0	. . .	. . .
Adult literacy rate (percent) 1974	62.0	60.0	75.0
Life expectancy at birth 1975	48.0	59.0	70.0
Housing-access to electricity (percent of all dwellings 1970)	. . .	43.0	87.0
Passenger cars (per thous. pop.) 1970	2.0	27.0	82.0
Radio receivers (per thous. pop.) 1970	. . .	41.0	150.0
TV receivers (per thous. pop.)	0.7	33.0	114.0
Newsprint (kg/yr per cap.) 1970	0.4	4.1	10.4
Number of daily newspapers	170.0	31.0	10.0
Total newspaper circulation (thous.)	1,800.0	583.0	490.0
Newspaper diffusion rate (per thous. pop.)	7.0	63.0	203.0
Cinema seating capacity (per thous. pop.)	. . .	27.8	27.3
Total reported 1974 advertising expenditures (millions of U.S. dollars)	40.0	36.6	43.0
Gross national production 1974 (billions of U.S. dollars)	15.4	6.6	4.3
Advertising as percentage of GNP 1974	.26	.56	1.0

NOTE: Figures without years refer to the last available years or to a
recent period for which comparable data for the three nations are
available. Data should be treated cautiously and are used only to
give a general picture of how these nations compare on several indicators generally considered relevant to the development process or to
advertising. Refer to original sources below for technical notes out-
lining the concepts, definitions, and methods used to facilitate
comparison.

SOURCES: Data have been extracted from various authoritative reference
materials, including: UNESCO, Statistical Yearbook 1975 (Paris:
UNESCO, 1976); World Bank, "Social Indicators Data Sheets" for
Indonesia (26 January 1978), Malaysia (8 June 1978), and Singapore
(22 April 1975), prepared by World Bank headquarters, Washington;
World Bank, World Development Report, 1978 (Washington: World Bank,
August 1978); Press Foundation of Asia, Asian Press and Media 1976/
1977 Directory (Manila: Press Foundation of Asia, 1977); and Starch
INRA Hooper and International Advertising Association (IAA), World
Advertising Expenditures 1976 Edition (Mamaroneck, New York: Starch
INRA Hooper, 1976).

Table 13

Several Consumer Characteristics in the Markets of Malaysia, Singapore, and Indonesia, 1970-76

| | Malaysia | | | Singapore | | | Indonesia |
	'70-71	'72-73	'75-76	'70-71	'72-73	'75-76	1976
Literacy percent literate in at least one language	74%	74%	77%	76%	80%	84%	83%
Urbanization percent living in market centres	18	19	19				
other urban areas	20	20	20				
"Class" percent living in household earning M/S $1000 or Rp150,000 & above	2	3	5	8	13	31	2
$501-1000 or Rp75,001-150,000	5	6	14	19	30	39	9
$301-500 or Rp50,001-75,000	14	13	18	28	33	20	12
$151-300 or Rp20,001-50,000	30	28	26	28	19	7	43
Up to M/S$150 or Rp20,000	41	36	30	7	2	1	33
(not disclosed)	8	13	7	10	3	1	*
"Ownership" percent having in homes							
motor car	11	11	17	20	25	26	6
motorcycle	20	21	31	17	15	15	18
TV set-black & white	17	20	32	54	67	74	33
-color	...	...	*	...	...	8	...
radio set-with batteries	64	64	54	74	76	53	69
-without batteries			22			44	
tape recorder	5	6	22	15	21	38	36
refrigerator	13	15	22	52	64	79	12
air conditioner	1	1	2	4	5	5	...
electric sewing machine	...	*	2	...	3	5	7
Home ownership % living in own home	67	67	74	46	48	49	...
Newspaper reading % read yesterday	44	41	45	60	61	70	31
Cinema going % went in past 7 days	16	19	15	15	20	20	8

= less than 0.5 percent

TES: The Survey Research Group (SRG), an organization specializing in market and social research in
utheast Asia, collected these data during continuous surveys of a representative cross-section sample
the adults in Malaysia, Singapore, and Indonesia. Indonesian data were not collected before 1976,
d the above figures are from three major cities- - Jakarta, Surabaya, and Medan- - only. SRG syndicates
antitative and qualitative research to such clients as mass media, advertising agencies, and advertisers.
e U.S. dollar equals approximately 2.4 Malaysian or Singaporean dollars, or 415 Indonesian rupiah.

JRCE: Dr. Newell Grenfell, chairman, SRG, provided these data during an interview in Kuala Lumpur,
laysia, May 18, 1977.

Table 14

Media Trends in Southeast Asia

	Newspapers 1973 1979	Television 1973 1979	Radio 1973 1979	Cinema 1973 1979
Singapore	61 88	45 62	34 31	20 26
Peninsular Malaysia	41 50	21 41	57 50	19 19
Hong Kong	64 66	77 84	33 46	21 12
	1975 1979	1975 1979	1975 1979	1975 1979
Thailand (Bangkok)	78 64	62 64	60 60	23 18
	1976 1979	1976 1979	1976 1979	1976 1979
Indonesia(Jakarta)	38 43	38 45	41 41	7 8

NOTE: All figures are based on media index surveys conducted by Survey Research Group, a major research organization with offices throughout Southeast Asia. Figures relate to adults (15 years and older). TV and radio audiences refer to people viewing or listening "yesterday", i.e. the day before the survey interview took place. Readership of daily newspapers is based on reading or looking at any issue of any daily "yesterday." The cinema audience is defined as those who went to the cinema "in the past 7 days." Thailand and Indonesia data are for Bangkok and Jakarta only since national media index surveys are not yet conducted. Peninsular Malaysia refers only to West Malaysia and exclude Sabah and Sarawak states in East Malaysia. Note the relatively high level of newspaper readership in Singapore and television viewing in Hong Kong. Also keep in mind that even low percentages, such as TV reach in Jakarta, can translate into large audiences. Jakarta's total adult population, for example, is more than twice that of Singapore.

SOURCE: "SRG Survey Highlights Southeast Asian Trends," SRG News, No. 33, March 1980, p.4.

Table 15

Media Trends in Rural Malaysia, 1974-80

Percentage of àdults (aged 15-plus) that:	1974	1975	1976	1977	1978	1979	1980
Watched television yesterday	16	19	21	25	24	35	44
Listened to radio yesterday	52	50	52	49	46	54	53
Read daily paper yesterday	17	27	32	34	35	39	42
Read journal in past 2-4 weeks	19	23	30	31	27	23	27
Visited cinema in past week	13	10	8	9	12	13	13

NOTE: These data from the Survey Research Group suggest that the growth of mass media - - at least in Malaysia - - is certainly not limited to urban areas. The proportion of rural adults watching television on an average day has risen particularly rapidly.

SOURCE: "SRM Highlights Malaysia's Rural Development," SRG News, no. 36, December 1980, p. 3.

media penetration is not limited to a few urban areas. Again, such patterns are probably showing up in rural areas elsewhere.

Advertising and Colonialism

The profound penetration of Southeast Asia began more than 350 years ago when the Dutch East India Co. gained political sovereignty over parts of what is now Indonesia in 1602. Later, Holland's European great power competitor, Britain, gained a foothold to the north when the British East India Co. acquired the island of Penang in 1786. By 1819, the company's agent, Sir Stamford Raffles, had founded Singapore as a free trade center to serve expanding British commercial interests.[17]

Through these early colonial efforts, the indigenous peoples were integrated into an international division of labor.[18] Advertising domination structures apparent in modern, politically independent Malaysia, Singapore, and Indonesia were developed through colonial patterns and processes created initially through Western political, military, and economic power and later supported by more subtle communication and cultural power.

While extracting various raw materials to meet the requirements of their metropoles, the European "mother" powers were having a considerable impact on indigenous living conditions and socialization processes through their laissez-faire, open-door policies. Christianity, the English language, pluralism, Western culture, mass media, and political, military, legal, and educational systems were among the diverse spin-off effects that the presence of formal colonialism had on Southeast Asia.

One unique "contribution" of the British was their creation of Singapore as a regional center for their trading, military, and political activities, including transnational movement of labor to support the colonial effort.[19] Materials from the mines, plantations, and forests of the nearby hinterlands were transferred to the Centers of Europe via Singapore. Such an entrepot and middleman status made Singapore significantly different from its less commercially active neighbors. The colonial powers—initially Britain but later others, especially the United States and Japan—and the "westernized" elites and trading classes in Singapore and in the hinterlands who cooperated with the expatriates prospered from such a structure. Under such a colonial system, communications and other forms of interaction between the indigenous people were next to impossible since the British and the Dutch had nearly a monopoly over communications, political, military, and economic power within their sphere of influence. Under colonial policies and paternalism, the hinterlands of Malaysia and Indonesia were virtually forced to rely on Singapore's capital, facilities, services, and communication channels for interaction with the outside world.[20] Some of these early dependency relations continued in different forms in postcolonial Malaysia and Indonesia.[21]

During formal colonialism, an especially important business organization was created by the Center to support its expanding capitalist system. The giant export-import trading agency or commercial house, headquartered in Europe but with operations throughout the colonies, was established to facilitate the colonial economic presence.[22] The trading agency managed the production, low-processing, and exporting of raw materials from the hinterlands to London and Amsterdam and beyond. It also supervised the distribution and sale of the "mother" nations' manufactured goods within the Periphery societies. As the Center's requirements and world political and economic conditions changed, the trading agencies found themselves increasingly needing more complex infrastructures and specialized support services including transportation, communication, and financial services. With the end of formal colonialism, advertising has been one of these modern, Western-created services that has gained great importance as the dominating Centers sought new ways to maintain the enforced integration of the Peripheries into their economy.

The TNAA, however, did not arrive on the Southeast Asian scene in a major way until more than a decade after World War II. The region was virtually asleep in terms of advertising as a socioeconomic and communication institution based on a deliberate mix of art *and* science and designed to disseminate mass messages throughout society.[23] Traditionally, word-of-mouth had always been the most effective means of persuading people to do anything. The early colonial businessmen soon realized that the persuasive techniques that worked back home in London or Amsterdam could also be applied to different societies. Early advertising consisted simply of posters, handbills, and newspaper advertisements, usually in the official colonial language and heavily concentrated in a few coastal areas. The messages were frequently identical to materials used in the Center nation, and they were designed to reach the small expatriate community comprised of colonial administrators, businessmen, planters, and soldiers. The masses, especially those inland, were far removed from the colonial marketplace and, therefore, from its media and advertisements. Not only did indigenous villagers not have access to the day's very limited communication channels, but they also were illiterate and were outside the cash economy. They could never afford luxury imported goods.

The colonial powers, too, were not interested in communicating or dealing directly with the indigenous people. Their "divide and rule" policies in Southeast Asia and elsewhere were designed to isolate the rural-based indigenous groups from the urban-oriented commercial groups, which included not only expatriates but also the overseas Chinese. The latter minority controlled trade within the region and served as middlemen for the expatriates in their business dealings with the local population.[24] The

Chinese became an unusually important tool in the historical colonial pattern. Following the independence of Malaysia, Singapore, and Indonesia, both local and foreign-born Chinese would serve as a prime bridgehead through which the TNC could follow in the footsteps of the great trading houses and penetrate the Peripheries. The sizable presence of a relatively affluent, tightly knit Chinese community throughout the region made the Chinese an easy scapegoat for the governments of "plural societies" like Malaysia and Indonesia. Since independence, the indigenous peoples in these societies have become increasingly frustrated with their inability to "catch up" to Westerners and the Chinese.

Initially, both the Dutch and the British were pretty much content with an international division of labor that had their respective colonies specialize in providing a variety of raw materials and agricultural products—especially tin and rubber—that required a very low degree of processing. They did not see the hinterlands as potential markets nor as areas worthy of their manufacturing investment. This gradually changed, especially after World War I, as a larger number of local people were integrated into the colonial market system and as the "mother" nations' firms sought overseas expansion opportunities.

Because of its special status as a strategically located colonial base, Singapore understandably was ahead of the rest of the region in terms of commercial and communication activities, including advertising. The influential English-language *Straits Times,* for example, was founded in 1845 to serve colonial needs for regional shipping and other news. In 1897 it became the first newspaper in the region to publish an advertising supplement in full color. Prominent trading houses such as Guthrie and the Borneo Company advertised their principals' imported goods in that particular issue, and these corporations remain influential advertisers in Singapore today.[25]

Before World War II disrupted colonialism, Western factories had begun modest local operations in the region. Progress was slow but gradually products made by such giant TNCs as Unilever, British-American Tobacco, Coca-Cola, Singer, Goodyear, Dunlop, Ford, ICI, Bata, Heineken, Philips, and National Carbon (now Union Carbide) gained popularity. Aggressive advertising and other marketing techniques helped insure that even those outside the major urban colonial centers would come to think of these corporations' "imported" goods as symbols of British-made, Dutch-made, or American-made quality.

Given a Western-controlled colonial environment, it is easy to understand how modern European and American advertising easily gained entry into the region as simply another spin-off institution within a larger comprehensive colonial development package. Newspapers gradually developed—first to serve narrow expatriate commercial interests, then the commercial *and* cultural needs of local minorities, especially the Chinese, and much later the broad political needs of the indigenous masses.[26] As in other developing economies, early admen were closely associated with printing and newspapers, and they functioned more as advertising space brokers or sellers than as space buyers.[27] The early advertising agencies did not operate as objective counselors who advised advertisers how to most efficiently and effectively sell their goods to specific target groups. The pioneering ad agencies tended to be run by expatriates who had at least a vague notion of how European advertising agencies worked or by Chinese who dabbled not only in selling ad space but also in outdoor signmaking, printing, and other business activities. The latter had the problem of convincing local businessmen that advertising was a necessary part of marketing.

Given this overview of advertising as a service that evolved out of the Western colonial presence in Asia, let me now describe the TNAA scene in detail in Indonesia, Malaysia, and Singapore before turning to the special case of China.

Notes

1. Michael J. Ball, "Marketing in Southeast Asia." Paper delivered at Bonnier Marketing Conference, London, August 30, 1973, p. 5.
2. "Change Alley" is a narrow lane in Singapore where travelers coming to Singapore have historically gone to change their money. Today, the alley is a popular attraction for tourists who wish to bargain for souvenirs. See Peter Kum, "Madison Avenue to Change Alley: A Route Full of Misconceptions," *Media*, January 1977, p. 26, for a symbolic use of Change Alley as something opposite from Madison Avenue. In a more general context, it refers to Singapore's traditional role as a center of entrepot services for Southeast Asia.
3. ASEAN was formed in 1967 by Malaysia, Singapore, Indonesia, the Philippines, and Thailand to promote social, cultural, and economic cooperation among these neighboring states. With the notable exception of Singapore, all members are primarily producers and basic processors of raw materials such as oil, rubber, tin, timber, copra, palm oil, and bananas. Singapore stands out as a commercial center for the region, and it has growing financial and manufacturing sectors. Throughout its first decade, ASEAN has been struggling with tariff cutting schemes and other means through which to encourage intraregional cooperation.
4. Statement from the Survey Research Group, an expatriate-founded organization of six companies engaged in market and social research in Malaysia, Singapore, Indonesia, Thailand, Taiwan, Hong Kong, and the Philippines. Its founder company, Survey Research Malaysia, began in 1964. The Group's clients include TNAAs, TNCs, government agencies, and mass media who purchase its consumer research to help with their business and communications planning. The Group has been responsible for introducing Western ideas of marketing research as a scientific method into its host-nations. See "The Survey Research Group" (Kuala Lumpur: The Survey Research Group, no date). For an excellent discussion of the role of commercial research resources in understanding mass communication in a Third World context, see Newell Harvey Grenfell, "Mass Media Audiences in Peninsular Malaysia: An Illustration of the Value of Audience Analysis in a Developing Country," (Doctoral dissertation, University of Malaya, April 1976). Grenfell is a founding member of the Survey Research Group.
5. "ASEAN: Five Good Markets in a New Light," *Commerce America*, 17 July 1978, p. 4. For a discussion of Japan's relationship with Southeast Asia and with the United States as the world's dominant power, see Jon Halliday and Gavan McCormack, *Japanese Imperialism Today* (New York: Monthly Review Press, 1973). For a more sympathetic view, see Alvin D. Cox, "Japan

and the Southeast Asian Configuration" in Sudershan Chawla, Melvin Gurton, and Alain-Gerard Marsot, *Southeast Asia under the New Balance of Power* (New York: Praeger Publishers, 1974), pp. 80–93.

6. Ball, "The Role of Advertising and Advertising Agencies in Developing Countries" (Paper prepared for Marketing Communications, Far Eastern Workshop, Manila, October 1971), p. 6.

7. "Know-how. That's how we got to be the biggest agency in Southeast Asia," an Ogilvy & Mather advertisement in *Media*, August 1980, p. 30.

8. The TNAAs often organize their global activities along regional lines. I use the term *Asia/Pacific Region* to refer to that vast area stretching from approximately Iran east to Japan and south to Australia and New Zealand. SSC&B:Lintas uses the same term to describe this geographic area. Other agencies use slightly different terminology. For example, Leo Burnett considers Southeast Asia under its Australia/Far East region, which reports to a regional managing director in Sydney, who in turn reports to the president of Leo Burnett International in Chicago. McCann-Erickson considers Southeast Asia as part of its Pacific Region, which reports to the regional director in Tokyo, who also serves as president of McCann-Erickson-Hakuhodo.

9. The American agencies are Ted Bates, Leo Burnett, Compton, Kenyon & Eckhardt, Marsteller, McCann-Erickson, Needham, Harper & Steer, Ogilvy & Mather, JWT, and SSC&B:Lintas. The Japanese agencies are Dentsu, Hakuhodo, and Chuo Senko. The Australian agency is Fortune, which is a partner in the London-based DFS Dorland Fortune (DDF) International group, which in turn includes the American agency Dancer-Fitzgerald-Sample (DFS).

10. In Bangkok, second unit agencies have been established by both O&M and SSC&B:Lintas. For an article reflecting the indigenous concern over "unfair competition" from these giants, see "Big Is Bad, Say Thai Agencies," *Media*, September 1980, p. 1.

11. For insight into the sizable Japanese presence in Southeast Asia, see Raul S. Manglapus, *Japan in Southeast Asia: Collision Course* (New York: Carnegie Endowment for International Peace, 1976).

12. John Shadwell, Marketing Manager, Leo Burnett Pty, Ltd., Sydney. Personal correspondence with the author, 5 July 1978.

13. Ball, Sydney. Personal correspondence with the author, 4 April 1978.

14. *SSC&B:Lintas World Review 1977*, p. 22.

15. Ball, "The Role of Advertising and Advertising Agencies in Developing Countries," pp. 10–11.

16. Ball, "The Day of the Asian Has Arrived," *Media*, August 1980, p. 8.

17. The literature on the history, politics, and economics of Southeast Asia and specifically Malaysia, Singapore, and Indonesia is vast. For a general introduction to the Indonesian scene, see such works as J. H. Boeke, *Economics and Economic Policy of Dual Societies as Exemplified by Indonesia* (Haarlem: Tjeenk Wellink, 1953); Bruce Glassburner, *The Economy of Indonesia* (Ithaca: Cornell University Press, 1971); G. D. Legge, *Indonesia* (Englewood Cliffs, N.J.: Prentice-Hall, 1964); Ruth McVey, ed., *Indonesia* (New Haven, Conn.: Yale University Press, 1963); and J. M. van der Kroef, *Indonesia in the Modern World* (Bandung: Masa Baru, 1956). For works on Malaysia and Singapore, see Gordon P. Means, *Malaysian Politics* (London: University of London Press, 1977); Donald and Joanna Moore, *The First 150 Years of Singapore* (Singapore: Donald Moore Press Ltd., 1969); Milton E. Osborne, *Singapore and Malaysia* (Ithaca: Southeast Asia Program, Cornell University, 1964); Thomas H. Silcock, *The Economy of Malaya* (Singapore: Eastern Universities Press, 1970); and Richard D. Winstedt, *A History of Malaya* (Kuala Lumpur: Marican, 1968). For a concise overview of the entire region, see Frank H. Golay, Ralph Anspach, M. Ruth Pfanner, and Eliezer R. Ayal, eds., *Underdevelopment and Economic Nationalism in Southeast Asia* (Ithaca: Cornell University Press, 1969); G. M. Kahin, *Governments and Politics of Southeast Asia* (Ithaca: Cornell University Press, 1965); and Michael Leifer, *Dilemmas of Statehood in Southeast Asia* (Singapore: Asia Pacific Press, 1972).

18. For example, see J. S. Furnivall, *Netherlands India* (London: Cambridge University Press, 1967); V. Kanapathy, *The Malaysian Economy: Problems and Prospects* (Singapore: Donald Moore Press, 1970); J. J. Puthucheary, *Ownership and Control in the Malayan Economy* (Singapore: Eastern Universities Press, 1960); S. Tas, *Indonesia: The Underdeveloped Freedom* (Indianapolis, Ind.: Bobbs-Merrill Co., Inc., 1974), especially chapters 2 and 3.

19. For an overview of Singapore's unique colonial history and its development as a city-state, see Iain Buchanan, *Singapore in Southeast Asia: An Economic and Political Appraisal* (London: G. Bell and Sons Ltd., 1972), and T. J. S. George, *Lee Kuan Yew's Singapore* (London: Andre Deutsch Ltd., 1973).

20. For an overview of colonial economic development and the rise of Western manufacturing and related services, see G. C. Allen and Audry G. Donnithorne, *Western Enterprise in Indonesia and Malaya. A Study in Economic Development* (London: George Allen & Unwin Ltd., 1962).

21. See, for example, K. S. Jomo, "Class Formation in Malaya: Capital, the State and Uneven Development," (Doctoral dissertation, Harvard University, 1977); Marc Lindenberg, *Foreign and Domestic Investment in the Pioneer Industry Programme, Malaysia, Political, Economic, and Social Impacts* (Doctoral dissertation, University of Southern California, 1973); Rex Mortimer, ed., *Showcase State. The Illusion of Indonesia's "Accelerated Modernization"* (Sydney: Angus and Robertson, 1973); Wayne Robinson, "Dominance, Dependence and Underdevelopment: The Case of Indonesia," *Political Science* 27, nos. 1 and 2 (July/December 1975), pp. 55–81; and Franklin B. Weinstein, *Indonesian Foreign Policy and the Dilemma of Dependence* (Ithaca, N.Y.: Cornell University Press, 1976).

22. In colonial Indonesia, a group of ten great trading houses were widely known as the Dutch "Big Ten." Like the old established business houses of the British, these transnational enterprises were engaged in a wide variety of activities, including banking, shipping, plantation management, insurance, mining, manufacturing, and importing of consumer goods. They included: Internatio, the Borneo-Sumatra Company, George Wehry, Lindeteves, Jacobson van den Berg, and Harmsen and Verwey. After Indonesian independence, these Dutch enterprises continued to dominate the Indonesian economy until Sukarno finally nationalized them in 1958 and split them into independent units under government bodies. This action helped destroy Dutch economic influence, but it also severely weakened the Indonesian economy since indigenous personnel were unable to efficiently maintain the enterprises. Corruption in the state enterprises was rampant, and the Chinese were able to increase their economic power within the Indonesian economy by assuming some of the tasks historically handled by the Dutch. In Malaysia and Singapore, similar large trading houses prospered but they were not nationalized, and they continued to be very influential within the economies of both Malaysia and Singapore. Major, long-established agencies include Guthrie, Sandilands, Buttery, Sime Darby, Inchcape Group (formerly best known as the Borneo Co.), the Boustead Group, and the East Asiatic Co.

23. For a history of the close links between advertising in Malaysia and Singapore, see: The Advertisers Association, *A Review of Advertising in Singapore and Malaysia during Early Times* (Singapore: Federal Publications, 1971).

24. See, for example, Hildred Geertz, "Indonesian Cultures and Communities," in McVey, *Indonesia*, pp. 24–96; Guy F. Hunter, *Southeast Asia: Race, Culture, and Nation* (New York: Oxford University Press, 1966); Jin-Bee Ooi, *Land, People and Economy in Malaya* (London: Longmans, 1963); Victor Purcell, *The Chinese in Malaysia* (Kuala Lumpur: Oxford University Press, 1967); Purcell, *The Chinese in Southeast Asia* (London: Oxford University Press, 1965). For a political science approach to pluralism, see: Cynthia H. Enloe, *Multiethnic Politics: The Case of Malaysia*. Ph.D. dissertation, University of California at Berkeley, 1967; Alvin Rabushka, *Race and Politics in Urban Malaya*, Stanford: Hoover Institution Press, 1973; and K. J. Ratnam, *Communalism and the Political Process in Malaya*, Singapore, University of Malaya Press, 1965.

25. The Advertisers Association, *A Review of Advertising in Singapore and Malaysia during Early Times*, pp. 11–12.

26. Compared to the Malaysian and Singaporean press, the Indonesian press is complex and unusually political and nationalistic. For an introduction to newspapers and Indonesian media generally, see such works as: Judith B. Agassi, *Mass Media in Indonesia* (Cambridge, Mass.: Center for International Studies, Massachusetts Institute of Technology, 1969); Robert H. Crawford, *The Daily Indonesian-Language Press of Djakarta: Analysis of Two Recent Critical Periods.* (Doctoral dissertation, Syracuse University, 1967), especially chapter 4; Crawford, "Indonesia," in John Lent, ed., *The Asian Newspapers' Reluctant Revolution* (Ames: The Iowa State University Press, 1971), pp. 158–78; Adaham Hasibuan, "Genesis of a Press: Economic Aspects of the National Press in Indonesia," *Gazette* 3 (1957), pp. 29–46; Mastini

Hardjo Prakoso, "A Short History of the Newspaper in Indonesia," *Katalogus Surat-Kabar: Koleski Perpustakaan Museum Pusat 1810–1973* (Jakarta: Museum Pusat, 1973), pp. xii–xvii; Nono Anwar Makarim, "The Indonesian Press: An Editor's Perspective," in Karl D. Jackson and Lucian W. Pye, *Political Power and Communications in Indonesia* ((Berkeley: University of California Press, 1978), pp. 259–81; Oey Hong Lee, *Indonesian Government and Press During Guided Democracy* (Hull, Britain: Center for Southeast Asian Studies, University of Hull, 1971); John H. Sullivan, "The Press and Politics in Indonesia," *Journalism Quarterly*, 44 (1967), pp. 99–106; Astrid Susanto, "The Mass Communications System in Indonesia," in Jackson and Pye, *Political Power and Communications in Indonesia*, pp. 229–58; and J. M. van der Kroef, "The Press in Indonesia: By-Product of Nationalism," *Journalism Quarterly* 31, no. 3 (1954), pp. 337–46.

The press in Malaysia and Singapore has been more commercially oriented than the press in Indonesia. Virtually all media in both Malaysia and Singapore evolved from the same political, economic, and historical circumstances, and newspapers often had sister operations in the neighboring state. For an introduction to the rise of the press in the two nations, see such works as: Nik Ahmad bin Haji Nik Hassan, "The Malay Press," *Journal of Malayan Branch Royal Asiatic Society* 36, no. 1 (1963), pp. 37–78; Russell H. Betts, *The Mass Media of Malaya and Singapore as of 1965: A Survey of the Literature* (Cambridge, Mass.: Center for International Studies, Massachusetts Institute of Technology, 1969); Paul P. Blackburn, *Communications and National Development in Burma, Malaysia and Thailand: A Comparative Systemic Analysis.* (Doctoral dissertation, American University, 1971); Cecil K. Byrd, *Early Printing in the Straits Settlements 1806–1858* (Singapore: Singapore National Library, 1970); Monghock Chen, *The Early Chinese Newspapers of Singapore, 1881–1912* (Singapore: University Malaya Press, 1967); John A. Lent, "English-Language Mass Media of Malaysia: Historical and Contemporary Perspectives," *Gazette* 21, no. 2 (1975), pp. 95–113; Elliott S. Parker, "A Potted History of Malaysian Journalism," *Leader, Malaysian Journalism Review* 2, no. 3 (1973), pp. 31–32; William R. Roff, *The Origins of Malay Nationalism* (New Haven: Yale University Press, 1967), especially pp. 43–55 and 157–77; Peng-siew Tan, "Malaysia and Singapore," in Lent, *Asian Newspapers' Reluctant Revolution,* pp. 179–190; and Zainal-Abidin bin Ahmad, "Malay Journalism in Malaya," *Journal of the Malayan Branch Royal Asiatic Society* 19, no. 2 (October 1941), pp. 244–50.

27. The advertising agency itself is a peculiarly American organization, although advertising itself has been an activity of most societies. For a concise historical overview of the development of both advertising and the modern advertising agency, see John S. Wright, Daniel S. Warner, and Willis L. Winter, Jr., *Advertising* (New York: McGraw-Hill Co., 1971), pp. 20–39, and the American Bicentennial-related materials in *Advertising Age,* 19 April 1976.

Part III
National Case Studies

6

Indonesia: Advertising in a Sprawling Archipelago

> Certainly we could live without drinking Coca-Cola or smoking foreign-brand filter-tip cigarettes, but it is very difficult. These foreign companies engage in advertising, and because of their advertising impact they are creating their own demand.
>
> —Mohammad Sadli[1]

"Modern" advertising—meaning Western-defined and imported— arrived in the sprawling archipelago called Indonesia to serve the growing needs of nonindigenous manufacturers and distributers. By 1938 the advertising agency as a specialized business organization had reached Indonesia.[2] Lintas International Ltd. was founded in London in 1930 to meet the growing international requirements of Unilever, a company formed when Lever Brothers joined forces with the Margarine Union. It became a highly-diversified giant Anglo-Dutch TNC which, in 1938, started an in-house advertising agency called Lintas in Batavia (now known as Jakarta) to handle its expanding soap and margarine advertising.[3] This was approximately twenty-five years before a professional, wholly owned and operated indigenous Indonesian agency would be in any economic position to even modestly compete with a TNAA of Lintas's vast resources, built up through decades of association with Unilever's worldwide marketing activities.

While other Western-style advertising agencies were all but nonexistent during Dutch colonialism and throughout most of Sukarno's rule, Lintas was busy working exclusively on Unilever's brands and developing resources that today are second to none in Indonesia. The agency handles dozens of products, including Lux and Lifebuoy soaps, Rinso detergent, Blue Band margarine, and Pepsodent toothpaste. By 1970, the parent Unilever organization wanted to tap American advertising expertise so it sold 49 percent of its transnational agency network to SSC&B, a New York agency founded in 1946. As a result, Lintas offices in Jakarta, Kuala Lumpur, and elsewhere began taking non-Unilever clients as a means of diver-

153

sifying and increasing business. By the end of the 1970s, this new parent TNAA—SSC&B:Lintas—was being acquired by the New York-based Interpublic Group of Companies, the world's largest advertising conglomerate.

Sukarno's "Old Order"

World War II (the Japanese occupied the Netherlands East Indies from 1942 to 1945), Sukarno's revolution against the Dutch, and growing economic and political instability severely disrupted all commercial activities. By 1955 at the Bandung Conference, Sukarno was speaking out strongly against the ongoing dangers of foreign influence to independent nations:

> I beg of you not to think of colonialism only in its classic form which we of Indonesia, and our brothers in different parts of Asia and Africa, knew. Colonialism has also its modern dress, in the form of economic control, intellectual control, and actual physical control, by a small but alien community within a nation. It is a skillful and determined enemy, and it appears in many guises. It does not give up its loot easily. Wherever, whenever, and however it appears, colonialism is an evil thing, and one which must be eradicated from the earth.[4]

To a large extent, Sukarno practised what he preached about abolishing contemporary colonialism, which he labeled NEKOLIM (neocolonialism and imperialism). TNCs such as Unilever, BAT, Dunlop, and Faroka were put under control of various government agencies as Sukarno actively promoted "Socialisme a la Indonesia," particularly after 1958. By that year, Dutch economic power had been expropriated, the big Dutch commercial houses had been indigenized, and Suharto promoted greater statism (rather than *asli* entrepreneurship) and anti-Western policies.

While Sukarno was trying to end foreign domination and make Indonesia's thousands of islands and diverse peoples into a unified, sovereign state through his "konsepsi" of "Guided Democracy," authoritarianism increased and the PKI—the Indonesian communist party—gained influence. Journalists and others who favored Western liberalism or policies contrary to those of Sukarno were silenced. For example, in 1956 prominent publisher Mochtar Lubis of the *Indonesia Raya* courageously spoke out against widespread inefficiency and government corruption and was put under arrest until after Sukarno's overthrow in 1966. Under Suharto's "New Order," Lubis briefly returned to journalism before being forced to close his newspaper. He (and several other journalists) left Indonesian journalism and moved into other businesses, including the emerging advertising business. In 1970, he established P. T. Fortune, an agency affiliated with the Australian agency of the same name that was part of the DDF international TNAA network.

Between Lintas's establishment before World War II and Fortune's formation early in the New Order, a few so-called advertising agencies (then known as *biro reklame* in Indonesian) had begun operations, but their influence was nil. Modern Indonesian advertising did not really begin until 1963 when Sukarno allowed Intervista Advertising, an indigenous business, to operate. Despite intensely anticapitalistic policies, a "crush Malaysia" stance within the region, and a philosophy of *berdiri di-atas kaki sendiri* ("standing on one's own feet"), Sukarno realized that some foreign ties had to be maintained. He allowed a Western-educated Indonesian intellectual named Nuradi—now well-known as the *bapak* ("father") of Indonesian advertising—to establish an agency to service key foreign clients, such as Pan American Airlines, and the government-owned (but foreign-managed) Hotel Indonesia that Sukarno erected for the Fourth Asian Games in 1962.[5] While Lintas was kept busy handling a full range of Unilever products, Nuradi was servicing a few local accounts such as Garuda airlines, plus a few prestigious TNC clients, such as BAT, that were struggling to stay in business amidst growing government restrictions and economic instability.

Throughout the turbulent Sukarno years, little real advertising was necessary since it was a seller's market. As a Unilever Indonesia executive explained: "In the 1950s, even if we spit on a piece of paper it would sell."[6] Foreign corporations, too, were harassed, and highly visible advertising campaigns were politically, as well as economically, risky. A more basic reason for advertising's problems during the period was the nation's general economic condition. Inflation was rampant: virtually all consumer goods, even basic necessities like rice and fuel, were expensive and scarce, and the vast majority of Indonesians were too poverty-stricken and preoccupied with daily survival to pay attention to advertisements. The media, too, were suffering critical economic problems and were being aggressively used by Sukarno as a means of keeping political control and fostering nationalism. Dutch and Chinese language papers, which traditionally had served the commercial and cultural interests of these relatively prosperous minorities, were banned, and the Indonesian language papers that survived were forced to become "tools of the revolution" (like Radio Republik Indonesia) and to be more concerned with selling the state's ideology than with advertisements or news.

Television, which Sukarno had implemented in time for the Asian Games, began using simple advertising slides or poster cards for ten seconds in March of 1963.[7] But the bulk of its very limited broadcasting day was devoted to government propaganda in the form of documentaries, mass rallies, and other political programs. At no time during Sukarno's rule did the number of television sets in the whole nation exceed about thirty-seven thousand or spread beyond three or four major cities.[8] Also, advertising was never a major factor in funding Televisi Republik Indonesia (TVRI). In 1965, for example, revenue from commercials accounted for less than one-fifth of TVRI's income.[9] Television set license fees were the major source of support for television, but funding was not a serious problem under Sukarno since all broadcasting served as a tightly controlled, monolithic voice for the government. It was not until the time of the New Order that radio-TV advertising became important. By 1971 advertising had become a more important source of revenue than licenses and direct government subsidy combined.[10]

Despite the absence of a thriving advertising industry and a free market economy, the charismatic Sukarno in many ways was Indonesia's self-appointed advertising man. Through his powerful rhetoric, attractive personality, and sophisticated use of symbols and slogans, Sukarno for years managed to sell Indonesian nationalism and his policies via slogans like "unity through diversity" and symbols such as the state philosophy of *Pancasila* ("Five Principles"). He not only fought to end the years of oppression under colonial domination, but he also made the people proud to be Indonesians. He stood up to the United States when he told it "to hell with your aid," and he focused international attention on the Third World nations, which he called the "New Emerging Forces." But, as Stephen Sloan has noted, eventually "the politics of slogans replaced the politics of solutions as measured by performance."[11] The virtual collapse of the economy combined with external pressures to produce widespread domestic unrest among the impoverished masses. Finally, political tension between the conservative military on one hand, and the militant PKI on the other, led to a showdown. Following GESTAPU, the abortive communist coup of September 30, 1965, the masses and the army had had enough of the "politics of disorder."[12] Suharto and the army acquired the real power, and Sukarno faded away.

Suharto's "New Order"

The sudden and violent shift from ORLA (*Orde Lama,* "Old Order") to ORBA (New Order) was dramatic: the once-popular national hero/president was removed from power, the PKI and Sukarno's party banned, the army firmly entrenched, confrontation with Malaysia and the West ended, and totally different development plans adopted. Because of their relative affluence and their alleged Communist sympathies, the Chinese in Indonesia were victimized as a "foe." At the same time, however, Chinese money that had left the nation during Sukarno's years was repatriated and used to help finance new industries in cooperation with the military and foreigners.[13]

The drastic change in leadership, the shift to Western-influenced policies, and the return of a free market system had immediate effects on the fledgling advertising industry and the badly neglected economy. Nuradi explained the situation in the late 1960s:

> after an uninterrupted period of thirty years of utter economic chaos bordering on total collapse—the unsophisticated Indonesian business community and the equally unsophisticated consumer community, both of which had never known conditions other than that of a seller's market and both of which have never experienced a situation of sharply competitive marketing and selling, were suddenly exposed to an onslaught of some of the best and some of the worst examples of the most aggressive marketing and selling attacks, pouring forth through the channels of mass communications media.[14]

Nuradi's comments before the Asian Advertising Congress in Jakarta in 1974 are worth citing at length because they reflect the frustration of both foreigners and Indonesians that somehow New Order advertising desperately needed to raise its standards:

> Every single one of the social, economic, administrative and political components that make up our living, producing, and consuming community is in need of being taught . . . taught not only what advertising is all about . . . but also, and this is of equal importance, how to look on advertising; how to respond and react to advertising; how to use advertising as a tool, and how not to become a tool of advertising; how advertising can become a virtue as well as a curse. Because of the magnitude of the tasks it has to accomplish, embracing all strata and all segments of the community throughout the length and breadth of the vast territory of Indonesia, it is perhaps true to say that what we have on our hands is not simply a job of education, but a mission, an evangelistic mission if you will, to spread the gospel of advertising so that the message is delivered where it should be brought home, so that it penetrates most effectively where it should register most firmly. The frustrating question that we are left to ponder is this: in a country that suffers so palpably from a shortage of experienced advertising talent *who* is it that we should call upon to do the missionary work, to spread the gospel?[15]

Neither the advertising industry, the government, nor the consumers were ready for the influx of foreign aid, investment, and advertising that hit Indonesia once the door to the West was reopened. Suharto adopted a liberal policy toward foreign investment that was the reverse of Sukarno's self-reliance stance. Ties with the West were reopened and massive injections of foreign capital were seen as the best way out of the nation's general economic problems. Creditor nations formed the Inter-Governmental Group on Indonesia (IGGI) to fund Western-style economic growth plans emphasizing industrialization, foreign investment, technology, and imported expertise. The liberal Foreign Investment Law no. 1, 1967, the decision to return expropriated businesses (and major advertisers) to their

original foreign owners, and the decision to permit nongovernmental commercial radio stations were among the important factors that fostered the
economic growth and political stability necessary for the rapid expansion of
advertising. Together, these and other factors combined to turn Indonesia
into an investor's paradise almost overnight. The United States and other
Western nations, including Japan, were delighted with the new policies, as
S. Tas has explained:

> Obviously the West has an interest in seeing Indonesia develop and
> modernize. The interest is primarily of a political nature. The West . . .
> has an interest in seeing the world develop peacefully, for every instance
> of unrest or human suffering gives the Communists and their soulless
> allies a fresh opportunity to rock the boat. But there are also economic
> aspects. It is in the interest of the West for Indonesia to become prosper-
> ous. The higher the income of the people there, the greater will be their
> purchasing power and the more attractive will the country be as a mar-
> ket. In the long term, this is much more important than the quick profits
> which are to be made from it, as from other underdeveloped countries.[16]

Additional policies were particularly conducive to the growth of advertising. Earlier during the Suharto rule, the government decided to make
television (as well as radio) a truly mass medium that would reach into
remote villages and support the government's development policies. Television facilities quickly expanded. For example, between 1964 and 1967,
the total TV transmission time had remained at 1,183 hours a year. This
included 183 hours of advertisements. In 1968, transmission jumped to
1,560 hours, including 220 hours of advertisements.[17] Throughout the
early 1970s, growth by several indicators was even more rapid, as table 16
shows. Much of the new TNC investment was placed in consumer goods,
such as Coca-Cola, Gillette razor blades, Fuji film, Johnson cleaning agents,
sweet condensed Indomilk, Ajinomoto food preparation, Bayer drugs and
insecticides, and Palmolive soap, that were expertly marketed by television
in their home nation.

In addition to TVRI as a vehicle by which to spread development news
and information and promote economic growth, the government also saw
the medium as a channel of entertainment in post-Sukarno Indonesia.
According to a 1973 TVRI report, "the people are tired of being told what
to do" and "they hunger for entertainment or amusement to forget their
daily problems of life."[18] A large majority of the imported entertainment
were series, films, and cartoons imported from the United States and
broadcast in English.[19] They also were sponsored by advertisers selling
imported goods or products made by joint-venture firms.[20] In 1976, for
example, approximately 73 percent of all advertisements were either for
imported products (10.5 percent) or products of joint-ventures (62.5 percent). Only 27 percent of products advertised were Indonesian goods.[21] In

Table 16

Growth of Television in Indonesia, 1969-73

	1969	1973
TV coverage area (sq. km.)	18,500	72,100
TV coverage in millions of people	22.5	40.0
Estimated number of TV receivers	80,000	300,000
Type of broadcast in total hours		
Entertainment	680	2,610
News/Information/Culture	800	1,700
Advertising	260	470
Total	1,740	4,780
TVRI facilities		
Total studios	2	6
Total broadcasting stations	4	22

SOURCES: Compiled from Table 141, Television Coverage; Table 142, Total Hours of TV Broadcasts Classified into Entertainment, News/Information/Cultural and Advertising; Table 143, Growth of TVRI Studios and Broadcasting Stations; and Table 144, Estimates of Growth in TV Receivers, in Indonesia Handbook 1974, Jakarta; Department of Information, Republic of Indonesia, 1975.

June of 1977, for example, sponsored programs on Jakarta television were paid for by these major TNCs:

Sunday morning feature film by Brisk, Signal-2, Lux, Ultra Milk, Hi Top, and Tancho
Sunday: "Kojak" by Mitsubishi
Tuesday: "Mannix" by S. C. Johnson
Friday: Coca-Cola
Saturday: Quiz program by Kao Feather
Saturday: Serial Film Akhir Pekan by Palmolive and Tancho[22]

A major advertiser like Unilever was actively advertising products outside of Jakarta, too. For example, that same month Unilever was sponsoring programs on these non-Jakarta stations:

Unjang Pandang: "Mannix," "Wild, Wild West," and "Kojak" (all 26 episodes)
Palembang: "Adventures in Paradise," "Mannix," and "Bonanza"
Medan: "Mannix," "Tammy," and "Bonanza"[23]

One of the commercials shown views in Unjang Pandang that month was a Lux commercial featuring American actress Natalie Wood in a campaign using Unilever's global "screen stars use Lux Toilet Soap" strategy.[24]

While advertising on TVRI was given greater importance under the New

Order, radio was not forgotten. In 1966, the government's Radio Republik Indonesia (RRI) stations were allowed to introduce "experimental advertising" to augment their revenue.[25] More significantly, the government authorized continuation of the hundreds of "amateur" or "pirate" stations that had spontaneously developed around the nation during Sukarno's final months. These stations, initially supported by various military units and sometimes operated by students, played a crucial role in generating widespread anti-Sukarno feelings. In 1969, 45 of these private, commercial stations were operating and by 1976 the number had expanded to 347.[26] While these stations were not allowed to engage in politics under the New Order and had to relay RRI news, they became very popular within their limited broadcasting area. They had to rely heavily on advertising for their revenue but they often were able to attract larger audiences than RRI because of their popular light music, entertainment, and discussion formats.

Government-run broadcasting received a major boost in 1977 when the American-built domestic satellite system, Palapa, became operational. In addition to bringing Jakarta television to almost all of far-flung Indonesia, the highly sophisticated communications system was designed to provide better telephone, radio, telex, and military facilities to all twenty-seven provinces.[27] It also strengthened Jakarta's power as *the* center of Indonesian information and improved services for TNCs in remote areas.

Within a few years, then, broadcasting had not only become commercialized but it had also acquired modern technology that permitted it to disseminate government—and commercial—messages and consumerism to remote corners of the archipelago. A statement from Minister Sadli suggested that Indonesia, like other Third World nations, had no choice but to open itself up to foreign technology and investment if a modern communication system and economic growth were to be encouraged: "Newspapers here are not so widespread, but radio and television in the last five or seven years have been commercialized. Our state-owned radio and television company needed income to run, so it accepted commercial advertising. That was a compromise with a social price."[28]

Historically, Indonesian newspapers have been the major advertising channel, but they have always been concentrated in Jakarta and a handful of other urban centers. About 83 percent of the population lives in rural areas, and this "silent majority"—a term used by the government itself—has always been largely ignored by the print media.[29] Estimates are that between 50 and 70 percent of the total Indonesian press circulation is limited to metropolitan Jakarta.[30] Two daily newspapers—*Kompas* and *Sinar Harapan*—handle about 50 percent of all newspaper advertising in Indonesia.[31]

Prior to the New Order, advertising expenditures in Indonesia were perhaps only $1 million a year, but between 1969 and 1972 they were estimated to have increased more than tenfold, and average annual advertising expenditure growth was at least 20 percent.[32] By 1977, approximately $70 million—80 percent in Jakarta—was spent on mass media advertising.[33] Tables 17 and 18 show how advertising expenditures boomed during the 1970s and how broadcasting became an increasingly important channel for advertising messages. Print media expenditures increased considerably, and the press remained the largest single advertising channel, but percentagewise it declined somewhat, especially relative to radio.

Long-established TNCs like Unilever, and new foreign manufacturers, particularly Japanese and American, took advantage of the various joint-venture arrangements, tax incentives, duty-free imports, remittance

Table 17

Total Advertising Expenditure in Indonesia, 1973-78

	1973	1974	1975	1976	1977	1978 (est.)
In millions of U.S. Dollars	18.5	23.1	28.9	36.1	43.4	52.0
Annual growth in percent		25%	25%	25%	20%	20%

SOURCE: Figures supplied by John Ormerod, manager, Lintas, Jakarta. I interviewed him on July 1 and September 19, 1977, and he had this table prepared for me.

Table 18

Media Expenditure in Indonesia, 1972-77

(In U.S. Dollars)

Media	1972 million	%	1973 million	%	1974 million	%	1975 million	%	1976 million	%	1977 million	%
Press	6.6	48	7.7	45	7.9	37	9.4	35	11.9	37	14.6	38
Cinema	1.2	9	1.5	9	2.4	11	2.4	9	2.9	9	3.1	8
Radio	2.2	16	3.1	18	4.9	23	6.4	24	8.3	26	10.0	26
TV	3.7	27	4.8	28	6.2	29	8.5	32	9.0	28	10.8	28
	13.7	100	17.1	100	21.4	100	26.7	100	32.1	100	38.5	100

NOTE: Approximately 60 percent of the press expenditures are in Jakarta newspapers; 40 percent cinema advertising in Jakarta cinema houses; and 65 percent of television advertising on Jakarta's central station. Radio advertising is split approximately 85 percent to private stations and 15 percent to the government's RRI stations. Because of its size and ties with Unilever, Lintas is able to afford its own media monitoring services. These figures are probably the most accurate of any on Indonesia advertising. Note, however, that they are conservative compared to so-called official totals.

SOURCE: Figures supplied by John Ormerod, manager, Lintas, Jakarta. I interviewed him on July 1 and September 19, 1977, and he had this table prepared for me.

guarantees, and other incentives offered by the government during the early Suharto period. An irresistible advertising bonanza followed, and one result was that "within a short period hordes of managers from a variety of advertising agencies began to fill up the suites of the Hotel Indonesia" trying to get in on the new opportunities.[34] These foreigners brought their own assumptions about Indonesian consumer habits and quickly picked up others. This statement from one TNAA expatriate in 1974 reflects the type of environment in which admen perceived themselves operating:

> Due to the limited income which the majority of the population receives, nearly all money is spent on consumption. Since social security as in developed countries does not exist in Indonesia, one would expect at least a minimum amount of money to be saved in order to take precautions against unemployment, sickness, etc. This, however, does not happen even in cases of sudden additional income. Indonesians seem to live only for the present, ignoring the unpredictable tomorrow. Peasants spend their profits on parties and all sorts of consumer goods, although they might be forced to borrow money at high interest rates to survive until the next harvest.
>
> Many Indonesian businessmen do not use their first returns on investment for developing and maintaining their firms on a sound financial footing, but for buying a big house and a luxury car. The latter reflects the status-consciousness of the urban population.
>
> Any product which can act as a status symbol and is in reach of the consumer has good chances on the market. But it must look expensive. This is different in rural areas where the orientation to western consumption patterns does not yet exist. Money for the peasants is simply a means for survival or, if more is available, for enjoyment and religious sacrifices.[35]

The TNAAs' Arrival

In addition to the well-established Lintas and Lubis's new agency, Fortune, other TNAAs arrived to take advantage of the potentially rich Indonesian market amidst the new free-market environment. Partly under pressure from major Center nation clients, additional TNAAs—some with offices already established in nearby Singapore, Kuala Lumper, Manila, or Hong Kong—"followed the flag" into Indonesia, especially around 1970. Fortune arrived to serve its major regional client, Cathay Pacific airlines; Dentsu wanted in to serve Toyota and Kao Feather; McCann-Erickson arrived to help Coca-Cola, Goodyear, and Gillette; Hakuhodo was interested in servicing Mitsubishi and Matsushita; and JWT arrived to help Pan American. Expatriates, of course, came with the TNAAs. In 1970, no work permits had been issued for advertising specialists, but by 1977 the number totalled eighteen.[36]

Outside of the pioneering Lintas, O&M has been the most successful

TNAA in Indonesia. The American agency entered through its 1971 acquisition of S. H. Benson, London, and its foreign offices, including Kuala Lumpur and Singapore as well as Jakarta.[37] In 1972, P. T. Indo-Ad was established as an Indonesian entity run by O&M under a management contract, but indigenous admen loudly accused O&M of using Indonesians as fronts while actually owning the agency. A government report in 1975 noted that the new agency was so aggressive that it "flooded" the media with big orders, and indigenous protests eventually forced O&M to resort to calling itself a consultant for an Indonesian agency.[38]

Despite complaints, the agency prospered. In 1972, O&M had twenty staffers (including two expatriates), twenty-one clients, and capitalized billings of $500,000. By 1977, it had forty-two staff members (including three expatriates), forty-two clients, and billings approaching $5 million.[39] That year it probably was the country's fastest growing agency, and its blue-chip clients included such giant TNCs as BAT, Beecham, Unilever, S. C. Johnson, ICI Paints, and Bayer. Three of O&M's top fifteen global clients—Unilever, American Express, and S. C. Johnson—were major Indo-Ad clients in Indonesia.[40]

None of the TNAAs, despite the atmosphere of Indonesia as a liberal, open economy, has had an easy time in Indonesia. Like other foreign businesses, agencies have been frustrated by poor communications, corruption, unclear and unenforceable government policies, and a lack of market information about consumers outside of a few large cities. The TNAAs also complain that local agencies demand financial assistance, training facilities, exposure to international advertising trends, and the prestige of a "big" foreign name, but offer the TNAAs little in return. One TNAA executive spoke for others when he voiced this general frustration with Indonesia: "The situation in Indonesia is indeed most disturbing. This beautiful country is the most backward and unpredictable in Southeast Asia when it comes to business and making advertising."[41]

Another expatriate described it this way:

In Indonesia, it is hell [producing good advertising]. There is virtually no expertise in the production area and the facilities and communications are grossly inadequate. . . . Competence in advertising skills of nationals in Malaysia and Singapore are much higher than Indonesia. The nationals in Mal Sing are better educated and have worked beside a stream of skilled expatriates. The restrictive work permit policy in Indonesia has forbidden the same opportunity for Indonesians who are themselves deliberately keeping expatriates out. The standard of advertising in Indonesia is the lowest in Southeast Asia as a result, and I suspect will remain that way for several years to come.[42]

During the early years of the New Order, advertising agencies often imported advertisements from outside Indonesia and simply translated them into Bahasa Indonesia or else did creative work "offshore," usually in nearby Singapore.[43] Several agencies tried to establish representative offices in Jakarta, but their efforts were subject to intense pressure from the Persatuan Perusahaan Periklanan Indonesia (P3I, the Indonesian Advertising Agency Association). The organization had been established with government help in 1972 to try to bring some order to the chaotic young advertising industry.

Corruption is—and always has been—a major problem in Indonesia, and incentives for advertising corruption are strong. Wheeling and dealing between agency and media and between advertiser and agency is common, as it is in many countries. During my field work in Indonesia, for example, the Indonesian advertising manager of a Western TNC and an account executive of a TNAA-affiliated agency lost their jobs when they were caught sharing kickbacks from radio stations. One expatriate adman told me: "The problems of corruption invade every sector of the economy including advertising, and thus reflect the morality of the people. Until this changes, nothing will change."

Some Indonesians blame corruption partly on culturally insensitive TNAAs. A spokesman for the indigenous advertising industry has said:

> One main problem still unresolved is the role of the multinational agencies. We realize that the advertiser, planning to spend hundred thousands of dollars on advertising to support his marketing efforts, would make sure that it will be handled competently and effectively. Unfortunately, several multinationals tend to capitalize on their fears by deliberately minimizing the role and potential of the national companies.
>
> With various less than honorable means some have tried to maintain their domination of the advertising industry. According to PPPI sources, almost two-thirds of the total billing are in the hands of a few multinationals. It is understandable that they yield [sic] considerable power. They more often than not practically dictate their terms to the media and advertising contractors. Since government policy is such that advertising agencies are required to be national companies, they find fronts for their operations. This is deplorable because in the long run it will ruin the chances to work out an acceptable form of cooperation between the multinationals and the bonafide national companies. What we would like to see is a concerted effort to transfer their marketing know-how and sophisticated techniques to Indonesians and find equal partners among the national businessmen as a conduit for their accounts. Not mere fronts or glorified errand boys. To be able to establish such a relationship their first task would be to understand the Indonesian personality. Although this sounds quite simple and elementary the gap in communications between multinationals and nationals stems from a misappraisal of the indigenous way-of-life and way-of-thinking. To do business requires an indepth understanding of the market and an insight in the cultural dynamics of the society at large. It is slightly more difficult than bribing your way around but it is certainly worthwhile and more profitable.[44]

Allegations of corruption advertising became a public issue in 1973 when Dentsu reportedly tried to bribe Indonesian Ministry of Trade officials after the Japanese TNAA's request for a license to operate a representative office in Jakarta had been rejected.[45] Since then Dentsu has maintained an extremely low profile and has operated under a technical assistance agreement through P. T. Faris, a Chinese Indonesian agency.

Other TNAAs, including Leo Burnett and Ted Bates, have not been able to even find a means to enter the Indonesian market, and both Grant and JWT have had to close their Jakarta operations.[46] The case of JWT in Jakarta illustrates the high political, as well as economic, risks that a TNAA sometimes finds itself taking to gain entry into a difficult market like Indonesia, where local elite "door openers" are so important to foreign businesses' success.

In 1974, John Sharman, then JWT's executive vice president, arranged for the TNAA to manage P. T. Thomertwal, which already was run by expatriates as P. T. IAP and ACE, a branch office of a Singapore agency.[47] Its president was the prominent printer of government-backed publications. Its general manager was a Sri Lankan adman and businessman.[48] Despite such influential bridgeheads and a staff in 1975 that included six expatriates, the management contract agreement failed and JWT pulled out in 1976. The agency, however, continued under the new name of Selindo. By 1980, it had signed an agreement under which Advertising, Marketing, and Communications (AMC), a well-connected Malaysian advertising agency, would manage it. AMC is the Malaysian representative of Dentsu and a member in the Worldwide Advertising and Marketing (WAM) consortium.[49]

Sharman explained JWT's withdrawal from Indonesia:

> The earlier promise of rapid growth of the Indonesian economy, which attracted some multi-national advertisers to invest there, was mostly not realized and the total advertising volume continued to be very small. Trained national talent was in very short supply and the remuneration level of the very few advertising professionals available was escalating at a fast rate. It was difficult to induce good expatriates to go to Indonesia and their cost was enormously high (first year $60,000 to $75,000) particularly relative to low advertising expenditures. Under these circumstances it became obvious that the immediate future offered little chance of satisfactory growth in revenues relative to the high investment needed.[50]

JWT's withdrawal from Jakarta was hasty. Details of its internal problems are sparse, and the parties involved obviously consider the subject sensitive.

Despite JWT's problems, the Indonesian market obviously is attractive to some TNAAs. In 1977, for example, seven TNAAs were active in the country, and their overall impact on indigenous advertising was substantial. Table 19 lists Indonesian agencies associated with these TNAAs and compares them to major indigenous agencies without formal ties. Of the

Table 19

Summary of Major Advertising Agencies in Indonesia, 1977-78

I. Transnational

Agency	Founded	Ownership	Billings*	Staff Total	Staff Expatriate	Total No. Accounts	Major Accounts
Delka Utama	1967	Local with Hakuhodo, Tokyo, association a/	. . .	. . .	1	. . .	Sanyo, Sony, National, Mitsubishi Colt
Faris Advertising	1969	Local with Dentsu Tokyo, technical assistance agreement b/	$1,928,000	27	2	. . .	Toyota, Suzuki motorcycles, Kao (soaps), P. T. Yasonta (Sharp products)
Fortune	1970	Local with a management agreement with Australia's Fortune Group, Sydney, which is part of DDF International	$1,687,000	24	1	12	Cathay Pacific Airways, Nestle (Lactogen, Dancow, Milkbrand condensed milk, etc.), Bristol-Myers (Mum, Clairol, Vitalis), Peugeot, P. T. Rhodia Indonesia (Phenergan Expectorant & Cream)
Hikmad & Chusen	1970	Local with a management agreement with Chuo Senko, Tokyo c/	$1,500,000	15	3	21	Honda Motorcycles, Kanebo cosmetics, Ajinomoto seasoning, Matsushita (National batteries and home electrical goods), Tancho toiletries, Kimia Farma drugs), Batik Keris (cloth)
Indo-Ad	1972	Local with a management agreement with Ogilvy & Mather International, New York City	$3,167,000	42	3	40	American Express, British-American Tobacco, Bayer, Beecham, Carnation, Cadbury Schweppes, Cavenham, Citizen watches, Dunlop, Guinness, Hilton Hotel, ICI paints, Joanne Drew (figure salon), Johnson & Johnson, S. C. Johnson (Clear, Glade, Pledge), Konimex, Max Factor, 3M, Pakistan Intl. Airlines, P. T. Perusahaan Bir Indonesia (Beer Bintang), Philips, Union Carbide (Eveready), Renault, Sheaffer pens, Warner Lambert Parke-Davis (drugs), Unilever (Sunsilk preparation), Eresindo Jaya (Gordon's Gin, Sanostol), Gilman (Girard Perregaux watches), Merck (drugs), Pfizer (drugs), Metropolitan Development (real estate), Unilever (Sunlight detergent, new products)

Agency	Established	Affiliation/Status	Billings				Major clients
		Lintas Intl. Ltd., London, and intimate ties with Unilever N.V. d/					Lifebuoy, Rinso, Pepsodent, Signal-2, etc.), Seiko, Australian Trade Commission, British-American Tobacco, Friesche Vlag (powdered and condensed milk), Johnson & Johnson (Band Aids, baby powder and shampoo, Stayfree, etc.), Bayer, Singer, Heineken beer, Ultra-Milk, Essaven
Perwanal Utama	1970	Local with a management agreement with McCann-Erickson Worldwide, part of The Interpublic Group of Companies (IPG), New York City f/	$1,687,000	29	2	32	Coca-Cola Indonesia (Coke, Fanta, Sprite), Goodyear, Gillette, Richardson-Merrell (Vick's Vaporub, Formula 44), Rado watches, San Miguel Beer, Tobacco Exporters Intl. (Dunhill, Peter Stuyvesant cigarettes)

II. Local

Agency	Established	Affiliation/Status	Billings				Major clients
Adforce	1973	Local	$1,687,000	25	0	. . .	Indo-Milk (condensed milk), Viva cosmetics, Pepsi-Cola, BMW
Adhiwarna Cipta	1975	Local	400,000	17	0	36	P. T. Indokaya Nissan Motors (Datsun), Hotel Indonesia Sheraton, Sinar Harapan (newspaper)
Circle 5 g/ (also called Libelle)	1974	Local	. . .	. . .	0	. . .	Sakura (film), Mi-Won, Anabrin
Inter Admark	1975	Local	. . .	. . .	0	. . .	United Tractors, Singapore Intl. Airlines (SIA), Polaroid (cameras and sunglasses)
Intervista	1963	Local	$3,133,000	55	0	. . .	British-American Tobacco, S. C. Johnson, Chase Manhattan Bank, Texwood jeans, CIBA, 7-Up, JAL, UNICEF, Palmolive, Bayer
Inscore Zecha	. . .	Local, but affiliated with Zecha Associates, a regional advertising and public relations agency based in Hong Kong	. . .	. . .	0	. . .	Mazda, plus various public affairs and research clients (including government bodies)
Matari	1971	Local, but history of special affiliation with Kenyon & Eckhardt, New York h/	$2,169,000	61	1	. . .	P. T. Astra Intl. (Honda cycles, Daihatsu cars, etc.), Astra Motor Sales (Toyota), Windusurya/Inter-Delta (Kodak), Rama Surya (Westinghouse products), P. T. Eresindo Trading (Dewar's White Label scotch, Borden's Klim, etc.) Dana paints, KLM, Tang juice, Wella

(haircare products), Konimex (drugs), Philip Morris (Marlboro and Abdullah cigarettes), Sinar Sosro (Teh botel -- bottled tea), Sahid Jaya Hotel, Setia Karya/Cussons Intl. (baby and toilet soaps)

Agency	Year established	Ownership	Gross billings				Major clients
Merpati Mas	1975	Local i/	$ 250,000	19	0	19	In-house agency for the Rodemas Group of Companies: Dino detergent, Sasa seasoning, Panda (General Electric licensed air conditioners and refrigerators)
Prima Advera	...	Local	...	...	...	1	Garuda airlines, Bajaj scooters
Selindo	1972	Local, but expatriate management from former association with J. W. Thompson, New York City j/	$2,400,000	27	4	23	Pan American, Mortein insecticide, Imperial Cigarettes, Olivetti, Kraft
Tempo	1952	Local	$1,000,000	...	1	...	In-house agency for pharmaceutical company of same name which makes numerous drug products, including Dr. Fritz Bode brand drugs such as Bodrex and Bodrexin

* = Estimate

NOTES: Most of these agencies are members of the Persatuan Perusahaan Periklanan Indonesia (PPPI), the advertising agency organization officially recognized by the Indonesian government. "Accreditation" in the strict sense of the term as it is widely used in more industrially advanced nations does not apply to the Indonesian advertising scene. The PPPI does not set clear-cut standards of conduct and competency in the way that the "4As" organizations of the more advertising-rich societies do for their members.

All of these agencies are based in Jakarta. A few of the big agencies are able to afford representatives in several other major Indonesian cities, particularly Jogyakarta, Medan, Surabaya, Bandung, and/or Ujung Pandang. Indonesian regulations require that advertising agencies must be 100 percent locally owned. Management or technical assistance agreements between an Indonesian agency and a foreign agency are allowed under some conditions.

In Indonesia, as elsewhere in the region, "local" ownership frequently means "Chinese" rather than other ethnic groups.

<u>a</u>/ In about 1967, Hakuhodo entered the Indonesian market through its own representative office in Jakarta. Later, to meet Indonesian legal requirements, it affiliated with a local agency, P. T. Delka Utama.

<u>b</u>/ P. T. Faris, an Indonesian agency, began in 1969, but it had no formal affiliation with Dentsu until 1974. Severe pressure from the Indonesian advertising organization forced Dentsu to operate only through a local agency and sharply curtail its Indonesian activities and expansion plans.

<u>c</u>/ Chuo Senko opened an office in Jakarta in 1970. By 1976, it had found an Indonesian agency partner, which incorporated as P. T. Hikmad and Chusen.

<u>d</u>/ Since 1978, the precise ownership arrangement of Lintas' Jakarta office as an "advertising department" of its major client, Unilever, has been unclear. On paper and under Indonesian regulations, the agency is totally owned by Unilever and is not allowed to do any non-Unilever business. Despite this "restructuring," the agency continues to maintain close ties to the SSC&B: Lintas International advertising network, which is 51 percent owned by Unilever and 49 percent by SSC&B, New York. The agency now calls itself Unilever Advertising Indonesia.

<u>e</u>/ The number of expatriates involved in Lintas is probably higher than three because the agency traditionally has had access to Unilever's marketing and other specialists who are allowed into Indonesia as foreign experts.

<u>f</u>/ In 1971, Perwanal Utama, an Indonesian agency, began affiliation with McCann under a management agreement. In 1979, this arrangement ceased and McCann became associated with Intervista, Indonesia's leading local ad agency.

<u>g</u>/ The number "5" stands for the five Southeast Asian nations' local agencies that operated as a loose, regional group in the mid-1970s. Only Indonesia's Circle 5 agency is believed to be still in business.

<u>h</u>/ Matari no longer has any official "special agreements" with Kenyon & Eckhardt Group, but informal, mutually beneficial contacts continue. For example, a media placement agency affiliated with Matari maintains a representative in the Grant, Kenyon & Eckhardt office in Singapore. The business is called P. T. United Multi Media, Inc., Jakarta.

<u>i</u>/ Formerly briefly associated with Marklin, a Hong Kong based regional agency that did business in Kuala Lumpur and Jakarta through its Singapore office. In 1976, its Singapore office went out of business due to poor financial management.

<u>j</u>/ Inter-Asian Publicity Co. (IAP), Bangkok, was founded in 1967 by a young American, William Heinecke. Prior to merger with Ogilvy & Mather in Thailand in 1974, IAP had financial interests in IAP/Ace in Singapore, IAP/Kace in Kuala Lumpur, and P. T. IAP in Jakarta. The latter agency became affiliated with J. Walter Thompson, New York, in 1974 under the name P. T. Thomertwal. In 1976, its association with JWT was terminated and its name changed to P. T. Selindo Multi Marketing & Advertising. Expatriate management has continued despite the reorganization.

SOURCES: These facts and figures about key Indonesian agencies were obtained from a very wide variety of often conflicting sources, including personal interviews in Jakarta with agency executives and others knowledgeable about Indonesian advertising. This information should be treated cautiously, and it is presented merely to suggest general patterns within the industry. Billing data are estimates only since agencies generally do not make their billings public.

ten biggest agencies for which estimated billings were available, eight had formal affiliation with a TNAA. Only Adforce and Nuradi's Intervista did not have expatriates working with them. By the end of the 1970s, even fiercely independent Intervista had acquired TNAA formal links. It became an "associate agency" (with no ownership) of McCann-Erickson, which previously had had a technical assistance agreement with Perwanal Utama, a local agency.

Full-service facilities, expatriate expertise, and many of Indonesia's major advertisers (Unilever, BAT, the Astra Group, Union Carbide, S. C. Johnson, Bayer, Honda, Mitsubishi, and Konimex) tended to be concentrated in the agencies having TNAA links. Three of these agencies in 1977 were Japanese-affiliated, and of the five non-Japanese TNAAs in Indonesia, four had American ties, and one—Lubis's Fortune—had Australian. Tables 20 and 21 indicate how several of these TNAAs have fared in terms of billings and gross income.[51] Comparable trend data for the strictly Indonesian agencies are unavailable.

Tensions

As the TNCs and the TNAAs moved into Indonesia, the totally unprepared local advertising agencies understandably wanted a share of the greatly expanded advertising pie. Their efforts, however, were set back not only by their agencies' inability to provide comparable service to the TNAAs, but also by the problems the government had in controlling the new industry. Various government agencies, particularly the Ministries of Trade and of Information, were not equipped to oversee the industry and they were involved in intrabureaucratic disputes over who should control advertising and the TNAAs and how that control should be maintained.[52]

In 1972, the government helped organize the P3I, which began with twenty-seven member agencies and grew to about forty in 1977. Most members, however, were very small operations without full service facilities or trained personnel. Many members were engaged in a number of business activities, and advertising tended to take second place to other commercial activities. While a Lintas or an Indo-Ad had vast resources to handle campaign planning, creation of concepts, design and production of all advertising material, general marketing advice, merchandising and promotion design, media planning, media buying, media control, and research consultation, most P3I members were struggling to provide even basic client services amidst an exceptionally competitive atmosphere. Tension was inevitable between the P3I, which felt local agencies were increasingly frustrated with the status quo and wanted to band together to eliminate all traces of foreign agency domination, and the TNAA-affiliated agencies, which strongly believed they were helping upgrade Indonesian advertis-

Table 20

Major Transnational Agency Billings in Indonesia, 1970-77

(In U.S. Dollars)

Agency	1970	1971	1972	1973	1974	1975	1976	1977
Fortune	. . .	. . .	1,264,392	1,200,000	. . .	. . .	. . .	1,687,000*/
Indo-Ad			500,000	2,000,000	3,000,000	4,000,000	4,500,000	5,000,000
Lintas	749,000	1,089,000	2,757,000	2,778,000	3,569,065	5,202,000	6,188,766	7,568,996a/
Perwanal Utama		100,000	250,000	500,000	1,000,000	1,250,000	1,500,000	1,687,000*/
Thomertwal (Selindo)b/			190,000	400,000	778,000	1,700,000	2,400,000	. . .

*/ = estimate

NOTES: These data are presented to give a rough picture of how the transnational agencies or local agencies affiliated with TNAAs have grown in the post-Sukarno, New Order Indonesia. Unfortunately, local agencies are reluctant to make any billings figures public, and even those data released by the TNAAs must be treated cautiously. Advertising agencies, like most businesses in Indonesia, often keep two or more sets of books for tax and other purposes. Overall, the figures suggest how "modern" advertising agencies' billings have dramatically increased over a relatively short period.

a/ Lintas data, as reported in Advertising Age, include both media and capitalized fees. In 1977, for example, billings of $7,568,996 included $4,376,300 in media and $3,192,696 in fees.

b/ Commenced operations in 1972 as a branch office of P. T. IAP and Ace with head office in Singapore. In 1974, the agency became affiliated to JWT and took on the name of P. T. Thomertwal. In 1976, affiliation with JWT ceased and the agency reorganized as P. T. Selindo Multi Marketing and Advertising, but management remained the same. Thomertwal no longer qualifies as a TNAA, but its management is expatriate, non-Indonesian.

SOURCES: Billings obtained from information supplied directly by the agencies, estimates from sources knowledgeable about Indonesian advertising, and from annual "International Agency Sections" of Advertising Age.

Table 21

Major Transnational Agency Gross Income Figures in Indonesia, 1973-77

(In U.S. Dollars)

Agency	1973	1974	1975	1976	1977
Indo-Ad	300,750	477,250	519,788	. . .	. . .
Lintas	475,573	626,540	917,193	1,063,875	1,349,613a/
Thomertwal (Selindo)b/		176,187	257,283	. . .	. . .

NOTE: In Indonesia, even more than in either Malaysia or Singapore, TNAAs' income figures are far more difficult to obtain than the annual billings. These data for a five-year period should be treated cautiously since exchange rates vary. Figures for the Japanese TNAAs and other major agencies, including the Fortune Group's office and the McCann-Erickson partner - - Perwanal Utama - - are unavailable.

a/ Since 1978, Lintas legally has operated as an advertising department of Unilever, and it has not been able to make any profits from non-Unilever clients in Indonesia.

b/ Only available income figures for P. T. Selindo are for the period 1974-76, when it was affiliated with JWT and known as Thomertwal.

SOURCES: Data are compiled from annual "International Agency Sections" of Advertising Age, 1974-78. They are either estimates or reported voluntarily by the agencies themselves.

ing's low professional standards. P3I, for example, would not allow Lintas to become a member since it was foreign-owned. In addition to antiforeign feelings, some P3I members also were anti-Chinese. Several of the more successful Indonesian agencies were either local Chinese-owned or associated, and the *asli* (indigenous Indonesian) admen resented the stiff competition that this "denationalized" minority group presented.[53] More generally, *asli* businessmen resented the close ties that some Chinese businessmen had not only with foreign investors but also with Indonesian generals and influential bureaucrats.

These anti-Chinese and economic nationalist feelings became a public issue in Indonesia in 1973 when pressure from P3I and the government forced Matari, a successful local Chinese agency, to cancel its plans for a management contract relationship with Grant International (now called Kenyon & Eckhardt). Matari had planned to bring in an Australian expatriate with TNAA experience in Kenya, Zambia, Nigeria, and Australia to help train Matari and other agencies' staff.[54] Matari was not very popular with some *asli* admen because of its reputation as somewhat of a house agency for the Astra International Group of Companies. As much as sixty percent of Matari's business has come from this giant business group under cukong (overseas Chinese middlemen) reported to have close ties to top generals.[55] On behalf of this influential client, Matari has handled its advertising for Toyota cars, Kodak film, Daihatsu cars, Honda motorcycles, and Xerox copying machines. As Astra grew, so did Matari, and such commercial success bred considerable resentment.[56]

A more general source of considerable advertising tension in Indonesia has been the concentration of virtually all major advertisers, national media, agencies, and government offices in Jakarta. Indonesia probably has at least 150 so-called advertising agencies, but 70 to 80 percent of them are concentrated in the capital city. All sources of power, including advertising, are based in Jakarta. As one Indonesian adman explained:

> It is common believe [sic] among the business community in Indonesia that at least 50% of all business transactions are conducted in Jakarta, 65% of money are [sic] circulated in Jakarta, and 80% of the total advertising expenditures spent in Jakarta. But these figures should be adjusted by taking into consideration that most of the head offices of the trade industry in Indonesia are located in Jakarta, imports and transhipments are mainly via Jakarta and media which cover most of the major cities and trading centers are all located in Jakarta. Media in other major cities are all local, at the most it [sic] covers the province where the city is located. The leading top ten media, top ten advertisers and top ten advertising agencies are naturally located in Jakarta—perhaps it can be stated with a few exceptions that the top 10 of everything is located in Jakarta.[57]

The "honeymoon" between foreign investors generally and the Indonesian people (and also the tenuous alliance between students and the government) was largely brought to an end with the "Malari" demonstrations in Jakarta in January of 1974.[58] Students and others took to the streets during Japanese Prime Minister Tanaka's goodwill visit, and their violent protests were antiforeign, especially Japanese; antibureaucracy, especially the Western-educated technocrats who had pushed for greater reliance on foreign investment; and antimilitary, especially toward the generals who were widely suspected of profiteering from business deals with Chinese and foreigners.

Thirty-foot outdoor advertisements (for Toyota, an Astra-distributed vehicle, and Sanyo) atop the Nusantara Building, Jakarta's tallest, were the center of some of the demonstrations. For example, in December 10, 1973, students from the "National Pride Committee" hoisted the Indonesian flag atop the Japanese-built building to protest foreign domination as symbolized by the two Japanese products. One newspaper reacted by calling the students' action patriotic in light of the hurt that the advertisements had inflicted on Indonesian pride:

> We ourselves view the two Japanese billboards as being in conflict with our own advertising ethics. Advertisements must be constructive, conforming with the Indonesian identity and the norms prevailing in the Indonesian society. Advertisements must not do damage to society and create psychological effects which are harmful to the nation's identity.[59]

Following the disturbances, some eight hundred people were arrested, nearly a dozen publications closed, and various other steps taken to suppress dissent. In response to some of the critics, Suharto ordered government officials to move from *gaya hidup mewah* ("luxury style of living") to *hidup sederhana* ("simple, plain life-style") and reduce their conspicuous consumption. The import of luxury cars, for example, was stopped, and the government generally expressed its concern that policies do more to help the *asli* businessmen. Officials reiterated the Minister of Trade's decree no. 314/Kp/XIII/1970, which limited the number of expatriates and required all foreign companies to terminate their domestic trade and service activities on December 31, 1977, in order to open more opportunities for domestic firms and Indonesian (usually interpreted to exclude Chinese) entrepreneurs.[60]

After the Malari demonstrations, advertising was increasingly seen by the government and its critics as an important part of a larger system that generated frustration—particularly in Jakarta where conspicuous consumption was most visible and people were confronted daily with perhaps two thousand advertising messages.[61] Minister of Information Mashuri in 1974 suggested the government's growing awareness of the social effects of advertising:

> Ads come to the home of every family, to the man in the street, to schools and other public places; they establish themselves a steadily firmer posi-

tion in the minds of people; they tend to leave an image that holds for long no matter how attractive, less attractive, or even distasteful they are. They pervade the inner cells of the community. In an era of advanced technology and sophisticated media, advertising ceases to be only a service in the interest of a salesman; it is itself a media conveying messages as influential in molding attitudes as they are powerful in motivating human behavior. This being the case, the problem of advertising covers a field much wider in scope than simply that of promoting business operations.[62]

At one point, for example, the government—fearing commercial exploitation of the concept "modern" by tobacco and alcoholic beverage advertisers—ordered a major Dutch TNC brewery to stop a campaign that associated modernity with its product. P. T. Perusahaan Bir Indonesia had to drop the slogan *Terdjunlah kedunia modern ini djadikanlah Bintang baru minuman anda* ("Join the modern world when you drink new Bintang beer") and shift to a less controversial image.

To help reduce public frustration and change the government's image of indifference to the poor, the government responded to public dissension by banning TV commercials "concerning goods/services which exhibit high living" (such as luxury housing development projects or fancy cars).[63] The government also urged the TNCs, particularly the Japanese, to maintain lower profiles. Some advertisers voluntarily reduced their outdoor advertising budgets, but at the same time shifted expenditures to less visible areas of sales promotions and to print media, which generally was less accessible to the poor.[64] In 1977, however, Lubis told me that consumerism was stronger than ever in Indonesia and that Malari had had no impact on advertising or anything else. "It [Malari] was a real victory for the Japanese," he said.[65] An American adman with Indonesian experience told me:

> The 1974 riots do not appear to have caused any discernable cultural or business negatives that have remained to 1977. I saw heavy pro-Western bias in product growth and consumption trends. Advertising is growing—so that I don't see an "anti" attitude. The expat [expatriate] problem in the trade sector is primarily toward the Chinese who dominate the business world—"Jews of the Far East." Such attitudes, riot or no riot, are normal when an "outside" group controls, so visibly, a major part of the business world. It's an extra reason to inflame passions of the "have-nots" beyond their normal rage against poverty. And so much easier than going against the generals! After all, the agitating communists are not surfacing (the few not in captivity) so where else can the spleen be vented?
>
> I have no basis of comparison as to the level of Japanese advertising pre-1974. I did see a great deal of advertising for cars, motorcycles, MSG (monosodium-glutinate), radios, TV. They do use billboard advertising. Wherever they are, Japanese tend to be clannish and low profile as a people. After all, they were not exactly gentle invaders of Southeast Asia, and I am sure they remember that fact. This does not preclude them from being aggressive marketers.[66]

Despite regulations forbidding foreign ownership of a service industry like advertising and requiring that any expatriates must conduct education and training programs so that Indonesians can then replace them, foreigners have continued to exert influence on advertising. Under various technical assistance and management agreements, such as the one O&M had with P. T. Indo-Ad or Chuo Senko with Hikmad and Chusen, foreigners played leading roles in local agency operations. In several cases, advertising agencies—foreign-affiliated and strictly Indonesian—have prominent figures backing them. Although unsuccessful, the JWT experience with Thomertwal is an example of a TNAA alliance with a bridgehead. Another is McCann-Erickson's technical assistance agreement in the 1970s with Perwanal Utama, an agency owned by the influential Diah family. B. M. Diah also owns the long-established *Merdeka,* a Jakarta daily, and he is a former minister of information and ambassador. His son, Nurman, is chief executive of Perwanal Utama and also is involved in running the family's publishing business.

Although legal ownership of TNAA-linked agencies is in the hands of Indonesian nationals (with the notable exception of Lintas),[67] the administrative and creative decision making processes are often controlled by non-Indonesians. To this extent, then, these agencies are not autonomous operations. They remain dependent agencies, and, in some cases, if expatriates left the scene, the agencies would fall apart. This is because expatriates are more actively involved in the day-to-day operations of some agencies than they are in training programs specifically designed to provide Indonesians with the skills and entrepreneurial attitudes needed to replace the foreigners. In some cases, too, the Indonesian bridgeheads tend to take a short-term view of their agencies and they encourage (or at least allow) their expatriate personnel to run operations in hopes of maximizing profits.

Despite compliance with the letter of Indonesian law, the TNAAs generally have always been suspected of arranging what are variously called "Ali Baba" arrangements, "bogus Indonesian companies," "dummy corporations," and "sleeping partnerships."[68] Confirming such alliances, is difficult, of course, but the fact that so many Indonesians talk about and believe that such partnerships exist is revealing.[69] As one Indonesian ad-man said in 1978: "Most foreign agencies are operating either illegally and or [*sic*] under disguise!"[70]

Indo-Ad, for example, is an agency frequently cited as being something other than a genuine Indonesian-run agency. The O&M International executive who established that TNAA's "associate agency agreement" with Indo-Ad has explained how his agency has managed to be so successful in Indonesia:

We have learned some tricks I don't wish to share with anyone. But I will say: (a) the key to our success is *not* to get involved with the military or well-known public figures, (b) to work harder and better than any other agency is the only reason anyone gets to be number one anywhere, (c) Indo-Ad is *not* a "front" in that we own no equity in Indo-Ad whatsoever.[71]

He has also said:

Indo-Ad is wholly owned by Indonesians and we manage the agency under legal contract. We are successful because we have better local partners, because we send in better expatriates, because we have been there longer than anyone else, because we know the market better, because we are not naive and because we work at it.[72]

More generally, he added:

we share profits with local employees, run pension and health schemes, do good works for governments, such as anti-drug campaigns and other volunteer causes. And we don't align ourselves with any political party or prominent figures. We stick to our business and don't stick our noses into politics.[73]

The TNAAs are not particularly pleased with what they feel is a less than warm welcome from Indonesians. One O&M executive who formerly managed the agency's Singapore office told me:

Our management agreement with P. T. Indo-Ad works satisfactorily and we are serving our clients well and making a profit at the same time.
    It is true that the government doesn't welcome us, because they don't welcome *any* service industry. Of course the advertising industry *resents* us because they cannot match our professionalism and they never will.[74]

Another expatriate, working in Jakarta, was critical of P3I leadership: "They want to get the foreigners out and keep the standards down."

Not all indigenous admen agree with the P3I's hard line against foreign influence on Indonesian advertising. Several told me that P3I leaders used their position for personal political and business connections that profit their own agencies. One Indonesian called those in control of the organization "adventurers" and "slime" and said trying to upgrade the industry's standards through P3I is like "beating your head against the wall." Another told me he gave up active participation in P3I when the organization would not implement even basic minimal requirements for membership. He said his suggestions were rejected by those who said he wanted to keep the small agencies out of the organization.

By the late 1970s, it seemed as though nothing had really changed in Indonesian advertising. The same problems that developed during the early years of the New Order have continued. In June of 1978, Lintas did become the last of the TNAAs to publicly comply with Indonesian regulations regarding foreign ownership of advertising agencies. It had the choice of either remaining wholly owned by Unilever N. V. and operating strictly as a house agency and no longer taking non-Unilever business, or of selling its operation to Indonesians. The TNAA's London-based chairman and chief executive explained:

> We obviously have no means by which we can operate outside national laws, and foreign ownership is no longer allowed in Indonesia. It is not, in our experience under these circumstances, easy to sell an illegal organization. We have made acceptable arrangements for all our clients and our staff. As might be expected with a largish business, it was a complex operation. We have been in and out of Indonesia a couple of times now, and we know from experience there is always tomorrow.[75]

Legally, therefore, Lintas no longer has an office in Jakarta. Unilever, however, has an advertising department that is virtually identical to the agency widely known in Jakarta as Lintas. The operation's overall strength was hardly affected by the reorganization since Unilever's business is increasing by about 15 percent a year, and in 1977 it accounted for 74 percent of Lintas's business in Jakarta.[76] As "Unilever Advertising Indonesia," the Lintas operation remains a strong influence on Indonesian advertising. This is because Unilever is the nation's largest advertiser—spending at least $5 million annually on advertising and promotion—and its influence on the media is substantial.[77] Lintas has emphasized how clients in Southeast Asia want to be sure their advertising appropriations go far:

> Indonesia, the least advanced market of all, is a significant example. In a country where clients actively involve themselves in the buying function, Lintas in Jakarta is probably the only agency *to deal direct* with all media over Indonesia. Everyone else appoints sub-agents, uses company salesmen or the like. There is also little monitoring available. Again Lintas has much and more to offer. The agency size means that it can afford to operate its own monitoring services.
> On the whole, SSC&B:Lintas pioneering and long experience with Unilever in Southeast Asia means: (a) credibility and efficiency of media plans, (b) more strength when negotiating with the media industry.[78]

As table 22 shows, seven TNCs controlled about 35 percent of Indonesia's TV advertising expenditures, and Unilever is by far the largest advertiser. In 1976, its expenditures were larger than the next four TNCs *combined.* The table also shows how the major advertisers tend to use agencies having a TNAA affiliation.

Despite P3I and official government rhetoric about the need to end the gap between the TNAA-affiliated agencies and the non-TNAA-affiliated agencies, the government's overall approach to foreign investment and the relative strength and vast resources of the TNAAs seemed to widen further

Table 22

Major Television Advertisers in Indonesia, 1976

	Names and Brands	Expenditures (In Thousands of Rupiah)	Agency
1.	Unilever Indonesia (Lux, Rinso, Blue Band, etc.)	580	Lintas, Indo-Ad
2.	S. C. Johnson (Raid, Pledge, Off, etc.)	130	Indo-Ad Intervista
3.	Perusahaan Bir Indonesia (7-Up, Sunkist, F&N drinks)	115	Intervista
4.	Coca-Cola (Coke, Fanta, Sprite)	110	Perwanal Utama
5.	Nestle (Milo, Milkmaid, Lactogen)	100	Fortune
6.	IndoMilk (IndoMilk, Orchid Butter)	95	Adforce
7.	Bayer Farma & Agro Chemical (Refagan, Tonkim, and Creswil)	95	Indo-Ad

Total	1,225
Total TV Expenditures	3,500 (100%)
Percent of above 7 advertisers	1,225 (35%)

NOTE: Many of the major TV advertisers also are among the biggest overall advertisers in Indonesia. In addition to the above seven major corporations, other Indonesian advertisers, often in media other than television, include the giant Astra Group, Honda, P. T. Tempo (drug products), Sanyo, British-American Tobacco, National, Philips, Garuda airlines, ABC Batteries, Union Carbide, Garum Kretek (local cigarettes), Ayer Mancur (local medicine or "jamu"), Richardson-Merrell, Rodemas Group (Dino soap), Ajinomoto, Tancho shampoo, and Remaco (music cassettes). One U.S. dollar equals approximately 415 Indonesian rupiah.

SOURCE: Unilever, "Television in Indonesia" (Jakarta: Lintas Media Dept., 1977), p. 23.

the inequalities within the Indonesian advertising industry. By 1977, advertising symbolically seemed to return to its pre-Malari status when Indonesian security authorities once again allowed giant billboards atop the twenty-nine-story Nusantara Building in the heart of Jakarta's "miracle mile" business and government district.[79] This time the signs were not for Japanese products, but rather an American corporation (Kodak) and a local drug product (Inza). The reappearance of the billboards again symbolized perceived social injustice and consumption levels and urban lifestyles out of reach to the vast majority of Indonesian villagers still operating in a traditional, peasant economy.

Mochtar Lubis has summarized the unmistakable trend during Suharto's New Order:

> We are shuddering under the impact of international consumerism. Every night on TV and in the cinemas, the commercials entice our people to join the great bandwagon of wasteful consumerism, to buy goods they do not really need, to want more, to buy more, to waste more. In the world of "free market forces," where your only protection is your own strength, Indonesia is but a weak link in the great chain of international finance, international marketing, and international technology.[80]

Yacob Oetama, editor of *Kompas,* the largest and most prestigious newspaper in the country, has also recognized that Indonesia's basic problem is that it wants independence *and* foreign assistance, in advertising and everything else. He has concluded: "We are caught in the dilemma of our system. There's a conflict over social justice and market forces."[81]

Recent developments indicate clearly that tensions over advertising continue within Indonesian society. A joint Indonesian-American study in 1979 reported:

> Commercials present a dilemma for Indonesian television. They were introduced in 1963, shortly after the first broadcast, but today they occupy the tenuous position of a necessary evil. What role they may have, if any, in the future of the Indonesian television system is a matter of debate. Meanwhile considerable efforts have been expended in an effort to minimize any undesirable social effects. The question is a difficult one because the benefits of commercials are also recognized. In addition to stimulating commerce, especially the local television production industry, advertising provides substantial income.[82]

Over the years, the government's policy on TV advertising has fluctuated greatly, and a number of experiments with different formats have been tried. For example, for more than a year commercials were allowed only for one hour (5:00 to 6:00 P.M.) and, with satellite relay links, this made it possible to exclude the more rural, outer islands from the possibly harmful effects of Jakarta advertising. But under pressure from commercial interests, the policy gradually changed and commercials were allowed in two half-hour segments before and after satellite transmission. By late 1978, virtually all outer island viewers were exposed to advertising, and this inevitably has raised questions about commercial influences on prevailing rural and Islamic norms.[83]

Gradually, pharmaceutical advertising on TV was put under tight controls and actions taken to limit the number of commercials per product per month so that certain advertisers could not longer flood the airwaves.

By the early 1980s, the negative effects of advertising had become a significant public issue. In 1981, free-market forces sustained a major setback—at least temporarily and probably through Islamic political pressures—when President Suharto surprised everyone with his announcement that effective in April of that year all television commercials would be banned. *Media* offered this explanation:

> A number of reasons are being advanced to explain the ban. Chief among them seems to be official concern that television advertising is helping to raise people's expectations too high. Indonesia's advanced system of domestic satellites means television is now available in every village throughout Indonesia's 13,000 islands and within reach of the 147 million population. Television commercials for consumer goods help generate a desire among people to move to the "good life" in Jakarta and other major cities. The government seems keen to lower these expectations.[84]

The long-term consequences of this decision—on the finances of government television, on advertising agencies that have found TV advertising a lucrative field, on advertisers who find television an effective sales tool, on rural *and* urban people's expectations, and on Indonesian national development generally—remain to be seen. Talk persists, for example, that the government will eventually lift the television ad ban or even allow a private commercial station in Jakarta and other urban centers.

Indonesia also continued to have serious misgivings about nontelevision aspects of advertising. In 1980, for example, the Indonesian Press Council, chaired by the Minister of Information and with members from both private media and the government, put into effect a policy that limited the size of newspapers to twelve pages and the volume of their advertising to no more than 30 percent of total space. The action is likely to have several effects. Jakarta's dominant dailies—the morning *Kompas* and the afternoon *Sinar Harapan*—should be hurt (at least until they can increase their diversification), and smaller papers should be helped by a more equitable distribution of advertising among the country's papers, many of which are politically well-connected but economically weak. Alternative advertising channels, particularly commercial radio, should be greatly helped by the television ad ban, and businesses will certainly be reexamining their distribution networks.[85]

Indonesia, then, is a classic example of an Asian developing nation that continues to struggle with some intense difficulties posed by outside pressures, including advertising, television, and sophisticated satellite systems. Given the government's emphasis on economic growth, media development, and foreign investment as part of a larger development package to speed-up progress, problems of avoiding dependence have been inevitable and are likely to continue.

Notes

1. Cited in Manglapus, *Japan in Southeast Asia: Collision Course* (New York: Carnegie Endowment for International Peace, 1976), p. 78. Sadli, former minister of mines and head of the government's Foreign Investment Committee, is a prominent Indonesian economist who has played a major role as economic development advisor to Suharto.

2. This date appears in *Lintas:Jakarta*, a promotional brochure distributed by the agency and undated.

3. Unilever's operations in Indonesia and worldwide are extremely complex. In Indonesia, for example, the firm consists of five legal bodies, separately incorporated, but managerially forming one entity under the name of Unilever Indonesia. It not only manufactures soaps, margarine and other foods, and toilet preparations, but it also is involved in timber operations in East Kalimantan. For an overview of Unilever in Indonesia, see "Short Notes on Unilever Indonesia," Jakarta: Unilever Indonesia, February 1975. For insight into the organization's worldwide activities, see *Unilever Report and Accounts 1977* (London: Unilever Ltd., 1978); *What Unilever Is* (London: Information Division, Unilever Ltd., 1977); and Sir Ernest Woodroofe and G. D. A. Klijnstra, "Summary of Written and Oral Statement," in Department of Economic and Social Affairs, *Summary of the Hearings Before the Group of Eminent Persons to Study the Impact of Multinational Corporations on Development and on International Relations* (New York: United Nations, 1974), pp. 446–55.

4. Cited in G. M. Kahin, *The Asian-African Conference, Bandung, Indonesia, April 1955* (Ithaca, N.Y.: Cornell University Press, 1956), p. 44.

5. Personal interview with Nuradi, managing director, Intervista Advertising Ltd., Jakarta, 8 July 1977.

6. Personal interview with R. M. Hadjiwibowo, an Indonesian director, Unilever Indonesia, Jakarta, 3 August 1977.

7. For background on the early days of TVRI, see Astrid Susanto, "The Mass Communications System in Indonesia," especially pp. 243–46, and *Televisi di Indonesia. TVRI 1962–1972* (Jakarta: Direktorat Televisi, Departemen Penerangan, 1972).

8. See table 2, "Perkembangan Jumlah Pesawat Televis Masa 1962–1972," in *Televisi di Indonesia,* p. 59.

9. In 1963, license fees brought in Rp679,590,000. Advertising (*iklan*) brought in Rp163,269,000. The total, in *uang lama* (Old Order money), was Rp842,859,000. See table on "Penerimaan Pengeluaran Televisi R. I. 1963–1970," in *Televisi di Indonesia,* p. 146. $1 = Rp10,000.

10. By 1971, TVRI's income of Rp654,282,000 included Rp367,477,000 from advertising, Rp235,251,000 from license fees, and Rp51,554,000 from government subsidy. See *Televisi di Indonesia,* p. 146. The totals are in New Order money. $1 = Rp415.

11. Stephen Sloan, *A Study in Political Violence—The Indonesian Experience* (Chicago: Rand McNally & Co., 1971), p. 40.

12. Theodore J. Lowi uses this phrase in reference to a rigid, inefficient society's disorder, which he argues serves a useful purpose by bringing about the rebirth of public order and new opportunities for effective political action and constructive change. See his *The Politics of Disorder* (New York: Basic Books, Inc., 1971).

13. For discussion of the power achieved by the Chinese through New Order dealings with the military and foreign investors, see Richard Robison, "Toward a Class Analysis of the Indonesian Military Bureaucratic State," *Indonesia,* no. 25 (April 1978), pp. 17–39. His argu-

ment is that the restoration of the market system and the development of capitalism has not produced a "strong national asli bourgeoisie," but rather a military bureaucratic state with close ties to both foreign and domestic Chinese capital.

14. Nuradi, "Comments by Mr. Nuradi." Remarks made as a panelist discussing "Advertising Education in Asia" at the Ninth Asian Advertising Congress, Jakarta, 5 November 1974, p. 2.

15. Ibid., pp. 2–3.

16. S. Tas, *Indonesia. The Underdeveloped Freedom* (Indianapolis, Ind.: Bobbs-Merrill Co., Inc., 1974), p. 357.

17. Extracted from table 33, "Total TV Transmission Hours Classified as Entertainment, News/Information/Culture and Advertisement for 1962–1971," in *Indonesia Handbook 1972* (Jakarta: Department of Information, 1973), p. 204.

18. Ibid., p. 65. This TVRI document also includes a listing of "positive" and "negative" impacts" of television programs, see pp. 66–68.

19. This point and the fact that television time is relatively expensive and therefore only major advertisers like Unilever, Toyota, and Bayer can afford it are emphasized in Alfian, "Some Observations on Television in Indonesia," in Richstad, *New Perspectives in International Communication* (Honolulu: East-West Communication Institute, 1976), pp. 53–60.

20. While the imported entertainment programs appeared to have a heavy American bias, the situation is quite different for advertisements themselves. Approximately 18 percent of advertisements are American, but Holland accounts for 21 percent; Japan 15 percent; and Indonesia 19 percent. The remaining are other European nations, Australia, Korea, and Hong Kong. Indonesia has had a liberal open-door policy on the importation of foreign-made commercials (but they are supposed to use Indonesian language voice-overs), and this probably accounts for the "grab bag" mix of commercials on the air in 1977. Personal interview with Rosmaniar, head, Advertising Section, TVRI, Jakarta, September 9 and October 14, 1977.

21. Rosmaniar, "Jumlah Iklan Menurut Klasifikasi (Pemasangan) 1976." (A report by the Advertising Section to the head of TVRI Central Station, Jakarta, no date).

22. Extracted from Unilever, "Television in Indonesia" (Jakarta: Media Department, Lintas, 1977).

23. Ibid.

24. JWT handles Lux advertising in most markets around the world. Since JWT itself is not operating in Indonesia, Lintas handles the account, although it may use advertising materials, such as a Natalie Wood TV commercial, produced by JWT.

25. Personal interview with Thomas Sugito, director, Radio Republik Indonesia (RRI), Jakarta, July 21, 1977. For details of RRI's policies and expansion plans, see Direktorat Jenderal Radio-Televisi-Film, *Radio Republik Indonesia 1976* (Jakarta: Departemen Penerangan (Information), 1976), esp. pp. 136–38 on *komersialisasi* of RRI.

26. In 1976, the government operated 48 RRI stations, and there were 477 non-RRI stations in Indonesia. These included 347 commercial stations, 92 district government stations (radio siaran pemerintah daerah), and 38 noncommercial stations (universities, religious groups, etc.). See "Radio Siaran Non RRI di Indonesia," *Radio Republik Indonesia 1976*, p. 208.

27. The Palapa satellite system was installed in time for the May 1977 national elections, as were a number of public television receivers at subdistricts, particularly on Java. Although the satellite's installation has focused attention on Indonesian television, including plans for educational television, the system will be of special benefit to the military and to Pertamina, the state oil corporation, which need reliable communications between Jakarta and the outlying regions. TNCs also will benefit since the system should improve the nation's overall business and commercial infrastructure. A number of TNCs, too, have profited directly from contracts related to the satellite and supporting facilities. For an introduction to Palapa and the controversies surrounding its establishment, see Rebecca Jones, "Satellite Communications: Indonesia's Bitter Fruit," *Pacific Research and World Empire Telegram* 7, no. 4 (May/June 1976), pp. 1–5, Arthur C. Miller, "Indonesia's New Communications Satellite, *Transtel Indonesia*, no. 18 (1977), pp. 47–51.

28. The then Minister of Mines Sadli is quoted in Manglapus, *Japan in Southeast Asia: Collision Course*, pp. 78–79.

29. For a discussion of the "vocal minority"—the 17% of the population living in urban

areas—and the "silent majority"—the 83% in rural areas—see "Rural Development Support Information Policy," in Department of Information, *Indonesia Handbook 1974* (Jakarta: Department of Information, 1975), pp. 75–83. For a more detailed discussion of government actions to improve communications with the villages, see F. Rachmadi, "Constraints on the Effective Mobilisation of Public Opinion in Support of Development." (Indonesian Country Paper presented at 26th Consultative Committee Meeting, Colombo Plan, Kathmandu, November 18, 1977.)

30. Rachmadi, head of research, Ministry of Information, has said that in 1977 Indonesia had sixty-five dailies with a total circulation of about 1.7 million copies daily. Seventeen of these were published in Jakarta, and they accounted for almost 56 percent of the nation's total daily circulation. See his paper cited in the previous note. Other sources have suggested an even greater concentration of circulation in Jakarta. For example, the government's *Indonesia Handbook 1973* (Jakarta: Department of Information, 1974), p. 188, reported that "about 70% of the total circulation of the Indonesian press is spread in the Metropolitan City of Jakarta, which is the hub of political and economic life of the country."

31. Personal interview with Iskandar, advertising manager, *Sinar Harapan*, Jakarta, August 16, 1977. He said four newspapers are the major advertising outlets:

Newspaper	City	Circulation	Advertising Columns (1976)
Kompas	Jakarta	260,000	7,545,485
Sinar Harapan	Jakarta	160,000	7,816,485
Pikiran Rakyat	Bandung	50,000	. . . .
Berita Buana	Jakarta	130,000	1,975,000

32. Virtually all figures of what Indonesia spends on advertising in a year are estimates. Reliable figures have not been maintained by the PPPI or the government, and agencies are very sensitive about releasing their annual billings or income figures. Estimates based on mass media expenditures in Jakarta tend to be somewhat accurate, but these figures often do not—or cannot—take into account expenditures elsewhere throughout Indonesia. In addition, corporations spend large amounts of money on various promotions, demonstrations, film programs in rural areas, etc., and there is no way to realistically total all of these expenditures. Rather than quibble over various "guesstimates," I think the major point to keep in mind about Indonesian expenditures is that they have skyrocketed since Suharto came to power. It doesn't matter much whether the "guesstimate" of annual expenditure is $50 million, $60 million, or $120 million. The important thing is that there has been an advertising boom in Indonesia and that various media and interest groups concentrated in Jakarta have reaped most of the benefits. The "official" estimate of expenditures is probably the figure reported at the Asian Advertising Congress, but my feeling is that this estimate is consistently higher than reality. For example, the Indonesian country report given at the Asian Advertising Congress meeting in Sydney in 1976 said: "From an estimate $40 million U.S. spent in 1974, 1975's total billing reached the $80 million marks while this year (1976) the estimate is $120 million. We do not anticipate the same growth rate over the next couple of years, but expect a gradual levelling off in the late seventies. If in 1973 only two advertising agencies were billing $1 million and over, at present at least eight agencies are in this category. More and more advertisers are also spending more than $500,000 annually as their advertising expenditures." This 1974 figure of $40 million was reported to the International Advertising Association (IAA). Lintas's figures in table 17 may be conservative but are easier to document.

33. This figure is an estimate obtained through correspondence with IAA member Ken Sudarto, head of Matari Advertising, Jakarta. He estimated the media expenditures based on:

> National: $55 million (mainly Jakarta)
> Regional/Local: $15 million (partly Jakarta)
> Total: $70 million (approximately 80 percent Jakarta).

He also estimated that the top leading agencies have billings ranging from a minimum of $1.5 million to a maximum of $5 million annually. He said about ten other agencies have billings between $250,000 and $1.25 million annually.

34. "Biro Iklan Harap-Harap Tjemas," *Tempo*, 25 March 1972, p. 44.

35. Hellmut Schutte was Lintas's client service head when he made these comments in his *Marketing in Indonesia* (Jakarta: P. T. Intermasa, 1974), p. 84. This book was prepared largely for foreign businessmen interested in opportunities in Indonesia. He concluded (p. 103) with this optimistic note about the "trickle-down" theory: "He (marketing manager) will not always find it easy to operate in Indonesia, a country which is not yet accustomed to modern business techniques and therefore gives rise to many frustrations. Patience is one of the main considerations of life in Indonesia and a good sense of ḫumor is often required. But the marketing man who can realistically assess the potential and the trends of the Indonesian market and skillfully uses his marketing tools is bound to win. Indonesia has developed rapidly during the last years and additional money from oil revenues will pour into the country where political stability will ensure economic growth at an accelerating rate. It will, however, take some time until the new wealth percolates through and increases the income of the Indonesian consumer."

36. Figures provided to me by Direktorat Pembinaan Sarana Perdagangan, Ministry of Trade, Jakarta, 22 September 1977. Figures do *not* include at least three work permits for Lintas personnel, who qualify for such permits as Unilever marketing specialists.

37. In personal correspondence on 13 June 1978, Michael J. Ball, executive director international, Ogilvy & Mather International, explained that the old S. H. Benson network in Southeast Asia was: ". . . a poorly run group of offices which were able to survive with mediocre work because mediocre work was the industry norm in the region. We determined to introduce new standards and did so. We sent in new managers and new creative directors to every office. We made available all our international body of knowledge. We instituted training programs for local staff and we sent a number overseas for extended periods. Now, their work is judged by the standards of New York, London and Sydney and it compares favorably."

38. In 1974, the Department of Information conducted a study of the status of advertising in Indonesia. See "Laporan Penelitian Periklanan di Indonesia." (Report of the Proyek Penelitian dan Pengembangan, Jakarta: Departemen Penerangan, 1975), p. 5. The issue of foreign influence on indigenous advertising has long been a controversial topic in Indonesia, and numerous press reports starting in about 1972 have commented on tensions between local agencies and foreign competitors. For an overview of some of the local agencies' problems, for example, see a series entitled "Dunia Usaha Periklanan: Berkembang dalam Kesemrawutan," which appeared in *Suara Karya*, the Golkar daily, over several weeks in November 1976.

39. Basic information on P. T. Indo-Ad provided through correspondence and personal interviews with Harry Reid, the agency's general manager in 1977, and Emir H. Moechtar, "president director" of the agency; and "A Profile of P. T. Indo-Ad" (Jakarta: P. T. Indo-Ad, May 1977).

40. See *Ogilvy & Mather International Annual Report 1977*, pp. 3 and 9. Because P. T. Indo-Ad is considered "independently owned" and "associated with Ogilvy & Mather International by management agreement," the agency does not include Indonesian operations in its *Client List 1978*, a booklet produced by the agency's headquarters in New York. Interestingly, however, Indonesia *is* cited in the client list by country in the TNAA's 1977 annual report.

41. This particular adman described working in Indonesia as "a very hot potato" and said "as long as the Indonesian government won't let international advertising agencies retain even a minority equity it is not really surprising to see them uninterested in trading or entering the country." He insisted that his comments remain unattributed.

42. Personal correspondence with Kenneth L. Brady, chairman and chief executive, Ogilvy & Mather (New Zealand) Ltd., Auckland, 9 December 1977. Brady formerly managed O&M's office in Singapore and is familiar with advertising throughout Southeast Asia. By 1980, he had become chairman of Meridian, O&M's second agency group in Southeast Asia.

43. Early during the "New Order," major advertisers like Coca-Cola and Toyota created advertisements for Indonesia outside of the nation itself. For example, both of these advertisers relied heavily on the creative work of their advertising agencies' offices in Singapore.

44. "Advertising as a Modernizing Agent in a Rapid Changing Society: A Brief Report on the Advertising's Industry Status in Indonesia." (Report prepared by the Indonesian delegation to the Tenth Asian Advertising Congress in Sydney, Jakarta, October 29, 1976), pp. 3–4.

45. See "Dentsu Advertising Ltd. Berusaha Supa Pejabat2 Deperdag," *Harian Nusantara*, 8 November 1973, p. 1. For other press reports of Dentsu's efforts to conduct business in

Indonesia see, for example: "Beberapa Biro Iklan Asing Beroperasi Secara Ali Baba," *Berita Buana*, July 9, 1973, and "Deperdag Larang Dentsu Advertising Ltd. Buka Perwakilannya di Indonesia," *Harian Nusantara*, 7 November 1973, p. 1.

46. In personal correspondence on January 6, 1977, O&M's Brady told me: "Burnett, Grant and Bates have all attempted on more than one occasion to establish themselves in Indonesia. They are interested in Indonesia but have failed in their attempts and lost heavily financially, as did J. Walter Thompson. McCann-Erickson is losing money every day they stay there. Lintas is profitable."

Grant was in Jakarta for about a year, but it was losing money and left. In a personal interview with William Mundy, regional vice president of Grant, Kenyon & Eckhardt, Singapore, 1 December 1977, I was told that the agency had no plans to return to Indonesia. Mundy said, "It's a complete hassle. Three-quarters of your day is spent in hassles and only one-fourth in advertising."

In 1978, Bates was on the merger trail internationally and was trying to affiliate with an Indonesian agency. See Bernice Kanner, "Bates Links Up with Shop in Japan," *Advertising Age*, 23 October 1978, p. 43.

47. The precise nature of JWT's involvement in Indonesia is unclear. One senior JWT official emphasized to me that the TNAA had no equity holding in P. T. Thomertwal and was only managing the agency under a management contract. Another JWT executive, however, told me that "the reason why we stayed so short a time in Indonesia was because we were not a majority shareholder and our partners' way of doing business and ours differed." Two press reports, too, have said that JWT had "assumed full management control" and had an "equity position" in the Jakarta agency. See "JWT Takes Control in Indonesian Shop," *Advertising Age*, 8 July 1974, p. 56, and Philip H. Dougherty, "Advertising: Buying Prime Time," *New York Times*, 26 June 1974, p. 69.

48. Maurice Karunaratne. I interviewed him in Jakarta on 27 September 1977. His creative director was Paul Wachtel, an American who previously had worked for IPA and Ace in Singapore.

49. "Jakarta Agency in Zecha Fold," *Media*, March 1980, p. 25.

50. Personal correspondence with John Sharman, chairman of JWT's executive committee and its chief operating officer, New York, 8 June 1978.

51. Evidence on the profitability of the TNAAs in Indonesia is conflicting. Agencies like Lintas and P. T. Indo-Ad obviously are making money in Indonesia. Roberts (see note 66), in personal correspondence on December 8, 1977, told me, "While the volume of advertising is low, a properly managed agency can be quite profitable—more so than in the U.S. as a percentage to billing or income."

Lintas's business has always been profitable, and its Jakarta manager, John Ormerod, told me in an interview on 1 July 1977, that 2 percent profit is considered good in London, but that Lintas Jakarta makes 5 percent. See, for example, Table 20.

Agencies like McCann-Erickson and Dentsu probably are in Indonesia more to service major transnational clients than to make a big profit, but their activities in Indonesia obviously contribute to the agencies' overall profits and growth. Theodore D. O'Hearn, McCann-Erickson Worldwide executive vice president for international operations, told me in correspondence on 23 May 1978: "Each McCann office is set up as a separate profit center. In other words, each manager of each operating unit has the responsibility for generating a profit on an annual basis. Not all offices make money. But this is for a number of various reasons. We don't start out with the philosophy that some offices should make money and that in so doing they should subsidize other offices."

Regarding the Southeast Asian market, he continued: "Philosophically, McCann attempts to staff *all* offices at the same professional level of excellence. In other words, we don't feel that the smaller markets should in any way be shortchanged professionally. McCann has established a worldwide standard of excellence and we strive to bring all offices regardless of their size or ranking up to a standard level of professionalism.

"With regard to Indonesia, I agree that this is a potentially rich market which, although it has been disappointing to international entrepreneurs thus far, should blossom in the years ahead."

52. In practice, during the early New Order years, the Ministry of Information (Departemen Penerangan—Deppen) was heavily involved in matters relating to advertising agencies.

Since 1976, the Ministry of Trade (Departemen Perdagangan—Deperdag) has exercised greater interest in overseeing advertising agency development. Of course, Deppen continues to have an influence on advertising generally since press, television, and radio content fall under its jurisdiction, but Deperdag has become more active in advertising agencies as they influence domestic trade.

53. The Chinese in Indonesia comprise only about 3 percent of the population, but their economic power historically has been disproportionately high. For a summary of Indonesia's long-festering anti-Chinese problems, see Ralph Anspach, "Indonesia," especially pp. 129–133, in Frank H. Golay, Anspach, M. Ruth Pfanner, and Eliezer R. Ayal, eds., *Underdevelopment and Economic Nationalism in Southeast Asia* (Ithaca, N.Y.: Cornell University Press, 1966); and John O. Sutter, "Indonesianisasi," Southeast Asia Program Data Paper no. 36 (Ithaca, N.Y.: Cornell University, 1959).

54. "Matari Advertising Meng-orbit Kedalam Konstelasi Periklanan Internasional." Press release issued by Matari Advertising, Jakarta, August 31, 1973. Press reports of the conflict between Matari and P3I include: "Matari Advertising Dipimpin Tokoh CGMI," *Harian Nusantar*, 29 September 1973, p. 1; "Reaski Pimpinan P3I Tentang Kasus Matari," *Harian Nusantara*, 1 October 1973, p. 1; "Matari Adv. Disokors Hingga Clearance Kopkamtib," *Harian Nusantara*, 3 October 1973, p. 1; "Matara Ad Sedia Tangguhkan Management Contract Dgn Grant," *Sinar Harapan*, 3 October 1973, p. 1; and the P3I met on 12 September 1973, and discussed the association between Matari and Grant International, Toronto. See "Risalah Rapat Pengurus, Harian Pengurus Besar PPPI, Tanggal 12 September 1973." Minutes of the Executive Committee of P3I, Jakarta, 12 September 1973.

55. Ken Sudarto, president, Matari Advertising, Jakarta, in a personal interview, 2 August 1977, told me that about one-third of his agency's business came from the Astra Group, but that as much as 60 percent had come from the group in earlier years. Astra is a huge industrial conglomerate. For an introduction to its diverse projects and products, see "Astra: A Dedication to Indonesia's Development" (Jakarta: P. T. Astra International, Inc., 20 February 1977). For a discussion of Astra as a Chinese business group in alliance with "asli politico-bureaucratic leaders," see Robison, "Toward a Class Analysis of the Indonesian Military Bureaucratic State," especially pp. 34–36. For a report of Astra's connections with General Ibnu Sutowo, former head of Pertamina, see "Pertamina Bankruptcy: Widening Ripples Threaten Banks and Business in Indonesia," *New York Times*, 9 April 1977, p. 25.

56. P. T. Astra began in 1957 in Jakarta as a trading and export corporation. When the Suharto government encouraged foreign and domestic private investors, P. T. Astra, run by a talented Chinese business family, was in a position to get various import licenses, contracts, and other concessions. Much of its influence evolved from its motor vehicle division, established in 1969 to handle Toyota and Daihatsu. In 1971 it became the local partner for Honda motorcycles. Later, it became sole distributor for a variety of engineering and industrial equipment, including Komatsu heavy equipment and Xerox machines. In 1970, it employed 575,000 people. By 1976, it had become probably the nation's largest private employer with some 7,351,000 workers. Matari, as Astra's major agency, also grew rapidly. From its start with two employees in 1971, the agency expanded to more than sixty in 1977, and it was one of the most successful local agencies.

57. Ken Sudarto, "Matari: The Advertising and Media Scene in Indonesia" (Jakarta: Matari Advertising, April 1978), p. i.

58. For a summary of the impact of Malari on domestic politics, see D. Sujati, "The Wake of the Malari Caper," *Far Eastern Economic Review*, 15 November 1974, pp. 9–10 (Indonesian '74 Focus section). For a general overview of Indonesian politics in that important year, see Gary Hansen, "Indonesia 1974: A Momentous Year," *Asian Survey*, February 1975, pp. 148–156. For effects on the media, see Derek Davies, "Consensus in the Negative," *Far Eastern Economic Review*, 25 February 1974, pp. 12–14. For a perspective on the role of students in Indonesian politics, see Arief Budiman, "The Student Movement in Indonesia: A Study of the Relationship between Culture and Structure," *Asian Survey* 18, no. 6 (June 1978), pp. 609–25, and Andrew H. Gunawan, "The Role of Students in the 15 January 1974 Incidents," *Southeast Asian Affairs 1975* (Singapore: Institute of Southeast Asian Studies, 1975), pp. 65–70. The Malari demonstrations were sparked by the visit of Japan's Tanaka. For insight into the anti-Japanese tensions in Indonesia, see Manglapus, *Japan in Southeast Asia: Collision Course*. For a more sympathetic treatment of Japanese investment in Indonesia, see Centre for Strategic and International Studies, *Japanese-Indonesian Relations in the Seventies*. (Papers presented at

the First Japanese-Indonesian Conference, Jakarta, December 6–9, 1973), and Masashi Nishihara, *The Japanese and Sukarno's Indonesia* (Kyoto: Center for Southeast Asian Studies, Kyoto University, 1976).

59. "Advertisement Which Hurts National Pride," an editorial in *Abadi*, 12 December 1973, U.S. Embassy, Translation Unit Press Review, no. 233 (Jakarta, 12 December 1973), p. 3.

60. For background on this basic government trade policy, see "Decision of the Minister of Trade Concerning Fields of Activities for Foreign Commercial Enterprises and Services and Their Agencies," no. 08/H.O./3/71 (Jakarta: Department of Information, March 1971). See also, *Doing Business in Indonesia* (New York: Business International Corporation, 1968); "Further Restrictions on the Involvement of Foreigners in the Trade Sector," *Indonesian Commercial Newsletter*, no. 43 (15 December 1975), pp. 1–4; "Nationalising Foreign Trading Activities," *Indonesian Commercial Newsletter*, no. 60 (23 August 1976), pp. 1–2; and "Transfer of Trading Activities Being Handled by Expatriates into Indonesian Hands," *Indonesian Commercial Newsletter*, no. 64 (18 October 1976), pp. 3–5.
Decree no. 314 meant that all domestic trading activities of approximately nineteen TNCs and 17,000 "foreign-domestic" trading companies had to be handed over to Indonesians as of January 1, 1978. The policy affected such major foreign corporations as Unilever, IBM, Dunlop, Bata, BAT, ICI, Singer Sewing Co., and Siemens. Most complied with the policy by choosing an Indonesian dealer as their sole agent.

61. Hellmut Schutte, "Advertising for Consumer Goods," *Management dan Usahawan Indonesia*, Edisi 7 (June 1973), p. 30, estimated that consumers in highly industrialized, Western nations see about seven thousand advertising messages daily, but in Jakarta perhaps "only" two thousand per day and much less in rural areas.

62. Mashuri, "Message by the Minister of Information to the Ninth Asian Advertising Congress." (Paper delivered in Jakarta, November 5, 1974), p. 2.

63. See Article 19 of Sumadi, "Decision of the Director General for Radio-TV-Film, Department of Information, no. 11/KEP/Dirjen/RTF/1975, on Regulations on TVRI Advertisement" (Jakarta, 1 September 1975). This and other advertising-related TVRI policies are published in *Ketentuan & Tarif Iklan (Regulation and Tariff on Commercial Broadcasting)* (Jakarta: TVRI, 1 November 1975).

64. M. Panggabean, director, development of trading infrastructure, Ministry of Trade, Jakarta, told me in a personal interview on 21 September 1977, that after Malari the government called in representatives of the Japanese Embassy, Jetro, and the Japan Club and talked frankly to them about the need to lower their nation's visibility in the Indonesian market. He said that the government has managed to lessen the Japanese presence.

65. Personal interview with Mochtar Lubis, Jakarta, 29 September 1977.

66. Personal correspondence with Dewey Roberts, St. Thomas, Virgin Islands, 8 December 1977.

67. Because of its historic links with Unilever, Lintas in Jakarta has always operated as an advertising department of that TNC, which is 100 percent foreign-owned in Indonesia. Since 1978, Unilever has not been allowed to directly distribute its own goods in the domestic Indonesian market. Like other foreign manufacturers, it has had to make use of Indonesian distributors.

68. Throughout Southeast Asia, the "Ali Baba" arrangement refers to an alliance between indigenous businessman ("Ali") who nominally owns an enterprise but in reality holds the shares for some outsider ("Baba"), frequently Chinese. In such an arrangement, a "Baba" obviously must find someone locally that can be trusted. In Indonesia, the government often refers to "the economically strong," the Chinese, and "the economically weak," the indigenous peoples.

69. See, for example, "Domestic Advertising Agencies Threatened," *Indonesian Observer*, 16 September 1972; "National Advertising Agencies Complain," *Indonesian Perspectives*, November 1972, p. 19; "Symbiosis Mutualistis Dibidang Periklanan," *Harian Kami*, 2 October 1973, p. 2; "Foreign Advertising Firms Hold Markets," *Jakarta Times*, 29 October 1974; and "Multinational Companies Controlling the Market of Advertising Servicers in Indonesia," *Indonesian Commercial Newsletter*, no. 22 (31 January 1975), pp. 3–5. For the P3I perspective on national control of advertising, see A. M. Chandra, P3I chairman, "Dasar Pemikiran Pembinaan Periklanan di Indonesia," a statement from the Persatuan Perusahaan Periklanan Indonesia, Jakarta, 5 February 1975.

70. Sudarto, "Matari: The Advertising & Media Scene in Indonesia," p. 28.

71. Personal correspondence with Michael J. Ball, executive director international, O&M International, Sydney, 17 July 1978.

72. Personal correspondence with Ball, 4 April 1978.

73. Ibid.

74. Personal correspondence with Kenneth L. Brady, Auckland, New Zealand, 6 January 1977.

75. Personal correspondence with S. R. Green, SSC&B:Lintas International, London, 7 April 1978.

76. Personal correspondence with John Ormerod, Lintas, Jakarta, 7 July 1978.

77. Unilever Indonesia does not make public its annual advertising expenditures. Based on conversations with Indonesian advertising personnel, I estimate that the giant advertiser spends at least $5 million per year on advertising and promotion. One TNAA-affiliated agency head estimated Unilever's expenditures at as much as $7 million a year. Much of the corporation's promotion efforts never appear in the mass media. They take the form of so-called company organised media—film shows, demonstrations, house-to-house visits, and extensive use of posters and advertising on buses and bus shelters. Expenditures in these areas are unlikely to be recorded through an advertising agency's billings figures, but in a poor, rural nation like Indonesia they are very important.

78. Frank Galbraith, "SSC&B:Lintas in Southeast Asia: Credentials and Profiles." (Report on the agency's operations in Thailand, Malaysia, Singapore, and Indonesia, Kuala Lumpur: SSC&B:Lintas, April 1977), pp. 5–6.

79. For several years after Malari, Kopkamtib (the military's Command for the Restoration of Security and Order) would not approve any requests for billboard space atop the controversial Nusantara Building, which had been built with Japanese reparation funds. Several admen told me that the security agency refused an inquiry from Xerox's agency, Matari, that it be allowed to use the space. The reason given was that, although Xerox is an American product, its Indonesian agent, PT Astra-Graphia, had Japanese ties. This suggests how sensitive the Japanese presence continues to be in post-Malari Indonesia.

80. Ironically, this statement comes from a man who heads an Indonesian agency that has a close relationship to a TNAA. It also comes from a man who was a sharp critic of Sukarno's policies and who has been critical of post-Sukarno developments. The statement is from Lubis's "Between Myths and Realities: Indonesia's Intellectual Community Today," *Asian Affairs*, September/October 1977, p. 45.

81. Personal interview with Yacob Oetama, *Kompas* editor, Jakarta, 27 July 1977.

82. Alfian, Andrew Arno, and Godwin Chu. "Television Commercials," in Alfian and Chu, eds. *Satellite Television in Indonesia*. (Honolulu: East-West Communication Institute, and Jakarta: LEKNAS/LIPI, 1979), p. 179.

83. Alfian and Chu, pp. 63–64 and 179–182. Also see Chu and Alfian, "Programming for Development in Indonesia," *Journal of Communication*, Autumn 1980, pp. 50–57.

84. "Suharto Blows the Ad Fuse," *Media*, February 1981, p. 1. Also see "Bila Iklan TVRI Ditiadakan," *Tempo*, 17 January 1981, pp. 20–22, and "Komentar2 Ttg Penghapusan Iklan TVRI," *Sinar Harapan*, 6 January 1981, p. 1 and 12.

85. "Advertising Restrictions Pose Serious Problems for Firms in Indonesia," *Business Asia*, 23 January 1981, pp. 1–2.

Around the world, the need for greater production in farming is required to keep up with world population growth. With this added demand, the farmers of the world have to come up with more efficient methods to work the land. Since 1890 Kubota has been involved with the ever-increasing demands of man, working to develop new products and technology to satisfy these needs.

The tractor is replacing the horse, buffalo and ox in the preparation of the land for agriculture. Not only is the tractor faster, but also it does a much better job of tilling and breaking up the ground and old roots, so that more oxygen and fertilizer can reach the roots and help produce bigger and better crops. That is what Kubota is all about: our complete line of agriculture equipment is designed

to give the farmer bigger and better crops, with less effort than ever before. Your Kubota dealer can show you our complete line-up of energy-and-time-saving tractors. When it comes to tractors, come to Kubota.

⊗ KUBOTA

Modern efficiency for today's farmer.

Please write: Kubota, Ltd., Agricultural Machinery Export Headquarters, 22, Funade-cho, 2-chome, Naniwa-ku, Osaka, Japan.

Bangkok Office: Thaniya Bldg., 4th Floor, 62 Silom Road, Bangkok, Thailand Phone: 234-7880, 234-7882 Telex: 82369 KUBOTA TH Cable: IRONKUBOTA BANGKOK **Jakarta Office:** Skyline Building 8F JL. M.H. Thamrin No. 9, Jakarta, Indonesia Phone: 363977 Telex: 46630 KUBOTA JKT **Taipei Office:** 8th Floor, Johnson Bldg. 17th, Jenai Road, SEC. 3, Taipei, Taiwan Phone: Taipei 7812309 Telex: 21015 KUBOTA TP Cable: IRONKUBOTA TAIPEI

REGIONAL JAPANESE TRACTOR AD

A common transnational corporate message is that imported goods and services promote economic growth and introduce new products and technology. This Kubota machinery ad was created in 1980 by Dentsu, the largest ad agency in Japan and the world. The message was designed to tell readers of the *Far Eastern Economic Review,* an influential regional news magazine, that the Japanese transnational is committed to the development of Asian agriculture. Transnational corporate campaigns directed at decision makers are not controversial compared to aggressive consumer goods campaigns directed to the masses and using a variety of highly visible media and promotional techniques. Particularly in Southeast Asia, Japanese advertisers have to be very conscious of local sensitivities. In countries like Indonesia and Thailand, Japan continues to be perceived as an exploiter. (Courtesy of Dentsu, Inc.)

JOHNSON & JOHNSON AD

Advertising does not simply sell products. It can also educate and change attitudes. For example, transnational agencies point out that they help people stay healthy, clean, and happy. This Johnson & Johnson ad, created by SSC&B:Lintas for use in Thailand, suggests that the American talcum powder makes babies dry and mothers happy. According to the agency, "Johnson & Johnson is a household name in the East, proclaimed and purchased by mothers from Borneo to Bangkok, where our fast-moving and very successful agency creates advertising that maintains a 30 percent share of the total talcum powder market, and no less than 60 percent of the non-mentholated baby powder market." (Courtesy of SSC&B:Lintas International Ltd.)

十進制郵政服務
郵費表
METRIC POSTAL RATES

1980年8月5日開始生
Effective 5 August 1980

十進制
百多個國家已採用
千萬不要落伍
It's a Metric world —
Don't be left behind!

ROYAL MAIL

PUBLIC SERVICE AD FROM HONG KONG

In Asia, as elsewhere, governments have turned to professional advertising to help sell family planning and other social aims. When Hong Kong "went metric," for example, the government turned to SSC&B:Lintas to help ease the transition. The agency created a theme ("It's a metric world—don't be left behind") aimed at Hong Kong's "strong international awareness and desire to conform to worldwide trends." An integrated communications campaign was developed using posters, leaflets, and an animated commercial showing children of all countries delighted with their new metric unity. This particular message showed how the metric system related to postal rates. (Courtesy of SSC&B:Lintas International Ltd.)

These further ads shall be placed in the Straits Times and Berita Harian.

Your Rain Forest is worth millions of dollars. In tourism.

Nowadays, more and more tourists are interested in visiting our National Parks. They go there for a very good reason. Most countries have killed off their wildlife, and now their peoples go to great lengths to see wild animals in their natural habitat.

We are lucky to have a unique Rain Forest — 130,000,000 years old: one of the richest in the world. And Malaysia is one of the areas in the world where such large tracts of virgin natural forest still exist.

This is where the Orang Utan is found: where the many beautiful species of butterflies and birds live. And these are only a few items of the wealth of our natural flora and fauna.

Destroy them now and they will be gone forever. We still have our Rain Forest. We musn't fritter it away.

Not only does the Rain Forest earn money for Malaysia in tourism: it plays an important part in our lives. Wild animals, wild plants and wild countryside are part of the

natural eco-system: the life support system of our planet. The stability of this system is essential to man's enjoyment and survival.

The World Wildlife Fund Malaysia is preparing campaigns to help save the Rain Forest by promoting successful ways towards forest conservation: by

studying the most efficient way for development and preservation to go hand in hand: by encouraging the development of more National Parks and reserves.

All this requires your goodwill and support. Save our Rain Forest for the enjoyment it can give us, for the money it can earn us in tourism.

Help save our rain forest
We hold it in trust

World Wildlife Fund Malaysia

World Wildlife Fund Malaysia,
P.O. Box 769, Kuala Lumpur
I share your concern over the future of the Malaysian Rain Forest.   Signed
I am interested in the WWFM and what it does. Please send me a brochure.
Name
Address

The Pelandok. Sang Kanchil— a living legend. Will he still be here tomorrow?

Malaysia's culture is inextricably linked with the Rain Forest, a unique heritage of which we should be proud. Where else did we get our mengkuang, the dyes for our early batiks, the myths and legends for our literature?

One popular character is Sang Kanchil, the mousedeer — known for his wit and adventures with other animals in the forest. He has been the source of many interesting

and enjoyable evenings. We are lucky to still have him around. And we owe it to our children to keep him around

His home has been, is, and will always be, the rain forest. If we do away with it, we do away with him.

Of course we are not saying that we should stop opening up the forest for development. What we need to do is to plan carefully.

The World Wildlife Fund Malaysia has several campaigns towards that — the study of how development and preservation can go hand in hand, the establishment of more National Parks and reserves, the promotion of successful ways towards forest conservation.

These plans need your support and goodwill. Keep Sang Kanchil a living legend.

Help save our rain forest
We hold it in trust

World Wildlife Fund Malaysia

World Wildlife Fund Malaysia,
P.O. Box 769, Kuala Lumpur
I share your concern over the future of the Malaysian Rain Forest.   Signed
I am interested in the WWFM and what it does. Please send me a brochure.
Name
Address

We do not want to kill off our national emblem, do we?

The tiger, a beautiful magnificent animal which we have adopted for our national emblem. Also a much misunderstood animal. Feared for his ferocity, killed for his skin, accused of being a man-eater.

Normally the tiger is not a man-eater. If he does turn into one, it is because he has been wounded accidentally or wilfully by traps or gunfire. When confronted by a human he is scared. But when cornered, he naturally fights for his survival and attacks in self-defence. Normally, he keeps himself to himself in his home — the Rain Forest. And if we take away his home, he'll have to look to somewhere else for his food — domesticated ground. By saving the rain forest we are not only doing it for the tiger. We are doing it for ourselves.

Our Rain Forest is important because wild animals, wild plants and wild countryside are part of the natural eco-system: the very life support system of our planet. And the stability of this system is essential for man's enjoyment and survival.

Malaysia is lucky to have one of the last surviving large tracts of rain forest in the whole world. Help preserve it.

There are plans for campaigns to help protect and preserve. The WWFM is helping to finance the preservation of the tiger who is in danger of extinction.

Other plans in hand are to encourage the establishment

of new National Parks and reserves and to study how best development and preservation of the forest can go hand in hand. But it needs your support in all ways. Let us not kill off our national emblem

Help save our rain forest
We hold it in trust

World Wildlife Fund Malaysia

World Wildlife Fund Malaysia,
P.O. Box 769, Kuala Lumpur
I share your concern over the future of the Malaysian Rain Forest.   Signed
I am interested in the WWFM and what it does. Please send me a brochure.
Name
Address

In 10 to 15 years time, Malaysians could be without their favourite fruit—the durian. Because the life of this fruit bat is in danger.

The fruit bat feeds off the flowers of the mangrove for half the year. For the other half, it feeds off the flowers of the durian, pollinating them at the same time. But clumps of the mangrove have been indiscriminately chopped down. So, no mangrove, no bat. No bat to pollinate, no durian.

We can see that the survival of our wildlife and our forest is essential to our enjoyment.

Our Rain Forest is important because wild animals, wild plants and wild countryside are part of the natural eco-system, the very life support system of our planet. And the stability of this system is essential for man's enjoyment and survival. Help to preserve them.

There are plans for campaigns to help protect and preserve. The WWFM is preparing several campaigns to encourage the promotion of laws and regulations for protection at all levels, to study how best industrial

development and preservation of the forest can go hand in hand, to promote the formation of more Forest

Reserves. All this requires your goodwill and support. Help save our Rain Forest for the durians we enjoy.

Help save our rain forest
We hold it in trust

World Wildlife Fund Malaysia

World Wildlife Fund Malaysia,
P.O. Box 769, Kuala Lumpur
I share your concern over the future of the Malaysian Rain Forest.   Signed
I am interested in the WWFM and what it does. Please send me a brochure.
Name
Address

WORLD WILDLIFE ADS FROM MALAYSIA

Individual ad agencies or their professional associations sometimes donate their services to help the government or nonprofit organizations spread public service messages. Ogilvy & Mather, for example, has assisted the World Wildlife Fund in Malaysia and elsewhere. In Kuala Lumpur, the O&M office produced these newspaper ads to promote the establishment of more national parks. (Courtesy of World Wildlife Fund Malaysia)

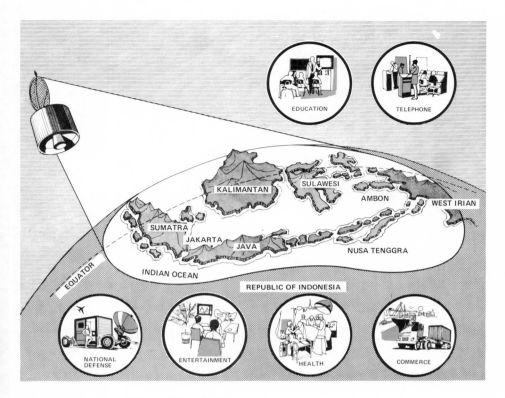

INDONESIA'S SATELLITE SYSTEM

Indonesia is the first Asian nation to own and operate its own satellite system. Since 1976, the American-built "Palapa" system has linked the country's thousands of islands and brought advanced telecommunications to the world's largest archipelago. The system has many public and private applications, as this illustration shows. For example, the new system has given every province the capability to receive television transmission from Jakarta and elsewhere. By 1981, the government had become so concerned that national broadcasts of TV commercials were creating tensions in rural areas that a ban on TV advertising was announced by President Suharto himself. Whether Indonesia's costly government-run television system can afford to forego advertising revenue remains to be seen. The Palapa system is regionally significant because Indonesia is encouraging its ASEAN neighbors to use its satellite services. (Courtesy of Hughes Aircraft Co.)

terdjunlah kedunia modern ini

djadikanlah Bintang baru minuman anda

Utjapkan BINTANG

Djika minum bir Bintang, Anda terdjun kedunia baru ... penuh gairah hidup, orang^2 modern, gagasan^2 baru, bir Bintang! Murni ... asli ... lain daripada jang lain. Nikmatilah rasa njaman dan relax ... minumlah Bintang. ... Utjapkan Bintang.

BBB.175.-3/'71

terdjunlah kedunia modern bir BINTANG baru

BINTANG BEER AD FROM INDONESIA

In Asia and elsewhere, the greatest controversies surrounding advertising regulations have centered around alcoholic beverages, pharmaceuticals, and tobacco. Governments increasingly believe that advertising for these products can introduce foreign life-styles, affect public health, and foster other negative influences. In predominantly rural, Islamic Indonesia, for example, the government has become sensitive to aggressive advertising, frequently by transnationals. The Ministry of Information has had to respond to religious and political pressures that maintain that various products and ads affect indigenous social and cultural life. Bintang (Star) beer once had to drop a major campaign that used the theme "Enter the modern world when you drink new beer Bintang" ("Terdjunlah kedunia modern ini djadikanlah Bintang baru minuman anda.") Tensions between the government and the advertising industry often develop when policies do not exist or are ambiguous and when communication between policymakers and admen is poor. (From *Televisi di Indonesia: TVRI 1962–72,* a publication prepared by the Ministry of Information, Jakarta)

FRONTPAGE DIVERSITY

In Malaysia, the government licenses newspapers to publish in a variety of languages that serve the country's Malay, Chinese, Indian, and expatriate readers. This 1981 photo shows Malaysian front pages in Chinese, English, Tamil (an Indian language), and Malay (both Jawi and Romanized scripts). Malay, or Bahasa Malaysia, is the sole official language, but Malaysia's most successful newspapers have always been in English and Chinese. Compared to the non-Malay population, Malays are less affluent and literate and tend to live in rural areas. Governments of plural societies have tremendous problems creating national unity and developing policies affecting media, education, and culture. (Courtesy of Dr. Duane Ebnet)

LIQUOR AD FROM MALAYSIA

To be effective, advertising in a multicultural society must be based on a very deep understanding of the target consumer. Simply importing advertising concepts and translating them into local languages can be risky. This Ogilvy & Mather liquor ad created in Kuala Lumpur is clearly designed only for the Chinese consumer in Malaysia. According to O&M, the ad "brings together his passionate love of gambling, particularly horse racing, his profound respect for omens and external influences that govern his luck, and his desire for symbols of material success." The promises of this ad are impossible to translate into neat English, and the brand name does not even appear in the copy since "Johnnie Walker Black Label" is difficult to phonetically or idiomatically put into Chinese. To a Malaysian Chinese, the product is known as Square Bottle Whiskey. (Courtesy of Ogilvy & Mather, Malaysia)

DUMEX SIGN

The selling of baby food products is an extremely competitive business, and one in which a handful of transnationals have skillfully used a variety of promotional techniques. Some of these have drawn such criticism that by the 1980s mass consumer advertising of infant formula was generally no longer done. In Malaysia and Singapore, for example, Dumex—made by Denmark's East Asiatic Co.—is a major competitor to Nestlé. During the 1970s, Dumex posters like these were highly visible, even in rural areas. (Courtesy of Consumers' Association of Penang)

7

Malaysia: Advertising in a Multicultural Society

> Malaysian society is so open to external influences and maintains such an active network of external transactions, information flows, and personal contacts that they constitute an important total influence in its political affairs. Malaysia is the polar opposite of a hermit kingdom, in fact and in aspiration. Not withstanding the passing of political colonialism, Malaysian elites have not turned their backs on foreign contacts nor expressed any desire to be self-contained.
>
> —Professor Milton J. Esman[1]

In sharp contrast to Indonesia under Sukarno, Malaysia has never been a closed, anti-Western, anticapitalist society. Under the leadership of British-educated Tunku Abdul Rahman, the nation's first prime minister, and each of his several successors, Malaysia has never pursued goals that were incompatible with those of Center nations. In fact, Malaysia has always been receptive to external advice, communications, and investment. Western concepts like "development" and "modernization" tend to mean about the same thing to Malaysian policymakers.

Highly significant increases in political sophistication, nationalism, awareness of TNCs, and ethnic consciousness—especially among some young, educated vernacular Malays—have occurred by the 1980s, but Malaysia remains basically very much an open, Western oriented, free enterprise society that on the surface is at ease with imported patterns, values, and institutions. Economically, in particular, Malaysia is heavily foreign controlled. Building upon development patterns set by the early European trading agencies, TNCs have invested substantially in Malaysia.[2] According to the government's *Third Malaysia Plan (1976–1980)*, in 1970 more than 63 percent of share capital was in non-Malaysian hands. By 1975, noncitizens still controlled nearly 55 percent of the corporate sector equity. By 1977, more than five hundred TNCs of various types, sizes, and national origins had invested more than $416 million in Malaysian manufacturing.[3] All of these corporations including Colgate-Palmolive, Goodyear, Johnson & Johnson, Sanyo, Beecham, ICI, Dunlop, Unilever, and Nestlé brought with them their marketing (including advertising) skills to help generate brand loyalties, greater sales, and foreign consumer patterns.

The Growth of Modern Advertising

Historically, in Malaysia and in Singapore, as in Indonesia, local elites and expatriates had long had access to a variety of imported, "mother" nation goods, usually supplied through the large European-based trading agencies, which did some advertising in the early colonial newspapers. Imported products like Guinness Stout, for example, were advertised in colonial Malaya as early as 1904,[4] but it was not until around independence in 1957 that local manufacturing began to flourish, and advertising was right behind.

Initially, Malaya's businesses and communications were under the colonial influence of Singapore, where most of the giant trading agencies and other expatriate-controlled entities which oversaw the area's markets and media were regionally based. Most of the colonial policies affecting politics, economics, and information originated in Singapore or were disseminated to Malaya via Singapore, in its unique role as a colonial city where British expatriates forged close relationships with Chinese traders. It was natural, then, that modern advertising would progress faster in Singapore than in the neighboring hinterlands.

In 1948, the first signs of advertising as something other than a hit-or-miss activity appeared in Singapore with the formation of the Association of Accredited Advertising Agents.[5] One of the founding member agencies, Masters Ltd., eventually acquired international affiliation and later evolved into Ogilvy & Mather. Established in 1928, Master was the largest local agency and had been established by a European who lived in Singapore all his life. In 1952, the advertisers formed their own professional association. Twenty major corporations that were beginning to advertise heavily in both Singapore and Malaya organized themselves into the Malayan Advertisers Association.[6] Leading members of the Association included Nestlé, Shell, Lever Brothers, and Fraser & Neave, the latter a Singapore firm that has had the Coca-Cola franchise since 1936 and that handles other soft drinks, and is brewing beer in partnership with Heineken of Holland.

By 1965, tensions between the governments of Singapore and Malaysia had increased, and Singapore left the Federation.[7] Agencies and advertisers in these two politically separate entities, however, continued to have very close relations for almost a decade after Singapore's separation. In

1974, pressure from the Malaysian government forced the two organizations of the advertisers and agencies to establish separate bodies in each nation.[8]

Like the commercial sector generally, Malaysia's media, too, has always been influenced by Singapore.[9] Many of the region's early newspapers were not only in English (rather than Malay, the indigenous language), but they also were printed in Singapore. Gradually, the more successful of these—including the prestigious *Straits Times* and the *Nanyang Siang Pau*—had sister operations in both places. By 1965, as Russell H. Betts had written, the so-called free press in Malaya and Singapore was experiencing "the pervasiveness of the money-making motive" and "the lack of inter- and intra-language stream commercial competition."[10] Betts observed that the press: "has become a profit-making business centered on entertainment for the reader and policies designed not to 'rock the boat' of financial success. Moreover, the pervasiveness of this profit-making motive not infrequently dominates to the point of undermining any serious attempt to fully and accurately cover the news."[11]

Unlike the Indonesian press, which has its origins as a political communication tool, the press in Malaysia and Singapore has evolved as a commercial tool. Because of this, the English- and Chinese-language press chains in Singapore and Kuala Lumpur encouraged the growth of advertising and stood to gain economically from foreign corporations, which considered advertising as a necessity rather than a luxury, and from general efforts to upgrade professional standards.

Gradually, then, an alliance of government policymakers, mass media owners, foreign investors, and TNAAs evolved from the area's colonial development patterns. At the heart of the alliance was a close working relationship between foreigners and the Chinese. But, as Donald and Joanna Moore have noted, the foreigners were in control:

> British manufacturers, anxious for foreign markets, began to appoint agents overseas whose task was to promote the sale of their principals' goods. In order to do this, they were granted, usually, the sole right to import their goods, and so developed the agency house system which is still one of the pillars of the Singapore economy. British goods were carried in British bottoms to British merchants in a British settlement. It was a beautiful system, remarkable alike for its efficiency and simplicity. And even today, when the practice of British manufacturers placing their agencies in Chinese hands is commonplace, by far the greater proportion of British agencies are held by British companies, or Singapore companies in which Europeans play a crucial role.[12]

The first TNAA to enter this colonial setting was a Chicago-based agency, Grant. It established wholly owned offices in Singapore in 1955 and in Kuala Lumpur in 1958. Grant's president spoke frankly about the motives for expanding into developing Asian markets:

American manufacturers are increasingly interested in foreign trade. In addition, advertising done for companies in the countries served helps to stimulate business and raise the standards of living. Work done abroad by advertising men from this country [the United States] makes friends for America and is an important contribution to the national interest.[13]

He urged other American agencies to establish their own networks:

It is because the opportunity is great and the job to be done so vast that we hope other advertising agencies in this country will look around in foreign lands and develop opportunities for their successful operation abroad. It would help us as well as them, and it would benefit the U.S. in many ways.[14]

Clients like Esso and Colgate-Palmolive were among the major TNCs to take advantage of Grant's facilities in Kuala Lumpur. The pioneering American TNAA was "an instant success" and it had more business than it could handle.[15]

Government-Private Sector Alliance

Other TNAAs bringing similar sophisticated Western advertising skills and resources, including a heavy reliance on English-language advertising materials, soon arrived on the scene to intensify advertising competition, especially after the government had taken steps to establish an investment climate favorable to foreigners. Unlike Indonesia, neither Malaysia nor Singapore had any qualms about allowing wholly owned foreign advertising agencies staffed by expatriates.

While agencies were developing and the manufacturing sector was expanding, the mass media, particularly broadcasting, were growing. The British had left an efficient radio service (and information department), and it was expanded to explain the new government's development programs and to try to develop a national consciousness among the diverse Malay, Chinese, and Indian communities, each with its own culture, religion, language, newspapers, and government-run vernacular radio broadcasts.

Commercial broadcasting gradually evolved from the government's desire to increase industrialization. The head of the commercial division in the Ministry of Information has said:

Every facet of industrial planning was looked into minutely. A World Bank Mission even recommended that the national radio system should lend a hand in creating consumer demand for locally-made goods. The mission felt that although there were sufficient newspapers in the country, they neither had the reach nor the circulation to carry the advertising message effectively. Until the Malay, English, Chinese and Tamil [an

Indian dialect] newspapers grew in circulation and the populace became more literate, public service radio should help to carry the advertising messages. Adoption of this recommendation immediately got the government directly involved in advertising communication. But since public radio represented the voice of the government, especially in an underdeveloped environment, it was decided that all radio commercials must be in consonance with a specially drawn up advertising code. That was in 1962.[16]

By late 1963 television was started, and the first televison commercial—for Benson and Hedges cigarettes, a British TNC product—appeared in December of 1965.[17] By 1967, television advertising revenue had surpassed radio advertising revenue.[18]

Advertising naturally expanded under such a receptive government. Unlike in Indonesia, the government made no effort to nationalize foreign-owned property, abolish the colonial language (English), ban American movies, break up the entrenched trading houses, or sever diplomatic relations with the West.

In Malaysia's case, then, as with Singapore, there has been neither a break between political colonialism and independence nor even much rhetoric about "imperialism," "socialism," "self-reliance," or "moderation." Functioning as centers in the Periphery, Malaysia's leaders have been generally conservative, English-educated, upperclass elites from the three major communal political parties—United Malays National Organization (UMNO), Malaysian Chinese Association (MCA), and Malaysian Indian Congress (MIC). The leaders of these parties had played a major role in negotiating a peaceful, nonrevolutionary transition from colonial rule to independence and encouraging cooperation with foreigners in developing the economy. There was no abrupt change in the distribution of political or economic power, and a coalition of urban leaders remained in firm control via the Alliance Party (a coalition of UMNO, MCA, and MIC) and later an expanded grouping that today is called the *Barisan National* ("National Front").[19]

Development policies and plans under such an alliance relied on stability and harmony of interests for economic growth. Urban businessmen (primarily Chinese and foreign investors), an essentially laissez-faire economic system, and continued reliance on the export of a few raw materials were essential elements of Malaysia's basic development climate. Under Malaysia's style of development and democracy, progress was considered best promoted by the private sector, and colonial penetration patterns were not significantly altered.

Two basic reasons seem to account for Malaysia's postcolonial policies based on caution, accommodation, status quo maintenance, and interethnic cooperation. First, it was clearly in the interests of the rulers, including MCA leaders and businessmen, to keep the ethnic groups apart and to preserve the close ties with Center nations so as to maintain the lucrative markets for the nation's vast resources. Second, these elites thought that Malaysia's delicately balanced multi-ethnic population could not handle open, Western-style political processes. A delicate balance of power had to be maintained, and only a coalition of English-educated elites working together behind the scenes to encourage economic growth and to discourage widespread political activity could keep the fragile plural society together.

This development approach allowed urban Western-influenced advertising to thrive. As one writer put it:

> Advertising is all around us in Singapore and metropolitan Malaysia, catching our eyes, assailing our ears, working its subliminal way into our mind. It governs our lives, fashions our habits, sets our pace. Yet we knock it. Because it is fashionable to do so. It is a product of Western civilization which we are making an integral part of our own.[20]

By 1977, eight major TNAAs were competing in Malaysia.[21] By the early 1980s, several others, including Compton, Needham, Harper & Steer, and a second O&M unit, were operating. Despite the obvious complexities of preparing messages for Malaysia's multilingual peoples, the TNAAs liked the Malaysian environment, and they prospered. One Ogilvy & Mather executive has suggested why the TNAAs are so comfortable:

> here in Malaysia we are living in one of the last bastions of capitalism, of free enterprise and of competition—all essential prerequisites to the development of a healthy advertising industry. The pace at which change is taking place in business here is boldly set by an enlightened, adventurous Government and by what must surely be one of the most aggressive business communities in the world. Even the Deputy Prime Minister is on record as having said, 'You do not have to go abroad to become a millionaire' . . . . the advertising business in Malaysia will become even more competitive. This country is a cockpit of advertising. It is unlike virtually any market in the world and certainly unlike any other in Southeast Asia. Elsewhere in this region . . . a typical ad agency has perhaps 3 or 4 large clients and 20, 50, or 100 tiny ones. Here it is different. In Malaysia we have big companies well-run, profitable, international and local companies, and a relatively affluent population—the 4th richest population in Southeast Asia. The typical large agency in Kuala Lumpur has a relatively small list of large clients and an even smaller list of small ones. Clients move infrequently and are fiercely contested when they do. This is hardly surprising when so much is at stake.[22]

The TNAA's Dominance

The TNAAs have much at stake in Malaysia. Table 23 shows the advertising dollars that are at stake in Malaysia, and tables 24 through 26 suggest the degree of dominance that the TNAAs, compared to indigenous agen-

Table 23

Estimate on Expenditure on Advertising in Malaysia, 1968-76

(In Thousands of Malaysian Dollars)

	1968	1969	1970	1972	1973	1974	1975	1976
Newspapers	19,800	24,100	25,100	38,900	45,400	31,200	45,100	55,500
Magazines	(2,000)	(2,500)	(3,500)	4,800	10,600	8,800	8,200	8,400
Publications	(4,000)	(4,000)	(4,000)	(4,000)	(4,000)	(4,000)	(4,000)	(4,000)
Rediffusion	300	400	600	500	400	400	600	600
Radio	4,000	4,100	4,100	5,300	5,000	4,300	4,400	3,800
TV	5,200	6,300	8,000	9,300	7,400	9,300	9,300	11,500
Cinema	(7,500)	(9,000)	(11,000)	(12,000)	(12,000)	4,600	6,800	10,100
Outdoor	(6,000)	(6,000)	(6,000)	(6,000)	(6,000)	(6,000)	(6,000)	(6,000)
Total Media	(48,800)	(56,300)	(62,300)	(80,800)	(90,800)	(68,600)	(84,400)	(99,900)
Production	(4,900)	(5,600)	(6,200)	(12,000)	(13,500)	(10,290)	(12,660)	(15,000)
TOTAL	53,700	61,900	68,500	92,800	104,300	78,890	97,060	114,900
		+15%	+11%	+35% (2 yrs.)	+12%	-24%	+23%	+18%

Bracketed figures denote estimated figures.

NOTES: One American dollar is equivalent to approximately 2.4 Malaysian dollars. In 1976, therefore, total estimated Malaysian advertising expenditure was about $48 million in U.S. dollars. Display advertising has been monitored throughout the 1968-76 period. Costs do not reflect, however, frequency or special discounts or loadings for some special positions. "Classified" and "Shipping" advertising was monitored only in 1969, 1970, 1972, and 1975. 1969-72 averaged about one third of total expenditure, and 1975 about one quarter. Estimates for 1968 and 1973 are, therefore, made on the same proportionate basis as 1969-72, but 1974 is based on 1975.

Magazines: Monitoring of regularly published magazines started only in 1972. About 25 such publications were monitored in 1972. Figures for 1968-1970 are sheer guesses. Fewer "high cost" consumer magazines (but more low cost technical magazines) were available in 1968, so expenditures were lower both actually and as percentage of total expenditure than now.

Publications: This section is intended to cover programs, charity publications, and similar "on-off"-type publications. It has never been possible to monitor these. The figures are sheer guesswork and have been maintained at the same level throughout the years because these publications seem to have declined in relative importance in recent years. The amount of money spent on them is probably about the same, but it forms a smaller proportion of total expenditure.

Production: This heading includes all media production, press, radio and films and print production through advertising agencies. Based on 10% of total media billings 1968-1970, and 15% of total media billings for 1972-1976. This is based on rough "production Reserve" formulae used by agencies and assumes that non-agency expenditures would follow the same pattern.

Rediffusion is the government-licensed, but privately-owned wire broadcasting service that originates over two broadcast networks in Kuala Lumpur, Ipoh, Penang, and Butterworth in Malaysia. Rediffusion has "sister" stations in Singapore and Hong Kong. It began in Malaya in 1949. It is a unique advertising and entertainment in Malaysia and its programs are directed predominantly to a Chinese audience. The number of sets on service has been expanding by at least 5% a year throughout the seventies. Programs, such as Chinese serials from Hong Kong or locally-produced, are extremely popular.

SOURCE: Fred Kent, regional media director for Grant, Kenyon & Eckhardt, Singapore, provided me with these estimates which he prepared during May of 1977. His original sources included "FERO Monitoring Reports," 1968-72; "MIS Adex Reports," 1973-76; and the two major cinema advertising organizations, Pearl & Dean and Cathay Organization, 1968-73. I interviewed Kent on 15 November 1977.

cies (either Malay or non-Malay owned and managed), have over Malaysian advertising.

Obviously, the TNAAs are doing something right because they are clearly far better established than either local Chinese or the relatively few indigenous Malay agencies. Compared to the local agencies, the TNAAs have better—or at least more Westernized—creativity. For example, by 1978 Malaysian advertising had won two CLIO awards (the transnational advertising industry's "Oscars" for worldwide advertising excellence), and both involved commercials by the same TNAA, Ogilvy & Mather, working in 1973 for Dunlop and in 1978 for Union Carbide's Eveready batteries. Also, the TNAAs win nearly all of the annual Juita awards, which the Malaysian Ministry of Information presents to the producers of those commercials judged the best in promoting social responsibility. Winning such awards takes talent and facilities. Generally, the TNAAs consistently have better physical facilities, a bigger and better trained staff, larger billings and income, and more of the big-spending TNC clients. As table 24 shows, of the ten biggest agencies for which data are available, only one, Union Advertising, is *not* foreign-affiliated. Union is a pioneering Malaysian Chinese agency that began in 1945 as basically an outdoor advertising and commercial art shop. A major client is Yeo Hiap Seng, a giant Chinese manufacturer of sauces, canned foods, and soft drinks in Malaysia and Singapore.

Estimates are that the six or seven largest agencies handle about 85 percent of the total advertising expenditure in Malaysia. According to a report by a group of local (non-TNAA) agencies, "The remaining agencies are fighting, principally with each other, for the remaining 15%."[23] After newspapers, television is the most important advertising medium in the nation. Table 27 lists the ten largest TV advertisers and shows how this all-TNC group of advertisers makes heavy use of TNAA agencies. Approximately 95 percent of all TV advertising revenue comes from TNC or joint-venture firms and only 5 percent from local advertisers, such as Lam Soon, Amoy Canning, Kee Huat Radio, and Social Welfare Lotteries.[24]

As in Indonesia, some of the major TNAA clients in Malaysia are the same ones served by the agency in a number of other nations. For example, PTM Thompson, a joint-venture with JWT, handles Lux soap advertising in Malaysia in the same manner JWT offices do in most places where the Unilever product is sold; McCann-Erickson handles Coca-Cola, Gillette, Goodyear, and General Motors; Ted Bates services Colgate-Palmolive in Malaysia, just as it does in the United States; SSC&B:Lintas handles most of Unilever's advertising in Malaysia, just as it does virtually around the world; Leo Burnett handles Beecham advertising in Malaysia and elsewhere in Southeast Asia; and Hakuhodo handles National products, just as it does in Japan. Ogilvy & Mather in Malaysia has very strong ties to its parent TNAA. For example, of O&M's fifteen most important interna-

Table 24

Summary of Major Advertising Agencies in Malaysia, 1977-78

(in U.S. Dollars)

I. Transnational

Agency	Founded	Ownership	Billings	Total Staff		Total No. Accounts	Major Accounts
				Total	Expatriate		
Ted Bates a/	1964	Wholly owned by Ted Bates & Co., New York	$4,250,000	57	2	16	Colgate-Palmolive, Hong Kong Bank, British Airways, Malayan Breweries, Champion Spark Plug, General Electric, Volvo, Mazola, United Motor Works (distributors of imported heavy equipment), Warner Lambert, Trebor, Fraser & Neave
Leo Burnett b/	1966	Wholly owned by Leo Burnett Co., Chicago	$6,088,170	70	4	32	Malaysian Airline System (MAS), c/ Beecham, Rothmans, Carlsberg beer, Chupa Chups, Levis, Bata, Qantas, Mobil, Ford, Boeing, The Chartered Bank, Pepsi Cola, Van Houten, Boh Plantations, Kimberly Clark (Kotex, Kleenex), Diethelm (Handyplast), Eastern Agencies (Optrex, DOM liqueur), S. C. Johnson (Pledge, Glade, Raid)
Grant, Kenyon & Eckhardt	1958	75% by Kenyon & Eckhardt, New York; 25% local d/	$1,650,000	34	2	23	Nestles, Getz Corp. (Tang, Maxwell House), Yellow Pages, Sterling Drug, Imperial Tobacco, Sports Toto Malaysia (lotteries), Kelvinator, Cycle & Carriage (Mercedes-Benz), Wearne Bros. (British Leyland, Chrysler), Caltex (projects), Cadbury Confectionery, Helena Rubinstein
Hakuhodo	1973	49% by Hakuhodo, Tokyo, and 51% local (including 30% Malay)	$ 750,000	20	1	34	Matsushita Group of Companies (National products), Japan Air Lines (JAL), Boustead Trading (Kao Shampoo, detergents), Perbiba (housing developers)
McCann-Erickson	1965	Wholly owned by McCann-Erickson Worldwide, part of The Interpublic Group of Companies, New York City	$2,271,390	14	4	13	Coca-Cola, General Motors (Opel), Max Factor, Rothmans of Pall Mall, Kodak, Monsanto, Esso, Gillette, Goodyear, Wearnes (General Motors dealerships), Par Paints, Kentucky Fried Chicken

Agency	Year	Ownership	Revenue				Clients
Ogilvy & Mather	1971 e/	Wholly owned by Ogilvy & Mather Int'l, New York	$5,968,380	86	1	23	Nestles, Malayan Tobacco Co. (BAT), Borneo Motors (Toyota), Avon, Cavenham, Rolex, Pakistan Int'l Airlines, Citizen watch, Dunlop, Johnson & Johnson, 3M, Philips, Shell, New Straits Times, ICI, Union Carbide, Unilever, Upali, Tractors Malaysia (Caterpillar), Chesebrough-Ponds, Century Motors (Renault), Champion Motors (Volkswagen, Audi, Rover), Chase Manhattan Bank, Lam Soon, Metrojaya Dept. Store, Texwood Jeans, Orchard Motors (Vauxhall, Bedford, Holden), Caldbeck MacGregor (Johnnie Walker, Courvoisier), Guinness
SSC&B:Lintas	1961	70% by SSC&B:Lintas Int'l, London, and 30% local (Malay)	$4,340,853	51	1	16	Lever Bros. (Breeze, Planta, Lifebuoy, Close-up, etc.), New Straits Times, Dutch Baby Milk Industries, Boustead (Old Parr whiskey, J&B whiskey), Lipton Overseas, Flytox insecticide, Glucolin, Behn Meyer (trading house), Cycle & Carriage (Mitsubishi Colt), Remy Martin
PTM Thompson	1975	25% by J. Walter Thompson, New York, and 75% local (25% for each of three partners - MAS, Tourist Development Corporation (TDC), and PERNAS, the state trading corporation	$3,246,540	53	2	18	MAS (airline), c/ TDC (Malaysian tourism), R. J. Reynolds Tobacco Co. (Winston, Camel, More), Holiday Inn, McDonnell Douglas DC-10, Federal Industrial Development Authority (FIDA), Reckitt & Colman, Harpers Trading (Estee Lauder cosmetics, Aramis, Ariston domestic appliances), Lever Bros. (Sunsilk, Lux soap), Parker pens, Pernas-Sime Darby (Camus Cognac), 7-Up, Malayan Banking, Dunlop, Esin Canning
Asian Marketing Communications	1976	40% by Zecha Associates Ltd., a regional advertising/public affairs agency in Hong Kong, and 60% by Melewar Holdings, a diversified Malay investment holding organization	$1,000,000	22	2	16	Mopiko ointment, Suzuki motocycles, Mazda, Lion Dentifrace (all handled for Dentsu), Kuala Lumpur Hilton, IBM, Development & Commercial Bank, Behn Meyer, Anika Impot & Edgar Sdn. Bhd., Mobil

II. Local

Agency	Year	Ownership	Billings				Clients
Associated Publicity	1969	Local	$ 875,000	23	0	7	National iron, battery, & home appliances (by Matsushita Electric), Kumpulan Barkath (Hacks sweets, Sunquick), City Motors (Alfa Romeo cars), Ajinomoto
Idris, Lim Associates	1975	Local (Malay), including 25% equity with Urban Development Authority (UDA); loose affiliation with MANA f/	$ 467,000	15	1	. . .	East Asiatic Co. (refrigerator), North Borneo Trading, P.K.N.S. (Selangor State Development), United Estates Project (housing development)
Kace	1971	30% local, 70% Hagemeyer (trading house)	. . .	16	0	27	Hagemeyer (Timex, BIC, JVC Nivico), Trebor sweets
LC Internada	1975	60% local (Malay) 40% Guthrie Berhad g/	$ 467,000	12	0	17	Asia Motor Co. (Mazda cars, STP products), Malaysia Industrial Development Finance Bhd., Lam Soon Oil and Soap, Amateur Photo Stores (Akai sound equipment)
Marketing and Advertising Management Services	1975	70% local through subsidiary of Bank Pertanian Malaysia, and 30% foreign	$ 167,000	7	2	5	Bank Pertanian (agricultural banking)
Johan Design Associates	1976*	Local (Malay)	. . .	. . .	. . .	. . .	Toshiba, Tourist Development Corporation, Bank Bumiputra, Malayan Manufacturers (Komatsu)
Rochdale Public Relations	1974	Local	. . .	18	0	. . .	MCIS (insurance), Jaya Puri (hotel), Secuba Holdings (Yamaha small tractors)
Ronald Quay Associates	1974	Local	$ 417,000	19	0	. . .	United Detergent Industries (Tiger detergent), Dow Chemical, AIA (insurance)
Trang Creative	1974	Local (Malay)	. . .	16	0	12	(not available)
Union Advertising	1945	Local	$ 833,000	24	0	51	Raleigh Cycles, Social Welfare Lotteries, Sissons paints, Yee Hiap Seng (canned food and drinks), Jack Chia (Tiger Balm and headache

Wings Creative Consultants	1976*/	Local	. . .	0	Honda, Beecham (product development), Matsushita air conditioners, Bang Bang jeans, Shriro (China) Ltd. (Nikon, Hasselblad)
Mascom Associates	1975	Local (Malay) with UDA holding 66% equity	. . .	0	(not available)

* = Estimate

NOTES: Most of these agencies are accredited as full-service agencies and belong to the Association of Accredited Advertising Agents (4As) of Malaysia. All agencies are based in Kuala Lumpur, although several have "sister" agencies or branches in neighboring Singapore. PTM Thompson, for example, has a small representative office in Singapore. Singapore agencies with Malaysian branches are not listed here. For example, Tom Tan Associates and Henry Chia Associates are based in Singapore but maintain small Kuala Lumpur offices.

"Local ownership" refers to equity control by Malaysian citizens, whether ethnically Malays, Chinese, or Indians. Unless specified, "local" tends to refer to Malaysian Chinese ownership rather than Malay or Indian.

a/ Founded as part of Cathay Advertising Ltd., a regional agency based in Hong Kong but having branches in Kuala Lumpur, Singapore, and Bangkok. Ted Bates took over the organization in 1963. In 1974, the Cathay offices dropped its original name and its well-known dragon symbol, and took the name Bates.

b/ Founded as a branch of Jackson Wain, a large Australian agency, by Peter G. Beaumont in 1966 to serve clients like Qantas airlines. Leo Burnett, Chicago, took over in 1971, but Beaumont continued as managing director of the Kuala Lumpur operations.

c/ Leo Burnett originally handled the MAS account starting with its first campaigns in 1972. In 1975, part of the account shifted to PTM Thompson, in which MAS had 25% equity. In 1978, Burnett regained the entire account after it was resigned by PTM Thompson.

d/ Founded as a branch of Grant International, which in 1975 was bought over by the Kenyon & Eckhardt Group, New York City. In this particular context, "local" refers to Malaysians and expatriates working in the Kuala Lumpur office.

e/ In 1971, Ogilvy & Mather acquired the Kuala Lumpur and Singapore offices of S. H. Benson when it bought that London-based British TNAA. O&M's Southeast Asian regional coordinator is based in the Kuala Lumpur office.

f/ Marketing & Advertising Network of Asia (MANA) is a loosely-knit group of national or local agencies, including Idris Lim Associates, within the region.

g/ Guthrie Berhad, part of the London-based Guthrie Corp., has a 40 percent equity stake in LC Holdings, which owns the agency.

SOURCES: These basic facts and figures on major agencies in Malaysia were obtained from a very wide variety of sources, including personal interviews with agency executives and others knowledgeable about the Malaysian industry and questionnaires sent to agency heads in Malaysia, as well as Singapore and Indonesia. Advertising is a rapidly changing business and information about clients, staffing, billings, etc. quickly become out of date. For this reason, the information should be treated cautiously.

Table 25

Major Transnational Agency Billings in Malaysia, 1967-77

(in U.S. Dollars)

Agency	1967	1970	1971	1972	1973	1974	1975	1976	1977
Ted Bates	. . .	. . .	. . .	. . .	. . .	. . .	. . .	4,000,000 a/	4,250,000 a/
Leo Burnett	. . .	4,087,527 b/	4,487,201	5,007,000	5,835,000	7,853,000	7,315,000	7,174,000	6,088,170
Grant Kenyon & Eckhardt	650,000	700,000	900,000	1,300,000	1,846,000	1,838,000	1,280,750 c/	1,332,523	1,650,000
Hakuhodo	. . .	. . .	. . .	. . .	150,000	365,000	500,000	750,000	. . .
McCann-Erickson	900,000	1,980,000	4,315,000	5,583,000	4,022,000	3,342,000	4,209,000 d/	2,381,619	2,271,390
Ogilvy & Mather	2,224,000 e/	3,500,600 e/	4,130,000	3,917,000	5,388,000	5,417,246	6,315,272	7,882,663	5,968,380
SSC&B: Lintas	1,007,000	1,330,000	1,245,000	1,837,000	4,421,000	5,131,650	4,272,000	4,334,000	4,340,853
PTM Thompson f/	. . .	. . .	. . .	. . .	. . .	. . .	1,394,000	3,333,000	3,246,540

NOTES: These data are given to present a rough picture of how the transnational advertising agencies have grown over the decade 1967-77. Data should be treated cautiously since exchange rates vary and some billings are only estimates. Whenever figures conflicted, I used the higher total. Transnational and regional agencies operating in Malaysia through a correspondent or loose affiliation are not cited here. All of the above eight agencies involve non-Malaysian equity from the transnational agency headquarters. All of the eight have their Malaysian office in Kuala Lumpur. Hakuhodo, the Japanese TNAA, is the only one without American ownership.

a/ In excess of

b/ Operating as Jackson, Wain & Co., Burnett's predecessor in Kuala Lumpur.

c/ Formerly Grant Int'l Malaysia, it became part of Kenyon & Eckhardt's worldwide group in 1975.

d/ 1967-75 data are for both Malaysia and Singapore McCann operations.

e/ Operating as S. H. Benson, O&M's predecessor in Kuala Lumpur.

f/ In Malaysia, JWT operates through PTM Thompson advertising.

SOURCES: Hakuhodo figures obtained through personal correspondence with the agency's Kuala Lumpur office, June 18, 1977. Other data is compiled from annual "International Agency Sections" of Advertising Age in 1968 and the years 1971 through 1978, or from information supplied directly by the agencies and estimates from sources knowledgeable about Malaysian advertising.

Table 26

Several Major Transnational Agency Gross Income Figures in Malaysia, 1973-77

(In U.S. Dollars)

Agency	1973	1974	1975	1976	1977
Ted Bates	. . .	. . .	. . .	$ 600,000	$ 650,00[*]/
Leo Burnett	. . .	. . .	$1,058,000	1,076,000	912,780[a]/
Grant, Kenyon & Eckhardt	$537,000	$343,000	. . .	261,552	328,558
McCann-Erickson	. . .	501,000	631,000[b]/	357,060	340,560
Ogilvy & Mather	937,000	1,045,000	946,817	1,181,808	1,145,100
SSC&B:Lintas	637,686	787,845	630,000	652,000	667,095
PTM Thompson[c]/	. . .	. . .	209,000	500,000	486,750

* = Estimate

NOTE: TNAAs' income figures for a particular office are far more difficult to obtain - - even in estimate form - - than the annual billings. These data for a five-year period should be treated cautiously since exchange rates vary.

[a]/ Burnett income loss is probably due in part to the loss of part of the Malaysian Airline System (MAS) account to PTM Thompson, JWT's Malaysian partner.

[b]/ Includes both Malaysian and Singaporean operations. Figures after 1975 are for Malaysian office.

[c]/ JWT had 25 percent equity in this joint-venture agency. The other 75 percent was shared equally by three Malaysian government bodies, Pernas, MAS, and the Tourist Development Corp. (TDC).

SOURCES: Data are compiled from annual "International Agency Sections" of Advertising Age, 1974-78. Figures are either estimates or reported voluntarily by the agencies themselves.

tional clients, three—Unilever, Shell, and Avon—are handled in Malaysia. Several O&M clients in Malaysia are also the agency's clients in both Singapore and Indonesia. They are: American Express, Bayer, BAT, Cavenham, Guinness, Union Carbide, Unilever, 3M, and Philips.[25]

Over the more than two decades since the first TNAA arrived in Malaysia, some tensions between the foreign corporations and the government and between the foreign agencies and the local agencies have developed.[26] The clear domination of the advertising agency business by the TNAAs, particularly by wholly owned foreign operations, has produced some resentment from Malaysian agencies, both Chinese and Malay. Also, the lack of more than a handful of successful, Malay-owned or managed agencies has been part of the government's overall concern that the modern commercial sector has not had much participation from the indigenous people.[27] But these advertising-related concerns have not become major political issues. They have resulted in neither advertising industry action (as in Indonesia with P3I's strong campaign against foreigners) nor in government action (as in the Indonesian government's ban on foreign ownership of any domestic trading or service business).[28] The result is that advertising power—like economic power generally—has remained largely in the combined hands of foreigners and local Chinese, both of whom have largely been happy with the government's economic growth policies

Table 27

Major Television Advertisers in Malaysia, 1977

Name	Agency
1. Malayan Tobacco Company (MTC)	Ogilvy & Mather
2. Rothmans of Pall Mall	Leo Burnett, McCann-Erickson
3. Nestle's Products	Ogilvy & Mather, Grant, Kenyon & Eckhardt
4. Lever Brothers	SSC&B:Lintas, PTM Thompson
5. Colgate Palmolive	Ted Bates
6. Beecham	Leo Burnett
7. Bristol Myers	U. S. P. Needham
8. Warner Lambert	Ted Bates
9. Dumex (East Asiatic Co.)	Henry Chia Associates
10. Gillette	McCann-Erickson

NOTE: The Malaysian Ministry of Information considers the total expenditure
of individual advertisers on Television Malaysia confidential information.
The range between the biggest advertiser and the tenth biggest is estimated
to be from approximately $792,000 per year for MTC down to approximately
$333,000 per year for Gillette. All these TNCs advertise several different
brands and products on television. Henry Chia Associates is a Singapore
agency with a Kuala Lumpur branch. USP Needham is a TNAA with regional
offices in Singapore. It does not have a Malaysian office and, therefore,
either places through a Malaysian agency or else directly itself but at a
reduced commission since it is not considered a local agency. MTC is the
Malaysian British-American Tobacco operation. East Asiatic is a Danish
trading company that also makes Vespa scooters, Carlsberg beer, and Dumex
powdered milk products.

Many major TV advertisers also are among the biggest overall adver-
tisers in Malaysia. In addition to these ten corporations, other major
Malaysian advertisers, often in non-TV media, would include Malaysian
Airlines System, Johnson & Johnson, Dunlop, Borneo Motors (Toyota cars),
Fraser & Neave (Coca-Cola and other drinks), Bata (shoes), Pernas, and
Sports Toto. Virtually all of these corporations are active members of
the Malaysian Advertising Assn. (MAA).

SOURCE: Personal interview with Peter Kum, head, Commercial Division,
Malaysian Ministry of Information, Kuala Lumpur, May 28, 1977.

through the years. Neither group, then, has had its freedom to own and
manage advertising agencies impeded by indigenous Malay pressure—
official or otherwise. Despite the fact that government has always been
Malay-controlled, Malays have remained very much junior partners in
Malaysian advertising (and the private sector generally). The government
has not been especially concerned about "justice" or the redistribution of
power within the advertising industry per se. Issues of autonomy or
sovereignty seldom arise in Malaysia with reference to advertising or anything else. This is in sharp contrast to Indonesia, where these concerns are
prominent.

Advertising in Malaysia is closely tied to broader issues of intercommunal accommodation and mutual deterrence. A major reason for Malaysia's remarkably flexible, favorable policies toward the TNAAs undoubtedly has to do with the nation's extremely difficult and complex racial situation and the government's historic firm commitment to Western-style development patterns. The "moderate" and "pragmatic" Malaysian government has always been committed to real economic growth and free enterprise, and it has felt that in large measure these are only fostered through substantial foreign investment. This comment by then-Prime Minister Datuk Hussein Onn is typical of policy statements strongly supporting foreign investment and greater industrialization:

> To enable the pricate sector to play its due role fully and effectively, the Government will give high priority to the need to maintain at all times a favorable climate for investment in Malaysia. In the design and implementation of our policies and programs, especially those which affect private enterprise and initiative, the Government will take great care to ensure that they always prove helpful in enabling the private sector to continue to contribute, in a dynamic manner, to our development goals. A very important aspect of Malaysia's development strategy is the need for accelerated industrial development. One of our economic priorities is to step up the inflow of foreign investment in new industrial projects in the country. Malaysia has a long record of good relationship with foreign investors, and I would like to assure all potential investors that this good relationship will be maintained and improved upon.[29]

To change the "good relationship" between the TNAAs and Malaysia by, for example, requiring all agencies to become 100 percent Malaysian (or even Malay-only) businesses or restricting the use of "alien" languages other than the sole national language (Malay), as Indonesia has done, would risk losing favor not merely with the TNAAs, but, more important, with foreign investors generally. The government recognizes that the TNAAs are not only TNCs themselves but also are TNC servants. As long as the TNCs argue that they need professional advertising services that still are lacking in Malaysia, the government is likely to respond to these needs and allow the TNAAs to operate more or less as they always have.

In Indonesia the government loses nothing—politically or symbolically—by efforts to weaken the Chinese politically, economically, and culturally or to reduce advertising domination by foreigners. In Malaysia, however, the situation is different. The Chinese are a substantial 35 percent of the population, Malays about 53 percent, and other groups (mainly Indians) about 12 percent.[30] The Malaysian government would risk not only major economic disruption but also racial violence if it were to try to fully implement some of Indonesia's policies in such sensitive areas as national language, cultural identity, or domestic trading. A major change, such as a ban on foreign ownership of ad agencies, would certainly intensify already existing tensions and competition between the Malays and the Chinese over domestic trade. The Chinese would surely only get richer by moving in to fill any gap created by the exit of the TNAAs, since the Malay agencies—with few exceptions—are in no position to compete with the Chinese agencies (or, of course, with the TNAAs).[31] In a sense, then, the government uses dynamic ethnic tensions and "responsible" TNAAs to help maintain political stability and overall TNC confidence in the economy and at the same time prevent total control of advertising from falling into Chinese hands. A number of Malays told me in no uncertain terms that if they had to choose between Chinese or foreign domination of their nation's advertising, they would opt for continued foreign control. As long as political power remains in Malay hands, the Malays feel they are in a position to have some control over foreign-owned advertising agencies and other investments.

Any crackdown on the TNAAs in Malaysia would be resisted by the advertising industry as a whole. This is because the two professional associations, the 4As and the MAA, want the status quo maintained. Neither organization is controlled by Malays. The president of the 4As, for example, is Mrs. Janet Yeo, a Chinese who is managing director of the largest non-TNAA agency in Malaysia. The vice president is an expatriate, Peter Beaumont, managing director of Leo Burnett. He is widely regarded as the most influential ad man in Malaysia. Of the association's twenty-one member agencies in 1977, only about two could be considered "Malay" in terms of both ownership and management control by individual Malays. Of the association's nine officers and committee members, seven were expatriates with TNAAs and two were Chinese with local agencies.[32] The Malaysian 4As contrasts sharply with Indonesia's P3I, which, in the name of Indonesian nationalism, has tended to be very antiforeign and anti-Chinese and has sought special government protection for indigenous agencies. The 4As has tended to be heavily TNAA- and Chinese-influenced and it has not sought government involvement in the industry. Like advertising organizations in the West, 4As prefers voluntary self-regulation through industry codes and independent groups such as the Advertising Standards Authority Malaysia (ASAM).[33] The latter body, established by the Malaysian advertising industry to maintain certain standards, has been chaired since 1978 by Mrs. Paddy Schubert, a public affairs officer with the Kuala Lumpur office of Burson-Marsteller, the transnational PR firm. She formerly was the director of trade relations for Shell, chairman of the Malaysian Institute of Management, and vice president of the Malaysian public relations organization. ASAM's patron was Malaysia's first prime minister, Tunku Abdul Rahman, who at the time also was chairman of *The Star* English-language newspaper.

The 4As organization works closely with ASAM and also with the advertisers' interest group, the MAA. This organization has considerable influence with the government since it is run by the largest advertisers in the nation. Like the 4As, it is controlled by a coalition of foreign and Chinese commercial interests, and it avoids taking aggressive positions on controversies. All meetings are conducted in English (rather than the official national language), and for years its president was a Malaysian Chinese—James Peter Chin, head of communications for Dunlop Malaysian Industries. Of the eleven officers and Council members in 1977, for example, eight were Chinese, and they represented such major corporations as Rothmans of Pall Mall, Nestlé, Bata, Fraser & Neave, Lever Bros., Tractors Malaysia (Caterpillar dealer), and Malaysian Airline System (MAS).[34] The MAA's membership in 1977 totalled 174—97 ordinary members, including virtually every prominent TNC and local advertiser in Malaysia, and 77 associate members, including advertising agencies, research organizations, materials suppliers, and media. The latter included all major local and transnational media, including *Time* Magazine and *Reader's Digest*.[35] In addition to maintaining liaison with the government and with ad agencies and the media, the MAA sponsored educational and social programs.

Because of the harmony of interests between media, advertisers, and agencies, organizations like the MAA understandably do not want the basic system to be changed. The MAA does not actively seek government intervention in advertising and it opposes efforts to weaken the power of the TNAAs for fear the quality of its members' advertising may decline under "Malaysianization." An issue such as foreign domination of advertising that the P3I openly addresses in Indonesia would never be the subject of much debate in public forums or even within the industry.[36] Ethnic politics in Malaysia dictate that if and when such sensitive issues must be discussed, they are handled at senior levels and behind closed doors.[37]

Tensions

After the 1969 general elections, the nation's deep-rooted racial tensions came to the surface in violent riots in Kuala Lumpur. Like the Malari demonstrations in Indonesia, the Malaysian disturbances affected the whole society, including advertising. Significantly, however, developments since 1969 have *not* altered the basic structure of the Malaysian advertising industry. Modern advertising began in foreign hands, and it continues that way today. The Malaysian government has consciously and successfully implemented policies to ensure that the *content* of advertising messages, particularly on television, reflects Malaysian values and lifestyles and that all firms' *hiring practices* are more receptive to Malay participation. But it has not implemented policies that would place advertising agencies under majority ownership and managerial control of Malaysian citizens.

The 1969 riots, however, did force Malaysians and their government to more explicitly address the basic problems behind the nation's ongoing troubles. For more than a decade after independence, Malaysia's de-

Table 28

Peninsular Malaysia: Number of Poor Households, 1970

	Total			Rural			Urban		
	Total households (000)	Total poor households (000)	Poverty (%)	Total households (000)	Total poor households (000)	Poverty (%)	Total households (000)	Total poor households (000)	Poverty (%)
Agriculture	852.9	582.4	68.3	816.2	560.2	68.6	36.7	22.2	60.5
Mining	32.4	11.1	34.3	27.0	9.3	34.4	5.4	1.8	33.3
Manufacturing	150.2	48.5	32.3	66.2	28.8	43.5	84.0	19.7	23.4
Construction	35.0	12.8	36.6	15.5	6.9	44.5	19.5	5.9	30.2
Utilities	12.8	4.7	36.7	5.6	2.3	41.1	7.2	2.4	33.3
Commerce	162.3	49.2	30.3	74.1	30.8	41.6	88.2	18.4	20.9
Transport	61.3	22.4	36.5	26.1	11.7	44.8	35.2	10.7	30.4
Services	299.1	60.7	20.3	136.0	33.7	24.8	163.1	27.0	16.6
TOTAL	1,606.0	791.8	49.3	1,166.7	683.7	58.6	439.3	108.1	24.6

NOTE: "Poverty (%)" refers to the percentage of poor households in the total. Those in this category are below the income that the government
considers required for minimum subsistence or what is considered "poverty line income."

SOURCE: Table 9-1 in Third Malaysia Plan 1976 - 1980 Kuala Lumpur, Malaysia: The Government Press, 1976, p. 161

velopment strategies seemed to be working—at least physical violence and political conflict were minimal. Despite Communist terrorism and a state of emergency between 1948 and 1960 and the usual problems confronting any young society, Malaysia experienced a very impressive record of economic progress and stability.

In terms of the conventional American model of development, the Malaysian experience was both exciting and successful. Per capita income, for example, became the highest in Asia after Japan and Singapore. The nation's policymakers and planners were better educated, more efficient, and harder working than those in most developing nations. And Malaysia had an abundance of natural resources and an adequate infrastructure, originally designed by the British and still efficiently removing raw materials from the hinterlands and transferring them to Japan and the West.

Despite Malaysia's harmonious relations with the industrial world, its well-organized administrative system, its vast natural resources, and its obvious progress in terms of such traditional indicators as GNP, urbanization, and mass media diffusion, Malaysia has not been a very happy or unified nation. Paradoxically, poverty has existed amidst plenty, and genuine development—in terms of equality and distribution rather than economic growth—has not trickled down to the masses, particularly those Malays in kampongs. Tables 28, 29, and 30 make the fact of Malaysian poverty self-evident. The urban/rural gap and the Malay/non-Malay (especially Chinese) gap are revealed in these government statistics.

Pluralism plus a growing awareness of class is at the heart of Malaysia's internal problems. An understanding of advertising or any other aspect of contemporary Malaysian life requires an appreciation of how a dominant colonial system imposed its varied structures on Malaysia's diverse peoples and forced this mixture to exist under one political system. Malaysia, then, is a classic example of what J. S. Furnivall had in mind when he wrote about the "plural society" with its tensions and competing interests as distinct from a homogeneous society. The medley of peoples that Furnivall observed is present not only in excolonial Malaysia but also in Indonesia, Singapore, and many other developing nations.[38]

Although the riots of 1969 did not bring about a change in the alliance coalition's grip on political power, they did clearly indicate that the Malays, as well as the non-Malays, were dissatisfied with the government's distribution of both political and economic benefits. For quite different reasons, both groups felt they were second-class citizens. The Malays, as the underprivileged people in their own homeland, wanted to progress much faster economically, while the Chinese and Indians, as legal citizens, sought a greater measure of political power. Overzealous politicians and activists from both ruling and opposition parties and from all racial groups must share responsibility for the militant communalism which forced the government to restore order only through a state of emergency. Parliamentary

Table 29

Peninsular Malaysia: Mean Household Incomes, 1970
(in Malaysian Dollars)

Groups	Mean Household Income (per month)
Malay	172
Chinese	394
Indian	304
Others	813
Rural average	200
Urban average	428
All households	264

NOTE: $2.4 Malaysian equals approximately $1 U.S.

SOURCE: Table 9-5 in Third Malaysian Plan 1976-1980. Kuala Lumpur,
Malaysia: The Government Press, 1976, p. 179.

Table 30

Peninsular Malaysia: Households in Poverty by Race, 1970

	All Households (000)	Poor Households (000)	Poverty Incidence (%)	Percentage of Total Poor Households
Malay	901.5	584.2	64.8	73.8
Chinese	525.2	136.3	26.0	17.2
Indian	160.5	62.9	39.2	7.9
Others	18.8	8.4	44.8	1.1
Total	1,606.0	791.8	49.3	100.0
All rural	1,166.7	683.7	58.6	86.3
All urban	439.3	108.1	24.6	13.7

SOURCE: Table 9-6 in Third Malaysian Plan 1976-1980. Kuala Lumpur, Malaysia:
The   Government Press, 1976, p. 180.

democracy—which the British had carefully worked to implant through the Alliance coalition arrangement—was suspended for almost two years. Malaysia's shaken leadership had to find better ways to control ethnic tension and build new structures to ensure that further communal conflict—physical *and* political—would be minimized.

In addition to the "sensitive issues" and other antisedition actions, including use of the Internal Security Act, to curtail political dissent, the government in 1970 created a formal national ideology, the *Rukunegara*. Not unlike Indonesia's *Pancasila*, the *Rukunegara* was written to help foster responsible citizenship through adherence to five principles: Belief in God, loyalty to the King and to the nation, support of the Constitution, sovereignty of law, and good behavior and morality.

Post-1969 Advertising

The 1969 disturbances also made the government more aware of the need to control the *content* of mass media messages. Increasingly, the Malaysian government looked upon the media as tools by which to help change people's values, attitudes, and expectations. The press and the government-run Radio and Television Malaysia system could obviously play an important role in the overall nation building process, and the government intensified its use of these communications channels to emphasize national identity and to increase the use of the sole official national language, Bahasa Malaysia, so that more Malaysians could communicate with one another. Islamic principles and Malay *adat* (customs) also were given greater official stress, in part because of a resurgence of orthodoxy among Muslims.

Advertising, too, was not neglected by the government.[39] On December 2, 1971, at a joint luncheon given by the MAA and the Institute of Public Relations, the Minister of Special Functions and of Information expressed the government's growing concern that the content of Malaysian advertising was inconsistent with the new *Rukunegara* philosophy. Tan Sri Ghazali bin Shafie observed:

> You all know as well as I do that modern advertising and public relations go beyond merely introducing a business or product, but go on to promote it by creating what advertising executives or public relations officers deem as desirable images in the minds of consumers or clients. However, we note in our newspapers, magazines, radios and on television that the images created have very often little relation with our environment or what we hope to achieve in our society. There is, I think you will agree, a certain degree of mindless aping of bourgeois values and styles of the West. I have noticed that certain products are associated, through the mass media in this country, with lifestyles of the middle and

upper-classes in the West, and this is being continuously presented to the Malaysian minds as being something to model ourselves by.

This attitude applies not only to imported products, but it saddens me to observe that it extends to locally-produced goods as well. We are all aware that a certain prejudice continues to exist in this country to the effect that all foreign-made goods are superior to locally-produced ones. This prejudice is, of course, without any basis in fact, and it is a left-over of the colonial era.[40]

Ghazali urged the admen to stop encouraging "mindless imitation of alien lifestyles," to use "local settings, local emotions, and local identification" in their messages, and to eliminate the use of racial stereotypes.[41]

Over the next few years, the government spelled out in greater detail exactly how the advertising industry was expected to help the government solve its nation building problems by greater use of the national language (rather than English or one of the mother tongues of the non-Malay groups) and greater use of local models, themes, music, and settings to reflect Malaysian identity in advertisements. By 1977, for example, the government had fully implemented a policy requiring that all advertising films (cinema and television) be made in Malaysia and reflect Malaysian identity and that all non-Malay films have subtitles in the national language.[42] Through such a policy, the government not only stimulated the local film-making industry, but it also eliminated all imported commercials, most of which were "nearly all Caucasian and they evangelised foreign trends, norms, and values, some of which ran counter to Malaysian social and cultural sensitivities."[43] About 80 percent of the imported commercials used in Malaysia had been produced in the United States or Britain.[44]

Much of the government's campaign for "Malaysian identity" in advertising was implicitly aimed at the TNCs and their TNAAs, which frequently had relied heavily on the English language and on imported concepts and had largely neglected the relatively conservative Malay consumer.[45] One Ministry of Information official complained about advertising experts who did not adjust themselves to the Malaysian environment or shelve their foreign oriented values so that they could adopt perspectives that would be correct in the Malaysian context. He told these experts that it could be "imprudent to simply impose foreign values on the Malaysian society." He explained:

What is done in good faith can cause a great deal of harm. The long hair fad; the half-naked and topless females; streaking, etc., have for some time been sensational happenings in some Western societies, but it would be wrong to project these as wholesome symbols in commercials meant for our consumption. I would urge all creative people to help contribute to the evolution of the better Malaysian society. Their messages should help consumers to be better Malaysians rather than to encourage them to adopt lifestyles that would have effect on our national character. The guidelines to the society we seek to create are embodied in the Rukunegara and I would commend all creative people to thoroughly familiarize themselves with all the concepts that motivated the framing of the Rukunegara. The character of advertising must change with every change that takes place in society that it is supposed to serve.[46]

The TNCs and their TNAAs have been unhappy with what they considered as ultranationalistic government policies surrounding "Malaysian identity," or against advertising certain popular consumer goods. For example, they were not pleased when the government in 1980 banned all beer and liquor advertising on radio and television; would no longer allow commercials for women's products such as sanitary napkins to be shown on TV before 10:00 P.M.; no longer permitted the use of children in advertising of products not directly related to children; and prohibited the use of Caucasian models or even voices on radio or television. Regarding the Made-in-Malaysia policy, the advertising industry argued it cost them more money to create locally than to import materials from abroad. Overall, however, the policies have helped create more effective advertising, because it has forced the TNAAs to get to know the indigenous consumers better.[47] Ultimately, this meant more profits to both advertisers and their agencies. The TNAAs have had no major problems adjusting to the new policies since they historically have had a great competitive edge over indigenous agencies and they have had the resources to conduct research and hire and train Malaysians who could produce the type of Malaysianized advertisements required by the government. A statement in 1978 from the Ogilvy & Mather office in Kuala Lumpur suggests that in a multicultural setting communicating in local languages and images is very effective:

> Many advertisers in Malaysia, faced with the possibility of having to communicate to their audience in as many as five different languages or dialects, take the easy way out. Overseas campaigns are adapted, copywriting becomes mere translation. In filming, on-camera voice is not used despite its known effectiveness. Ogilvy & Mather create advertising which is understood by Malaysians and which reflects the character of Malaysia. An idea is originated and copy written in the language in which it will appear. On-camera presenter commercials have been used, even though, as in the case of [Nestlé's] Maggi Chilli Garlic Sauce, three separate filming sessions had to take place.
> We have conducted research which has proven that what you show is more important than what you say. This is given even more point by this fact: when a commercial goes out on air as much as 40% of the audience will not fully understand the words.[48]

By not taking the easy way out, the big agencies like O&M not only create advertising (for big clients like Nestlé) that is more relevant to Malaysia's unique plural society but also comply with the government's wishes that advertisements and messages generally reflect local rather than foreign ideas and concepts and help foster greater acceptance of the national language among the non-Malay population. In such a situation, the government is happy because advertising is cooperating with its efforts to project a national culture (some critics might say a *Malay* rather than a true, culturally integrated *Malaysian* culture that all citizens could identify with and support). TNCs and their agencies are happy because their advertising is better understood, and this ultimately increases its persuasive power and leads to more profits.

With its Made-in-Malaysia policies, the government did recognize the potential that advertising, like communications generally, has for nation building, and increasingly it has intervened in the mass media—whether operated publicly or privately—to both control the flow of information and to stimulate greater communication within the nation's still separate communities. The Malaysian government has directed its attention to eliminating some of the negative contents of the media and to encouraging the potentially powerful, positive effects they might have for the creation of a set of common values and goals that would help glue the society together and encourage a common Malaysian consciousness. Major areas, however, were left untouched by government action. Newspaper advertising is the most important channel of advertising in Malaysia, and as table 23 showed, totals more than twice the volume of television, radio, and cinema advertising *combined* but it was not directly affected by the Made-in-Malaysia policies. The private newspapers and magazines continued to import much of their advertisements, emphasize so-called Western images and values, and use non-Malaysian models. For example, while the government refused to permit Lever Brothers to use Television Malaysia for its international commercials featuring non-Malaysian stars like Brigitte Bardot, it did nothing to stop Malaysian women's magazines from using the TNC's Lux print media advertisements featuring Bardot.[49] Despite the government talk about the need for media generally to reflect Rukunegara principles and Malaysian identity, specific government action has largely been limited to the government-owned radio and television channels.[50] As one official said:

> In Malaysia, we feel it is the inability of advertisers to keep themselves in check that has made the interventions necessary. In most instances, interventions were last resort reactions, after very considerable abuse had been experienced. Sometimes this has resulted in over-reaction. In Malaysia, intervention has taken a different form. It was not legislation but merely the denial of the use of government media. Boiled right down, it was, if you would buy time in this media, your message must meet certain requirements. You are not compelled to use this media but if you want to, then you need to conform.[51]

Since the new rules applied equally to *all* advertising agencies—TNAA and local—they contributed in no way to a redistribution of advertising power in Malaysia.

"New Economic Policy"

As a post-1969 response to the growing Malay frustrations over their economic backwardness, the government did establish a twenty-year, socio-economic agenda for the nation's national development. Called the "New Economic Policy" (NEP), it stressed national security and also presented a "two-pronged" approach leading to an overriding end called national unity, or *bersatu*. By 1990, the government hopes to have eradicated poverty regardless of race and to have "restructured" society to eliminate the identification of race with economic function.

The NEP's most controversial and specific objective is its intention to guarantee a fairer distribution of the ownership and control of wealth in the nation:

> The NEP has set as its target the ownership and management by Malays and other indigenous people of at least 30% of commercial and industrial activities in the economy and an employment structure at all levels of operation and management that reflects the racial composition of the nation by 1990. Since restructuring is planned to result from growth, Government policy was directed towards assisting the Malays and other indigenous people to participate fully in the growth of commerce and industry. The Government adopted interrelated programs for this purpose. These included training, advisory assistance, credit facilities, a scheme of preferences for contractors and suppliers among the Malays and other indigenous people as well as the purchase and reservation of share capital in trust for them.[52]

In effect, the NEP requires the government to help Malays become entrepreneurs and enter those nonagricultural occupations, including service industries like advertising, that traditionally have been controlled by non-Malays and foreigners.[53] At the same time, however, it implicitly stresses that the government will *not* accomplish such an objective by taking wealth away from non-Malays. Instead, the government and the private sector will work together to make the "economic cake" larger. This will require massive government expenditures on new public enterprises to give special assistance to Malays *and* continuation of the government's long-standing policies supporting conventional economic growth through TNCs. The government has emphasized that while foreign corporate ownership will decline percentagewise to 30 percent by 1990, in *absolute terms* it will increase by more than 10 percent annually. Therefore, despite greater centralized planning and more direct government involvement in the private sector, the role of foreign investors will be more important than ever before. Clearly, without continued heavy investment by the TNCs, the NEP cannot succeed. Ironically, if the NEP *does* succeed, it could well mean more profits for the Chinese businessmen and foreign investors, whose goods and services would be more accessible to increasingly less poor Malays. Greater spending power would stimulate greater competition and consumer demand, a situation which often creates a need for more advertising. Since the TNAAs continue to dominate the advertising industry, they likely will continue to expand under the NEP.

This expansion of the TNAAs is expected because the government's policy regarding Malay involvement in advertising and other business activities clearly has not been to "rob Peter to pay Paul."[54] The 30 percent Malay equity participation share required in the NEP is to come from an "expanded cake" rather than by the government's taking away share capital from existing non-Malay (including foreign) businesses. Much of the growth of the Malay share was to be held by public enterprises rather than by Malay individuals. This has meant that a sharp increase in state ownership was necessary to build up a Malay capitalist class.

A number of government-financed Malay companies and statutory bodies with access to privileges that ordinary private entities do not receive have been established since 1969. Two of these—Pernas (Perbadanan Nasional Berhad, the National Corporation) and the Urban Development Authority (UDA)—have become directly involved in establishing advertising agencies intended to encourage the entrance of more Malays into advertising, but their impact on the industry has been mixed.

In 1969, Pernas became a giant conglomerate and industrial holding company for *bumiputras*. Under the leadership of prominent Malay prince-politician-businessman Tengku Razaleigh Hamzah, who later became Minister of Finance, Pernas got itself heavily involved in more than fifty joint ventures and other activities with foreigners and local businessmen. To increase *bumiputra* financial and managerial participation in the Malaysian economy, Pernas became involved in everything from Goodyear tires and Cadbury chocolates to the Kuala Lumpur Hilton and trade with China and other socialist states.[55] In 1974, Razaleigh saw advertising as an important modern service industry that Malays should be involved in, and he worked through the JWT office in Manila to interest the American TNAA to enter Malaysia. In 1975, a joint venture between JWT and three Malaysian public enterprises, including Pernas, was arranged.[56] The following partners each had 25 percent equity in a new agency called PTM Thompson:

Pernas Securities Sdn. Bhd., a wholly owned subsidiary of Pernas,
Tourist Development Corp. (TDC), the government tourist promotion agency which until 1972 was the Department of Tourism,
Malaysian Airline System (MAS), the government airline, which originally was in partnership with the Singapore government in Malaysian-Singapore Airlines (MSA). In 1972, each government established its own separate national carrier.
JWT, the New York-based TNAA.

In announcing the partnership, JWT's president, Don Johnston, said, "JWT's involvement in Malaysia is a recognition of the country's great economic growth. Malaysia with a population of 11 million is one of Southeast Asia's most viable markets, with a high standard of living and a stable democratic government."[57]

Because of its close government and JWT connections, the new agency rapidly expanded.[58] In 1975, it had a thirty-five-person staff and billings of $1.42 million. By 1977, PTM Thompson had a fifty-three-person staff, billings more than $3 million, and a Singapore office. An unusually high 42 percent of its billings came from the public sector,[59] and the agency's government-related clients have included MAS, TDC, Pernas, and the Federal Industrial Development Authority. Affiliation with JWT clearly helped PTM Thompson acquire TNC clients. For example, Lux soap and Parker pens, two products handled by JWT offices in numerous nations, were PTM Thompson accounts, ant the agency boasted:

> A director from each partner sits on the Board of PTM Thompson. In addition the Chairman of The Company is nominated by PTM. Because of the position of these key people in their respective business fields, PTM Thompson have a unique advantage over other international advertising agencies in Malaysia. No other agencies have on their board of directors such individuals at the centre of Malaysian business and government affairs.[60]

Although JWT legally had only 25 percent control of the agency, it seemed to have considerable management control. The founding general manager was Ian Dawson, an Australian with JWT experience in London and Australia. He had first come to Malaysia in 1972 on a pilot survey for JWT. The first creative director was an Englishman, Kenneth Smith, who had had TNAA experience with Foote, Cone, & Belding, Leo Burnett, and Ogilvy & Mather. From 1971 to 1973 he had been O&M's creative director in Malaysia, and in 1977 he succeeded Dawson, whom JWT transferred to Australia to head its Melbourne office. Later he was promoted to regional directorship of JWT's Southeast Asian operations.

From JWT's perspective, the joint-venture in Malaysia has worked well, although the agency has no similar government affiliations elsewhere and is not contemplating other such arrangements. The agency made a profit in its first full year in operation,[61] and in less than three years it became one of Malaysia's top five agencies. From the government's perspective, the arrangement probably was not working as well as intended. For example, by 1978, MAS, probably Malaysia's largest single advertiser, was no longer a client of its own agency.[62] Because of misunderstandings between MAS and PTM Thompson, the airline's advertising worldwide was being handled by Leo Burnett, which had handled all of the account prior to PTM's establishment. (By 1980, the importance of JWT's presence in Malaysia was somewhat diminished because the TNAA had established a wholly owned, full service office in Singapore. Previously, much of JWT's business in Singapore and other parts of the region had been handled through PTM Thompson.)

In addition to the advertising venture with JWT, the three Malaysian government agencies also established at the same time a public relations firm, PTM Communications.[63] Zecha Associates, a Hong Kong-based regional advertising and public affairs agency, held 20 percent of the equity, and the Malaysian partners 80 percent. The chief executive was Austen Zecha, an Indonesian born, American educated, Dutch-American citizen. He had Southeast Asian journalism experience and had been both an advisor to the late Robert F. Kennedy and a communications manager for Exxon and Mobil in New York City.

PTM's joint venture with Zecha ended in 1976, when he established a new agency, Asian Marketing Communications (AMC), by taking PTM's major private sector accounts and some staff with him. Zecha's new Malaysian partner was a prominent Malay businessman, Tunku Abdullah, who was the son of the first Malaysian king and brother of the present sultan of the state of Negri Sembilan. Tunku's conglomerate, Melewar Holdings group, held 60 percent of the equity and Zecha 40 percent.[64] In addition to finding a well-connected Malay as a partner, Zecha also became Dentsu's representative in Malaysia and AMC handled placement for such Dentsu clients as Mazda, Suzuki motorcycles, Mopeiko, and Lion Dentrifrice.[65] By the early 1980s, AMC had expanded into Indonesia and was establishing other links throughout Southeast Asia.

The experiences of JWT in alliance with the Malaysian government and Zecha Associates, first with PTM and later with Tunku Abdullah, seem classic examples of what Galtung had in mind when he wrote about penetration from the top as a way in which the elite in dominating nations penetrate the elite of the dominated nations. Through internationalized bridgeheads who are integrated into the ruling class, the government bureaucracy, and the core of the capitalist world economy, foreigners are able to enter a Periphery nation like Malaysia and develop a harmony of interest between themselves and a small local elite.[66] Without high ranking bridgeheads, foreign businessmen like Zecha and TNAAs like JWT and Dentsu clearly would not be able to operate very effectively, if at all, in Malaysia.[67]

Other TNAAs, and TNCs generally, also recruit bridgeheads, presumably well-rewarded, and use their political and business connections. For example, the only Japanese TNAA with its own operations in Malaysia is Hakuhodo. It owns 49 percent of a joint venture agency with two prominent Malaysian businessmen, a Chinese owning 21 percent and a Malay owning 30 percent and serving as the agency's chairman. The latter is Junus Sudin, managing director and deputy chairman of the New Straits Times Group, the most prestigious and successful publisher in Malaysia.[68] Junus has close ties to Tengku Razaleigh who, in 1972, through his Pernas affiliation, served as intermediary in the government's successful efforts to bring the newspaper group under local control.[69] Junus's close ties to the government are indicated by the fact that he has been head of Pernas

Securities, which has 25 percent interest in PTM Thompson, and managing director of Petronas, the national oil corporation.

Outside of Hakuhodo and PTM Thompson, the only other TNAA agency in Malaysia in the mid-1970s that had complied with the NEP's goal of 30 percent Malay ownership was SSC&B:Lintas. In 1977, it restructured itself to permit Malay participation, and it arranged for a prominent Malay businessman and director of several major companies to acquire 30 percent equity. Although O&M remained 100 percent foreign-owned, it did have a prominent Malay as its Malaysian chairman. The vice-chairman of Guinness Malaysia, a major O&M client, served in that capacity. Other board members were four Malaysian Chinese and the expatriate managing director. By 1981, another TNAA, Grant, Kenyon & Eckhardt, had named a prominent Malay businessman as chairman of its Kuala Lumpur operations.

Although the Pernas involvement in a TNAA-affiliated business is the most important example of direct government involvement in the agency business, another major state owned public corporation was also involved in advertising. This was the Urban Development Authority (UDA), established in 1971 and directly responsible to the Prime Minister's Department. UDA has been involved in the NEP's efforts to restructure society through urban development and the creation of a Malay commercial community in cities such as Kuala Lumpur, which historically have been dominated by Chinese.

To encourage the entrance of Malays into advertising related businesses, UDA established three joint ventures:

Firm	Activity	Date Established	% UDA Equity
Idris, Lim Associates	advertising	March 1975	25%
Instadt	photography	November 1974	51%
Mascom Associates	advertising	May 1975	66%

UDA is represented on each entity's board of directors, and its financial commitment (loan, equity, bank guarantees, etc.) to the three businesses has totalled about $159,000. UDA's goal is to relinquish its share of equity to individual Malays within three years, but in these particular businesses this has not been possible because of their instability.[70]

Idris Lim Associates, for example, has had its problems. It began as a cooperative effort of Idris Sheikh Ahmad, a Malay adman with TNAA and London experience, and Francis Lim, a Chinese creative adman with Lintas experience. Idris held 45 percent of the equity, Lim 30 percent, and UDA 25 percent.[71] The multiracial partnership did not last long and by 1977 Lim had established his own business and also returned to Lintas as a consultant.[72] Idris's father, former chief minister of the Malaysian state of Perlis, then became a shareholder of what has become a wholly Malay-owned business. A comment from Idris suggests the problems that small, local agencies have had in Malaysia:

> We are not considered professionals because many in the industry today are still not honest with themselves. Many of them take on accounts because there is money to be made instead of finding out if the concept proposed and executed will work for the accounts. . . . They [Malaysian advertising people] may be printers, block makers, sign board makers or run photography and art studios. They will accept jobs which they pass on to other agencies and split commissions. By doing so they hope to make a fast buck. But in the long run they will fail on the job and the client will not trust not only that agency but the whole industry. Sadly enough, most of these so-called advertising agencies are local agencies. Where is the trust in locals because of the failures of a few? They spoil the market for the rest.[73]

During its early years, UDA conducted "crash programs" through which it could have an immediate impact on Malay urban life. Some of these activities were poorly conceived and have been financial failures because Malay businessmen, some with more political than entrepreneurial skills, did not have sufficient managerial expertise to run viable agencies. An UDA official told me that the government agency is "more cautious now" and has had to be "doubly certain" about how its funds are spent promoting new Malay businesses.[74] He also indicated that UDA was less than enthusiastic about additional investment in the advertising business.

In short, Malaysia's colonial history, its racial composition and long-simmering communal tensions, and the strong dominance of the TNAAs have worked to prevent Malaysians, or the government, from giving much attention to the structure of the advertising business. Advertising nationalism—or at least Malay nationalism—has certainly increased with reference to advertising content, but the structure of the industry itself has been given little attention, despite the government's plans that "at least 30 percent of commercial and industrial activities" should be owned and managed by Malays and other indigenous people by 1990.[75] Rather than address the problem of how to restructure the large, successful TNAAs that dominate the advertising industry, the government so far has generally chosen to concentrate its modest direct efforts on acquisition of equity in the joint-venture with JWT and in UDA's three advertising-related Malay businesses. This strategy has provided only limited opportunities for Malays, and it has not brought about a redistribution of advertising power. Only a handful of Malays seems to have benefitted, and the status quo has been preserved, with economic (and advertising) power largely remaining in Chinese and foreign hands.

As long as the government uses its own resources to try to build up advertising power for a few Malays and does not directly address the question of taking power from the Chinese and foreigners (as it is trying to do with some sectors of the economy), an uneasy alliance between Malay, Chinese, and foreign elites will probably continue. Each set of elites would lose much by any move toward a genuine restructuring of the advertising industry in Malaysia, and in the early 1980s each continued to work with one another on such relatively non-controversial "growth" efforts as an increase in the amount of color television transmission time.

Notes

1. Milton J. Esman, *Administration and Development in Malaysia* (Ithaca, N.Y.: Cornell University Press, 1972), p. 56. He has been an advisor to the Malaysian prime minister.

2. See, for example, Robert Bach, "Historical Patterns of Capitalist Penetration in Malaysia," *Journal of Contemporary Asia*, no. 6, (1976), pp. 457–76; Charles Hirschman, "Ownership and Control in the Manufacturing Sector of West Malaysia," *UMBC Economic Review* 7, no. 1 (1971), pp. 21–30; and E. L. Wheelwright, *Industrialization in Malaya* (Melbourne Australia: Melbourne University, 1965). For the Malaysian Government's perspective on investment—past and future, see its *Third Malaysia Plan 1976–1980* (Kuala Lumpur: Government Press, 1976). This document is highly readable and contains some useful data on foreign ownership and indicators of Malaysian development.

3. "Malaysia: Your Profit Centre in Asia" (Kuala Lumpur: Federal Industrial Development Authority (FIDA), February 1977), p. 18.

4. Stuart Middleton, "The Future of Advertising in Malaysia" (Speech by the managing director of Ogilvy & Mather International, Kuala Lumpur, to the Gombak Rotary Club, December 17, 1976, Gombak, Malaysia), p. 1.

5. The Advertisers Association, "*A Review of Advertising in Singapore and Malaysia during Early Times* (Singapore: Federal Publications, 1971), p. 26.

6. Personal correspondence with J. T. A. Rohan, Basingstoke, Britain, September 8 and 28, 1978. Rohan, as a representative of Shell in Singapore, was a founding member of the association. Later, he became Far East Director of S. H. Bensons International Ltd., which in 1961 bought over Masters. He said the association introduced educational courses and formed subcommittees responsible for the main media and "put pressure on media owners to provide audited figures of circulation, audience attendances, etc." When agencies like Benson and Grant entered the area they demanded that local agencies terminate their media-owning activities. He explained: "Up to that time advertising agencies could not survive on standard commission from clients' legitimate advertising work, and to make ends meet owned, published, and distributed trade journals; commercial directories; cinema concessions, bus back advertising franchise; etc. Masters, for example, had the franchise for the bus back advertising of the Singapore Traction Co., and accordingly collected 15% commission from their clients who were encouraged to use this medium, and 35% commission from the Singapore Traction Co. for operating the medium. The total of 50% commission from both parties is quite something! Many of the trade journals, commercial directors, etc. never saw the light of day, although companies subscribed to entries in the publications and supported the publications with advertising."

7. Iain Buchanan, *Singapore in Southeast Asia: An Economic and Political Appraisal* (London: G. Bell and Sons Ltd., 1972), pp. 20–21, has given this interpretation of Singapore's communally based separation from Malaysia and the growing antagonism between the close neighbors: "By 1965, it was apparent that Malaysia, as a workable concept of regional cooperation, had been rendered still-born by deep-seated internal conflicts—conflicts starkly expressed in the ideological and communal bitterness which underscored relations between the Federal and Singapore governments during the latter's 'Malaysian Malaysia' campaign. On August 9th, 1965, Singapore seceded from the Federation, to become 'forever a sovereign democratic and independent nation.' For both territories, a fundamental reappraisal of respective economic and political positions was inevitable. Separation merely highlighted Singapore's most intractable problems: its dependence upon a long-established colonial system, its top-heavy economic structure, its fluid social and cultural foundations, and its vulnerable place in a Malay-dominated world which—as Confrontation and Separation (and later, the post-Gestapu bloodbath in Indonesia and the 1969 Emergency in Malaya) all showed—was far from settled, either politically or economically."

8. In 1974, separate organizations were organized in each nation. Malaysian advertisers reorganized into the Malaysian Advertisers Association (MAA) and the agencies into the Association of Accredited Advertising Agents Malaysia. In Singapore, the organizations became the Singapore Advertisers Association (SAA) and the Association of Accredited Advertising Agents Singapore. James Peter Chin, head of communications for Dunlop and the first president of the MAA, has stressed the close links between the two nations. In a report to the annual general meeting of the MAA, 30 April 1977, he said: "Political demarcation cannot separate siamese twins especially when we shared the same umbilical cord! MAA and SAA are more than inter-related. We have a common history of advertising discipline, experience and know-how. We grew up together. We progressed and mature together . . . we are a couple of creative yo-yos moving up and down in the market place and bazaars of independent Malaysia and Singapore. We are two ánd yet one. We are one and yet two—in advertising, publicity, marketing!"

See also A. A. Larsen, "Malaysia: More Insertions for the Bumiputras," *Media,* November 1974, pp. 21–22. He analyzes increased government involvement in the advertising industry.

9. See, for example, Allington Kennard, "1845 to 1970: We're 125 Today," *Straits Times* (Malaysia), 15 July 1970, and John Lent, "English-Language Mass Media of Malaysia: Historical and Contemporary Perspectives," *Gazette* 21, no. 2 (1975).

10. Russell H. Betts, *The Mass Media of Malaya and Singapore as of 1965: A Survey of the Literature* (Cambridge, Mass.: Center for International Studies, Mass. Institute of Technology, 1969), p. 116.

11. Ibid., p. 114.

12. Donald and Joanna Moore, *The First 150 Years of Singapore* (Singapore: Donald Moore Press Ltd., 1969), pp. 234–35.

13. Quoted in "C'mon In—Overseas Is Fine, Grant Urges, Opening 25th Office Abroad," *Advertising Age,* 16 January 1956, p. 56.

14. Ibid.

15. Peter Kum, "The Malaysian Case History." (Paper prepared for the Advanced Summer Seminar on Transnational Communication Enterprises and National Communication Policies, East-West Communication Institute, Honolulu, August 6–19, 1978), p. 6.

16. Ibid., pp. 4–5.

17. Personal interview with Hugh Bowdewyn, former commercial manager for Radio and Television Malaysia (RTM), in Singapore, 18 November 1977. For an overview of the government-operated broadcasting system, see *Radio TV Malaysia* (Kuala Lumpur: RTM, Ministry of Information, 1975), esp. pp. 41–42 on the system's Commercial Division.

18. Since advertising was introduced into Malaysian broadcasting, it has become an important source of revenue. Revenues from both radio and TV set licensing and broadcasting commercials go directly to the Malaysian Treasury rather than to Radio and Television Malaysia. Government officials insist that broadcasting's objective is public service—not profit. From 1966 to 1976, broadcasting advertisements produced this revenue:

Year	Radio (in millions)	Television (in millions)	Total
1966	3.5	2.3	5.8
1967	3.4	3.6	7.0
1968	2.5	4.9	7.4
1969	3.8	6.1	9.9
1970	4.1	8.9	15.0
1971	4.8	9.4	14.2
1972	6.5	10.4	16.9
1973	6.4	9.9	16.3
1974	5.8	12.1	17.9
1975	6.0	13.5	19.5
1976	5.0	16.0	21.0

SOURCE: Personal correspondence with Kum, Commercial Division, Ministry of Information, Kuala Lumpur, June 6, 1977. One American dollar is equal to approximately 2.4 Malaysian dollars. This means, for example, that radio and TV commercials together produced about $8,750,000 (U.S.). License fees on receiver sets produced somewhat less than this amount.

19. For an overview of communal politics and the uneasy equilibrium between various political parties and ethnic groups, see Sevinc Carlson, *Malaysia: Search for National Unity and Economic Growth*, The Washington Papers, Vol. III, 25 (Beverly Hills: Sage Publications, 1975).

20. Peter Lim, "The New Role of Slogan in a New Society," *Straits Times*, 28 April 1968, p. 6.

21. This figure of eight does not include the Burson-Marsteller public relations agency operated by Marsteller, an American TNAA. Its activities in Malaysia and Singapore do not include full-service advertising, although the agency does give clients advice on advertising, particularly where corporate programs are required. Zecha Associates, a Hong Kong–based regional marketing communications business, which has part ownership in Asian Marketing Communications also is not included as a TNAA since its activities are more regional than truly transnational. Both of these agencies, however, use expatriates and have access to more resources than most Malaysian agencies.

22. Middleton, "The Future of Advertising in Malaysia," pp. 3 and 6.

23. This estimate is from "The Advertising Agency Situation in Malaysia," an informal report from several local advertising agencies presented to the Deputy Minister of Finance, Senator Rafidah Aziz, Kuala Lumpur. This meeting is cited in Vimala Madhavan, "Local Ad Agencies to See Dr. Mahathir," *The Star*, 6 October 1977, p. 23. Kum, "The Malaysian Case History," pp. 7–8, also refers to complaints of unfair competition from the TNAAs.

24. Personal correspondence with Kum, 6 June 1977.

25. Ogilvy & Mather International Inc., *Advertising Annual Report 1977*, pp. 3 and 9.

26. Some of the areas of friction between foreign and Malaysian national agencies are cited in Kum, "Madison Avenue to Change Alley: A Route of Misconceptions," *Media*, January 1977, and R. Letchmikanthan, "Malaysian Industry Heads Toward 'Better and Brighter' Future," *Media*, January 1977, p. 9.

27. For an overview of the problems of Malays entering the business world, see Oliver Popenoe, *Malay Entrepreneurs*. (Doctoral dissertation, London School of Economics, 1970).

28. Malaysian government agencies of course *are* concerned about advertising—particularly its content—and about advertising agencies—as a type of business. Ministries such as Information, Trade, Home Affairs, Health, etc. become involved in issues that affect the TNAAs from time to time. In general, however, I feel the government has given little attention to the TNAAs as a subset of foreign investors. No policies have been developed that pertain specifically to foreign-owned advertising agencies. Many policies affect all advertising agencies—local or transnational—and all foreign businesses, but the government has never singled out the TNAAs for study or special control. Like all foreign businesses, the TNAAs are expected to comply with the government's policies pertaining to Malay participation, but they have not been subjected to any particular pressure. A reason for this might well be that the government realizes that advertising as an industry employs relatively few people and in terms of volume of business is relatively small compared to most other service industries and to nearly all manufacturers.

29. Cited in "Malaysia: Your Profit Centre in Asia," p. 3.

30. *Malaysia 1974 Official Year Book* 14 (Kuala Lumpur: Ministry of Information, 1975), p. 22. These figures are for Peninsular Malaysia (West Malaysia) only. If the East Malaysian states of Sabah and Sarawak are included, the percentage of Malays declines somewhat. Population statistics are always a matter of controversy in Malaysia. The important fact to keep in mind is that roughly half of all Malaysians are Malays, speak Bahasa Malaysia as their mother tongue, and are Moslems. About half the population is non-Malay, speaks a mother tongue other than Bahasa Malaysia, and does not follow the Islamic religion. Most of this half is Chinese.

31. Data on local agencies are difficult to obtain, but of the "local" agencies listed in table 24 only Johan Design Associates is what I would consider to be a truly Malay agency that is competing on an equal basis with some of the TNAAs and the better Chinese agencies. In general, the Malay agencies—the few that exist—cannot compete for the major TNC accounts because they lack the full-service facilities, the professional staff, and the financial capital necessary to support the kind of services that the major advertisers in Malaysia expect from their agencies. Several local agencies have failed in recent years because they lacked the financial and managerial skills needed to keep an agency in the black. Local agencies have been hard hit by the media owners' policies since 1976 that require bank guarantees to cover as much as two months of billings. Kum, "The Malaysian Case History," p. 9, explained that

such policies were easy to comply with for the TNAAs because of their international banking connections, but local agencies had problems because local banks refused to furnish guarantees unless collateral worth a similar amount was given the bank: " . . . if a Malaysian agency wanted to furnish a bank guarantee worth $100,000, it would either have to surrender a land title or something similar worth that much or open a fixed deposit account for that amount with the bank concerned. This automatically restricted the servicing capacity of the Malaysian advertising agency. It would have to tie up more capital in the shape of fixed bank deposits the more business it managed to get." A major reason for such guarantees was the failure of Marklin, a regional agency. See Nicky Careem, "Marklin: Why It Collapsed in Malaysia and Singapore," *Media,* July 1976, pp. 14–15.

32. "List of Members of Association of Accredited Advertising Agents, Malaysia" (Kuala Lumpur: 4As, 26 April 1977). The expatriates did not always attend all 4As meetings. They often had their agencies represented by a senior Malaysian staff member.

33. An example of self-regulation was the industry's Code of Advertising Practice produced in 1974 and updated in 1977 to regulate advertising activities. See *Malaysian Code of Advertising Practice* (Kuala Lumpur: Advertising Standards Authority, 1974). The code was drawn up jointly by the 4As, the MAA, the Malaysian Newspaper Publishers' Association, and the Federation of Malaysian Consumers Association. The 4As and the MAA also cooperated to establish in 1975 the Audit Bureau of Circulations (Malaysia) to systematically obtain the audited circulation figures of newspapers and magazines.

34. Listed in *MAA Bulletin* 3, no. 6 (December 1977), p. 2. This is the official publication of the advertisers' association.

35. *Malaysian Advertisers' Association 1976 Annual Report* (Kuala Lumpur: MAA, 1977), pp. 3 and 11.

36. Because of the nation's history of racial tension and occasional violence, such as the May 13, 1969, riots in Kuala Lumpur, the government enforces a sedition regulation that prevents discussion of the following "sensitive" issues: (1) position of the Malay sultans and king (Yang di-Pertuan Agong), (2) Malay (Bahasa Malaysia) as the national language, (3) special rights for Malays (land, jobs, licenses, scholarships, etc.), and (4) citizenship for non-Malays.

37. In 1977, for example, while I was in Malaysia a small group of local agencies (Malay and Chinese) complained to the government about unfair competition from the TNAAs. Rather than bring the matter directly to the attention of the two advertising industry groups, the 4As and the MAA, the group went directly to the government and met with Deputy Minister of Finance, Senator Rafidah Aziz. She listened and referred the matter to Datuk Amar Taib, the Minister of Information. He had a private meeting with several representatives of local ad agencies and with representatives of such prestigious advertisers as Malayan Tobacco Company, Beecham, Pernas Sime Darby, Goodyear, and Dunlop. The results of the meeting were never made public, but the group apparently reached a consensus that the major problem of the non-TNAAs was insufficient capital accumulation—a cash flow problem. Participants agreed to do some more thinking about the possibility of some insurance arrangement being established to underwrite advertising transactions so that the local agencies could solve the problem of a lack of financial resources to service big TNC accounts. The handling of this sensitive issue over TNAA domination of the Malaysian advertising "pie" is typical of the way Malaysia has traditionally addressed communal problems. Senior government officials got personally involved, they called in key community and business representatives, and through secret discussion and accommodation the issue was at least discussed, if not resolved to all parties' satisfaction.

A second example from my time in Malaysia illustrates how policy changes can be made swiftly once senior government officials become personally concerned. By 1977, the government had become extremely worried about the rapid growth of drug abuse, particularly among Malay youth. Estimates were that the nation had 150,000 drug addicts and that about 43 percent were Malay. In a well-publicized UMNO speech, Prime Minister Datuk Hussein Onn cited Malay drug abusers as one of three Malay groups who were retarding Malay progress. See "We Must Not Fail: Hussein," *New Straits Times,* 12 May 1977, p. 1. A Cabinet Committee on Drug Abuse was established under Deputy Prime Minister Dr. Mahathir Mohamed. He met with key agency, media, and tobacco industry representatives to express his concern over the drug problem and the impact that tobacco advertising, particularly on television and in the cinema, was having on youth. He singled out several TNC cigarette campaigns as examples of advertising that glamorized smoking. As a result of the government leaders' clear concern over rising drug problems, the government late in 1977 imposed guidelines on all tobacco advertising. Scenes associated with pleasure, excitement, and fun; young, sensual, provocatively attractive women; the successful man; the sexually attractive man; music that is exciting; etc. were banned. The deputy minister of home affairs, Datuk Shariff Ahmad, personally reviewed existing cigarette commercial films dating back to 1973. Two TNCs—Malayan Tobacco Co. (BAT) and Rothmans—dominate nearly 100 percent of cigarette sales in Malaysia, and their advertising campaigns were directly affected by the new guidelines. For example, Mahathir reportedly had singled out MTC's John Player Classic campaign as one that especially glamorized smoking and suggested that cigarettes give people inspiration to do things that they would not otherwise be able to do. While in Malaysia, I saw several variations of this *inspirasi* advertisement developed for MTC by Ogilvy & Mather. One film showed a handsome male smoking and then getting inspired to compose music. Another film showed a handsome male smoker getting inspired to paint a beautiful woman's picture. By 1978, advertisers were not allowed to show any real people in their cigarette advertisements. All contents had to center on the cigarette itself rather than incidental events and scenes that are not brought about by smoking.

38. See, for example, J. S. Furnivall, *Colonial Policy and Practices* (New York: New York University Press, 1956). For various perspectives of the significant 1969 Malaysian disturbances, see Felix V. Gagliano, *Communal Violence in Malaysia 1969: The Political Aftermath*, Southeast Series no. 13 (Athens: Center for International Studies, Ohio University, 1970); Cheng Teik Goh, *The May 13th Incident and Democracy and Malaysia* (Kuala Lumpur: Oxford University Press, 1971); John Sliming, *Malaysia: Death of a Democracy* (London: John Murray, 1979); and National Operations Council, *The May 13 Tragedy* (Kuala Lumpur: Government Printer, 1969). The latter is the government's version of the disturbances.

39. See, for example, James Morgan, "Advertising Obligations," *1973 Asia Yearbook* (Hong Kong: Far Eastern Economic Review, 1974), p. 220. For one of the few studies conducted in Malaysia on advertising, see Agnes Mavis Bonney, "Patterns of Advertising in Malaysia Today" (Master of Arts thesis, University of Malaya, Kuala Lumpur, May 1974). She concluded (p. 182) that in Malaysia, "A kind of self-feeding, self-pandering process seems to be at work. The people creating the advertisements are themselves an elite, what one advertiser termed an 'a-typical' elite. They are either expatriates who, for all their goodwill and endeavor, are not able to understand the needs and aspirations of the local people, especially the local people of Malaysia who are so diversified; or Malaysians who represent the higher classes of society."

40. Tan Sri M. Ghazali bin Shafie, "Advertisements and Our Society." (Speech at the luncheon of the Advertisers Association and the Institute of Public Relations, Federal Hotel, Kuala Lumpur, 2 December 1971), p. 3.

41. Ibid., pp. 3–4.

42. The Made-in-Malaysia policies were developed over several years by the Ministry of Home Affairs, whose Board of Film Censors oversees the contents of all films in Malaysia. This table shows how the policies had an immediate impact on the commercials appearing on Television Malaysia beginning in 1972 when the government began levying a 5 percent surcharge on every imported commercial:

Year	Malaysian-made Commercials	Foreign-made Commercials	Total Commercials
1970	20	813	833
1971	23	698	721
1972	176	471	647
1973	389	104	493
1974	449	61	510
1975	436	67	503
1976	460	17	477

SOURCE: Personal correspondence with Peter Kum, head of the Commercial Division, Malaysian Ministry of Information, Kuala Lumpur, May 28, 1977.

For details of the Made-in Malaysia rules, see Harun Din, deputy chief secretary, Ministry of Information, "Rules: Made-in-Malaysia Films." (Letter to advertisers, advertising agencies, and production houses. Kuala Lumpur: Ministry of Information, 21 January 1974). Examples of rules include:

"Models used must be Malaysians and project the Malaysian Identity."

"No scene or shot that can be done in Malaysia should be shot overseas."

"Any service not available in Malaysia may be got from overseas provided prior approval is obtained from this Ministry."

"No racial group must be identified typically with a trade or vocation."

"No racial group, by mode of dress, environment or habitation should be shown disadvantageously."

"Lip to lip kissing scenes are not acceptable."

"Scenes propagating the 'Hippie' cult in any of its forms are not acceptable."

"Scenes of women in micro-mini skirts are not acceptable."

"Suggestive scenes and scenes implying eroticism are not acceptable."

43. Personal correspondence with Kum, May 25, 1977.

44. Ibid.

45. Malaysia is a Muslim state, and many of the government's regulations protect Malays and are based on Islamic moral values. Advertisements and other mass media contents often are criticized by Muslim individuals or groups for being contrary to the teaching of Islam. Since about the mid-1970s, the government has been subjected to increased pressure, due in part to a major upsurge of orthodoxy in Muslim nations. The Dakhwah (Muslim missionary groups) movement has become strong in Malaysia, and it is opposed to materialism. Advertisements, then, frequently offend devout Muslims and others. Alcohol and pork are prohibited by Islamic teaching, and advertisements for these products are especially sensitive. Pork products cannot be advertised on television or the national network of Radio Malaysia. Liquor advertisements are allowed only on Network II of Television Malaysia and the national network of Radio Malaysia. See "Advertising Code" (Kuala Lumpur: Ministry of Information, 1973).

Occasionally, advertisements that have been passed for television screening and shown on the air have to be removed because of public pressure, particularly from Muslims. Kum told me about two commercials that offended viewers: "Hello Sayang [Hello Lover, a hair product] . . . this ad was initially given the benefit of the doubt and accepted for screening. But there were protests from various sectors of the public as well as religious bodies. They objected strongly to the very strong implication of sex. Two young people are seen getting into an intimate clinch and then the male pushes a mirror out of alignment so that they can no longer be seen. People found this to be most suggestive."

"[R. J.] Reynolds [cigarettes] . . . some cultural groups complained about the length of hair on the main model. At certain angles, the hair did appear overly long, breaking the long hair rule."

46. Shariff Ahmad, deputy minister of information, was the influential Malay official who enforced the Made-in-Malaysia policies. In 1978 he became minister of agriculture. These comments are from his untitled speech given to the Advertisers Association monthly luncheon, Hotel Merlin, Kuala Lumpur, January 16, 1975. See translation of the speech in "Siaran Akhbar," Press release Pen. 1/75/81 (Pen) (Kuala Lumpur: Malaysia InformationOffice, 16 January 1975). For another speech see his "Advertising in the Context of a Malaysian Identity." (Speech at the Advertisers Association monthly meeting, Federal Hotel, Kuala Lumpur, 13 September 1973.

47. Middleton, "The Future of Advertising in Malaysia," pp. 3–4, emphasized: "The true facts of advertising here [in Malaysia] today are that the best selling cigarettes, best selling beer, best selling cars, best selling paints, best selling batteries and many other best selling market leaders happen to have been advertised in a Malaysian context with advertising created in Malaysia using Malaysian setting and Malaysian citizens to help sell them. This process is bound to continue—aided by Government regulations or not. Even in the technique of advertising itself I foresee more imaginative use of the indigenous languages. The national language and the Chinese dialects have for too long been a poor relation to the English language in advertising in Malaysia. Yet the inherent power of these languages is unquestionable, and it is a shrewd advertising man who finds out how to use the indigenous language to the best effect."

48. "What Ogilvy & Mather Have Learned About Creating Advertising That Sells in Malaysia," MAA Bulletin 4, no. 5 (October 1978), p. 12.

49. While in Malaysia, I saw a Lux magazine ad featuring Brigitte Bardot in *Jelita Magazine*, May 1977, p. 65. This women's magazine is published by the New Straits Times Group. I interviewed the Group's managing director, Junus Sudin, on 9 May 1977, in Kuala Lumpur. When I asked him about the desirability of publishing an ad featuring a foreign actress like Bardot rather than Malaysian models, he told me that in a multiracial society like Malaysia Caucasians are considered "neutral" and don't offend any particular group. Since 1978, however, Lux and its TNAA, JWT, have been using two Malaysian stars, Uji Rashid and Lan Yin, rather than foreigners. For a discussion of marketing of Lux and other soaps in Malaysia, see P. Y. Chin, "Toilet Soap: Growing Sophistication," *Malaysian Business*, January 1977, pp. 7–10. Lux controls at least 55 percent of the Malaysian soap market and has been sold in Malaysia since the early 1950s. See also, "Made in Malaysia," *Malaysian Business*, February 1973, p. 71.

50. A notable exception to the government's lack of interest in print media advertising in terms of whether it reflects Malaysian identity is a 1977 government report, "Report of the Committee on Advertising Guidelines" (Kuala Lumpur: Socio-Economic Research and General Planning Unit, Prime Minister's Department, 25 June 1977). The committee, chaired by the Unit's respected director, G. K. Rama Iyer, reported to the Malaysian Cabinet. In an interview with Iyer, Kuala Lumpur, 4 January 1978, I learned that the committee was established to consider Malaysian identity, particularly in print media and posters, and to develop a government response to the growing public concern over lewdness. Iyer said the committee was established after a particular poster incident in a Kuala Lumpur shopping center. The poster was a jeans advertisement, and the government received complaints from rural people and others who found the poster offensive. The committee's recommendations are confidential, but if accepted and implemented, they could mean greater government involvement in efforts to regulate the use of sex in advertising.

Iyer gave me a specific example of an advertisement that projected a positive identity. It was a TNAA-produced Nescafé instant coffee advertisement which showed a school teacher helping two Malaysian students as part of "The Nescafé Life." The caption under the major picture read: "Teaching is such satisfying work when you love children."

51. Personal correspondence with Kum, 24 March 1978.

52. *Third Malaysia Plan 1976–1980*, p. 30.

53. Shahreen Kamaluddin, head of the School of Mass Communication, MARA Institute of Technology, Shah Alam, Malaysia, in personal correspondence, 15 December 1977, explained that there were relatively few Malays in advertising, an industry that has been "a Chinese domain, jealously guarded as such." She said, "advertising is a new field and 'onlookers' do not know much about what a job in advertising entails. For those who know and don't go in, this could be because advertising is a challenging and demanding career where a person has to work under pressure—to meet deadlines and stand up to stiff competition from peers within individual set ups and among business peers as well as in the industry. Job entails defending beliefs [and] viewpoints and being able to stand up to criticisms levelled by clients and superiors. There is little job security at the early stages—pay is low until you hve proved yourself. . . . There are Bumiputras in most of the advertising setups but they are mainly graphic artists. There is no Bumiputra copywriter as yet. Some Bumiputras have set up their own companies where they are managers and creative directors, but these are few and far between. There are more Bumiputras as marketing trainees, executives in advertising/marketing departments."

54. This emphasis that government policies will always be fair to all and will not "rob Peter to pay Paul" is a common feature of officials' speeches. See, for example, "Prime Minister Outlines Functions of Urban Development Authority." (Speech by Tun Abdul Razak at the opening ceremony of the Urban Development Authority, Kuala Lumpur, 12 November 1971).

55. For background information on Pernas, see "Perbadan Nasional Berhad (Pernas)" (Kuala Lumpur: Pernas, 15 April 1977), and "A Review of Major Pernas Activities," *Suara Pernas* (magazine of the Pernas group), vol. 3, no. 2, 1975 ("Special Issue: Pernas After Five Years"). For a more critical view, see Pran Chopra, "The Dynamic World of Pernas: Business Plus a Philosophy," *Asian Finance*, April 15–May 14, 1977, pp. 59–65; James Morgan, "Man in the Hot Seat," *Far Eastern Economic Review*, 8 January 1972, p. 40; and Arun Senkuttuvan, "Throwing the Book at Pernas," *Far Eastern Economic Review*, 4 July 1975, pp. 48–53.

56. For an overview of PTM Thompson's operations and history, see "Thompson in Kuala Lumpur" (Kuala Lumpur: PTM Thompson, no date).

57. "JWT Opens Office in Malaysia," *Dialog News*, 16 December 1974, pp. 1–2.

58. Establishment of the new agency in 1975 created considerable unrest within the Malaysian advertising industry. Many admen resented the government's entrance into commercial advertising. The TNAAs were unhappy with JWT's entry into the Malaysian market because it would mean greater competition. Several TNAAs had been handling major accounts, such as MAS and TDC, and they feared these would shift to PTM Thompson. Even some Malays were unhappy with the joint venture because they suspected that JWT rather than Malays would dominate the new agency. In a personal interview with PTM Thompson's general manager, Ian Dawson, Kuala Lumpur, 31 March 1977, I was told that JWT in New York did run into "some flak" from other TNAAs who felt the agency had "capitulated" to the Malaysian government. Dawson said neither of JWT's initial fears about the Malaysian joint venture have come true. The agency has *not* been "dictated to" by politicians and the JWT senior vice president on the PTM Thompson board has *not* been outvoted by the Malaysian partners. Dawson said the agency's political connections are a "two-edged sword"—they can hurt as much as help. My view is that they clearly help.

59. Personal correspondence with Kenneth Smith, PTM Thompson general manager, 17 May 1977.

60. "Thompson in Kuala Lumpur," p. 3.

61. *JWT 1975 Annual Report*, p. 4.

62. MAS spends an estimated $2.5 million annually on advertising, but much of this amount is spent on media outside of Malaysia. Since MAS has a monopoly on domestic flights, the airline does not have to spend much inside Malaysia. Competition outside of Malaysia, however, is stiff, and advertising is an important factor in any national airline's success. Neither the airline nor the agency will explain in detail why MAS is no longer handled by PTM Thompson, but obviously there were serious problems between the agency and the airline. Despite the fact that MAS owned 25 percent of PTM Thompson, the agency decided not to bid for MAS business in 1978. Several sources told me that MAS was notoriously late in paying its bills and that the agency did not want to treat MAS any different from any other client. In 1978, MAS advertising campaigns worldwide were handled by Leo Burnett, Kuala Lumpur, but the corporate concept was conceived by the TNAA's Sydney office.

63. "New Ad, PR Agency Set Up," *Straits Times*, 4 December 1974.

64. For background on Tunku's business activities, see "Tunku Abdullah's Growing 'Empire'," *Malaysian Business*, April 1977, pp. 22–23. For background on AMC, see "Asian Marketing Communications Sdn. Bhd." (Kuala Lumpur: AMC, no date); "Bold New Venture with a Bright Future," *Asian Trade and Industry* 8, no. 11 (1976), p. 30; and "New Consultancy in Kuala Lumpur," *Media*, February 1977, p. 15.

65. In Kuala Lumpur and Singapore, Dentsu had been using Marklin Advertising Ltd., a Hong Kong–based regional agency, to service its accounts. When Marklin's operations in Malaysia and Singapore failed in 1976, Dentsu shifted to AMC in Malaysia. See note 31.

66. The backgrounds of the two princes are not dissimilar. Both, for example, attended Malay College, the English-medium, upperclass high school that the British established in Kuala Kangsar, Malaysia, to prepare the colony's elite to take over positions of administrative responsibility from the British. Both have also attended universities in Great Britain. Razaleigh is a member of the Kelantan royal family and is a political activist. He has been minister of finance and the treasurer and a vice president of UMNO, the ruling Malay party. At various times, he has held many of the most prestigious business and government positions in the nation. For example, he has been managing director of Bank Bumiputra; group chairman of Pernas and chairman of Pernas Securities; chairman and chief executive of Petronas, the national oil corporation; president of the Malay Chamber of Commerce of Malaysia; and chairman of the National Chamber of Commerce and Industry of Malaysia. While Razaleigh has shifted his attention from Malay business to government, Tunku Abdullah, a member of the Negri Sembilan royal family, has moved from government into business. He was in the civil service from 1952 to 1963, and was a member of Parliament from 1964 to 1974. His business activities, including joint-ventures, comprise a growing business empire that has been consolidated into Melewar Holdings Sdn. Bhd., a group of companies in construction, insurance, real estate, trading, tourism, and marketing services.

67. For an overview of the important role that past and present politicians and civil servants, predominantly Malays, play in mediating between the state and private enterprise, see Lim Mah Hui, *Ownership and Control in a Dependent Economy: The Case of Malaysia's One Hundred Largest Corporations.* (Doctoral dissertation, University of Pittsburgh, 1977). For a discussion of the emerging bureaucratic capitalists in Malaysia, see K. S. Jomo, "Restructuring Society: The New Economic Policy Revisited." (Paper delivered at the Fifth Malaysian Economic Convention, Malaysian Economic Association, Penang, May 25–27, 1978). According to Jomo, p. 15: "The bureaucratic capitalists today are drawn mainly from the ranks of leading politicians with business connections, businessmen with strong ties with those in politics or the bureaucracy, as well as present and former high level bureaucrats (including military and other government officers) in direct and indirect control of those enterprises set up or otherwise controlled by the state. This class then is to be found operating in both the public and private sectors. While the distinction between the two components is quite blur [*sic*] in reality, it is useful to retain in so far as it provides some insights into various issues such as the contradictions within the bureaucratic bourgeoisie. Also, although there are different modes of private appropriation available to individual bureaucratic capitalists—such as salaries, expenditure and other allowances, honoraria, graft, directorships, partnerships and so on—they may all be considered as belonging to a single class fraction."

68. Junus studied chartered accountancy in Australia under the Colombo Plan from 1955 to 1960. He was group secretary of the ICC Group of Companies in Malaysia and Singapore, 1969–72. He was secretary-general of the Associated Malay Chambers of Commerce of Malaysia, 1970–72, and also secretary-general of the ASEAN Chambers of Commerce and Industry.

69. John A. Lent, "Government Policies Reshape Malaysia's Diverse Media," *Journalism Quarterly,* Winter 1975, p. 666, noted the increasingly intimate ties between Malaysian newspapers and the government: "English-language newspapers, like their Chinese counterparts, have felt tremendous political and governmental pressure since 1970, chiefly in the area of ownership. In the fall of 1972, the Straits Times Press succumbed to the harassment, renamed itself New Straits Times Press and placed 80% of its ownership in the hands of the Malaysian state trading corporation, Pernas. As a result, the papers were controlled indirectly by the Malay political party, United Malay National Organization (UMNO), a member of the ruling National Front government."

Junus has been a leader in efforts to put the influential daily under Malaysian ownership and management. In a personal interview with him on 9 May 1977, in Kuala Lumpur, Junus emphasized that Pernas does not own the New Straits Times. He said that in 1972 the Straits Times Group sold 80 percent of the issued capital using Tengku Razaleigh as an intermediary. He said the Group now is 65 percent Malaysian-owned (about 55 percent Malay or Malay institutions and 10 percent non-Malays) and about 35 percent Singaporean-owned.

70. This information about UDA's involvement in advertising-related businesses is from a personal interview with Zakariah Md. Sohor, senior development officer, UDA, Kuala Lumpur, 4 May 1977. Zakariah sits on the boards of both Mascom and Instadt.

71. "Advertising Man with a Mission," *Malaysian Business,* 1 July 1975, pp. 4–5.

72. Personal interview with Lim, Kuala Lumpur, 14 April 1977.

73. "Advertising Man with a Mission," pp. 4, 5.

74. See note 70.

75. *Third Malaysia Plan 1976–1980,* p. 30. In a personal interview with Shaharuddin Harun, secretary, Foreign Investment Committee, Prime Minister's Department, Kuala Lumpur, 16 June 1977, and subsequent correspondence, I was told that the Malaysian government wanted at least 70 percent Malaysian equity in all new investments in the extractive and natural resource-based industries. In the manufacturing sector, "a more flexible approach" was being adopted, based on the merit of each investment. Regarding Bumiputra equity, he said the government's policy was that "the corporate sector, of which the advertising industry is but a component part, shall by 1990 have an ownership position of 70 percent Malaysian (with *at least* 30 percent Bumiputra) and 30 percent foreign." He explained: "In other words, there may be certain advertising companies within the corporate sector which may have 100 percent Bumiputra equity by 1990, just as there may be other advertising companies where foreign majority may be possible."

8
Singapore: Advertising in a "Global City"

> . . . an independent Singapore survives and will survive
> because it has established a relationship of interdependence
> in the rapidly expanding global economic system. Singa-
> pore's economic future will, as the years go by, become
> more and more rooted in this global system. It will grow
> and prosper as this system grows and prospers. It will col-
> lapse if this system collapses. But the latter is hardly likely to
> happen because that would be the end of world civilisation.
> —S. Rajaratnam,
> Singapore Foreign Affairs Minister[1]

Singapore is a unique Asian nation where commerce and advertising thrive. More significantly, it is one where questions about the role of foreigners in advertising or anything else are almost antinational since the city-state relies so heavily on foreign investment, and one-party politics tend to work against the public discussion of alternatives.

Always vulnerable because of its small size (less than 2.5 million people crowded into about 227 square miles), its lack of natural resources, and its historically open economy, Singapore became even more so after its forced separation from the Federation of Malaysia in 1965. For example, the goal of a common market with Malaysia was destroyed. Amidst the increased nationalism in neighboring Malaysia and Indonesia and the British military withdrawal by 1971, Singapore felt forced to reorient itself. Traditional entrepot relations with the neighboring hinterlands continued and Britain remained an important ally, but Singapore's leaders thought that to survive and prosper in what seemed to them to be an increasingly hostile region, the nation would have to become more globally oriented. The United States and Japan were among the new Center nation partners of Singa-pore, especially once confrontation with Indonesia was over and Suharto welcomed foreign investors.

Singapore's vulnerability continues, especially since private foreign capital and expertise freely enters and leaves, but the nation has rapidly transformed itself into a modern, efficient, sophisticated transnational service and distribution center for the region. The nation's leaders call Singapore a global city—a city that "electronic communications, supersonic planes, giant tankers, and modern economic and industrial organization have made inevitable."[2] Originally as a colonial city and now as a global city, Singapore has been heavily influenced by political and economic developments far beyond its island borders, but its government's philosophy is simple: "For us the alternative to an independent Singapore is bondage—interdependence yes; bondage never."[3]

A Global City

Colonialism made Singapore inevitable, as Western commercial interests needed a strategically located free port and commercial base from which to penetrate the region's resource-rich hinterlands. Today, as a strategically located global city, Singapore continues to use its only resource—human labor—to serve foreign economic needs through a wide range of sophisticated service facilities that rival most in the world. Foreign investors, including many of the early European trading agencies and also a wide variety of Japanese, American, and other enterprises, feel secure with Singapore's status and its "open door" policies. The latter promote predominantly tertiary activities that serve Center nations' interests and maintain long-standing relations of dependence between Singapore and the more affluent industrial world and between Singapore and its less affluent, less industrial neighbors.

Singapore's material progress and fast-moving, highly disciplined style of life contrast sharply with the situation in its Malay World neighbors, which are heavily burdened with basic urban-rural problems. In comparison to either Malaysia or Indonesia, Singapore is small, rich, urban, Chinese, corruption-free, Western consumer-oriented, technologically sophisticated, English speaking, highly specialized, and foreign controlled. To its neighbors, Singapore sometimes seems arrogant and is resented as being a parasite in their midst that is more interested in strictly economic development—especially "doing business"—than in political or cultural development that would create a genuine national consciousness and identity.

After its separation from Malaysia, Singapore—under the dynamic leadership of Prime Minister Lee Kuan Yew's People's Action Party (PAP) since 1959—capitalized on its location, its strong tradition of free enterprise, and its hard-working labor force (about 76 percent Chinese) and actively sought foreign investors, including TNCs who wanted a regional base for their labor- and technology-intensive manufacturing and modern service industries.

To encourage foreign investors, the government developed comprehensive policies—many of them tough and unpopular—that would quickly make Singapore a politically viable and stable nation with the disciplined workforce wanted by TNCs interested in long-term growth and profitability. Within a few short years, the government efficiently and strictly enforced policies in such diverse areas as public housing accommodations, family planning, compulsory English instruction,[4] labor union activity, and mass media ownership.[5] All of these major policy areas were heavily promoted in both the private media and in the government-run radio and television service, which is under the Ministry of Culture. Government information programs are well-coordinated in Singapore, and anyone stepping foot into the nation quickly becomes aware of such government campaigns as "Stop at Two" (promoting family planning and the two-children family regardless of sex), "Anti-Smoking," anti-long hair and anti-drug abuse, "Keep Singapore Clean and Pollution Free," "Save Fuel," "Use Your Hands" (promoting the value of dirty or heavy work), and "Buy Singapore-made Products."

The combined effects of the major PAP policies since independence have resulted in downplaying Singapore's "Chineseness," so as not to antagonize Malaysia or Indonesia, and in dampening any major political dissent so as not to stir up communal tensions and scare investors away. Singapore's political stability has evolved since 1960, and it has unquestionably contributed to the nation's dramatic economic growth and to a rise in the standard of living, as table 31 shows. By the mid-1970s, the government had become increasingly concerned about the nation's swift move toward "developed nation" status. It was actively lobbying before international banking and donor agencies and arguing that Singapore was a "middle-income developing country," not a "middle-class nation" or an "industrialized nation."[6] Despite evidence of continued economic growth and of a growing middle class in Singapore, the nation continues to exhibit inequalities by class and ethnicity and new social problems that have accompanied economic growth and greater materialism.[7]

Government-Private Sector Alliance

In Singapore, the government is clearly committed to the free enterprise system, within which TNCs and TNAAs operate most successfully from their perspective of growth, profits, and consumerism. During a time of growing government involvement in the private sector generally and increased direct government control over various aspects of advertising, Singapore stands out as an Asian nation that has *not* reverted to nationalism and that has unequivocally welcomed investment from TNCs, including TNAAs.

In Singapore, as in so many other developing nations, advertising was stimulated by government policies allowing commercials on the govern-

Table 31

Key Indicators of Standard of Living in Singapore
(Monetary Figures in Singaporean Dollars)

Year	Approx. Per Capita Income	Per Capita Savings (Fixed & Savings Deposits)	TV Sets	Telephone	Private Cars*	Buses*
1965	$1,500	$ 405	1 per 29 persons	1 per 22 persons	1 per 18 persons	1 per 1,166 persons
1977	$6,000	$2,770	1 per 7 persons	1 per 6 persons	1 per 17 persons	1 per 436 persons

Year	Modern Sanitation	Annual Per Capita Expenditure Furniture, Furnishings, & Household Appliances	Annual Per Capita Expenditure on Culture, Recreation, Entertainment & Education
1965	50% of population	$157	$126
1977	75% of population	$256	$367

Year	Daily Newspapers Circulation Per 1,000 Population	Annual Cinema Attendance Per Person	Radio and Television Licenses Per 1,000 Population
1968	148	14	49
1977	215	19	143

*/ In 1975, the Singapore government officially began discouraging private car ownership and improving public transportation services to reduce pollution and congestion in heavily urbanized Singapore.

NOTE: In 1965, Singapore withdrew from the Federation of Malaysia and became an independent nation. One U.S. dollar equals approximately $2.4 Singaporean. These statistics should be treated cautiously since Singapore has a relatively large, affluent foreign community, including diplomats and expatriates working with local and foreign firms.

SOURCES: Compiled from government data in The Yearbook of Statistics, Singapore 1977/78 (Singapore: Department of Statistics, 1978), p. 7, and "Standard of Living Rises as Economy Expands," The Mirror, 13 March 1978, pp. 4-5. The latter is an official publication of the Ministry of Culture.

ment-owned broadcasting service as a means of stimulating economic growth. Advertising began on Singapore radio, which had existed since 1935, in July of 1960, and on Singapore television in January of 1964.[8] Several years earlier, cinema advertising had become an important, well-organized advertising channel in both Singapore and Malaya, largely due to the arrival of Pearl & Dean, a British firm that took over the sale of cinema advertising time for the giant Shaw Brothers chain of theaters in both markets.

Compared to Indonesia and even to Malaysia, whose advertising development patterns in many ways parallel those of Singapore, Singapore's official policies affecting foreigners in the advertising business are essentially laissez-faire. Singapore is not promoting a "localization" policy in either rhetoric or practice. Lee Kuan Yew has made clear that expatriate professionals are needed and welcome:

> There is no way to embark on Singaporeanization without irreparable damage. I do not see us producing the number of engineers, management consultants, and decision-makers with the experience and judgment to fill these jobs, even if all the firms wanted us to, for at least 20 years. Before then, new advances in business and industry will bring in a new generation of experts and expertise.[9]

By 1977, for example, more than fifteen thousand "employment pass holders and foreign investors" were in Singapore as owners, managers, advisors, and technicians, and the prime minister estimated that a policy to remove them would, within a year, result in 30 percent of the workforce losing their jobs.[10] Since the United States is the largest foreign investor in Singapore, many of the expatriates are Americans.

In sharp contrast to both Malaysia and Indonesia, then, Singapore makes no economic nationalistic demands on a service industry such as advertising that backs and supports foreign investors. The government makes no distinction between indigenous and foreign advertising agencies, or capital generally. Expatriate work permits—an increasingly touchy topic in both Malaysia and Indonesia—are liberally granted. The small island nation in 1978 had about thirty-three expatriates in advertising agencies, while the much larger Malaysia and Indonesia each had about twenty-five.

In terms of regulations on media content, Singapore's policies are probably as strict as any nation. The Prime Minister, for example, is well-known for his mistrust toward the press and his stern views against aping the West's permissiveness and for his tight control of the press. He has told the media:

> It is not possible to sustain the moral fiber of your society if 'everything goes.' Everything does not go in Singapore. There are incentives and disincentives which will be applied. Some have a special responsibility—

people in the news media, the PR man who draws his posters, the producers of snippets for television or cinema advertisement. Only one
society is more exposed than us, Hong Kong. There, everything goes.
But nobody cares. Nobody is trying to build a nation in Hong Kong. If
they try, Peking will come down on them. Nor does Hong Kong have one
man one vote every five years.[11]

Other Singaporean officials also frequently speak out about their people
being overexposed to what is "bad" and about the need for "cultural in-
noculation" to promote a "rugged" and "resiliant" society that values hard
work and thrift.

Symbolic of Singapore's efforts to control alien influences was the government's much-publicized campaign against unkempt, long hair in the
early 1970s.[12] The government, too, has been extremely worried about
growing drug abuse and the health hazards of smoking tobacco. In 1971 it
implemented a blanket ban on all tobacco advertising.[13] But as long as
advertisements do not make unwarranted claims, avoid stirring up racial
and religious sensitivities, and do not use long-haired males and "hippie
life-style" themes, the government has not interfered in advertising to any
great extent.

The government seems to take the stance that there are certain costs that
Singapore has to pay because of its size, its openness to foreign investment,
and its unique geopolitical location. In the area of advertising, for example,
some foreign intrusion is simply unavoidable. Advertising and other contents from Malaysian radio and television spill over into Singapore, and the
government is all but powerless to keep them out.[14] Until the early 1980s,
cigarette commercials were allowed in Malaysia but not in Singapore. Any
Singaporean, however, could freely tune in one of Malaysia's two television
channels or four radio networks and expose himself to tobacco advertisements. In this case, Malaysian government policy clearly undermined Singaporean government policy.

The Singapore government has no particular restrictions against
foreign-made advertisements as long as they, like locally made messages,
meet the standards of ethical conduct specified in the Singapore Code of
Advertising Practice and the government's Radio and Television Singapore
Program Code.[15] Imported television commercials, for example, are allowed and commercials can be aired throughout the broadcast schedule.
This is in sharp contrast to Malaysia, where foreign-made commercials are
banned, and to Indonesia, where foreign advertising films are allowed but,
like any TV advertising since 1975, they could be shown only during a
relatively limited block of advertising time. In 1981, all television commercials were banned in Indonesia. Singapore Television's language policy also
is more open than that of either Malaysia or Indonesia. In Singapore,
advertising and other programs can be in any of the four officially recognized languages (Malay, Chinese, Tamil, and English), but the govern-

ment's bilingual policy has resulted in English and Chinese being the major languages of advertising and everything else. In Malaysia, the government tolerates the use of Chinese, Tamil, and English on one of its two television networks, but encourages the use of the national language everywhere. One TV network is reserved exclusively for Bahasa Malaysia, and any shots of copy on packs of labels must be in Jawi (Arabic) or Roman characters (not, for example, in Chinese or Indian characters). In Indonesia before the 1981 ban, the government required that the Indonesian language be used, although this frequently meant that an imported advertising film using obviously foreign models and settings would be used with a "voice over" or sound track dubbed into Indonesian.[16]

Singapore's liberal stance on foreign advertising obviously is a great advantage to the English speaking TNC advertisers and their TNAAs, which together have ready access to professionally produced commercials from their headquarters and other sources outside of Singapore. Such imported syndicated pattern material can be used at a fraction of the cost that it would take to originate materials in Singapore. As a result, advertisers have no incentive to produce advertising with Singaporean identity, and Singapore television and the media generally are full of foreign-made advertisements, often in English and using Caucasian models and Western settings. In 1977, for example, about 140 brands of jeans, many of foreign origin, were being advertised in Singapore, including on government-run television.[17] In Parliament, the minister of culture responded to growing public criticism of jeans advertising by saying:

> Acceptance of advertisements for telecast does not mean the station's or the government's full endorsement of the manner of presentation or of the product advertised. For example, acceptance of commercials promoting jeans does not mean government endorsement or otherwise of that apparel. We are only concerned with selling air time.[18]

By 1978, there was widespread talk that the government was so serious about improving Radio and Television Singapore (RTS) that it would remove broadcasting from under the Ministry of Culture and make it more commercial and autonomous. By the early 1980s, such a move had been implemented and broadcasting was freed of some government red tape.

From the perspective of the businessman, such a development is considered pragmatic and is obviously well-received. For example, two senior TNAA executives publicly praised the Singapore government during their visits to the nation. O&M's David Ogilvy told Singaporeans: "I've known for years that this is the best governed country in the world and after watching the television last night I know why. That's not meant to be funny. How lucky you are."[19] James Benson, international vice chairman of O&M, has said of Singapore: "It seems like the country is run by businessmen. Some of the government people may not take this as a compliment but I mean it as one."[20]

The president of the Advertising Media Owners Association of Singapore told me: "We'd like to see the best ads in the world so that local advertising people can learn and improve."[21] A Singaporean working for a TNAA said: "Singapore is very much a cosmopolitan place—a city of the world, and you can't achieve the status of city of the world if you have all these [government regulatory] obstacles."[22] The 1978 president of the 4As told me: "I don't think we should shut out the expats unless we're better. This closed-company kind of thing is bad for business."[23]

The president of the Advertisers Association told his organization:

I see ourselves inviting the best advertising brains from these countries [in Europe, United States, Australia, and Japan] to Singapore to explain the advertising practices in their respective countries. I see the Singapore Advertising Man as an International Advertising Man because increasingly Singapore's markets will be outside Singapore.[24]

While the Singapore government's attitude toward advertising generally is not widely criticized by either local or foreign advertising people, these same ad men *are* critical of government policies and the increasing nationalism (interpreted as both antiforeign and anti-Chinese) in both Malaysia and Indonesia. For example, one TNAA expatriate spoke harshly of the Malaysian government: "If it makes more restrictions, Kuala Lumpur won't become the ASEAN advertising capital but the ass-end capital!"[25] A Singaporean with a TNAA spoke about the "blind nationalism" in both neighboring nations and said "everything across the [Singapore-Malaysia] Causeway is political" and has racial overtones. An expatriate ad man emphasized that it was a pleasure being based in Singapore because the government was corruption-free and did not pressure advertising into reflecting an artificial "Singaporean identity."

Amidst such an environment of relative harmony between the government and the transnationally linked private sector, it is only natural that the foreign businesses and the advertising industry generally would prosper. In such a climate, too, it is easy to see how tiny urban Singapore might become saturated with advertising and be used as a base camp for the TNAAs.

TNAAs' Dominance

As tables 32 and 33 illustrate, advertising expenditures and the number of agencies in Singapore have increased dramatically since 1967, when the government was intensifying its efforts to attract labor-intensive invest-

Table   32

Estimated Expenditure on Advertising in Singapore, 1968-76

(In Thousands of Singaporean Dollars)

	1968	1969	1970	1972	1973	1974	1975	1976
Newspapers	13,200	16,000	16,800	24,100	30,200	35,400	43,700	51,800
Magazines	(1,000)	(1,500)	(2,500)	2,600	7,100	11,700	7,000	7,300
Publications	(3,000)	(3,000)	(3,000)	(3,000)	(3,000)	(3,000)	(3,000)	(3,000)
Rediffusion	600	600	800	600	700	800	700	800
Radio	1,100	1,800	1,800	1,400	1,200	1,200	1,600	1,200
TV	6,300	7,500	9,500	8,400	9,100	9,900	12,800	12,400
Cinema	(2,500)	(3,000)	(4,000)	(4,500)	(4,500)	1,800	2,200	1,500
Outdoor	(4,000)	(4,000)	(4,000)	(4,000)	(4,000)	(4,000)	(4,000)	(4,000)
Total Media	(31,700)	(37,400)	(42,400)	(48,600)	(59,800)	(67,800)	(75,100)	(82,000)
Production	(3,200)	(3,800)	(4,200)	(7,300)	(9,000)	(10,100)	(11,200)	(12,000)
TOTAL	34,900	41,200	46,600	55,900	68,800	77,900	86,300	94,000
		+13%	+13%	+20% (2 yrs.)	+23%	+13%	+11%	+9%

NOTES: Bracketed figures denote estimated figures. One American dollar is equivalent to approximately 2.4 Singaporean dollars. In 1976, therefore, total estimated Singaporean advertising expenditure was more than $39 million. Display advertising has been monitored throughout the 1968-76 period. Costs do not reflect, however, frequency or special discounts or loadings for some special positions. "Classified" and "shipping" advertising was monitored only in 1969, 1970, 1972, and 1975. 1969-72 averaged about one-third of total expenditure, and 1975 about one quarter. Estimates for 1968 and 1973 are therefore made on the same proportionate basis as 1969-72, but 1974 is based on 1975.

Magazines: Monitoring of regularly published magazines started only in 1972. About twenty-five such publications were monitored in 1973. Figures for 1968-70 are sheer guesses. Fewer "high cost" consumer magazines (but more low cost technical magazines) were available in 1968, so expenditures were lower both actually and as percentage of total expenditure than now.

Publications: This section is intended to cover programs, charity publications, and similar "on-off" publications. It has never been possible to monitor these. The figures are sheer guesswork and have been maintained at the same level throughout the years because these publications seem to have declined in relative importance in recent years. The amount of money spent on them is probably about the same, but it forms a smaller proportion of total expenditure.

Production: This heading includes all media production, press, radio, films, and print production through advertising agencies. Based on 10 percent of total media billings 1968-70, and 15 percent of total media billings for 1972-76. This is based on rough "production reserve" formulae used by agencies and assumes that nonagency expenditures would follow the same pattern.

Rediffusion is the government-licensed but privately owned wire broadcasting service that originates over two broadcast networks in Kuala Lumpur, Ipoh, Penang, and Butterworth in Malaysia. Rediffusion has "sister" stations in Singapore and Hong Kong. It began in Malaya in 1949. It is a unique advertising and entertainment channel and its programs are directed predominantly to a Chinese audience. The number of sets on service has been expanding by at least 5 percent a year throughout the seventies. Programs such as Chinese serials, either from Hong Kong or locally produced, are extremely popular.

SOURCE: Fred Kent, regional media director for Grant, Kenyon & Eckhardt, Singapore, provided me with these estimates which he prepared during May of 1977. His original sources included "FERO Monitoring Reports," 1968-72; "MIS Adex Reports," 1973-76; and the two major cinema advertising organizations:Pearl & Dean, and Cathay Organization, 1968-73. I interviewed Kent on 15 November 1977.

Table 33

Advertising and Related Services in Singapore, 1967-74

	1967	1972	1976
Number of establishments	91	150	297[a/]
Number of employees	858	1,077	2,358[b/]
Gross Receipts (in thousands of Singaporean dollars)	30,479	58,875	59,686

NOTE: In Singapore, government considers advertising and "related services" (publicity and market research services) as its industrial group 8391.

[a/]   Includes 182 advertising services

[b/]   Includes 1,355 in advertising services work

SOURCE: 1967 figures from personal correspondence with Lau Kak En, Department of Statistics, Government of Singapore, Singapore, 8 December 1977; 1972 figures from Report on the Census of Services 1972 (Singapore: Department of Statistics, June 1974), Summary table 1, p. 16; and 1974 figures from Report on the Census of Services 1974, vol. 1, Real Estate, Business, Social and Personal Services (Singapore: Department of Statistics, July 1977), table 1.1, p. 17.

ment and to shift from import substitution to export promotion.[26] For example, between the boom years of 1968 and 1976, annual growth in advertising expenditure was never less than 9 percent.

Despite its relatively small (but increasingly affluent and sophisticated) domestic market, Singapore obviously has always had great appeal to the TNAAs. By the time of its independence in 1965, Singapore already had seven TNAAs, some of which serviced Malaysia, Indonesia, or Brunei out of their Singapore offices. By the early 1980s, at least seven more TNAAs—including such American giants as JWT, BBDO, and Y&R—had entered the Singapore market.

One reason for such a relatively heavy concentration of TNAAs (and other service organizations) is that compared to most developing nations its people are receptive to new products and ideas, affluent, well-educated, and generally Western-oriented. But certainly a more important reason is the government's receptiveness to foreign businesses. This has meant that a service industry such as advertising has been able to develop around wholly owned foreign investments. The TNAAs have not had to find politically well-connected bridgeheads through which to operate since they can openly own and manage their operations without fear of what they perceive as interference from either meddling officials or xenophobic (or at least envious) local ad men. Foreign-owned agencies have not had to worry about finding local directors or hiring particular ethnic groups since the government gives little attention to the role of indigenous ad men in running the industry. As in Malaysia and Indonesia, the TNAAs in Singapore rely heavily on indigenous personnel to staff most positions, but senior posts are usually held by expatriate managers. Unlike in some developing nations, these expatriates do not have to maintain low profiles for fear of jeopardizing their position, and their agencies need no "fronts."

Both the government and the powers that be within the local advertising industry seem to welcome the TNAAs, and their ideas seem to be readily absorbed locally. An indicator of such penetration is that expatriates in Singapore are very visible in the industry's two major professional organizations—the 4As and the Singapore Advertisers Association (SAA).[27]

Another reason why the TNAAs have crowded into Singapore has to do with the island republic's strategic geopolitical location between two growing, but somewhat unpredictable, markets. Kuala Lumpur is only about 200 miles north of Singapore, and Jakarta is about 550 miles south. Singapore's efficient transportation, communications, banking, and other support facilities make it an ideal regional headquarters for a modern service industry like advertising.

Like other technical and professional consulting services, the TNAAs give Singapore high ratings as a clean, efficient, economically stable, and politically safe headquarters for Southeast Asia. To one extent or another, such TNAAs as the Fortune Group, JWT, Kenyon & Eckhardt, McCann-Erickson, Needham, Harper & Steer, Bates, Dentsu, Hakuhodo, Y&R, SSC&B:Lintas and Y&R use Singapore as headquarters for a wider market than merely Singapore. In 1980, for example, approximately half of Y&R's media billings in its new Singapore office were outside that country. (Hong Kong is probably the only place in Asia that has more TNAA offices than Singapore, and it was not surprising that when Ogilvy & Mather decided to diversify into transnational public relations in the early 1980s, the agency choose both Singapore and Hong Kong as sites for its first Asian public relations operations.)

A few other examples of regionally conscious TNAAs will show the middleman role that Singapore, as a regional source of advertising expertise and back-up facilities, plays between the region's Malay countryside and the advertising-rich, Center nations like the United Kingdom, the United States, Japan, and Australia. In addition to obviously serving the Singapore domestic market, a TNAA like McCann-Erickson uses its Singapore office to oversee regional activities for such major American clients as General Motors, Gillette, and Coca-Cola. The agency's Malaysian billings for Coca-Cola are even credited to its Singapore operation rather than to its Kuala Lumpur office.[28] USP Needham services such major TNC clients as Bristol-Myers and Carnation from its regional office in Singapore and has a senior "creative coordinator" appointed to oversee regional activities from Singapore. Leo Burnett handles Levi Strauss for both Malaysia and Singapore markets out of Singapore. Dentsu's Singapore office only recently became a full-service operation, but it has long been a key representative office for the area of Malaysia, Singapore, and Indonesia. Dentsu in Singapore handles various requests from the TNAA's headquarters in Tokyo, conducts surveys, collects information, and services clients.[29]

It is undeniable that both Malaysia and Indonesia have greatly improved their ability to plan, produce, and disseminate advertising materials and skills within their own borders. To a large extent, this changing pattern has occurred because the TNAAs have invested in executive, creative, and other capabilities that make their operations in Kuala Lumpur and Jakarta self-sufficient and at the same time more economical and more culturally sensitive. It also has occurred because of these two governments' concerns that their nations secure a larger share of the region's service, as well as manufacturing, activities. The feeling is that Singapore (like London, New York, Tokyo, and Sydney) for too long has profited unfairly from its higher level of development and its historic influence over intraregional business.

Singapore was particularly hurt by its forced separation from Malaysia in 1965 and subsequent policy changes. The Malaysian government's implementation of the Made-in-Malaysia advertising film policy adversely affected the Singapore advertising industry. Although it is impossible to quantify, my impression is that Singapore's importance as a regional advertising center has *not* declined. Whatever business it has lost from economic nationalism in Malaysia or Indonesia has likely more than been made up in Singapore's domestic advertising expansion and by the nation's success at becoming an important regional center for TNCs and their professional service and communications needs. Table 34 shows that eight of the ten largest agencies for which billings data were available in 1978, for example, are foreign-owned. Seven of the eight are TNAAs, most of which are also operating in Malaysia or Indonesia and all of which are American affiliated or owned.[30]

Until 1979, Batey Advertising—the largest agency in Singapore—was not a TNAA, but it was largely foreign-owned and operated and certainly did not qualify as a "locally oriented" agency. Its major client has been Singapore's largest and most prestigious advertiser, the government-owned Singapore International Airlines (SIA), and Australian Batey's international award winning advertising is seen around the world.[31] By 1980, however, even Batey Ads had become TNAA-linked after BBDO's Hong Kong–based holding company acquired a 25 percent interest.

The only two wholly locally owned and operated agencies among Singapore's top ten agencies are Starlight Advertising (whose biggest client is the

Table 34

Summary of Major Advertising Agencies in Singapore, 1977-78

(In U. S. Dollars)

I. Transnational

Agency	Founded	Ownership	Billings	Staff Total	Staff Expatriate	Total Accounts	Major Accounts
Advertising Associates a/	1965	Wholly owned by Australia's Fortune Group, Sydney	$1,666,670 */	29	3	...	Cathay Pacific Airways, Sime Darby, b/ Yeo Hiap Seng, Canada Dry, John Dewar's, France Scott Pte. Ltd. (Remy Martin, Cointreau and Haig), Sterling Drug, Boyle-Midway (Black Flag and Woolite), Cadbury Chocolate, Castrol
Ted Bates Ltd.	1954 c/	Wholly owned by Ted Bates, New York City	In excess of $1,420,000 */	33	1	44	British Airways, Wrangler jeans and sportswear, Rank Xerox, Ronson, Malayan Breweries (Tiger Beer), Meadow Gold ice cream, Hong Kong and Shanghai Bank, Tampax, General Electric Co., Development Bank of Singapore
Leo Burnett Pte. Ltd.	1964 d/	Wholly owned by Leo Burnett, Chicago	$4,337,745	50	4	...	Ford Motor Co., Kelloggs, Levi Strauss, Pepsi-Cola, Procter & Gamble, S. C. Johnson, Time Magazine, Singapore Tourist Promotion Board, Mobil Minolta, Qantas, Shriro (China) Ltd. (Revlon, Dunhill, Sunbeam), Van Heuten chocolates, Brands Essence of Chicken, Arrow shirts, Chartered Bank, Caldbeck Macgregor (Bacardi, Johnnie Walker, Courvoisier, other liquor and wines), Eastern Agencies (Wrights Coal Tar Soap, Optrex, Woodwards Gripewater, Dom Benedictine), Chupa Chups, Yaohan Dept. Store
Dailey, Naidu & Chan Intl.	1971	Majority local but small portion of equity with Dailey & Associates, Los Angeles e/	...	...	0	...	not available
Dentsu	1967	Wholly owned by Dentsu, Tokyo	...	3	1	...	(Dentsu in Singapore operates a representative office rather than a full-service agency. Any Dentsu home-office clients needing service in Singapore are referred to Advertising Associates, and the two agencies split any commissions for placement of advertisements in Singapore media. In Malaysia, Dentsu places through Asian Marketing Communications.)
Grant, Kenyon & Eckhardt f/	1955	60% owned by Kenyon & Eckhardt Group, New York City; 40% locally g/	$3,276,000	65	8	...	Bank Americard, Titoni watches, Esso, Handy Plast, Metro Dept. Store, Singapore Tourist Promotion Board, Wella hair care, Reader's Digest (corporate), Cold Storage (food and supermarket), Helena Rubinstein, Alitalia, Martell Cognac
Hakuhodo	1973	Wholly owned by Hakuhodo, Tokyo h/	$ 750,000	13	2	11	Kao (detergent and shampoo), Matsushita Electric (National products), Ajinomoto (seasoning), Glico (confectionery), Isetan Dept. Store, Toshiba (creative

Agency	Ownership	Year	Billings				Clients
Compton	50% by Compton, New York City; 50% by Guthrie Group, London i/	1964	$1,065,000	22	0	. . .	Guthrie Trading (Canon, Toshiba, Livita, Kanebo cosmetics, Vat 69, Bulova, etc.), Overseas Chinese Banking Corp. (OCBC), NTUC Travels and Welcome Supermarkets, Lee Jeans, Siemens (telecommunications), Jardine Sandilands (appliances and toiletries), Elizabeth Arden (skin care products)
McCann-Erickson	Wholly owned by McCann-Erickson Worldwide, part of The Interpublic Group of Companies, New York City	1964 i/	$1,479,995	26	1	. . .	Coca-Cola Corp./Lion (S) Pte. Ltd., General Motors Overseas Distribution Corp., Boustead Trading (Hennessy), Gillette Southeast Asia, Kodak, Hilton Singapore, Nabisco, Lever Bros., L'Oreal, Thomas Cook Overseas
Ogilvy & Mather	Wholly owned by Ogilvy & Mather Intl, New York City	1928 k/	$5,303,515	50	2	48	Alberto-Culver (hairspray, shampoo), American Express, Avon (cosmetics), Bayer (Bayon insecticides), Borneo Company (Rolex and Tudor watches, consumer products), Bosch, British American Tobacco (Singapore Tobacco Company development projects), Cavenham Foods, Chesebrough-Pond (Odorono, Vaseline Intensive Care lotion), Chubb, The East Asiatic Co. (Vespa scooters, shipping), Betz Corp. (Quaker, General Foods, Purex, Cuticura), Citizen watches, Guinness Stout, Moutrie (Texwood jeans), 3M, Pakistan Intl Airlines, Pan American Airways, Philips, Prodenta (Indonesia), Scott & Bowne (Scott's Emulsion, Vykmin), Sheaffer pens, Shulton (Old Spice, Breck), Sime Darby (corporate, Shoppers City), Straits Steamship, Straits Times Group (Publications), Temenggog (A&W fast food chain), Unilever, Union Carbide, Kandos chocolates
SSC&B: Lintas S.E. Asia Sdn. Bhd.	Wholly owned by SSC&B: Lintas Intl. Ltd., London	1975 */	$2,082,466	18	1	. . .	Lever Bros., Johnson & Johnson, JAL, Behn Meyer Trading, Industrial and Commercial Bank
USP Needham S.E. Asia Pte. Ltd.	Wholly owned by USP	1972	$1,000,000 */ j/	15	2	. . .	Wrigley's gum, Australian Trade Commission, Bristol-Myers (Clairol, Mead Johnson, Drackett Divisions), Vitalis, Mum-Ban deodorants), Carnation Co., Diner's Club, Century/Champion Motors (Audi, Renault, Volkswagen cars), Lipton Tea, Philip Morris Malaysia (Marlboro cigarettes), Setron (radio and TV sets), New Zealand Dairy Board, Boots Far East (baby products)

II. Local

Agency	Ownership	Year	Billings				Clients
Ace Advertising m/	Local	1953	. . .	. . .	0	. . .	Shell, Hagemeyer (trading house, including National products)
Argus	Local	1965 */	. . .	. . .	0	. . .	Sanyo (electrical goods), Garuda airlines, Longine watches

Agency	Year	Ownership	Billings				Selected Accounts
Batey Advertising n/	1972	Expatriates own majority equity	$6,000,000	50	7	9	Singapore Airlines (SIA), United Overseas Bank, Yardley cosmetics, Carrier air conditioners, Silvaroyal (Omega, Tissot watches), BP Oil, Volvo cars
Henry Chia Associates	1972	Local	$1,667,000 */	24	0	12	Dumex (baby food, full cream milk, analgesics), Jack Chia Group (toiletries, confectioneries), Amco Jeans, Triumph (undergarments), Linguaphone (language courses)
Fortune	1947	Local, plus Fortune owns small part of IMAA, a New York-based joint venture agency group o/	$1,001,224	23 in two offices	0	...	Pan American (cargo only), Boustead (trading), Diethelm, Singapore Carpet Mfrs., Rentacolor Pte. Ltd., Hotel Merlin
Interads	1972	Local, quasi-government ownership through Singapore Pools p/	$1,125,000 */	8	0	...	Singapore Sweeps and Toto (lottery), plus advertising, particularly about appointments, tenders, and notices, for other government-related agencies, including Housing Development Board, Public Utilities Board, Ministry of Defense, Port of Singapore Authority, Jurong Town Corp., Singapore zoo
Pace	1963	Local, but loose affiliation with Marketing & Advertising Network Asia (MANA), a regional agency network headquartered in Manila q/	$1,300,000 */	29	0	18	Roxy (S) Pte. Ltd. (Sharp electrical goods and Telefunken color TV), Bridgestone Tires, Yamaha
Starlight Advertising s/	1952	Local	$2,500,000 */	40	0	...	Seiko watches, Emporium Dept. Stores
Tom Tan Associates	1968	Local	$ 575,190	18	1	27	Honda (cars and cycles), KLM, Robinson & Company (department stores), Selangor Pewter, Jack Chia-MPH (pharmaceutical products)

*/ = Estimate

NOTES: Almost all of these agencies are members of the Association of Accredited Advertising Agents Singapore (4As).

"Local ownership" in Singapore advertising tends to mean Singaporean Chinese rather than any other ethnic group in the nation.

a/ The Fortune Group, based in Sydney, maintained a small office in Kuala Lumpur from 1969 to 1976, but it now handles Malaysian business out of its Advertising Associates agency in Singapore.

b/ Sime Darby, the giant trading house, once owned half of Advertising Associates. It continues to give some of its diverse advertising business to Advertising Associates, but the Fortune Group has acquired the total share holding of the Singapore agency.

c/ Cathay Advertising Ltd., a regional advertising agency started by an Australian woman in Hong Kong, began the office in 1954. Later, George Patterson, the large Australian agency, acquired an interest in the agency. In 1963, the entire regional operation was acquired by Ted Bates, New York, when it took over George Patterson.

d/ The agency began as a branch of London Press Exchange (LPE) in 1964. In 1971, Leo Burnett, Chicago, merged with Britain's LPE and Australia's second-largest agency, Jackson Wain. Their offices became part of Leo Burnett's transnational operations.

e/ Since about 1975, the agency has been a member of the Dailey International Group, which consists of about ten local agencies concentrated in the Pacific Basin and calling themselves the Trans Pacific Communications System (TPCS). Dailey & Associates usually holds a minority position in each of these agencies. It started in 1968 when Detroit's Campbell-Ewald, now part of The Interpublic Group of Companies g/ The Kenyon & Eckhardt Group considers itself a "multi-national agency" and says it pursues a "worldwide policy of national ownership." In the case of the Singapore operation, the 40 percent "local" ownership refers to locally held equity other than that held directly by the parent organization. Expatriates working in the Singapore office own some of this 40 percent.

h/ When it was founded in 1973, the Singapore office of Hakuhodo was 60 percent owned by the parent Japanese corporation and 40 percent by Singaporean interests. In 1974, Hakuhodo, Inc. gained 100 percent ownership of the local operation.

i/ The agency began in about 1964 as a house agency for Guthrie, the oldest commercial or trading house in the area. It continues strong with numerous investments in engineering services, marketing and import-export activities in Singapore and Malaysia. Later, Compton Advertising, the American TNAA, bought 50 percent of the equity, and the agency, known as Lash-Compton, became part of Compton's Asia-Pacific network, coordinated by the Sydney office of Compton Advertising Australia.

In 1978, the agency was renamed Compton Advertising (Singapore) Pte. Ltd. to emphasize its connection to the American TNAA, which that year acquired majority shareholding and expanded its services.

j/ Until December of 1975, McCann-Erickson in Singapore had operated as a branch office of McCann in Kuala Lumpur. The TNAA's Southeast Asia regional coordinator is headquartered in the McCann Singapore office, which maintains a very close working relationship with McCann's operations in neighboring Malaysia and Indonesia. The agency's Asia and Pacific regional headquarters is in Tokyo.

k/ O&M Singapore can trace its origins back to one of the area's first advertising agencies, Master's Ltd., which began in about 1928 and later became S. H. Benson, London. In September of 1971, O&M was established in Singapore through a takeover of Benson.

l/ USP Needham South East Asia, Singapore, provides clients with service in Singapore and elsewhere in the Southeast Asian region. The agency was established in 1972, after a previous association with S. H. Benson. It formerly was part of the International Needham Univas Network, which broke up in 1977. Its parent company, USP Needham Australia, has the American TNAA, Needham Harper & Steers, as its partner.

m/ Widely known as IAP & Ace, the Singapore agency was once associated with agencies in Thailand, Malaysia, and Indonesia, and JWT had some interest in the Singapore agency. In 1974, the Bangkok IAP (Inter-Asian Publicity) organization under American William E. Heinecke. merged with Ogilvy & Mather. In Jakarta, the agency evolved into P. T. Selindo, after an unsuccessful management association with JWT. The Kuala Lumpur operation was sold to (among others) Hagemeyer, a large Dutch trading house with years of experience in Malaysia and Singapore. By 1979, JWT had returned to Singapore with a wholly owned, full service office.

n/ Batey Advertising, which functions as virtually a house agency for Singapore Airlines, had its origins in McCann-Erickson, Singapore. Ian Batey had been account supervisor handling the Malaysian-Singapore Airlines (MSA) account for McCann in 1970. When the governments of Malaysia and Singapore decided to split the jointly-owned airlines into two separate national operations, Batey pulled out of McCann in 1972 and established his own agency to service SIA, the new Singapore national carrier. In 1979, Batey's agency had become 25 percent owned by BBDO's Hong Kong-based holding company.

o/ IMAA calls itself "a joint venture company incorporated in the U.S.A. and owned by a group of strong national advertising agencies in 19 strategically located countries around the world." It also has "branch office contracts" with agencies in about 30 other nations. Fortune in Singapore is a small shareholder of IMAA, rather than owned by it. Fortune is closely affiliated with another local agency, Asian Ad, which began in 1973 and handles Fiat, Jebsen & Jessen, Diethelm, Boustead, and Rollei. For nearly a year, the two agencies functioned as virtually one operation.

p/ Interads functions as a house agency for the Singapore government and primarily handles tenders and notices, appointments, and other advertising for government departments. It is run by a six person board of civil servants under the chairmanship of the Postmaster General.

q/ MANA began in 1976 as a regional network to compete with the TNAAs in providing advertising services within Asia. Pace Advertising, Singapore, was one of the seven original local agencies in MANA. MANA Chairman Antonio de Joya is president of Advertising & Marketing Associates, the largest locally-owned agency in the Philippines. In addition to MANA, de Joya has headed efforts to establish an Asian Federation of Advertising Associations.

r/ Starlight, one of the oldest agencies in Singapore, is widely known as a "Chinese agency." About 70 percent of its business is with Chinese businesses, many of which are small advertisers who do not use English-language media.

SOURCES: These facts and figures about major Singaporean agencies were obtained from a very wide variety of often conflicting sources, including personal interviews in Singapore with agency executives and others knowledgeable about Singaporean advertising. This information should be treated cautiously, and is presented merely to suggest general patterns within the industry.

local distributor of Seiko watches) and Henry Chia Associates (whose main account is Dumex baby food and pharmaceutical products, distributed by East Asiatic Company—the pioneer Dutch trading and shipping agency and a major Southeast Asian advertiser of consumer and other goods). Starlight, one of Singapore's oldest agencies, was founded in 1952 as a cinema advertising slide contractor by C. K. Liew. It has numerous small accounts from Chinese clients, who comprise about 70 percent of the agency's business.[32]

The other major indigenous agency was founded by English-educated Henry Chia, one-time press secretary to the Singapore chief minister, pioneer local public relations man, and former managing director of Leo Burnett's Singapore office. He left that TNAA in a dispute over expatriate control of the agency and in 1972 established his own agency by taking the Dumex account away from Burnett. He has emphasized that his *national* agency was "born out of an environment that was too strongly tinged with imported influences" and it creates every single piece of its advertising locally.[33] Chia has explained:

> Why this emphasis on "national"? Simply because being nationals, we are at a unique advantage in being able to tune in to the same wavelength as the local consumers. We are able to speak the same language. We are in an enviable position of spontaneously understanding religious, racial, and cultural sensitivities. And idiosyncracies, too. All this . . . comes naturally with us. And we do not mean translations of English copy. It goes far beyond this. It gets into the very fibre of conceptual approaches, weaving patterns to fit each required language group.[34]

Despite the success of these two local agencies, they are the exception rather than the rule. To a greater extent than in either Malaysia or Indonesia, advertising in Singapore is Western-oriented and TNAA-dominated. The biggest agencies tend to be TNAAs, and they have better facilities, better paid and trained staff (often expatriates), and more prestigious and bigger clients. For example, the government's own Singapore Tourist Promotion Board (STPB) spends nearly $2 million a year promoting the nation as a tourist center, and the STPB advertising account is shared by two TNAAs—Leo Burnett and Grant, Kenyon & Eckhardt.[35]

Also, as the trend data in tables 35 and 36 show, the TNAAs do far more business and make far more profits than most Singaporean-owned and operated agencies. Under Singapore's open door investment policies, foreign corporations do not have to worry about foreign exchange controls on capital brought into the nation, and there are no limits on the remittance of after-tax profits.

In Singapore, as in Malaysia and Indonesia, most agencies make their profits from commissions on newspaper advertising, but television—where the TNAAs excel—has become an increasingly important medium. Singapore televison advertising revenues almost trebled from S$3.5 million to S$9.5 million in the period 1964 to 1975, and by 1978 nine out of ten homes had television.[36] A comparison of tables 23 (chapter 7) and 32 shows that television advertising in Singapore has always attracted more advertising than in Malaysia, despite Malaysia's population being more than five times larger. Malaysia and Singapore are similar, however, in that TNCs dominate television advertising, and these large advertisers tend to use TNAAs rather than indigenous agencies. The latter seldom can afford the specialized skills and resources needed for TV production. Table 37 lists Singapore's ten biggest television advertisers and their agencies, all but two of which are TNAAs.

A comparison of tables 32 and 27 (chapter 7) shows how interrelated transnational advertising is between Malaysia and Singapore. Four TNCs— Nestlé, Colgate-Palmolive, Beecham, and East Asiatic (Dumex)—are among the top ten TV advertisers in both nations. A comparison of these two tables with table 22 on Indonesia (chapter 6) shows that several of that nation's top TV advertisers are among the biggest advertisers on Malaysian and Singaporean televison. These concentration patterns for advertisers and TNAAs are hardly surprising given the history of Southeast Asia and contemporary, TNC "global reach" trends.

Tensions

Some of the advertising-related problems in Singapore undoubtedly are a reflection of uneasiness over the government's policies, some of which impinge on the daily lives of everyone in Singapore.[37] Others are a reflection of the nation's multiracial composition and its lack of a clear national identity that all Singaporeans can agree upon.[38] For example, complaints about Singapore as a "cultural desert" are frequently heard, and one Singaporean scholar has concluded:

> Culturally, we are neither here nor there. We are exposed to the cultures of the East and the West. Consequently, many get confused. Can we create a national culture? It is not foreseeable at this stage. We would do better if we develop maximally what strong cultural heritage we have. There is also the constant danger of chauvinism evolving as a result.[39]

Other problems in Singapore are common to developing nations generally and are the result of Singapore's extraordinarily rapid transformation away from traditional values and cultural patterns and toward "modernization," or "Westernization."[40] Some problems can best be understood in the context of a concern that foreign life-styles and values such as materialism and permissiveness are fostering a hedonist cult and causing Singaporeans, particularly the young, to abandon their cultural traditions. Government

Table 35

Several Major Transnational and Local Agency Billings in Singapore, 1967-77

(In U.S. Dollars)

	1967	1970	1971	1972	1973	1974	1975	1976	1977
I. Transnational									
Advertising Associates	..	..	..	..	1,680,000	..	..	..	1,666,670*/
Ted Bates								1,420,000a/	1,420,000a/
Leo Burnett	1,099,430b/	4,937,134c/	3,412,000	3,001,000	2,665,754	3,627,367	3,611,591	4,179,620	4,337,745
Grant, Kenyon & Eckhardt d/	700,000	2,000,000	3,600,000	4,370,000	..	..	..	3,725,720	3,276,080
Hakuhodo	..	..	..	..	..	165,000*/	250,000*/	458,340*/	750,000*/
Lash-Compton	..	..	..	800,000	683,001	942,609	800,000	918,000	1,065,000
McCann-Erickson	326,000e/	..	..	..	..	..	..	1,081,880	1,479,995
Ogilvy & Mather	1,354,000f/	1,495,000f/	1,316,113	1,177,249	2,665,754	3,627,367	3,611,591	3,691,203	5,303,515
SSC&B:Lintas	..	..	..	..	..	..	905,000	1,554,888	2,082,466
USP Needham	..	..	..	..	..	..	..	..	1,000,000*/
II. Local									
Henry Chia Associates	..	..	..	..	625,000g/	875,000*/	1,250,000*/	1,416,670*/	1,666,670*/
Fortune	..	..	..	368,760*/	368,760*/	690,698*/	400,000*/	..	1,001,224*/
Pace	445,000e/	625,000*/	750,000*/	857,387	1,041,666	1,166,666*/	1,250,000*/	1,375,000*/	1,300,000*/
Singapore Graphic Associates	..	..	190,000	430,000	742,961	707,562	819,000	..	..
Tom Tan Associates	..	365,000*/	470,833*/	493,750*/	540,417*/	596,250*/	663,333*/	471,900*/	575,190*/

* = Estimate

NOTE: These data are given to present a rough picture of how the transnational advertising agencies have grown in Singapore over the decade 1967-77 and how they compare to several local agencies for which some comparative billings data are available. Figures should be treated cautiously since exchange rates vary and some billings are only estimates by agencies themselves or advertising industry sources. Whenever figures conflicted, I used the higher total.

a/ Estimated in excess of this figure.

b/ As a branch of the London Press Exchange (LPE).

c/ This figure represents combined office of Leo Burnett-LPE and Jackson Wain, the Australian partner of Leo Burnett, Chicago. In 1971, the office officially became a Leo Burnett branch.

d/ Up to 1975, the agency had been part of Grant International. Kenyon & Eckhardt bought the agency in 1975.

e/ 1968 figure.

f/ Until 1971, Ogilvy & Mather in both Kuala Lumpur and Singapore was a branch of S.H. Benson, which in 1970 was part of the Benson Needham Univas world network. By 1980, O&M had established a second group of agencies in the region called Meridian. Its offices included Singapore.

g/ Combined 1972 and 1973 billings.

SOURCES: Data obtained from a variety of sources, including information supplied directly by the agencies, estimates from sources knowledgeable about the Singaporean industry, and annual "International Agency Sections" of Advertising Age in 1968 and the years 1971 through 1978.

Table 36

Several Major Transnational Agency Gross Income Figures in Singapore, 1973-77

(In U.S. Dollars)

Agency	1973	1974	1975	1976	1977
Ted Bates	. . .	. . .	. . .	213,000[a]	213,000[a]
Leo Burnett	. . .	. . .	785,000	756,000	650,036
Grant, Kenyon & Eckhardt	. . .	900,000	800,000	726,390	700,024
Lash-Compton	102,134	150,817	128,000	144,000	159,750
McCann-Erickson[b]	. . .	. . .	. . .	162,180	221,875
Ogilvy & Mather	399,663	504,362	541,468	664,898	795,130
SSC&B:Lintas			146,000	268,000	313,465

[a] In excess of

[b] Until 1976, McCann-Erickson's Singapore operation was part of the Malaysian office, and figures indicating the split between the two offices are unavailable.

SOURCES: Data are compiled from annual "International Agency Sections" of Advertising Age, 1974-78. Figures are either estimates or reported voluntarily by the agencies themselves.

Table .37

Major Television Advertisers in Singapore, 1976

Name	Agency
1. Beecham	Leo Burnett
2. Borneo Co.	Ogilvy & Mather
3. Colgate Palmolive	Ted Bates
4. East Asiatic Co. (Dumex)	Henry Chia Associates
5. Fraser & Neave (Coca-Cola and other soft drinks)	McCann-Erickson
6. Guthrie (Canon, Toshiba, Kanebo cosmetics, etc.)	Compton
7. Nestle	Ogilvy & Mather, Grant, Kenyon & Eckhardt
8. Thong Sia (Seiko watches)	Starlight
9. Unilever	SSC&B:Lintas
10. Yeo Hiap Seng (Pepsi and other drinks and foods)	Leo Burnett

NOTE: This list includes, in alphabetical order, the top ten advertisers on Television Singapore in 1976. Most of these businesses do such a large volume of advertising for various products that they frequently employ more than one advertising agency. The agencies cited above are examples of the sole or the major agency used by each advertiser. The Singapore government considers the total expenditures of individual advertisers on Television Singapore confidential.

Many of the major television advertisers also are among the biggest overall advertisers in Singapore. In addition to these ten corporations, other major Singaporean advertisers, often in media other than television, would include Cathay Pacific Airlines, Singapore International Airlines (SIA), Sony, Philips, Sharp, several banks (OCBC, UOB, Chartered Banks, etc.), and several department stores (Metro, C. K. Tang, and Yaohan).

Many of the major advertisers in Singapore are also major advertisers next door in Malaysia. For example, Malayan Breweries and Guinness are large cinema advertisers in both countries. The major difference between major advertisers in the two markets is tobacco. Since 1971, Singapore has banned all tobacco advertising. In Malaysia, advertising from TNCs like Rothmans, Malayan Tobacco, and R. J. Reynolds remains a major source of media advertising revenue.

SOURCE: Personal interviews with numerous Singaporean advertising industry representatives, and Soh Siam Loh, "Our Top Ten Big Spenders When It Comes To Selling," Business Times, 24 February 1977.

leaders and concerned citizens are constantly speaking out against "the ugly Singaporean," "moneytheism," and Western consumer habits. Typical of these concerns were those expressed in 1977 by a member of Parliament and the executive secretary of the consumers' association:

> Indulgence in wasteful spending can be clearly seen in the market places, shopping complexes and restaurants. Our mass media, especially our television, have in no small way contributed to this unnecessary spending and wasteful habits among our citizens. We seem to be succumbing to the phenomenon common in developing countries, where imported products acquire snob value, mainly because they cost more and partly because people wish to ape life in the West in the mistaken belief that the West are the trend setters of fashion and a sophisticated way of life. Our television service appears to be guided only by the amount of revenue that advertisements bring in and is not concerned with the type of advertisements. This matter has been mentioned in the House before and seems to have fallen on deaf ears.[41]

Despite these concerns about Singapore's quality of life and the extent to which it is affected by adverse foreign elements, the basic development policies pursued by the government since 1965 have not been changed. A comment by the leader of the national trade union congress, which has intimate ties with the government, typifies the Singapore Establishment's response to much of the criticism:

> Tell our children to look around elsewhere in Asia, where things are quite different, where political witch-doctors condone privilege based on birth, colour, creed, and so on, and our young people will sing "Majullah Singapura" much more fervently than they do now. And do not allow our children to be confused by the humbugs and charlatans who claim to disdain material pursuits and material wealth. For it is material wealth, the producers of wealth, and the technology for wealth creation, which are responsible for our jobs and our standards of living. The skyline of modern Singapore and our new HDB townships are real monuments to the spirit of Singaporeans—not the germ-ridden slums which existed in the past. After getting these facts of life straight, we can get on to the quality of life, which ought to progressively improve.[42]

Given such attitudes on the part of Singapore's leaders, it is understandable why advertising nationalism in Singapore, unlike in Malaysia and particularly in Indonesia, has never become a political issue. Privately, of course, local agency owners and even Singaporeans working for the TNAAs complain about the influence that foreigneres have over Singapore's advertising industry. But local ad men have never gone to the government for special assistance, as they have in some other developing countries, even though they may believe that the TNAAs do take away their clients and may feel that they can never make it to the top of a TNAA simply because they are not Caucasian.[43] The frustration felt by local admen, who feel they are as competent as some of the better-paid expatriates who supervise them, are reflected in this bitter Singaporean's comments:

> There is no more frustrated lot than our local advertising personnel, comprising creative consultants, designers, copywriters, and photographers, to mention a few. Our advertising market is still, after long years, dominated by foreign ad men. A small group of these foreigners—distributed in a number of advertising agencies—have been cornering the bigger contracts in the market, often not because of their expertise, but because of their close ties with other expat executives in the commercial firms in Singapore. Our local executives would not feel so aggrieved if the standard of the expats' work was beyond the reaches of that available from local efforts. The contrary is often the case, and it makes one wonder how foreign admen could have been given the professional visit passes in the first place. The continued presence of mediocre foreign admen deprives our own people of proven worth of an enormous amount of advertising work, so much so that many have expressed the intention of changing their vocations out of sheer frustration or going abroad to seek greener pastures.[44]

Another Singaporean agreed: "without any question from the authorities concerned, employment passes are regularly renewed and even more expatriates are streaming in to find a place in the sun in this exotic island of the East with the greatest of ease.[45]

Henry Chia, one of the few Singaporean ad men to speak out against expatriates, told me about fly-by-nights:

> With few exceptions, the expatriate community in the ad agency business are the birds of passage. . . . They are here as discards (a strong but true opinion) or at best they look upon this country as their stepping stones to better positions at home or elsewhere. How in heaven's name can one really expect them to contribute?[46]

One TNAA managing director came close to agreeing when he told me his agency had problems getting committed expats: "They usually come in for two years, play a lot of golf, have a good time, and then move on."

The prime minister himself has spoken out against the harmful effects that the presence of expatriates generally can have on a nation like Singapore that actively encourages the introduction of Western industry and know-how:

> With Western industries have come Western technologists and executives, their wives and children, and their life-styles. Some of them give visible demonstration of the new hedonist cult. By their personal example, they add to the insidious daily erosion of conventional Eastern morality by so many Western television features, the cinema, magazines, and newspapers. The continuous appeal to the baser instincts is found in too many Western-made or Western-style TV advertisements, whether selling soft drinks or soaps.[47]

Not everyone in Singapore's advertising industry would agree with Lee Kuan Yew or with the view that expatriates are not helping train Singaporeans. For example, one local adman who had served on the Joint Education Committee, a cooperative advertising industry body which encourages professional training, argued that if it is true that:

> . . . the expatriates would rather feast and leech than teach, then so be it. After all we can't expect every man to be noble. But before we blame the expatriates for our own deficiencies, perhaps we should first shame our local elders into becoming involved and accepting what is after all our own responsibility. There are too many of us who are quick to pay lip service but slow to action, and when things do not materialise as they should, it is all too easy to look for scapegoats.[48]

These views suggest that in Singapore, as in many developing countries, the local advertising industry is splintered. Divisions, for example, exist by ethnicity (Caucasian vs. Asians, local vs. expatriate, indigenous group vs. alien group); by language (English vs. vernacular, official national language vs. all other languages); by education (foreign vs. local, local English-medium vs. local vernacular-medium); by training (TNAA trained vs. non-TNAA trained); by commercial success ("rich" vs. "poor" agencies); by staff resources (agencies with expatriates vs. agencies without expatriates); by client type (all or predominantly TNC business vs. all or predominantly local business); and by accreditation (agencies recognized as "professional" or "full-service" by either 4As or prestigious media vs. agencies not recognized).

Amidst such divisions reinforcing one another in a highly visible industry, it is easy to see how the better organized and more stable and experienced TNAAs could take advantage of such differences to maintain their domination over a nation's advertising capacity. In 1974, for example, several local Singaporean agencies unhappy with the 4As tried to organize themselves into a National Council of Advertising Practitioners. The objective was to strengthen national advertising through a locally controlled organization that would offset the TNAA-controlled 4As.[49] The organization never got started because the handful of small agencies could not agree among themselves on what standards of conduct and competency should be enforced.

As long as the local agencies generally remain unorganized as well as small, unprofessional, and isolated from one another by various cleavages, the gap between the TNAAs and the indigenous agencies in Singapore and elsewhere will not be reduced and Periphery nations' advertising dependence on the Center nations will continue as usual.

In the Singaporean context, then, suggestions that the government implement, say, a "made-in-Singapore" policy on advertising films, or require a degree of indigenous ownership in an agency, or change its expatriate employment policy, or give special assistance to local businesses would not be officially welcomed.[50] The local political and business establishment in Singapore was virtually created by association with foreigners and it does not want to take any action that might detract from the overriding objective of *economic* development. The government is extremely sensitive to implementing any policies that could tarnish Singapore's good name with the TNCs and risk its status as a showcase regional base for their activities, including a "softwares" production area like advertising.

Despite some local admen's complaints of foreign domination and unfair competition from the TNAAs, there has been *no* collective confrontation with the TNAAs, and the government has taken few, if any, specific actions that can be construed as supportive of efforts to consciously use advertising for purposes other than basically economic development and growth.[51] This almost "arm's length" relationship is in sharp contrast to situations in Malaysia, Indonesia, and a growing number of other nations where the governments—also strongly pro-Western and pro-foreign investment— have at least paid lip service to indigenous businessmen's desires for increased local ownership and management control as well as better and more formal training programs for locals. This has focused a degree of public attention on the fact that advertising, as very much an imported institution, has no real social goals and responsibilities other than to meet standards of good taste and honesty. To this extent, then, Singaporean national advertising as a salient public agenda item is lagging behind a number of other Asian countries where governments are very conscious of the possibility that the power of advertising could help accomplish more self-directed development patterns and promote a more integrated society.

Clearly, the government of Singapore is willing to pay a price for its dedication to rapid economic and social changes developed around liberal foreign investment policies, expansion of the middle class, and adoption of a consumption ideology.[52] In terms of advertising, the costs include continued domination of the local advertising industry by a handful of foreign-owned and operated agencies and a constant stream of imported advertising influences and materials, most of which originate in affluent Western societies where values are different from those either held by many Singaporeans or those which the government believes should be held by everyone. In terms of indigenous cultural development, the costs include continued conflict and confusion over life-styles and values—often perceived in terms of "Asian" versus "Western"—and uneasiness with growing reliance on the English language and the values and attitudes that inevitably accompany its use. In terms of politics, the costs seem to include apathy about political participation, political conservatism among professional and intellectual elites,[53] and an attitude on the part of a one-party, technocratic government that sees opposition to its benevolent policies as inconsistent with Singapore's progress.

Advertising, as part and parcel of Singapore's market economy system, certainly *does* contribute to the government's economic development goals for a Global City. By Western advertising standards, Singapore *has* been a remarkable success story due to the efforts of the TNAAs, which have freely crowded into Singapore and brought along their ideas of modern advertising and modern living. As one TNAA-produced advertisement for a new Toyota model proclaimed:

> Singapore is compact.
> Singapore is practical.
> Singapre is stylish.
> Singapore is fast-moving.
> Singapore is ahead of the rest.
> So is the Starlet.[54]

But by Malaysian or Indonesian standards, the Singapore government seems so preoccupied with what it sees as the more important economic growth issues of the day that it has ignored the needs of its own advertising entrepreneurs. More specifically, the *structure* of the Singaporean advertising industry has been neglected and the question of how advertising might be used to help solve the nation's noneconomic problems, some of which have been aggravated by foreign advertising influences, has largely been unaddressed.

Notes

1. S. Rajaratnam, "Singapore: Global City." (Text of address to Singapore Press Club, 6 February 1972, Singapore: Government Printing Office), p. 12.

2. See ibid., p. 3. For a Galtung-based analysis of Singapore's important role as "an intermediate processing center" for petroleum in the region, see Robert F. Ichord, *Southeast Asian Oil and United States Foreign Policy.* (Doctoral dissertation, University of Hawaii, December 1976).

3. Rajaratnam, "Singapore: A Viable Independence." (Extracts of a speech at the fourth annual dinner of the Alumni International Singapore on 9 November 1972), *The Mirror* 10, no. 46 (November 18, 1974), p. 8.

4. Singapore pursues a bilingual language policy in the schools, and about 86 percent of the students attend English-medium schools, where they study in English but also learn a second language, usually the mother tongue. For an overview of Singapore's communication problems from a linguistic perspective, see Eddie C. Y. Kuo, "Language, Nationhood and Communication Planning: The Case of a Multilingual Society," *Southeast Asian Journal of Social Science* 4, no. 2 (1976), pp. 31–42.

5. The Singapore government has tightened its control of newspapers in recent years. In 1971, for example, Lee Kuan Yew gained international notoriety when he shut down *The Eastern Sun* and the *Singapore Herald* as antinational influences. The same year, four editors from the *Nanyang Siang Pau,* a Chinese daily, were arrested and detained for stirring up Chinese racial feelings over coverage of China and opposition to the government's language and cultural policies. In addition to extreme sensitivity to Chinese language publications for fear they will glamorize Communism or threaten the government's bilingual language policy, Lee's government has been worried that newspapers will engage in "black operations" and receive subsidies from foreign sources. The 1974 Newspapers and Printing Presses Act and

amendments in 1977 give the government great control over newspaper management. For example, no individual can hold more than 3 percent of the ordinary shares of a daily newspaper, and the government can nominate those holding "management shares." These regulations have broken up the nation's two influential family newspaper empires. The Aw family, main owners of *Sin Chew Jit Pow*, and the heirs of Lee Kong Chian, of *Nanyang Siang Pau*, were required by law to sell most of their shares when their papers were forced to go public. For Lee's view of the press, see his "The Mass Media and New Countries," (address to the International Press Institute, General Assembly meeting, Helsinki, 9 June 1971), and "The Mass Media and Its Role in Developing Countries," (summary of speech by the Prime Minister at the Press Club Dinner, Hilton Hotel, Singapore, 15 November 1972).

6. See, for example, Soh Tiang Keng, "Singapore: No More a 'Poor' Nation," *Business Times*, 23 March 1977, and "Singapore, the 'Middle-class Nation'", *Business Times*, 28 March 1977.

7. For the view that Singapore has successfully achieved rapid economic growth and a more equitable distribution of income, see Peter S. J. Chen, "Social Stratification in Singapore," Working Papers no. 12, Department of Sociology, University of Singapore, Singapore, 1973, and "Growth and Income Distribution in Singapore," *Southeast Asian Journal of Social Science* 2, nos. 1–2, 1975.

8. Interview with Raymon T. H. Huang, commercial manager, Radio-Television Singapore, Singapore, 1 November 1977. He reports to the director of the Department of Broadcasting, which is under the Ministry of Culture. Prior to becoming commercial manager responsible for all broadcasting advertising, Huang was chairman of the Board of Film Censors.

9. I heard the prime minister make these comments in a Singapore address to the Political Association of the University of Singapore on "Higher Education and Singapore's Future," December 23, 1977.

10. Ibid.

11. Lee, "The Mass Media and Its Role in Developing Countries," p. 12.

12. For a discussion of Singapore's crackdown on long hair and other styles of living, see Willard Hanna, "Culture, Yellow Culture, Counterculture, and Polyculture in Culture-Poor Singapore," *Southeast Asia Series, American Universities Field Staff Reports* 21, no. 2, 1973, esp. pp. 7–9.

13. Under the Prohibition on Advertisements Relating to Smoking Act, 1970 (no. 57 of 1970), media advertising of tobacco products was banned. The only promotions allowed were simple point-of-sale materials with no copy message, branded tobacco company cars, and giveaways. The government has no statistics to indicate what effect this legislation has had on tobacco sales. Poh Beng Swee, "The Ban of Cigaret Advertisements on Mass Media in Singapore," an academic exercise for the Department of Business Administration, University of Singapore, 1971/72, estimated that tobacco companies were spending close to S$5 million a year on advertising and that 15–20 percent of total cinema ad revenue, 13 percent of television ad revenue, 20–25 percent of radio ad revenue, and 6 percent of press ad revenue came from tobacco. He also estimated that agencies, including Benson (now O&M) and Jackson Wain (now Leo Burnett), in Singapore lost an estimated S$600,000 on commissions after the ban. These two TNAAs had handled the bulk of Singapore Tobacco Co. (BAT) and Rothmans of Pall Mall advertising respectively.

14. To some extent, the spill-over effect influences Malaysia, too, although not all of even West Malaysia can pick up Singapore radio and television. While I was in Singapore in December 1977 and January 1978, Television Singapore was actively promoting its showing of the controversial American television series, "Roots." The eight episodes were sponsored by Amateur Photo, Singapore distributor of such products as Akai sound equipment. Sponsorship cost an estimated S$160,000, including heavy advance media publicity. More than half of Singapore's adult population saw at least one episode, according to a survey conducted by Survey Research Singapore. Many Malaysians in the southern part of West Malaysia also saw "Roots" since they are within range of Television Singapore. Other Malaysians, however, will never see the program because the Malaysian government decided that it was too expensive and the racial discrimination reflected in the series could create censorship problems. Because of its delicate racial problems, the government undoubtedly felt that such a program might have an adverse social impact on Malaysian viewers.

15. For insight into advertising practices, see Raymon T. H. Huang, "Advertising Codes

and Practices in Singapore including the Cultural Effect of Television Commercials." (Prepared for Tenth Conference, Commonwealth Broadcasting Association, Cyprus, 1974). See also, *Singapore Code of Advertising Practice* (Singapore: Singapore Advertisers Association for the Advertising Standards Authority of Singapore, 1976). This code, originally based on the British Code, is similar to one used by the Malaysian advertising industry. Indonesia has no such code. The Singapore code has been approved by organizations representing advertisers, ad agencies, and media. It is interpreted by the Advertising Standards Authority, which is an advisory council to the Consumers Association of Singapore (CASE). It was established in 1975 to encourage self-regulation of the advertising industry. CASE was founded to promote consumer education and protection by the National Trade Union Congress (NTUC), the labor organization that supported the PAP's rise to official power in Singapore. NTUC and the government both help subsidize CASE. Because of CASE's close NTUC ties, the organization has great influence on consumer affairs in Singapore.

16. A government study of fifty-one Indonesian television advertisements for August and September, 1976, found that more than 39 percent of the commercials used foreign actors and more than 37 percent reflected an "international" atmosphere. See Kelompok Kerja Penilai Siaran Iklan TVRI, "Laporan Final Penilaian Iklan Lewat Televisi" (Jakarta: LIPI/LEKNAS (Indonesian Institute of Sciences), November 1976), p. B2.

While in Indonesia in 1977, I often observed the commercials on Jakarta television during the 5:30–6:30 P.M. advertising hour. A number of the commercials placed by both foreign and local advertisers were obviously produced outside of the nation and for a Western audience. Examples of the numerous commercials I saw that seemed culturally out of place in the Indonesian context included an American-made Coca-Coca film showing young couples on a hayride; a Tancho hair cream commercial from Japan showing a couple playing in the snow; a commercial for an Indonesian food seasoning that showed a Caucasian couple dining by candlelight in a European villa; a Greenspot soft drink film showing Caucasians relaxing on a fancy yacht;   a local drug product's ad featuring a Caucasian model dubbed into Indonesian and talking about headache relief; a Manhattan shirt ad showing Caucasians golfing or traveling around New York City; and a children's medicine commercial showing a Caucasian child sleeping under heavy blankets.

17. This estimate of the number of jeans is from a personal interview with Dr. Philip Chen, general manager, Times Periodicals and president of the Advertising Media Owners Assn., Singapore, 25 November 1977.

18. Jek Teun Thong quoted in "Making Money Not Main Function of RTS," *Straits Times,* 24 February 1977. The minister also said that in 1976, "199 advertisements were rejected for showing on television. They included advertisements which made unwarranted or superlative claims, featured unkempt long-haired males or indecently clad females."

19. David Ogilvy, "How Much Do You Know About Advertising?" (Speech at a Singapore Advertisers Association luncheon, Singapore, 7 April 1978).

20. I heard Benson make this remark during a speech at a Singapore Advertisers Association luncheon, Singapore, 9 November 1977.

21. See note 17.

22. Personal interview with Mervyn Neo, account director, Ogilvy & Mather, Singapore, 17 November 1977.

23. Personal interview with Vince Khoo, then vice president of the 4As, Singapore, 22 November 1977. In 1978, he became president.

24. Patrick Mowe, in remarks at the Annual General Meeting, Singapore Advertisers Association, Holiday Inn, Singapore, 22 April 1977.

25. This comment is a reference to a much publicized speech by O&M's managing director in Kuala Lumpur in 1976. See note 4 in Chapter 7. The TNAA executive predicted that Kuala Lumpur would become the ASEAN advertising capital because it had "a pool of professional advertising talent that is simply unmatched in any other ASEAN capital city."

26. For a discussion of how Singapore's rapid economic growth and industrialization have spurred advertising, see Richard Barnes, "Boom in the Persuasion Business," *Singapore Trade & Industry,* December 1971, pp. 11–15, and Tsang Sau Yin, "Come Blow Your Horn," *Singapore Business,* July 1977, pp. 20–25.

27. Increasingly in recent years, major advertisers in Singapore and Malaysia have used English-educated, well-traveled, and TNC headquarters–trained local specialists rather than

import costly, less politically sensitive expatriates to oversee their advertising activities. Senior executive and marketing positions are often still in expatriate hands, but directing local advertising operations is an area where TNCs relinquish control to indigenous personnel who presumably are better acquainted with local media and local consumers' traits. Most of these local advertising people are local Chinese rather than Malay or Indian. In Singapore, the SAA appears to be run by an elite corps of these Westernized bridgeheads who work for TNCs and who share many of the same sophisticated interests and tastes of expatriate businessmen. For example, SAA's vice president is Dennis Khoo, a Chinese who manages Nestlé's operations in Singapore and previously was its advertising manager in Malaysia. He also has worked with Nestlé in Switzerland and Hong Kong. Some of the TNC bridgeheads have had experience with either the TNAAs or the media.

28. Personal interview with Hans van der Ros, managing director, McCann-Erickson, Singapore, 9 November 1977. The agency's regional headquarters for the Pacific and Asia are in Tokyo, but van der Ros functions as coordinator for the TNAA's combined operations in Singapore, Malaysia, and Indonesia. He said a very close working relationship is maintained between Singapore and the two neighboring offices, and McCann-Erickson has been upgrading its Singapore facilities since 1975 so as to better meet clients' requirements for a mixture of coordination and on-the-spot service.

29. I visited the Singapore Dentsu office on November 7 and 9, 1977, and met Tateo Toda, the TNAA's chief representative. In September of that year, for example, Dentsu had monitored expenditures on these Japanese items: twenty-five electrical home appliances, nine cars, thirteen cameras, six watches, seven cosmetics/toiletries, four heavy equipment, ten office equipment. ten medicines, ten services, and nineteen other items. Advertising expenditure for these advertised products and services that month totalled more that $320,000. This figure suggests that Japanese advertising is important in Singapore, but most of this total was handled by local agencies or non-Japanese TNAAs in Singapore. For example, in the former category would be an agency like Argus, which handles Sanyo, and Pace, which handles Sharp. In the latter category would be Compton, which handles such Japanese brands as Toshiba and Kanebo; O&M, which handles Citizen watches; and Leo Burnett, which handle Minolta and Yaohan (department stores). Hakuhodo is the only Japanese agency ith a full-service office in Singapore, and its relatively small billings makes it the least important of the TNAAs in Singapore. The weakness of the Japanese TNAAs in Singapore is symbolized by the fact that Dentsu does not even directly place its own advertising. It chooses to use another TNAA, the Fortune Group's Advertising Associates.

30. Advertising Associates is owned by the Fortune Group in Australia but is associated with America's Dancer-Fitzgerald-Sample (DFS) through the DFS Dorland Fortune group.

31. For background on Batey's agency, see "SIA and MAS: The Story of Splits, Common Sense and Success," *Media,* February 1975, pp. 14–15; Ilsa Sharp, "A Very Clever Nice Guy, *Singapore Business,* March 1977, pp. 60–63; and "A Way with Marketing: SIA Keeps Playing Its Big Trump Card," *Media,* February 1977, p. 8. In 1976, Batey won the coveted CLIO award in New York City for his "A Way with People" series. The campaign was judged the "best overall international print campaign." For examples of Batey's famous "Singapore Girl" ads and a list of his numerous international and other awards, see "Our Product," Singapore: Batey Advertising (Pte) Ltd., 1977. Regionally, Batey has handled such prestigious clients as Tissot watches, Volvo cars, and United Overseas Bank.

32. East Asiatic Co., a pioneer Dutch trading and shipping agency, is a major advertiser in Malaysia, Singapore, and Indonesia. Like many of the early colonial operations, it has diversified into industrial activities such as Dana paints and Dumex pharmaceuticals in Indonesia; Vespa scooter assembly in Malaysia, Singapore, and Indonesia; and Carlsberg beer in Malaysia. Henry Chia handles Dumex products, including baby foods and pharmaceuticals, in all three nations. The account is worth about $1 million, which is considered very large for a non-TNAA. The agency is headquartered in Singapore but maintains an office in Kuala Lumpur.

I interviewed Alfred Setoh, account director, Starlight Advertising, Singapore, 3 November 1977. For background on the agency, see "Get to Know Us" (Singapore: Starlight Advertising, 1975), and Soh Siam Loh, "Ad Agency that Never Turns Away a Client," *Business Times,* 21 April 1977, p. 10.

33. "Introducing a National Approach . . ." (Singapore: Henry Chia Associates, no date), pp. 7, 13.

34. *Ibid.*, p. 5.

35. Personal interview with Joseph Kong, assistant director, marketing, Singapore Tourist Promotion Board, Singapore, 8 December 1977. More than 1.7 million tourists visit Singapore every year, and the board conducts an aggressive promotional campaign to recruit tourists using such themes as "Shopping and Gourmet Paradise," "Clean and Green Garden City," "Multi-Racial Society," "Instant Asia," and "Singapore—Where the World Comes Together." The board's two TNAAs develop international campaigns using such transnational media as *National Geographic, Reader's Digest,* and *Time.*

36. TV revenues in Hon, "Advertising Industry in Singapore." Survey Research Singapore data show that nine out of ten homes have television and that about 63 percent of all adults watched television "yesterday." These figures are reported in "Singapore Media, Except TV, Shows Continuing Growth," *Advoice,* December 1978, p. 2.

37. For a summary of many of the frequently heard criticisms of the government's policies and practices, see such critical works as Buchanan, *Singapore in Southeast Asia: An Economic and Political Appraisal* (London: G. Bell and Sons Ltd., 1972), and George, *Lee Kuan Yew's Singapore* (London: Andre Deutsch Ltd., 1973). For a concise, sympathetic overview of Singapore politics, see Wee Teong-Boo, "Political Structure of the Global City," in his *The Future of Singapore—The Global City,* (Singapore, University Education Press, 1977) pp. 155–65. He does comment upon, for example, the government's "tendency to bureaucratic arrogance" and the passivity of many Singaporean intellectuals.

38. For background on the government's approach to nation building and Singaporean identity, see Jon S. T. Quah, "Singapore: Towards a National Identity," in *Southeast Asian Affairs 1977* (Singapore: Institute of Southeast Asian Studies, 1977), pp. 207–19.

39. "Foreword," in Wee, *The Future of Singapore—The Global City,* p. 9.

40. For an excellent overview of the impact of the West upon Asia and modernization in Singapore, see Syed Hussein Alatas, *Modernization and Social Change* (Singapore: Angus and Robertson Publishers, 1972).

41. Ivan Baptist, MP, quoted in "Mass Media Helping to Instill Wasteful Spending Habits," *Business Times* (Singapore), 17 February 1977.

42. C. V. Devan Nair, NTUC Secretary General, in a speech to the Singapore Teachers' Union third biennial delegates conference, Mandarin Court, Singapore, 28 May 1977.

43. Several local Singapore agencies gave me examples of how the TNAAs used pressure in various ways to take away their clients. In a personal interview with Sonny Ong, managing director, Asian Ad, 28 November 1977, I was told that his small agency had the Philips electrical account for a year, before it was taken over by O&M, which handles Philips in many markets. The shift came after O&M's chairman, John Elliott, New York, had visited Singapore and looked into the matter. Ong said the rationale given for account switch was that his agency was handling competing electrical products. Although the local Philips personnel were pleased with his work on the account, Ong said, international pressure was applied and Philips Singapore moved the account to O&M. Philips is an important client of O&M internationally and in Malaysia, Singapore, and Indonesia. Occasionally, a major TNC switches from a big name TNAA to a local agency. In Singapore, for example, O&M had handled Shell, which is one of the agency's top fifteen clients internationally. O&M's Kuala Lumpur office continues to handle Shell, but in Singapore it shifted from O&M to Ace, a local agency. Shell told me it was cheaper and faster to use a small agency rather than O&M, which told me that some international accounts are very prestigious but unprofitable in some markets.

44. "Mediocre Expats and Our Frustrated Admen," *Straits Times,* May 31, 1974. This letter to the editor of the nation's most prestigious newspapers was signed "Bean-eater." Its publication brought considerable public attention to the issue of expatriates in the advertising industry.

45. "When Will We See the Expats Go?" *Advoice,* November/December 1975, p. 4. This letter appeared in the official publication of the Singapore advertising industry under the pseudonym, "Bean Eater the Second."

46. Chia, Singapore, in personal correspondence with the author, early December 1977.

47. Quoted in Hanna, "Culture, Yellow Culture, Counterculture, and Polyculture in Culture-Poor Singapore," p. 8.

48. Patrick Ang, "'Detached Expats'—Statement Does Not Present a Fair View," *Advoice,* May 1978, p. 2.

49. Several local agency heads mentioned the unsuccessful efforts in the mid-1970s to

organize such a national organization. Apparently the proposal never got beyond the talking stage, and no one was able to provide me with any written documents about this proposed group.

50. Because of its ethnic composition, Singapore does not have the problem of a shortage of local entrepreneurs that both Indonesia and Malaysia face. Compared to other ethnic groups, the Chinese excel in all trading activities, not excluding advertising. Because Chinese have both political and economic power in Singapore, the question of giving "special rights" to the minority Malay and Indian groups never arises. The Singapore government is very active in various business activities, including state ownership of insurance, steel, banking, shipbuilding, and petrochemicals projects, that concern nearly every major sector of the nation's economy. The government, however, has not entered into any advertising agencies along the lines of either Malaysia's PTM Thompson or UDA's several joint ventures. Since 1972, the government has owned Interad Advertising Consultants, which functions as a house agency for government agencies, particularly the two government-operated games of chance, Toto and Singapore Sweep. These legal forms of gambling are operated by Singapore Pools, a wholly-owned government operation that runs the pools and makes sure that profits are used for community services such as sports promotion. The manager of Interads also serves as public relations manager for the pools. The agency maintains a low profile in Singapore and is not designed to compete with agencies in the private sector although, in effect, it does since government notices, appointments, posters, etc. could be prepared by commercial agencies. Interads is *very* successful. In a personal interview with manager Joseph Y. S. Chan, 16 November 1977, I learned that the agency's net profits have risen from S$44,000 in 1972 to about S$190,000 in 1977. The chairman of Interad's six-person civil service board is the Singapore postmaster general. The agency apparently has no social objectives other than to provide efficient, centralized advertising services to government agencies, which may or may not use its services.

51. By this statement, I do not mean to downplay the government's *very* active role in consumer education and in upgrading the contents of advertising in terms of honesty. Both CASE and the government encourage greater "professionalism," and this has the effect of improving the TNAAs' strength since professional standards and ethical conduct are essentially Western-defined concepts. Any efforts at discouraging unprofessional behavior on the part of advertising agencies is likely to help make the TNAAs stronger since it is the small, local agencies which tend to feel they have to pursue such unethical practices as kickbacks to survive. However, neither local nor TNAA is above discounting and giving commission rebates, which generally weaken the advertising industry because cost rather than quality of service is given priority by clients.

52. Government officials openly talk about the various inevitable costs of movement toward industrialization and the consumer society. See, for example, Lee Kuan Yew, "Progress at a Price," *The Mirror* 13, no. 44 (31 October 1977), p. 1. In this talk to an American group, the prime minister, for example, admits: "Amongst the more unexpected changes was the adoption of contemporary Western attitudes to work by our young. There is the same desire to avoid taking jobs which are considered demeaning or are dirty or heavy. However adequately compensated these jobs may be, young workers prefer less pay for easier, more pleasant conditions of work. So domestic service, garbage removal, road making, construction work exposed to the weather, these are now to be done by guest workers, though there is four per cent unemployment."

53. For example, Peter Chen, "Professional and intellectual Elites in Singapore," *Singapore Spectrum* 1, no. 1 (May/June 1978), p. 4, reports his findings that: "84% of the [professional and intellectual] elites interviewed expressed the view that, in the next ten years or so in Singapore, opposition parties cannot be a vital force nor can they play a constructive role in parliament. About 72% agreed with major government policies relating to public housing, transportation, and medical service and social welfare programmes. Also 76% of the professionals and intellectuals stated that they would do exactly what the government had done were they in government."

54. PTM Thompson advertisement for Borneo Motors, Toyota's distributor in Malaysia and Singapore. The ad appeared in the *Straits Times*, 28 November 1978, p. 32.

9

China: Advertising in a Socialist Society

The modern Marco Polos of Madison Avenue arrived in
China yesterday ready to impart the wisdom of the West in
exchange for the dream of finding the riches of the East.
—*The New York Times,* June 28, 1979[1]

No book about contemporary Asia could be complete without consideration of the People's Republic of China (PRC), the world's largest
market and its most revolutionary nation. Profound changes are sweeping
the country, and one indicator of the "new," outward-looking China is the
spread of modern advertising.

Before the 1949 revolution, during the period when foreigners exerted
great direct power over China, the Chinese people had been exposed to
foreign advertising, and influential transnational corporations like British-
American Tobacco had pioneered mass advertising in "old" China in the
early 1900s.[2] But under the Communists, foreign advertising had disappeared in the 1950s and domestic advertising had virtually stopped by the
mid-1960s.

Since 1979, the year of the PRC's thirtieth anniversary, authorities have
permitted foreign advertising to influence how the vast country communi-
cates both with itself and with the rest of an increasingly interdependent
world. The government slowly but surely has begun to use indigenous and
imported advertising as an institution of commercial information and mass
persuasion for two growth oriented purposes: to sell Chinese goods abroad
(such as Tsingtao beer in the United States) and to sell both Chinese *and*
foreign goods at home.

This chapter will explain how advertising—recognized universally as an
attribute of capitalist development and privately owned media—has become a factor to be reckoned with as China struggles to implement its
ambitious "Four Modernizations" (industry, science, agriculture, and de-
fense) policy to the year 2000. I will argue that China, like most of Third
World Asia, clearly is no longer immune to the pervasive influences of the
transnational corporations in communication and other areas and that

269

there are links between advertising on the national and international levels.

These issues are worthy of consideration because of the effects advertising could have on China's centrally planned economy and development needs and resources and on those of other Asian and developing societies. These are important because many nations continue to respect China's progress toward achieving self-sufficiency, meeting basic human needs, and maintaining cultural integrity. At the same time, however, there is growing concern that external influences, including transnational corporations and advertising, can constrain development by maintaining or even developing inequalities and contributing to tensions and conflicts over sovereignty, communication policies and plans, and sociocultural issues. How China, as a developing socialist society, copes with these interrelated problems and modernizes could help other nations formulate deliberate national development policies and appropriate communication plans.

By the early 1980s China clearly had not gone capitalist, but some free-market forces—including the profit motive and some private ownership of small business in urban areas, as well as increasing amounts of advertising, were being introduced, and mass consumer needs were gaining greater official attention. The Chinese certainly had not abandoned their Mao look for the gray flannel suits symbolizing Madison Avenue, but the door into a society of nearly one billion hard-working prospective consumers was far enough ajar for foreign advertising—on a case-by-case basis—to gain a toehold. Not only had new products (for example, Coca-Cola; Kodak film; Seiko, Citizen, Rado and Orient watches; Frisbee toy saucers; Winston and Marlboro cigarettes; Hitachi, Philips, Sanyo, and Sharp electrical goods; Mopiko medicine; Mitsubishi and Mercedes Benz trucks; and Boeing aircraft) and services (for example, American Express travelers cheques, Pierre Cardin fashions, pinball video machines, and Kaiser and Hughes technical assistance) arrived, but also transnational advertising personnel eager to appraise the market and spread their skills in hopes of future successes.

Transnational Ad Agencies

As China has opened up to foreign influences, emphasized consumer goods (and agriculture) over heavy industry, and inched toward a blending of socialism and some aspects of capitalism, and as the full normalization of economic and commercial relations with the United States has occurred, the transnational ad agencies have been eager to establish relations with Chinese trade officials and media—either directly or through Hong Kong–based intermediaries. By late 1980, *Advertising Age* had declared:

The race is on among multinational ad agencies to crack the huge China

market. So far the agencies have found that the Chinese are more interested in selling their products abroad than in allowing Western consumer goods into China in large numbers. However, each agency wants
to be well placed with a list of important Chinese contacts when that day
arrives.[3]

Interest in China has begun to pay off, and in 1981 at least five of the
major TNAAs—Y&R, McCann-Erickson, O&M, Leo Burnett, and
Dentsu—actively were working with various Chinese authorities. Table 38
suggests the kinds of activities that foreign ad agencies were undertaking.
McCann-Erickson, the first American agency to actually station people inside China rather than covering the country from headquarters or a nearby
Asian office (usually in British-run Hong Kong) has explained the impetus
for all the activity:

> Of major interest is the fact that virtually all media in China is now
> available for advertising by foreign marketers. They are invited to adver-
> tise with minimal limitation on product categories. Although advertising
> of "technological products" is encouraged, the interpretation of the term
> is broad and includes a wide range of consumer durables and even some
> indulgence products under certain conditions. Not only is a market
> emerging for foreign products but the means of communicating to end-
> users and consumers is now at hand.[4]

Reoriented Policies

What has happened comparatively quickly in China is that the government has unmistakably reversed long-standing policies against the normalization of relations with the United States and against "bourgeois"
advertising and economic self-reliance. Such policies had evolved over the
period 1949 through the Cultural Revolution and political turmoil of the
late 1960s. In 1979, *Beijing Review* offered this perspective:

> Since the start of the Cultural Revolution in 1966, commercial advertise-
> ments completely disappeared from the Chinese press because Lin Biao
> and the "gang of four" alleged these ads "are the practice of capitalistic
> businesses," when they took control of the country's mass media. For a
> period of time even window displays and showcases were banned. After
> the smashing of the "gang of four," attention was again given to design-
> ing show-window displays, but people were still not sure by the end of
> 1978 whether newspapers should run commercial ads, and no one tried.
> As there is no private enterprises' cutthroat competition in China, there
> is no need for ads or a big advertising industry as in capitalist countries.
> But this does not mean that there is no need for ads.[5]

By 1979, it had become obvious that China's new leadership, led by
Deputy Prime Minister Deng Xiaoping, no longer dismissed foreign assist-

Table 38

Major Transnational Advertising Agency Involvement in China

World Rank in Income	Agency	Headquarters	Office in China	Examples of Agency's Activity in China
1	Dentsu	Tokyo	Yes	First TNAA to arrange a friendly loose agreement with the Shanghai Advertising Corporation (SAC), 1979. Opened small representative office in Beijing, 1980.
3	Young & Rubicam	New York	No	Officials have visited China. Sells made-in-China goods through J.K. Gill, its U.S. West Coast office supplies and gift store chain. In 1980 headquarters trained two officials with SAC and the Beijing Advertising Corp. Has conducted outdoor poster campaign in China to increase its presence.
4	McCann-Erickson	New York	Yes	First Western agency to establish office in China through McCann-Erickson Jardine(China) Ltd., a venture with minority shareholder Jardine Matheson & Co., Hong Kong. Has agreements with SAC and Beijing and Guangdong Advertising Corporations. Has helped Coca-Cola place sports documentary on national Chinese television and obtained Beijing billboard site for Kodak film. Chinese clients include CAAC, China's national airline, and China International Travel Service.
5	Ogilvy & Mather International	New York	No	Handles China business through its Hong Kong office, whose "China Desk" head travels into China on a monthly basis. Has placed ads in China for such clients as American Express, Grundig TV sets, Rado Swiss watches, Texwood Jeans, and Mercedes Benz trucks. Has primary agency agreements with both Guangdong and Beijing Advertising Corporations to represent them in EEC and Australia and New Zealand. Has agreed to provide the Chinese advertising corporations with access to some of O&M's systems, information, and training. Appointed by R.J. Reynolds to launch Camel filter cigarettes in China. Has helped sell Chinese goods, including "Temple of Heaven Essential Balm", in West Africa. In 1981 managed the first Chinese campaign conducted by a U.S. agency in the U.S. and funded by the Chinese government. The ads promoted Chinese herbs and drinks for China National Native Produce and Animal By-Products Import and Export Corporation.
9	Leo Burnett	Chicago	No	Handles China business through its Hong Kong office. In 1980 signed agreement with Guangdong Advertising Corp. to handle that province's export advertising in Canada and Southeast Asia. Has filmed commercials in China for Seiko and Philips products. A commercial for Philips TV sets was the first "testimonial" commercial produced in China, and it showed a Chinese family extolling the virtues of their new set.

SOURCE: China activity information covers 1979-81 and is extracted from a variety of TNAA, media, and trade journal sources. In addition to these big five TNAAs, a number of other foreign agencies have approached the Chinese in hopes of doing business in or for China. These agencies, for example, include BBDO, DDB, N. W. Ayer ABH, Compton, Dailey & Associates, Hakuhodo, and Fortune. It is important to note that China does not have exclusive relationships with any TNAAs.

ance in advertising and other areas as incompatible with socialist ideals. China is decades away from being an advertiser's paradise, but clearly advertising has gained official stature. An obvious indicator of this is that foreign corporate advertisements have replaced political slogans as feature displays gracing huge billboards in downtown Beijing and elsewhere.

China's reoriented policies reflect the view that the mass promotion of goods (as much as of services and ideas) can assist the government in its efforts to develop and transform China into a modern, powerful nation. As *Wen Hui Pao*, a Shanghai daily, wrote:

> We must learn from foreign advertising, make things foreign serve China and draw on the strong points of certain countries' advertisements to help develop socialist advertising. We should use advertising as a means to educate and assist people and to promote understanding and cement ties between the masses and production and sales departments. Advertising is an art involving a wide selection of the people. Good advertising can make our cities beautiful, lift our spirits and make us feel proud of a thriving socialist economy or culture in a cheerful artistic atmosphere.[6]

Advertising, then, has been envisioned as a potential tool of social change in China, to be used along with other purposive communication tools long used in the country.[7] Even the *People's Daily (Remin Ribao)*, the official communist party newspaper, has begun publishing advertisements; jingles can be heard on the radio; television stations are accepting commercials; telephone directories in the major cities are taking foreign advertising; and space is for rent on large neon signs. By mid-1981, *China Daily,* the first national English-language daily newspaper in the PRC, was established by the *People's Daily* with the guidance of the publishers of Australia's *Melbourne Age* newspaper. Both domestic and foreign advertising was welcomed in the 8-page paper, published in Beijing but distributed to tourists and foreign residents throughout the country.

Significantly, then, the authorities have gingerly allowed more people to have contact with foreigners and foreign messages. The Chinese are no longer discouraged from listening to overseas radio broadcasts, studying foreign languages or great works by Western artists and musicians, or viewing the occasionally shown foreign film. Also, American magazines like *Time, Newsweek,* and *Reader's Digest,* or technical publications like *Scientific American* and *American Industrial Report* are now being imported into China. All carry transnational corporate advertising, but these publications as mass media remain unimportant because they are available only in limited numbers and are sold with foreign currency in a few urban areas only.

The Chinese have become convinced that at least some elements of foreign advertising contents and know-how can be imported and directed at decision makers and adopted for use. This has occurred even though the masses still have little discretionary income and are essentially rural-based. For example, China's gross national product per capita, as reported by the World Bank in 1980, was $230. About 63 percent of the labor force was in agriculture and relatively isolated from the increasingly cosmopolitan urban centers of Beijing, Canton, and Shanghai, where foreigners, businesses, media, and the state-owned advertising corporations tend to concentrate.[8]

It is important, then, to keep things in perspective. China clearly has not been flooded by advertisements or consumer goods—foreign or local. Hong Kong scholar Leonard Chu has offered this picture of contemporary China:

> Though the purchasing power of the Chinese people is generally considered far below the prices of the advertised items (that have appeared in China), most sponsors are aiming at those returned overseas Chinese and those with relatives or friends abroad. In fact, people in Hong Kong and elsewhere have been flooded with letters from their relatives asking for specific brands of TV sets, cassette radios or watches. Some of the brands are even unknown to the letter receivers. At Shumchun, the Chinese town bordering Hong Kong, people carrying TV sets on bamboo poles has become a common sight for the past year.[9]

Despite such scenes and the fact that Hong Kong visitors going into China are allowed to take in many foreign items, it must be remembered that the vast majority of Chinese peasants, workers, and soldiers has no access to foreigners or to their media or currency. Disposable income continues to be very limited. To the average person, consumerism amounts to little more than ownership of—or access to—perhaps a bicycle, a radio, a watch, and a sewing machine. Access to an electric fan, a TV set, a phonograph, a camera, a calculator, or a tape recorder is less common. Private ownership of a car is prohibitively expensive and even buying a bicycle takes about sixty-seven days' earnings for the average worker.[10] Literacy is far from universal, media are poorly distributed (except for radio), newsprint is in short supply (most newspapers have only four pages), and billboard space remains limited. Television continues very much in its infancy. Sets are frequently found in factories and other communal places rather than in private homes. (Interpersonal communication has always been extremely important in Chinese society, and it should not be forgotten that word-of-mouth advertising is very influential in all countries. As the Chinese come into greater personal contact with overseas relatives and tourists, it is safe to assume that they will learn about consumerism and more colorful alternative life-styles.)

In recent years, foreign businessmen have been busy positioning themselves for entry and expansion into China, and the Chinese authorities have been allowing greater individual initiative to national and provincial level state corporations and actively seeking foreign investment and advice. The latter has included some foreign advertising expertise (Japanese, as well as American) to help speed implementation of a China-style socialist modernization. Shanghai—China's New York City—has been designated as the center of the PRC's emerging import and export advertising industry, and in July 1979 the government enacted a long-awaited joint-venture law encouraging direct foreign investment and even allowing foreigners to repatriate some profits.

Such developments are obviously risky since they could contribute to the fostering of not merely rising expectations but also dangerous urban-rural gaps and various frustrations if the Chinese are "contaminated" too quickly with consumer goods and foreign ideas and values. But the government is gambling that the political and cultural risks are worth taking. The positive implications are for rapidly improving the standard of living by increasing light industry and textile production; expanding production and distribution, including advertising as a catalytic agent; increasing the quantity and quality of Chinese products at home and their sales abroad; and cementing various links (including military) with other nations and international organizations (including the World Bank) to ensure China's stability and economic growth.

Ogilvy & Mather has cautioned its clients:

It has to be remembered that China has been virtually cut off from the rest of the world for over 30 years. The people have only been told what's "good" for them and during the last decade, this has been exclusively the "Cultural Revolution". They have no idea about multinational companies, and the sort of products or services they can provide. There is an *astonishing* knowledge gap—even at senior government level. Nothing can be assumed in any business discussion.[11]

China has already begun to experience the problems that lack of knowledge about advertising in any society can aggrevate. In Shanghai, for example, TV sets were advertised on television, but people became upset because there was an inadequate supply and the quality of some of the locally made sets was very poor.[12] This incident reinforces other evidence that the Chinese are becoming increasingly aware of the need to improve the quality and the supply of their goods before advertising them.

The advertising now appearing in various Chinese media is very straightforward, factual, and usually technically oriented. Also, it must be in Chinese script and broadcast in the Mandarin dialect. The advertising of frivolous or luxurious products is not allowed, nor is the Western concept of sex in advertising. Again, O&M has wisely warned prospective advertisers:

Interpretation of advertising will be extremely literal and it is not desirable to attempt analogy, let alone humor of any kind. Moral standards are extremely high. Any manifestation of modern Western liberal attitudes is likely to give offense. Most younger Chinese have not been exposed to Western living standards and so care should be taken to avoid showing certain ordinary living conventions which could be quite confusing and just not understood in China.[13]

Regulations pertaining specifically to advertising are still in their infancy (although some concerns have been expressed over liquor, medicine, cigarette, and food advertising), and the authorities are unconcerned that Hong Kong and other capitalistic societies (particularly Japan and the United States) and their transnationals must inevitably profit from China's new directions and the potential market for "one billion toothbrushes and two billion armpits." A Hong Kong-based adman has explained why China has opened its doors to some foreign ad influences: "Two pressures have been contributing to a more liberal attitude. One is from manufacturers of Japanese products, especially consumer durables such as televisions, fridges, and watches. And the other is the desire to build up stocks of hard currency to progress with the four modernizations."[14]

Prospects for Western Advertising

Admen from the United States, Japan, and other industrialized countries, who for years have stood by watching the lure of China from offices in Tokyo, Hong Kong, and elsewhere in Asia, are eying the rise of Chinese advertising with intense interest since the PRC is about the last sizable potential market closed to their influences. Foreign businessmen have long seen China's "isolationist," "proud," "nationalistic," and "xenophobic" closed-door policies as stumbling blocks in efforts to spread commercial activities abroad in hopes of realizing the dream of One Great Market. The opening of China's doors, however slight, has created a feeling of considerable optimism (and, initially, euphoria) among those who want China to go the usual route of developing nations and welcome foreign investment and commercial media.

Charles Fullerton, former head of O&M in Hong Kong, has put the situation in more realistic proportions in 1978:

The amount of business which is available now—by Hong Kong people sending goods into China, for instance—in no way justifies the cost of advertising at present. But the long-sighted manufacturer has his eye to the future, to the early 1980s, and is building awareness of his product. This gives the advantage to the bigger manufacturers who can afford to do this, people like ITT in the field of television sets.[15]

The ultimate dream of the transnationals is that Marlboro Country,

McDonald's golden arches, and Coca-Cola's "smile" will be household images throughout China. For the present, however, the only money to be made is from advertising technical, industrial, and agricultural goods and services rather than the mass consumer goods so familiar to Western societies. China is planning to spend billions for foreign technology and capital goods, but the growth in both technical and economic cooperation with foreigners has not come as fast as many Westerners had predicted when China's modernization program was announced in the late 1970s.

Like any market, then, China carries risks. McGraw-Hill Publications, New York, which is actively promoting itself as an expert on China marketing, has told American businesses:

> Obviously, the People's Republic of China is an important new market for American manufacturers. But it's one thing to identify an important new market. And quite another to successfully capture a share of it. Selling industrial products in the PRC involves the same problems as selling them in the U.S. Plus the problems of a different language and culture. And a different political, economic, and foreign trade system.[16]

One cautious American corporation with impeccable communications credentials is Coca-Cola, maker of the world's most advertised single trademark. The giant soft drink manufacturer quietly worked for a decade to get back into China after the Communist takeover. A Coca-Cola executive explained, "The right way to enter the PRC is one step at a time and one day at a time."[17] In January 1979, Coke became the first American consumer product available in China when it was awarded the "sole privilege" of selling cola drinks in the Chinese market. The delicate nature of Coke's historic return to China was emphasized by a Coke executive: "It's a gentle business operation. We don't want to offend the Chinese or give them the impression that they've opened the door a little and there we come crashing through. Our relationship has to be built on respect and trust."[18]

In many ways, Coca-Cola was the logical transnational to turn to for Western marketing and technological advice since it has been operating highly successfully in nearly every country on earth (one notable exception is in the Soviet Union, where Pepsi-Cola is allowed).[19] The Chinese government was interested not merely in a soft drink, but it also wanted to tap the company's expertise in citrus and wine operations, food processing, glass-making, water purification, and other fields.

Initially, Coke was available only through foreign-currency tourist hotels and restaurants, but by 1981 Coke had constructed its own bottling plant in Beijing, and the drink became more widely available, although few average Chinese would want to pay its relatively high price compared to local drinks.

With the exception of point-of-sale advertisements in more than twenty cities and occasional print media institutional advertising on special occasions, Coke has not been able to reach the vast potential market via mass advertising. This, of course, can and likely will change. In September 1979, Coke's worldwide ad agency, McCann-Erickson, announced that it was the first American TNAA to do business with China's major state-run advertising agency, the Shanghai Advertising Corporation (SAC). McCann-Erickson has been permitted to establish a joint venture ad agency with Jardine, Matheson & Co. Ltd., the oldest and largest of the big Hong Kong trading companies.[20] Jardine seems the perfect minority partner for the American agency. It has been trading with China since 1832, when it was established in Canton, and it boasts "strong links since the founding of the People's Republic of China with the Central Ministries and Corporations, the provincial and municipal authorities and the growing number of new companies through whom business is channeled."[21]

The new company has opened a representative office in Beijing, and initial clients included the Civil Air Administration of China (CAAC, China's national airline) and the China International Travel Service. Ultimately, of course, McCann wants to do work directly in the country not only for Coca-Cola but also for its other major transnational clients. Progress was made toward this end in 1980 when McCann arranged for Coca-Cola to present an Olympics documentary on the Chinese national television network.

McCann's entry into China is hardly surprising since the TNAA has such a strong reputation for "following the flag"—whenever Coke entered a major new market, like Japan or Indonesia, McCann was close behind. The agency is interested in having its own operations in China to create basic product awareness and help ensure that Coca-Cola continues to project a uniform, high-quality brand image—even in a society where competitive advertising is nonexistent and where authorities might not be happy to have a foreign corporation compete aggressively with the one locally made cola or with other indigenous drinks.

Evidence of China "Opening Up"

While the entries of Coke and McCann into China are among the most visible and significant recent changes in the PRC, there are other indicators that foreign investment and advertising have become socially acceptable activities worthy of greater mass consciousness and official use in China.

In early 1979, authorities began domestic product advertising in newspapers for the first time since the Cultural Revolution started. An early print ad in a Tientsin daily promoted local toothpaste. Shortly afterward, ads from foreign businesses were allowed in Shanghai's daily *Wen Hui Bao* and, more significantly, in other media. The first foreign-made product advertised in *Liberation,* a Shanghai newspaper, was the American film *Convoy,* starring Ali McGraw and Kris Kristofferson and shown to capacity crowds in Beijing and Shanghai.[22]

Authorities appointed *Wen Wei Po,* a pro-Beijing newspaper in Hong Kong, as their sole agent coordinating the placement of ads through virtually all Chinese media, including publications, broadcasting, and billboards.[23] To date, most ads have been for China's government-owned consumer goods such as "Phoenix" and "Peony" skin creams and "Butterfly" hair oil, but an estimated 30 percent of foreign product advertising has been Japanese. About 40 percent of foreign product advertising comes from Hong Kong, but originates with businesses based elsewhere.[24]

In 1978, the government's oldest and largest ad agency, SAC, was reactivated and the following year it began soliciting foreign advertising. Established in 1962 to promote sales of Chinese exports, SAC had disappeared under pressure from the radical Gang of Four. Today it is stronger than ever with a staff of about 180.[25] It has even been advertising its "full and efficient services" in the *Beijing Review,* the English-language weekly, and in local media.[26] By 1979, SAC expected to take in more than $650,000 from its foreign advertising clients, which have included Toshiba, JAL, Pakistani Airlines, and British Leyland. The state-run agency has emphasized, however, that earnings from foreign clients or Chinese are not an objective: "Our aim is to exchange views, techniques, news, and products. We are not interested in fees. Our only duty is exchange. The trademark is a bridge."[27]

Regarding ads for foreign products, SAC has maintained:

> We believe that through advertising these foreign commodities in China we can help our respective organizations to select the best kind of equipment or technology which is required in their work. It also serves the purpose of increasing the exchange of technology and science with other countries. To serve this purpose, we pay great attention to selecting the most needed products to be advertised in China. And these are mainly products of industrial and mineral goods. As a rule we do not accept the advertisement for those commodities which are purely for individual consumption. Because we think these kinds of commodities are not needed in our own markets. So there is no point for us to advertise them among our people.[28]

SAC did not remain China's sole ad agency for long. By 1980, decentralization in advertising and other business areas was underway via a general liberalization of the country's internal trade structure. Advertising agencies were established in Beijing and Guangdong (Canton area) and elsewhere to handle foreign as well as domestic regional clients. (It should be noted that China has long owned China Advertising Company, a Hong Kong-based agency that has actively promoted Chinese exhibitions and advertising in the British colony. A wide range of China-made products have always been available in Hong Kong, and the Chinese government is one of Hong Kong's major television advertisers.)

In January 1979, radio commercials were permitted and in March that year a commercial was allowed for the first time on Chinese television. The spot appeared during a live women's basketball game on Shanghai television. It featured a popular Chinese basketball star and several teammates drinking a local soft drink, Xingfu Cola ("Lucky" Cola). Ironically, Lucky Cola's shape and logo, including the familiar Coke-style script underscored by a dramatic curve, bear more than a slight resemblance to the popular American soft drink.[29]

In Hong Kong, Singapore-born and Australian-trained entrepreneur Robert Chua's production company was hired to handle production of advertising films and sales for China in partnership with *Wen Wei Po*. The firm was telling foreign businesses interested in advertising on television in Canton, the important commercial center ninety miles into China from Hong Kong, that:

> On the average week day 6 million viewers are watching Kwangtung TV and on weekends that number swells to over 10 million. Around 50 percent of all those viewers have friends or relatives in Hong Kong. So whilst your product may not be available in mainland China just yet your audience could still have access to it. And think of the investment you'll be making. As China gradually opens her doors to trade and imports your product will be well on the way to being established.[30]

In April 1979, on the first night of commercials from Canton, the Hong Kong offices of two American TNAAs had products advertised. Rado watches (handled by O&M) bought a 30- and a 60-second spot, and Marlboro cigarettes (handled by Leo Burnett) bought three 15-second spots. Of the nine imported products on the air when Canton commercials were introduced, five were for cigarettes. By 1980, Chua had signed contracts to place Citizen watch "time-checks" on China Central Television (from Beijing) and a Seiko-sponsored sports program on Guangtung Television (from Canton).[31]

In addition to serving as a buying agent and commercial film producer for Kwangtung Television, Chua was also helping the Canton Railway Authority install closed-circuit TV on the Hong Kong–Canton express and in the border town station of Shumchun. Ads promoted products such as Rothmans cigarettes and Coca-Cola, which are sold on the train.[32]

In late April 1979, China established its first formal link-up with a TNAA. A friendly loose agreement between SAC and Tokyo's Dentsu was worked out in which both parties agreed to exchange marketing information, have ad hoc consultations on export-import ads, and sell ad space, time, and locations for one another. One of their first joint efforts was the use of outdoor advertisements and neon signs to promote Japanese goods in Shanghai.[33] By 1980, Dentsu had established a small office in Beijing.

Billboards for foreign products were permitted for the first time during the June 1979 badminton world cup championship in Hangzhou. Billboards were allowed around the stadium to advertise such consumer non-durables and minor luxury items as Marlboro, 7-Up, and Hennessy cognac.[34] Also significant, downtown billboards in Shanghai, Canton, and in Beijing were made available for foreign advertisers. Smith Kline, an American pharmaceutical and medical equipment corporation, was among the first to rent billboard space in Shanghai and Beijing.[35] Kodak was another early billboard user in Beijing. Its first billboard used huge photos of an Apollo astronaut on the moon, an oil rig, and the familiar yellow Kodak film box plus logo. McCann helped Kodak acquire the space.

A steady stream of TNAAs began approaching the Chinese in the late 1970s with various proposals and goodwill gestures. In mid-1979, for example, executives from three major agencies—N. W. Ayer, Compton, and Doyle Dane Bernbach (DDB)—spent a well-publicized two weeks in Shanghai and Beijing giving seminars on how American research and other advertising-related skills could help in the sale of Chinese goods in the United States. A DDB official predicted: "Long term, I see happening in China what happened in Japan. There'll be a consumer economy. But it takes a long time to build trust and respect. There may be nothing for the first five or ten years. It's a long-term investment and this is Step One."[36]

O&M is probably one of the very few transnationals already making money from the Chinese. In May 1979, the New York-based TNAA quietly was awarded the assignment of selling such China-made goods as carpets, brandy, and proprietary medicines. The account could be worth "many millions of dollars within five years," according to O&M's Hong Kong manager. The TNAA's first specific job was to promote Chinese goods in Nigeria, a market that O&M has been active in since British colonial days.[37]

Another New York TNAA, Young & Rubicam, also has done business with China, although very little in advertising. The agency owns J. K. Gill, a west coast U.S. gift and office supplies chain that for some years has been selling Chinese handicrafts and other items bought at the Canton Fair. Y&R's chairman has visited China twice, and the PRC's leading light industry officials have visited Gill's offices in Portland.[38]

Like other transnationals, Y&R has no qualms about doing business with any centrally planned state. One of its executives explained:

the socialist system does recognize the need for successful growth and profits. The difference in this respect between our system and their system is disagreement about the way in which these profits should be employed, and to whom they should go, but it is *not* the issue of whether or not there should be *any* profits. Whether or not Young & Rubicam can have a fully owned, profit-making agency in a socialist country is, I think, beside the point. What is more important is that long-term, all of us have responsibilities as citizens of the world in addition to the countries we work in.[39]

Idealism notwithstanding, the TNAAs realize that the whole of their global operations is stronger than the sum of their individual offices. This means that TNAA activity in China will not be very profitable immediately by itself, but within a global context the long-term benefits of a China presence will be well worth the effort. This explains why both McCann-Erickson and Dentsu rushed to establish representative offices in Beijing rather than try to do business with China from offices outside the country.

Bigger Concerns

Ironically, advertising has emerged in China—and expanded elsewhere in Asia—at a time when UNESCO and a number of developing nations and consumer advocates elsewhere are taking an increasingly critical look at the presumed social effects of advertising and on the links between transnational corporations, communications, mass culture, and development plans that emphasize consumption and economic growth.

Many of advertising's critics are impressed by theoretical developments in the dominance-dependency area. They argue that advertising, as a unique socioeconomic and communication activity, is a crucial factor behind how and why information and cultural influences generally flow one way (West to East, North to South, urban to rural, rich to poor, top to bottom, and so forth) and continue in the hands of a comparatively few affluent nations and influenial, largely private groups. In virtually all societies where advertising is practised, pressures are increasing for more government regulation, and advertising is increasingly being considered in a broader context of all inter- and intranational communication and of pressures to foster a "new international economic and information order."

Defenders of the private-business perspective generally maintain that advertising's spread subsidizes costly media operations (state-run, as in China's case, as well as private) and stimulates economic growth. It also helps make it possible for people to raise their living standards (and expectations) and to gain access to new or better goods, services, and life-styles, many of which originate in high production/high consumption societies like Japan and the United States.

Western advertising specialists strongly reject the stereotype image of the adman as "a commercial fanatic promoting wastage and excess, prepared to pollute the minds of the community as a preliminary to selling products which pollute its environment" and argue—as the Chinese do—that advertising can be used to spread useful information and promote social benefits that improve the long-term welfare of any community.[40] The TNAAs adamantly reject charges that America dominates the world's advertising and emphasize that they understand that Western-style campaigns created in New York or London can no longer simply be exported around the world. The chairman of Y&R has explained: "a funny thing happened on the way to worldwide domination. The rapid expansion of large multinational companies ran hard into strong countervailing forces, and in the wake of that confrontation, vigorous national feelings began to assert themselves. Despite numerous attempts to bury it, nationalism does not die easily."[41]

The TNAAs, then, in the rush to expand into China or anywhere else, have had to pay increasing attention not merely to technical know how but also to local sensitivity and nationalism. They recognize that a Hong Kong-, Madison Avenue- or Ginza-accented China gives rise to a host of cultural concerns and political risks, and that their fragile China links exist only through the explicit approval of the government.

The questions raised by the role of advertising in China are endless and fascinating. For example, are China's people really ready for an influx of foreign (or even domestic) advertising influences, no matter how carefully regulated or culturally sensitive? Is it conceivable that consumerism could become China's next great movement or mass campaign? How—and how much—can Western-style advertising foster a "great leap forward" for the average Chinese in a commune or factory? In terms of television viewing habits, how does communal viewing compare with the private home viewing found in most countries? How important will consumer product advertising become in comparison to industrial advertising? Will the opening up of China to imported technology and investment dollars introduce influences that will disrupt China's attempts to avoid such presumed evils of the free market system as consumerism and self-indulgence, the profit motive, class conflict, and Western values and life-styles? As an expensive medium like television expands, will China, like many other Third World nations, become dependent upon both foreign programming and transnational corporate advertising? Can China design a national, self-reliant advertising system consistent with modernization *and* socialism that, for example, might emphasize information rather than persuasion; indigenous rather than foreign values; interpersonal rather than mass communication; the needs of the many at the bottom of Chinese society rather than a few party leaders and bureaucrats at the top; and so forth?

Obviously, some of these questions are already attracting greater explicit attention outside and inside China. For example, scholar John K. Fairbank has asked: "With all due respect to one of America's inexpugnable claims to fame, we may also wonder whether Coca-Cola can really hit the spot in Honan province. In summer Shanghai, yes, but will it increase crop acreage in Lin Hsien, or irrigate more than the purchaser?"[42]

Within China, too, these kinds of questions about the effects of advertising are gradually being raised. Closer scrutiny is being given to tobacco and pharmaceutical promotion and the link to poor public health, and in the early 1980s *Beijing Review* published a cover story directed at those who are convinced that China is on a path leading to a consumer society. The Chinese weekly concluded: "Obviously, people here have not yet begun to go in for consumerism and wasteful habits, chase after money or worship material possessions. This is a thing we are happy about because a "consumer society" is not necessarily a society which brings people happiness. What many a Chinese wishes to see is a comfortably off, yet simple and honest society."[43]

Finally, one of the more complex questions about the future of advertising in China has to do with the political future of Hong Kong. In 1998, the New Territories part of the colony could revert to China when Britain's 99-year lease expires. Only time will tell whether the Chinese will take back the territory, or work out some means of continuing the status quo so that the Mainland can continue to take advantage of Hong Kong's Western-oriented commercial and communications services, including advertising.

Conclusion

Ultimately, advertising and development in China depend on political factors, and only time will tell what kinds of impact advertising and, more broadly, modernization will have on the Chinese.

Reliable, quantifiable information about communication in China remains skimpy, and the government's policies continue in a state of flux. More specifically, China's advertising plans are not clearly articulated within the broad complex of the society's needs, aspirations, and resources. More important, it must be recognized that all policies and plans could be readjusted at any time by forces less ideologically flexible or tolerant to the West than those in control of China during the relatively stable late 1970s and early 1980s.

Application of Galtung's theory to China, then, will require more time and far better information. China might well turn out to be unique among Asian developing nations in that its senior officials have explicitly invited foreign admen into the country but at the same time have deliberately limited their sphere of influence. The notion of Western-style commercial media and Galtung's bridgehead concept might have little application in China, where the party, government, media, advertising corporations and trade organizations are part and parcel of one more or less unified power structure in which competition is minimal. In more overtly competitive, capitalistic developing societies, difficulties and changes have been posed by a sudden influx of outside commercial influences, including advertising, television, capital and expatriates, and—more broadly—Western values and organizations. But the resulting social or political problems seem to have been most pronounced in societies where there is a sharp distinction and competition between the public and private sectors, where economic gaps exist between different classes, and/or where the population is not culturally homogeneous.

Galtung himself, half-facetiously perhaps, has argued that Chinese history since the 1949 revolution has been "a progressive oscillation between distribution and growth-oriented strategies." Writing on this Chinese "zig-zag" development model, he has conjectured that the present nine-year growth stage might end around 1985:

> Around that time a new turning point might come—give or take some years—growth would have petered out. Because of the results and discontents caused by the inequalities engendered by it, there would be new demonstrations in that square in Beijing, Coca-Cola bottles will be smashed against the McDonald's Hamburger (Japan, Inc.) stands, now introduced so that the Chinese can have fast food and not waste too much time that could be used more productively, the Gang of Four will be resuscitated, Mao will come up and Chou down, and so on, and so forth.[44]

The results could be much different, of course, if Galtung's prediction does not come true. If China sticks with a policy oriented toward economic growth and if the deliberate introduction of modern advertising and foreign business influences as socialist development tools does succeed in making a better life for the masses, China conceivably could increase its credibility as a model for other nations struggling to find a workable middle road between dependence and independence.

Regardless of what happens in and to China over the long run, the late 1970s and early 1980s will likely be remembered as the landmark period of China's great leap outward toward Madison Avenue.

Notes

1. Philip H. Dougherty, "3 Agencies Take Pitch to China," *The New York Times*, 28 June 1979.

2. Sherman Cochran, *Big Business in China: Sino-Foreign Rivalry in the Cigarette Industry, 1890–1930* (Cambridge, Mass.: Harvard Univ. Press, 1980).

3. Dennis Chase, "China Admen Tightening Y&R Ties," *Advertising Age*, 15 December 1980, p. 62.

4. McCann-Erickson Jardine (China) Ltd., "Advertising in China" (New York: McCann-Erickson, 1980), p. 1.

5. "Commercial Ads in Newspapers," *Beijing Review*, 9 March 1979, p. 31.

6. Translation of Ding Yunpeng, "Put Advertising in Its Proper Perspective," an article in Shanghai *Wen Hui Bao*, 14 January 1979, by Foreign Broadcast Information Service, *Daily Report: People's Republic of China*, 24 January 1979, p. E18.

7. For an introduction to communication in China, see Goodwin C. Chu, ed., *Popular Media in China: Shaping New Cultural Patterns* (Honolulu: East-West Center, University Press of

Hawaii, 1978); Chu, *Radical Change through Communication in Mao's China* (Honolulu: University Press of Hawaii, 1977); and Alan P. L. Liu, *Communication and National Integration in Communist China.* (Berkeley: University of California Press, 1971).

8. The World Bank, *World Development Report, 1980* (Washington: The World Bank, August 1980), pp. 111, 147, and 158.

9. Leonard Chu, "Advertising Returns to China," *The Asian Messenger* 4, nos. 2 and 3 (Autumn 1979/Spring 1980), p. 56.

10. Estimated in a table of social indicators in "Teng's New Deal," *Newsweek,* 5 February 1979, p. 43.

11. Ogilvy & Mather Hong Kong, *How to Advertise in the People's Republic of China* (Hong Kong: Ogilvy & Mather, November 1979), p. 6.

12. Warren Unna, "Advertising: China's Link between Communistic and Capitalistic Ideas?" *Advertising Age,* 11 June 1979, p. S-9.

13. Ogilvy & Mather Hong Kong, *How to Advertise in the People's Republic of China,* p. 9.

14. John Roddy of John Roddy-FCB, Hong Kong, quoted in "The China Bandwagon Rolls . . . with a Warning," *Media,* May 1978, p. 15.

15. Quoted in "The China Bandwagon Rolls . . . with a Warning."

16. "McGraw-Hill Helps You Do Business in the People's Republic of China," an advertisement in *Advertising Age,* 25 June 1979, p. S-23.

17. Ian R. Wilson, President, Pacific Group, The Coca-Cola Company, quoted in Pat Cariseo, "Coke's China Entry: Painstaking Progress," *Atlanta Business Chronicle,* 6 August 1979.

18. Wilson quoted in Paul Troop, "Discovering a Continent," *The Atlanta Journal,* 20 December 1978, p. 15-D.

19. For a discussion of the politics of the transnational soft drink industry and details of sophisticated promotional techniques used to achieve market expansion, see J. C. Louis and Harvey Yazijian, *The Cola Wars* (New York: Everest House, 1981).

20. See Bernice Kanner, "McCann Joins Other Shops in Lining Up China Business," *Advertising Age,* 1 October 1979, p. 1, and "Interpublic Group Unit to Help China Advertise," *Wall Street Journal,* 27 September 1979, p. A14.

21. "Your Bridge to Trade with China," an advertisement for Jardines in *Far Eastern Economic Review,* 5 October 1979, p. 51.

22. See, for example, David Holly, Los Angeles Times Service, "Ads Return to China," *Honolulu Advertiser,* 10 March 1979, p. A14, and a translation of Georges Biannic's AFP report of 6 February 1979 on "Commercial Advertising Reappears in Shanghai Media" by Foreign Broadcast Information Service, *Daily Report: People's Republic of China,* 6 February 1979, p. E16.

23. Kamaluddin Sayed, "Chinese Media to Accept Ads," *Advertising Age,* 5 March 1979, p. 2.

24. Lois Bolton, "Chinese Ad Unit Determines Society's Needs, Not Wants," *Advertising Age,* 20 August, 1979, p. S-13.

25. Information from Chinese advertising authorities in "Interview at Shanghai Advertising Corporation," transcript of a meeting between the Chinese and a group of visiting Canadian scholars led by Dallas Smythe, Simon Fraser University, 23 May 1979.

26. See, for example, "Do You Want to Promote Your Business?," an advertisement for SAC in *Beijing Review,* no. 10, 9 March 1979), p. 32.

27. Quoted in Bolton, "Chinese Ad Unit Determines Society's Needs, Not Wants."

28. SAC official quoted in "Interview at Shanghai Advertising Corporation," p. 2.

29. See "China Advertises Cola Drink on TV," *The New York Times,* 12 March 1979; "Xingfu Cola Hits the Spot," *Honolulu Advertiser,* 12 March 1979, p. A-8; Bolton, "Coke Apparent Victim of Oriental Pragmatism," *Advertising Age,* 25 June 1979; and "Advertising in China," *Advertising Age,* 20 August 1979, p. S-12.

30. "Robert Chua Productions Are the People to Talk to If You Want to Talk to 10 Million Mainland Chinese," an advertisement for Robert Chua Productions and *Wen Wei Po, Media,* May 1979, p. 5.

31. "On the China Trail," *South China Morning Post,* 28 October 1980, p. 2 (RCP—TV Studios Supplement).

32. "Chua Will Help Put China on TV Rails," *Media,* June 1979, p. 6.

33. Mat T. Matsuda, "Chinese, Dentsu Agree to Advertising Exchange," *Advertising Age,* 14 May 1979, pp. S-1–2.

34. "China Opens Its Doors, an *IOCU News,* May/June 1979, article reported in *AMCB,* June 1979, p. 13.

35. "Peking Opens the Door to Foreign Admen," *MAA Bulletin* 5, no. 5 (October 1979), p. 4.

36. Neil R. Austrian, president of DDB, quoted in Dougherty, "3 Agencies Take Pitch to China."

37. "Chinese Hand O&M Consumer Products," *Media,* June 1979, p. 1.

38. See, for example, John Revett, "Occidental Overtures to Mainland China," *Advertising Age,* 20 November 1978, p. 28AW; "Carnation, Other Coast Marketers, Eye China," *Advertising Age,* 25 December 1978, p. 29; and Bernice Kanner, "Marketers Gearing Up China Blitz," *Advertising Age,* 13 August 1979, p. 82.

39. Alexander Brody, "It's the People that Count," a reprint supplied by Young & Rubicam, New York, from *Madison Avenue,* March 1973, p. 5.

40. A. E. Pitcher, Ogilvy & Mather, "Professionalism at Work on Social Projects," *Viewpoint,* Winter 1978, pp. 16–19.

41. Edward N. Ney, "The World of Advertising Is Not One World." (Speech to the American Association of Advertising Agencies, Chicago, 10 November 1977).

42. John K. Fairbank, "The New Two China Problem," *The New York Review of Books,* 8 March 1979, pp. 3–6.

43. "More Consumer Goods—An Important Aim in Readjustment of the National Economy," *Beijing Review,* no. 47 (24 November 1980), p. 28.

44. Johan Galtung, "Is There a Chinese Strategy of Development?" (Paper presented for the Alternative Strategies and Scenarios subproject of the Goals, Processes and Indicators of Development Project of the United Nations University at a workshop in Geneva, May 29–30, 1979), pp. 11–12.

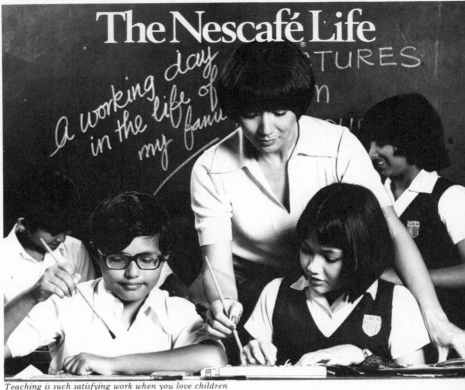

The Nescafé Life

a working day in the life of my family

Teaching is such satisfying work when you love children

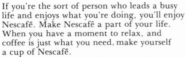

Click ...   *... whoosh ...*   *... stir ...*   *... mmmm*

If you're the sort of person who leads a busy life and enjoys what you're doing, you'll enjoy Nescafé. Make Nescafé a part of your life. When you have a moment to relax, and coffee is just what you need, make yourself a cup of Nescafé.

Black or white, Nescafé gives you delicious, natural coffee freshness, fast. It adds that extra enjoyment to a full life. Make it a part of your life — the Nescafé life.

Enjoy natural coffee freshness fast with Nescafé

NESTLÉ COFFEE AD

Few advertising and public policy issues have attracted more attention in recent years than the international controversy over the marketing of infant food. Nestlé, for example, has been boycotted and its activities in developing countries closely scrutinized. In Malaysia and Singapore, the Swiss-based transnational sells formula products such as Lactogen and Nan, but it also sells consumer products like instant coffee. This Nescafé ad, prepared by Ogilvy & Mather in Kuala Lumpur, seems to go out of its way to support social development efforts by noting that teaching is satisfying work. In Malaysia and elsewhere advertisers are increasingly aware of the social value of reinforcing cultural traditions and the political value of supporting government policies. (Courtesy of The Nestlé Company)

REGIONAL KOMATSU AD

First as a British colony, then as part of Malaysia, and now as an independent republic, Singapore has thrived as a regional commercial and communications center for foreign businesses. This Komatsu ad was prepared for the *Far Eastern Economic Review* by the Singapore office of Hakuhodo, Japan's second largest ad agency. The ad promotes Singapore as Komatsu's "key operation centre in South East Asia" and stresses how the Japanese corporation's Singapore operations use a satellite to link up with headquarters in Japan. Transnational ad agencies and their clients have flocked to Singapore because facilities for communications are excellent and there are no regulations against wholly-owned subsidiaries. (Courtesy of Komatsu Singapore Pte. Ltd.)

"SINGAPORE GIRL" AD

Probably the most widely acclaimed advertising from Asia in recent years has been the "Singapore Girl" campaign for Singapore Airlines (SIA). The theme was created for the government airline by expatriate Ian Batey of Batey Ads, Singapore. During most of the 1970s, his operation was a rare example of an agency without transnational agency links that had great success at attracting prestigious transnational clients. Like many independent, "hot" agencies, however, Batey eventually felt he had to have direct ties to a foreign agency. By 1979, BBDO International, Inc., New York, had acquired part ownership in the award-winning agency. (Courtesy of Singapore Airlines Ltd.)

MIND YOUR OWN BUSINESS

All of us in the ad business have an obligation to the public and to one another. This obligation involves advertisers in making promises that are honest and intelligible, in using good manners and taste and in using fair methods of selling. All of us should be dedicated to advertising that is professional, ethical and clearly-worded.

All too often advertising comes under attack because high standards are not adhered to.

Be responsible: it's the best way of minding your own business.

ADVERTISING STANDARDS AUTHORITY OF SINGAPORE
Trade Union House, Shenton Way, Telephone 984169,916555

ADVERTISING STANDARDS AD

Advertisers, media, and ad agencies find it in their own best interest to support self-regulatory bodies rather than wait until the government has to step in and take measures that might adversely affect the advertising industry. One of the best organized self-regulatory bodies in Asia is in Singapore. The Advertising Standards Authority of Singapore (ASAS) has ties to consumer and trade union groups and includes representatives of agencies, advertisers, and media. It sets standards, publicizes a code of ethical advertising practice, and deals with complaints from the public and from within the industry. In a number of developing countries, however, codes either do not exist or are difficult to enforce. (Courtesy of the Advertising Standards Authority of Singapore)

COKE CARTOON ABOUT CHINA

Fears about the possible impact of Western-style advertising and consumerism on China under Teng are reflected in this American cartoon from 1979. That year, Coca-Cola returned to China after an absence of thirty years. Shortly thereafter, Coke's transnational ad agency became the first American agency to establish an office in Beijing. McCann-Erickson entered the unique China market through a joint venture with Jardine Matheson & Co., Ltd., Hong Kong. (Courtesy of John Trever, *Albuquerque Journal*)

HONG KONG STREET SCENE

In Hong Kong, every form of advertising imaginable beckons tourists and more than 5 million local residents to buy Western and Asian goods and services. Except for Japan, Hong Kong has the liveliest, most competitive advertising and commercial environment in Asia. Hong Kong is a British colony that (like Singapore) has historically served as a center of foreign trade and communications. Many transnational advertisers, ad agencies, and media have offices in Hong Kong. Agencies like Ogilvy & Mather and Leo Burnett use the colony as a base from which to try to expand into neighboring China. Hong Kong is such an important Asian business center that China itself has long had a state-owned ad agency there to aggressively promote made-in-China goods. (Courtesy of the Hong Kong Tourist Association)

McCANN-ERICKSON BILLBOARD IN CHINA

In China, billboards and other major media are gradually becoming available for foreign advertisers, with the Japanese the most evident. This L'Oreal billboard in Guangdong (Canton) for French cosmetics and perfumes was arranged through McCann-Erickson. The agency has also done billboards in China for such clients as Kodak film and Rado watches. Much of the imported advertising in China continues to be oriented more toward visiting businessmen and tourists than toward local Chinese. (Courtesy of McCann-Erickson Jardine (China) Ltd.)

CHINESE CIGARETTE AD

Despite the fact that China has the world's highest tobacco consumption rate, Chinese cigarette advertising is not hard-sell. Advertising for state-made cigarettes and other consumer products tends to be more informative than persuasive. As this ad for "Double Happiness" brand cigarettes illustrates, made-in-China ads are simple and dull compared to most Western advertising. Note, however, that even this straightforward ad suggests that smoking is a desirable social activity. (Courtesy of Ta-Kung-Pao, *The Chinese Export Commodities Fair*)

CARD NO. 1

**HONG KONG
WEN WEI PO.**
香港文匯報

**ROBERT CHUA
PRODUCTIONS**
蔡和平製作有限公司

9 Suffolk Road, Kowloon Tong,
Kowloon, Hong Kong.
Tel: 3-383641 (5 lines)
Telex: 85761 RCPHX
Cable Add.: "ROBERTCHUA" H.K.

GUANGDONG
GUANGZHOU

HONG KONG

MAP OF CHINA

TV COMMERCIAL RATE

TIME	DURATION (seconds)	PRICE IN HK DOLLARS		REMARKS
		Rotation	Fix Position	
A RATE	10	$2,100	$2,600	Sat. Sun.
	15	$2,600	$3,200	& Public
Between 1900 to 2130	20	$3,200	$4,000	Holiday
	30	$4,300	$5,400	20%
	60	$7,200	$9,000	Surcharge
B RATE	10	$1,700	$2,100	
	15	$2,100	$2,600	
Before 1900	20	$2,600	$3,200	
After 2130	30	$3,400	$4,300	
	60	$5,800	$7,200	

Volume Discount

50 — 150,000	2.5%	450 — 600,000	12.5%
150 — 250,000	5%	600 — 800,000	15%
250 — 350,000	7.5%	800 — 1,000,000	17.5%
350 — 450,000	10%	1,000,000 over	20%

Market Description

Total population	60 Million
Total TV Sets	600,000
TV Coverage area	Whole Guangdong and some edging area of neighbouring provinces.
Viewership	12 Million (Weekend, Sunday & Public Holiday)
	8 Million (Weekday)

CHINESE TV RATE CARD

Hong Kong television producer and entrepreneur Robert Chua is probably the most influential middleman in the expanding relations between China and the outside world of modern advertising. Along with a pro-Beijing newspaper in Hong Kong, Chua is actively promoting his services as exclusive advertising agent for foreign advertising on Chinese television in Guangdong (Canton), Sichuan, and Henan. His rate card for Guangdong Television, which has had commercials since 1979 and serves an area that is relatively consumer conscious because of its proximity to Hong Kong, is shown here. Chua secured the first commercial contract for China Central Television (Beijing) when he arranged for Citizen watches of Japan to make time-check spots. (Courtesy of Robert Chua Productions)

Part IV

Conclusions

10
Dependency Implications

My findings on the TNAAs in contemporary Malaysia, Singapore, and Indonesia show that the structure of past and present advertising relations between several advertising-strong industrialized nations and these Southeast Asian nations is one of dominance. The presence of market-hungry TNAAs is, and always has been, overpowering to indigenous agencies, and my data generally confirm the theoretical explanations of First and Third World interaction suggested by Galtung's model.

This chapter will detail how advertising in these three nations exhibits the general interaction structure that Galtung hypothesized. China will be given little attention since transnational advertising is too new a phenomenon upon which to base any conclusions.

Advertising Interaction Structure

Through exploitation, fragmentation, and penetration, the United States and—to a far lesser extent—Britain, Japan, and Australia function as advertising "top dogs," or Center nations in relation to Malaysia, Singapore, and Indonesia. Predominantly American-owned (but, interestingly, *not* American staffed) TNAAs have been able to take advantage of the relatively young and underdeveloped state of advertising (and media, government, and business generally) throughout Southeast Asia. As industrialization has increased and as advertising has become both "Americanized" and "transnationalized," the TNAAs have rushed into the untapped mass markets of the region. Because of a substantial head start over local agencies, the TNAAs have often found ready and lucrative outlets for their commercial messages, creative and managerial knowledge and skills, and foreign-determined professional values and behavioral patterns.

In each of my first three cases, the TNAAs have shaped and controlled the structure of the entire national advertising industry. For example, while establishing domestic branches to support their expanding organization, the TNAAs also were introducing a virtually new service organization called the modern advertising agency. They also were at the same time operating as agents of economic penetration through their intimate ties to major TNCs and the market economy generally; as promoters of professional, Madison Avenue-style business values; as transmitters of Western lifestyles; and as political actors supporting orderly maintenance of stability and system reinforcing development policies. Such policies are focused on economic growth strategies.

The overall consequences include a unidirectional flow of advertising influences and values from the West to these Third World nations, as well as an aggravation of domestic tension and dependency. In this study, the latter means that Center nations provide transnationally linked advertising services on which those in control of Malaysia, Singapore, and Indonesia rely. In each of these nations, dominant, Western-oriented, well-connected, urban elites believe that TNAA services are indispensable and unavailable anywhere else. Dependency also means that existing advertising exchange patterns represent a continuation of the general relationships that originated during these societies' colonial periods. Compared to the United States and other advertising Centers, these three ex-colonies are vulnerable peripheral areas with a substantial measure of advertising inequality within and between them. Their enclave advertising investments—like other foreign investments—are largely unintegrated into the indigenous economy. This is particularly the case in Indonesia, where a large percentage of the population is isolated from the concentration of commercial, media, and political developments centered in Jakarta.

As Periphery nations, Malaysia, Singapore, and Indonesia provide the transnational power structure with advertising-related raw materials. These include invaluable market data on audience ratings and consumers' needs and wants that are useful to both TNAAs and advertisers (not to mention governments) as they develop strategies to effectively and efficiently reach large numbers of people.[1] Center nations, on the other hand, provide the very basic means of production, including the creative and technological advancements that make for "good" advertisements—as defined by Western admen. The TNAAs import a complex managerial organization, including expatriate advisors or managers, capital, supplies and equipment, prestigious reputations, and—most important—creativity in the form of advertising concepts, themes, symbols, graphics, music, copy, and other ingredients that go into advertising production. Without these latter means of labor-intensive creative production, the TNAAs would not have much advantage over their local competitors. With such administrative, technical, and material resources, however, the TNAAs have a very great competitive edge over indigenous agencies.

The following sections will take a closer look at advertising relations in Malaysia, Singapore, and Indonesia and will give particular attention to their dynamics over time. The basis for the analysis is a refinement of the researchable static and dynamic propositions about the TNAAs enumerated in chapter 3.

Static Propositions

1. *Major decisions in advertising agencies in the Periphery are controlled more by foreigners than by local citizens.*

My data suggest a clear, built-in division of labor within most of the major advertising agencies of all three of my cases. With few exceptions (Intervista in Jakarta, Starlight in Singapore, and Union in Kuala Lumpur), the most prestigious and senior positions in the leading agencies are held by noncitizens. In the case of the TNAAs, the key posts of managing director and creative director are usually held by foreigners, whose loyalties understandably are with the TNAA organization and its "mother" nation rather than with the Periphery host nation. For virtually all the TNAAs, the Center provides the locus of overall corporate decision making in major areas of administration, finance, and research, and it has its position of strength reinforced by a variety of transnational interaction patterns.

The TNAA's home offices seem to have considerable influence in defining advertising for these Periphery nations, and they ultimately make the challenging choice decisions, enforce discipline, and set priorities for operating methods, movement of senior personnel, capital, technology, and prestigious accounts. The TNAA's Center-based headquarters—whether in New York, Chicago, London, Tokyo, or Sydney—also usually determine accountability, arrange formal training, establish an agency's professional standards, coordinate common accounts, distribute research, and generally oversee long-range planning efforts and set goals. A few examples from Ogilvy & Mather, which has offices in all three nations, will illustrate the influence that a parent organization can have.

The O&M offices in Malaysia, Singapore, and Indonesia report to the parent corporation's executive director international, who is based in Sydney but frequently travels in the region and reports directly to O&M's chairman at international headquarters in New York City. The expatriate managers in each of these nations follow the same principles of management developed at O&M headquarters. They each have a 187-page manual that covers "everything from how to get great advertising to how to prevent embezzling."[2] By constantly preaching O&M's worldwide principles, the TNAA tries to ensure the same level of service and a unanimity of purpose in all of its seventy offices. O&M's chairman has explained: "It is all too easy for an agency with a lot of offices all over the place to become a mere holding company. But that's no good. Clients don't hire holding companies. Clients don't want to see basic differences of style between offices. One agency indivisible."[3]

To help the agency become "indivisible," O&M conducts its own formal training, including advertising management programs for present and potential office heads. The director of the program is based in New York. To conduct the various training activities at the local level, O&M always has sixty or seventy expatriates working around the world as "disciples," spreading what the agency believes in.[4]

An example of an O&M disciple is Australian Kenneth Brady, who joined the agency in Melbourne in 1969. Since then he has served as managing director of O&M's associated company in Jakarta; manager of the agency's Asian Desk at New York headquarters; managing director of the Singapore office; chairman of O&M in New Zealand; and, most recently, chairman of Meridian, O&M's new second agency group in Southeast Asia.

A TNAA like O&M maintains control over its sprawling operations not only by posting its people directly in the field but also by taking advantage of "international management supervisors," who enforce quality control on big international accounts and spread the agency's knowledge. It also uses its founder's great prestige, and David Ogilvy himself remains active in the agency. For example, O&M's chairman has said:

> Our International Creative Council, headed by David Ogilvy, reviews our creative work from all over the world twice a year. I can tell you that it is electrifying for copywriters in Kuala Lumpur, or art directors in New York, to get a memo from David Ogilvy praising or criticizing their advertisements. Without doubt this Council has helped raise our creative standards.[5]

O&M staff—local as well as expatriate—clearly identify with Ogilvy personally, and they want to reflect their parent corporation's values and experiences. I recall visiting the O&M office in Singapore and seeing a huge color photo of Ogilvy in the reception area. Along one corridor to executives' offices, I saw framed copies of quotes from Ogilvy's "Magic Lantern" presentations based on advertising research on "how to create advertising that sells." Also prominently displayed on one wall was a personal letter from Ogilvy praising a newspaper advertisement created by the office for Singapore tourism. An indicator of the importance that the agency's Malaysian office gives to Ogilvy as a model is its publication—in the Malaysian national language—of Ogilvy's best seller, *Confessions of An Advertising Man*. The agency distributes this Bahasa Malaysian translation as a public relations tool.

Not all the TNAAs are as well coordinated or commercially as successful as O&M, but all are influenced by home-office policies and practices and by the expatriates who frequently staff their overseas offices. Although an agency like O&M has a local board of directors in Malaysia, Singapore, and Indonesia, major decisions are often made far away from these places by people who are neither citizens nor residents of the society in which such decisions might ultimately be implemented. Such integration and centralized decision making in the Center are facilitated by regular exchange of materials, use of telephone and telex, frequent top-level meetings among TNAA executives, and periodic visits by Center nation experts to Periphery operations. In 1978, for example, Ogilvy visited O&M offices in Australia, New Zealand, Malaysia, Singapore, and Thailand. He also became chairman of the agency's Frankfurt office.

The opening words from a speech by a senior J. Walter Thompson executive illustrate how mobile TNAA managers like Ogilvy are: "It's a small world. Ten days ago I attended intracompany meetings in New York and Washington; thereafter I spent a long weekend with my children in England; then I managed to put in a few days' work in my office in Tokyo and now I am here in Sydney surrounded by advertising professionals from all over Asia."[6]

Well-paid and travelled TNAA executives like this one and other specialists regularly make decisions about whether new ideas, techniques, capital, technology, research, personnel, and so forth will be made available to host nations through the parent TNAA's various branches or "daughter" companies. Whenever such resources are provided to the TNAA office in the Periphery, it is encouraged to test them in the local market and transfer the results back to TNAA headquarters for further development and for possible application elsewhere through "common creative denominators."[7]

Malaysia, Singapore, and Indonesia—as Periphery hosts—either imitate or obey those rules and regulations, resources and discoveries which are provided and controlled by TNAA managers and stockholders in the Center. Of course, bridgeheads in these nations will be consulted about some decisions and sometimes will even be allowed to own stock in the local operations.[8] But such "concessions" to what Galtung has termed "the highly formal equality" in which local elite are given not only the same standard of living as the Center elite but also "representation in the bodies of policymaking" are not a serious threat to the Center's control over decision making and policy implementation.

Table 39 uses the case of Malaysia to give examples of various TNAA bridgeheads. The brief biographical material on these local advertising elites suggests the quality of indigenous personnel that the TNAAs generally can attract. Many have been educated in the British tradition and trained abroad. Most have travelled outside their nation and held more than one "glamorous" job that brought them into frequent contact with foreigners or at least other local elites who share similar business and cultural values. Professionally and socially, these generally outgoing elites spend much of their time with expatriate clients and supervisors, and they seem to have few problems communicating with foreigners. In Galtungian terms, they spend their time supporting the presence of the TNAAs and carrying out standardized tasks using Center models while expatriates all but monopolize the advertising processing requiring greater skill and edu-

Table 39

Examples of Transnational Advertising Agency "Bridgeheads" in Malaysia

Agency	Position	Ethnicity	Biographical Information
Leo Burnett	Account Director	Malay	Graduated from Univ. of Western Australia with B. S. in Industrial Psychology. First Malaysian to hold post of district sales manager for Qantas Airways, Kuala Lumpur. Experienced as a marketing consultant with management consultant firm.
Leo Burnett	Art Director	Malay	Won first prize in government's Dewan Bahasa dan Pustaka mural design competition in 1961. In 1965 represented Malaysia at Commonwealth Arts Festival, the Fifth International Contemporary Art Exhibition in New Delhi, and Warath Festival in Sydney. His works are part of Melbourne Art Gallery's permanent collection. Studied advertising design at Art Center of Design in Los Angeles and graduated with distinction. He has worked in Burnett's major U. S. and British offices.
Grant, Kenyon & Eckhardt	Research Executive	Chinese	Graduated from University Science Malaysia with honors degree (sociology). In 1973 joined the Malaysian Center for Development, an agency within the Prime Minister's Department, as an assistant research director. Joined Lintas in 1976 as media planner and research executive. Shifted to Grant, Kenyon & Eckhardt in 1977.
McCann-Erickson	Creative Director	Indian	Joined McCann in 1977 from Lintas, where had been creative director since 1975. With Lintas had worked in Jakarta office on "special projects" and regularly made working visits to London and Europe. In 1975 visited the New York office together with ten other Lintas creative heads. Attended 1978 Cannes Film Festival.
McCann-Erickson	Media Manager/ Account Supervisor	Chinese	With Beecham, 1970-72; O&M, 1973-74; Lintas as media manager and account supervisor, 1975-76.
McCann-Erickson	Account Supervisor	Chinese	Joined McCann in 1975. Group Product Manager, Sterling Drug, 1973-75. Administrative Officer, National Cash Register, 1970-73.
McCann-Erickson	Account Director	Chinese	Five years with O&M prior to joining McCann in 1978. Previously spent five years with Colgate Palmolive in Malaysia, and IBM in Singapore, Sydney, and Kuala Lumpur.
Ogilvy & Mather	Producer	Indian	Well-known actress, former Radio Malaysia broadcaster.
Ogilvy & Mather	Joint Creative Director	Chinese	Copy chief at O&M until 1977, when he joined PTM Thompson. Rejoined O&M in 1978. Former freelance film director.

Agency	Position	Ethnicity	Background
SSC&B: Lintas	Head of Client Services	Malay	Studied in Melbourne. Joined O&M (then Benson) in 1965. PR manager of Malayan Tobacco Co., 1968-73. Assistant to director of culture, Ministry of Culture, Youth & Sports, 1973-75. Former president of Malayan Sportwriters Assn. and chairman of Malaysian Arts and Theater Council.
SSC&B: Lintas	Media and Research Director	Chinese	Graduate of Taiwan University. Started career as sales representative with two large international companies. Joined O&M (then Benson) in 1963 as account executive and spent a year in Sydney and Hong Kong with Benson offices. Joined Lintas in 1973 as an account director. Has made working visits to Lintas London and Rotterdam. In 1976 attended agency's International Media Seminar in New York.
SSC&B: Lintas	Commercial Director	Chinese	Graduate of British College of Commerce. Worked in Britain for five years as cost accountant, financial and management consultant, "troubleshooter" accountant and auditor with several large British companies. Financial accountant for a large international company in Malaysia, 1972-74. Joined Lintas in 1974.
SSC&B: Lintas	Audio/Visual Manager	Chinese	Four years as Radio Malaysia broadcaster. Promoted to senior copywriter/production supervisor in the Commercial Division of Ministry of Information. Joined Lintas as radio/film manager in 1975. Left in 1972 to become manager of a local production company. Rejoined Lintas in 1975. Has travelled to Europe, Australia and Hong Kong on film production assignments.
SSC&B: Lintas	Copywriter	Malay	Started career in 1962 as a film production assistant with Singapore-based film company. In 1962 became "trainee copywriter" for O&M (then Benson). In 1966 joined McCann as copywriter, radio producer and creative administrative assistant. In 1971 joined O&M as copywriter. In 1972 moved to Lintas and spent 1973 on a working visit to Lintas Jakarta.
PTM Thompson	Media Director	Chinese	Graduate of University of Malaya with honors in Economics. Former marketing executive with the Straits Times Group. Former head of the Group's Research Division in Singapore and later marketing services manager for the New Straits Times in Kuala Lumpur. Media manager of SSC&B: Lintas before joining Thompson in 1975.
PTM Thompson	Account Director and Area Representative for Singapore office	Chinese	Experience in several local Singapore and transnational agencies, including Grant K&E and Leo Burnett as account service manager. Was one of the first group of students to sit for the local Singapore Intermediate Certificate of Advertising. Has completed British-recognized diploma work in advertising, public relations, and marketing.
PTM Thompson	Chairman of the Board	Malay	Director-general and deputy chairman, Tourist Development Corp., one of the three government agencies that are in this joint venture with J. Walter Thompson, New York.

NOTE: Most of this information pertains to the years 1976-78. Names of particular individuals in these positions have been withheld. I use these examples, based on personal interviews and printed materials from agencies and trade sources, as a "rough" indicator of the kind of indigenous people working closely with the TNAAs. Similar "bridgehead" patterns can be seen in Singapore, Indonesia, and other societies where the TNAAs do business.

cation. As the table shows, many of these elites have jumped from one TNAA to another, and this is an indicator not only of the instability of the agency business generally but also of these elites' frustration and of their search for more money and more prestige. Job stability is nonexistent. Raids by one agency of another's top personnel are not unusual.

A local employee trying to change the TNAA system and gain greater power for himself or for indigenous personnel within the agency would either be isolated or fired for "making trouble" for the TNAA management. Usually, of course, a local staffer would not even consider advocating structural changes in how the TNAAs operate. Well-paid and usually effectively socialized and integrated into the international advertising system, he goes about his routine duties of manufacturing effective advertising to communicate with his fellow nationals and keeps quiet, content with the salary, prestige, and sometimes ostentatious life-style that employment with a TNAA gives him. Only rarely does anyone seem to buck the system. An exception to this rule is the case of Henry Chia in Singapore. He left a top post with Leo Burnett to risk setting up his own agency and he has spoken out against foreign influences on national advertising.[9]

2. *In the Periphery, indigenous advertising personnel, and government policymakers concerned about the regulation of advertising, have little interaction with their counterparts in other periphery nations.*

This proposition follows from Galtung's thinking about the "feudal interaction structure" and, in particular, from his rule that "interaction between Periphery and Periphery is missing in imperialism."

In general, regional advertising groupings have not been successful, and local agencies in all three nations (and most certainly in China) are largely isolated from the outside world.[10] They are simply too busy surviving to have much to do with their colleagues in neighboring nations. Despite the close geographical, historical, and cultural proximity, Malaysia, Singapore, and Indonesia have little advertising interaction except at the TNAA level. In other words, indigenous agencies in Malaysia have little contact with indigenous agencies in Indonesia, but TNAAs maintain close contact with their sister operations elsewhere. For example, O&M in Jakarta is in frequent touch with O&M in both Singapore and Kuala Lumpur and with O&M in such Centers as New York, London, and Sydney. Also, senior TNAA executives at headquarters are in regular contact with their peers in other agencies. Professional organizations like the 4As and the New York–based International Advertising Association (IAA) promote intra-elite interaction and foster an informal consortium through which the TNAAs work together to promote their common global interests.

In Southeast Asia, only major agencies like O&M or SSC&B: Lintas can afford to bring their office managers together to exchange ideas in regional meetings. These sessions are often held in Singapore, and the meetings are limited to a few senior expatriate personnel and up-and-coming local executives. The primary objective of these intraregional gatherings is to find ways to better meet the corporate parent TNAA's goals of faster growth, greater profits, and more efficiency.

Through imported films and print media advertisements, imported professional advertising journals and various reports, and visits from TNAA advertising experts, local advertising personnel—even those not directly employed by TNAAs—learn a great deal about advertising in Center nations. But these same people have little personal contact with either advertising materials or personnel from elsewhere in the region. Part of the reason is certainly the gap between these nations' levels of advertising development. Malaysia and Singapore, for example, certainly look more toward London, New York, or Sydney than they do toward Beijing, Jakarta, or Bangkok, all of which many Malaysians and Singaporeans perceive as years behind themselves. In the case of Malaysia and Indonesia, for example, despite their shared national language, the two nations exchange little advertising.[11] In some cases, the governments' protectionist policies discourage imported materials. Malaysians, for example, cannot see TV commercials made in the United States, Britain, Japan, *or* Singapore *or* Indonesia because of a ban on all nonlocally made advertising films. Also, the governments of both Malaysia and Singapore prevent each other's daily newspapers from being circulated within their borders. Also, regarding expatriate admen, governments make no special provision whereby advertising experts from within the region could enter a neighboring nation to give advertising training or counsel on a less restricted basis than the expatriate from thousands of miles away.

Advertising interaction between Malaysia and Singapore has especially diminished in recent years as the Malaysian government has tried to go its own way and forget Singapore's pre-1965 status as part of Malaysia. Members of each nation's 4As and advertising associations continue to have contact with each other through business links and personal "old boy" networks, but these will diminish as Malaysia and Singapore politically pull further apart and as younger advertising personnel replace the "old guard." The latter remembers not only the days when Malaysia and Singapore were virtually one market but also when both were British colonies. My guess is that the Malaysian advertising men of the future will increasingly be Malays who are more inward-looking and nationalistic. The Singapore advertising men of the future will continue to be Chinese, but they will be very transnationally oriented compared to admen in Malaysia. Predictions about the Indonesian admen are more difficult to make, but I see nothing in the immediate future that will change the present situation in which Indonesia is far behind Malaysia and Singapore and relatively isolated. China, of course, is extremely isolated and far behind even Indonesia in terms of exposure to transnational advertising influences.

A basic reason Periphery advertising interaction at industry and government levels is missing in the region's plural societies has to do with the old colonial maxim of "divide and rule." Malaysia and Singapore historically had close interaction in advertising and everything else because of a common "mother country," colonial administration, elite language (English), and set of foreign-controlled businesses. Under colonialism, a real alliance between Malaysia and Indonesia was virtually impossible because Indonesia had a different colonial master (Holland); a different ethnic mix (fewer Chinese); and a different language environment. Indonesians, for example, have never used much English or relied on English-language media since Sukarno had such great success at implementing a single national language. More recently, factors such as Sukarno's "confrontation" policies and anti-Chinese sentiments have also worked against these nations directly getting closer together.

Professionally, advertising personnel do assemble every two years somewhere in Asia for the Asian Advertising Congress, but these gatherings tend to be one-shot social meetings rather than work sessions. Also, the congress has always been heavily influenced by non–Third World factors. For example, Center nations like Japan and Australia are considered "Asian" nations by the congress, and TNAAs and transnational media personnel are well represented in attendance and on the official program. Their organizations can afford to send representatives to such meetings and they are presumed to be more knowledgeable about the latest advertising developments. It was not until late 1978, after years of talking, that an official, Asian-oriented advertising organization was established. Called the Asian Federation of Advertising Associations (AFAA), the organization was started largely through the efforts of a few Filipinos, and it is too early to say whether it will have any impact on the region.[12]

In short, the hypothesized advertising relations illustrated in Figure 2 with one Center and three Peripheries fit the present reality in Malaysia, Singapore, and Indonesia.

3. *For its transnational advertising, the Periphery nation depends largely on only one advertising Center nation.*

Evidence validating this proposition is strong. All TNAAs in these three nations are owned or somehow formally affiliated with TNAAs in one of only two Center nations—United States and Japan. In practice, the United States almost monopolizes these nations' advertising interaction with the outside world since the Japanese agencies are relatively weak, particularly in Malaysia and Singapore.

Such a situation supports Galtung's contention that in the feudal interaction structure "Periphery interaction with other Center nations is *missing.*"[13] Big power, industrialized nations like West Germany, the Soviet Union, Holland, and France have a degree of military, political, economic, and cultural influence on Southeast Asia, but in terms of advertising agencies their influence is virtually zero. These Center nations may have some influence on Malaysia, Singapore, and Indonesia through the advertisements that their corporations and governments place, but their influence through their own agencies is nonexistent. In short, Malaysia, Singapore, and Indonesia almost *have* to deal with the United States if they want outside advertising agency interaction. These nations cannot pit one advertising Center nation (say, the United States) against another advertising Center nation (say, Britain or Japan). The reason is that the United States is *the* super-Center of advertising. Nations like Britain, Japan, and Australia are relatively distant second-class Centers. Galtung's feudal Center-Periphery structure, then, needs to be modified slightly for advertising. The rule, "if you stay off my satellites, I will stay off yours" does not apply to advertising.[14]

The Japanese TNAAs—all three of them in Malaysia, Singapore, and Indonesia—maintain only a very modest presence *anywhere,* and nowhere (except in Japan, of course, and possibly in China) are they serious competitors to American agencies. Japan as an advertising power, then, is overrated given the reality in these particular nations. Japan surely is a Center nation vis-a-vis Southeast Asia in terms of economic exchange, but when it comes to advertising agency influence in Malaysia and Singapore and, to a lesser extent, Indonesia, Japan is certainly only a minor Center nation. This is understandable since advertising agency work in the region is overwhelmingly dependent on English, which is not used very much in Japan, and on Western values, some of which conflict with Japanese culture. Just as Japan has never exported its culture and communication software in a big way (for example, through a Japanese transnational news agency), it also has not exported much advertising influence through Japanese TNAAs. This pattern holds true for Japanese advertising activities not only in the region but globally. For example, Dentsu and Hakuhodo maintain operations only in a few key markets where Japanese economic interests are sizable, but these are the same markets where American agencies also are very active. Japan, then, does not have "its" Periphery advertising nations, America "its" Periphery advertising nations, and so forth. As *the* advertising Center nation, the United States is more or less free to extend its advertising trade relations in almost all directions. Other Center nations and, of course, the Periphery nations do not have the organizations or the power to carry out such transnational advertising interaction. The latter nations must be content to interact with the outside world largely via the American TNAAs.

4. *Advertising subimperialism is maintained in the Periphery through a bilateral arrangement in which the Center nation builds on already existing structures and uses another nation as a go-between partner to maintain the status quo in the region.*

Data from Malaysia, Singapore, and Indonesia support Galtung's important hypotheses about go-between and "favorite country" relations and about the United States as the super-Center in Southeast Asia. Present

situations within and between these particular nations confirm that the
United States has largely become the strongest advertising power in this
region by building upon already existing structures, including advertising
agencies, largely developed by Britain during its colonial rule. Although its
overall power has declined since formal colonialism, Britain remains a
Center in this region. More important in terms of advertising, Britain
functions as a go-between nation vis-à-vis the United States, as advertising
super-Center, and the Peripheries of Malaysia, Singapore, and Indonesia.
Figure 6 illustrates these contemporary go-between advertising relations.
In figure 3, Galtung hypothesized that Japan served as America's favorite
country in maintaining control over Southeast Asia. My data on advertising, however, show that Britain—not Japan—is generally America's advertising partner in this politically and economically important region. China,
however, could be an important exception. Indications are that McCann-
Erickson and Dentsu, in their Beijing operations, are not the competitors
one might expect. Instead, each seems to share the common objective of
their clients—all want to work together to convince the Chinese authorities
that China should be opened up to more foreign influence and that there is
ample room for both American and Japanese ad agencies.

A closer examination of the special relationship between the United
States and Britain in terms of advertising reveals parallels with other types
of harmonious partnership relations between these two advertising-rich,
English speaking powers. Jeremy Tunstall, for example, has observed that
a special media relationship exists between these nations, and that "Britain
has been, and is, a lynch-pin in the worldwide spread of American
media."[15] Such a description certainly fits advertising in Malaysia and Singapore, to a lesser extent in Indonesia, and to an even greater extent in
Hong Kong. Historically, the British influence has been significant, not
only in spreading English and media models but also in establishing some
of the early ad agencies and advertisers in colonial outposts, including
Hong Kong.

The British heritage is not as strong in Indonesia as it is in either Malaysia or Singapore. This is understandable since modern advertising did not
arrive in Indonesia in any major way until the early 1970s, several years
after British influence had peaked in the region.

Personnel in senior posts with the TNAAs in Malaysia, Singapore, and
Indonesia tend to be from Britain, Australia, or New Zealand. In addition
to historic "mother" nation and white Commonwealth ties, the major reason for the lack of American TNAA personnel in the field in Southeast
Asia has to do with economics. American admen seem reluctant to give up
well-paying secure jobs in the United States for a "hardship" assignment in
distant Malaysia, Singapore, or Indonesia. The latter is considered an especially difficult post for any expatriate. Expatriates from Australia, New
Zealand, Britain, and other Western European nations seem more adven-

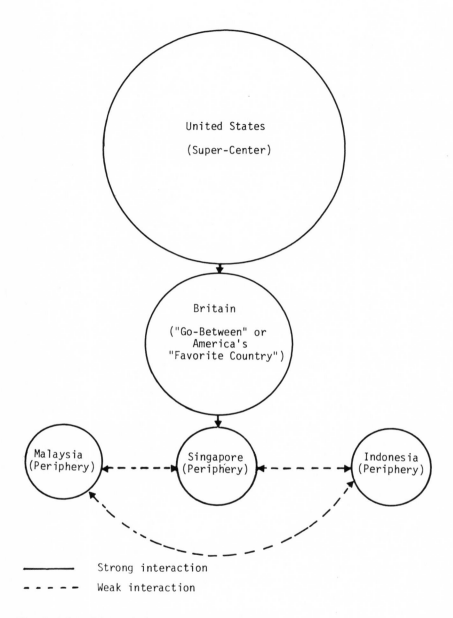

Fig. 6. Advertising relations in Southeast Asia.

turous than Americans and more familiar with the realities of the good life in places like Kuala Lumpur or Singapore. These non-American Westerners also often can be hired at lower salaries than Americans.

Based on interviews and visits to TNAAs, I observed that almost all of the American-owned or affiliated agencies are actually managed by non-Americans. The Japanese agencies have only Japanese managers, but other TNAAs have a grab bag of English speaking expatriate managers and creative specialists. As the head of Ogilvy & Mather once explained: "Americans have no monopoly on talent. We grab it where we can find it."[16]

As long as the expatriates direct profitable operations, maintain close contact with regional and global headquarters, follow corporate policies and procedures, and provide services up to "international standards," TNAA home office executives see no reason to directly intervene by, say, imposing expensive Americans on Southeast Asian offices. Most of the American TNAAs seem to consider the region still pretty much within the old British sphere of influence, and they have no qualms about taking full advantage of British-oriented expatriates, many of whom enjoy Asian work. For example, a "very American TNAA," like McCann-Erickson, relies heavily on white Commonwealth expatriates. In 1977, its representative in Jakarta was an Australian who had worked for a TNAA in London and Melbourne and had set up O&M's office in Auckland. Its Kuala Lumpur manager was an Englishman who previously had managed McCann's office in Portugal. Its Singapore managing director was Dutch. Most of the expatriate admen in Malaysia, Singapore, and Indonesia have worked elsewhere in the region or elsewhere in the Third World and frequently for other TNAAs.

These examples indicate how difficult it is to distinguish between British influence, Australian influence, American influence, and so forth. These English speaking nations have all been subjected to similar advertising and cultural patterns and processes over time and, in many ways, they are involved in trading and other relations of common interest. In the case of advertising influence, it is accurate to say that in all three nations there is a very substantial penetration of American owned agencies and white Commonwealth (largely British) influence via expatriate advertising specialists employed by agencies and TNCs and via educational experiences provided in Center nations. Indonesia does not have the British flavor that Malaysia and Singapore do, but the differences are not particularly relevant. Regardless of whether a TNAA is American owned or British owned, American managed or British managed, the effects of Western influence upon the individual agency, the national advertising industry generally, and the host nation as a whole are essentially the same. As one TNAA executive from Australia said:

I don't care where expatriates come from and, in fact, four of the five managers of our Southeast Asian offices are British, not Australians. But that only happens to be true right now and we have had more Australians, New Zealanders, and even an American. I don't think our advertising is influenced by any particular country. Our objective is to run the best advertising for the market and we use mostly nationals to produce advertising which effectively reaches other nationals.[17]

The evidence is strong, however, that the TNAAs' managers, local employees, and advertisements are under the influence of a combination of British and other Commonwealth personnel *and* American advertising models, standards and ownership. In this sense, then, it is accurate to say that advertising in Malaysia, Singapore, and Indonesia is dominated by a mixture or coalition of Anglo-American interests.

This finding is consistent with Galtung's view that the world has more than one Center, and that differences exist between the capitalist Centers and the socialist Centers, as well as between nations within either of these two major divisions. In the case of advertising, I have already explained how the centers of the United States and Britain play different roles vis-à-vis Malaysia, Singapore, and Indonesia. Distinctions between these three Peripheries need to be made if advertising interaction is to be understood in more precise terms. To understand feudal interaction, then, it is important to understand why some Periphery nations are more unequal or more dependent than other Periphery nations.

My research shows that Hong Kong (and also Singapore, compared to its two neighbors) are generally more tightly intertwined with the transnational power structure and with Center advertising. Like their TNC clients, a number of the TNAAs have used, and continue to use, Hong Kong or Singapore as a regional base.

A number of factors account for Singapore's great desirability as a TNAA base. Its central location, efficient transportation and communication facilities, sophisticated shopping facilities, its heavily Westernized and English speaking population, its political stability, and its foreign investment oriented government combine to make Singapore an ideal global city that plays a strategic processing or go-between role between industrial nations like the United States, Japan, and Britain and its less industrialized neighboring hinterlands.

Figure 7 accurately reflects Singapore's unique position midway between several different Centers and the Peripheries. Figure 8 applies this Galtungian structure to the case of McCann-Erickson's operations to show how a major TNAA uses Singapore as a go-between in its relations with Indonesia. In the illustrated interaction relation, the gap between the super-Center, the United States, and the extreme Periphery, Indonesia, is enormous, and Singapore serves as a willing intermediate layer between

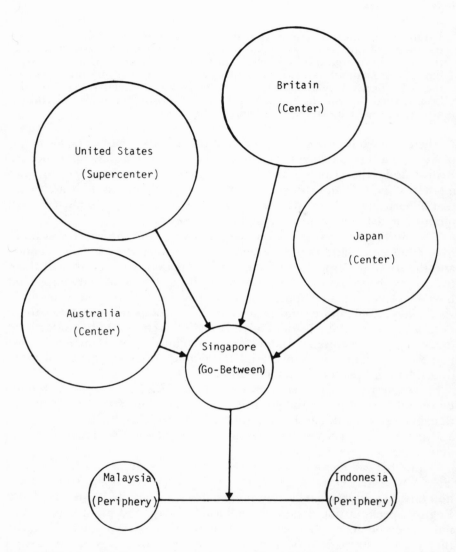

Fig. 7. Singapore's Go-between Status in a Multi-Empire World of Advertising, 1977. NOTE: The arrows stand for vertical interaction relations. Super-Center United States and the less important other Centers use Singapore as their go-between. By substituting Hong Kong for Singapore, and China for Malaysia and Indonesia, China's relationship to the rest of the world can be illustrated.

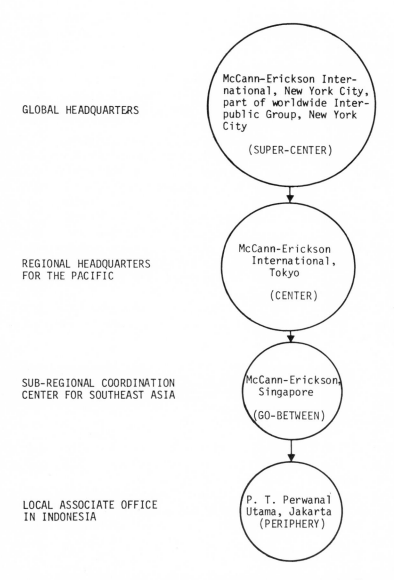

GLOBAL HEADQUARTERS

McCann-Erickson International, New York City, part of worldwide Interpublic Group, New York City

(SUPER-CENTER)

REGIONAL HEADQUARTERS FOR THE PACIFIC

McCann-Erickson International, Tokyo

(CENTER)

SUB-REGIONAL COORDINATION CENTER FOR SOUTHEAST ASIA

McCann-Erickson, Singapore

(GO-BETWEEN)

LOCAL ASSOCIATE OFFICE IN INDONESIA

P. T. Perwanal Utama, Jakarta
(PERIPHERY)

Fig. 8. Transnational Advertising Agency Go-between Relations in Singapore. NOTE: By 1980, McCann-Erickson had acquired a new indigenous partner, Intervista, in Indonesia, but the same patterns illustrated here continued.

the Center (and its ally, Japan) and Indonesia. In terms of advertising processing and advertising progress generally, Singapore appears to be at least one cycle "behind" the Center and at least one cycle "ahead" of Indonesia. For example, Japan and the United States have had color television for years; Singapore acquired it next, and then Indonesia. Advertising ideas, as well as technology, often trickle down to Singapore or Hong Kong from the Centers. Later, these reach the more isolated Peripheries such as Indonesia and perhaps even China.

In the case of McCann-Erickson, the regional manager in Singapore oversees the TNAA's activities in both neighboring Indonesia and Malaysia. In 1977, for example, he visited P. T. Perwanal Utama's Jakarta offices once a month, and the McCann expatriate in that office normally referred "major policy decisions" to Singapore for "guidance purposes."[18] McCann's chief in Singapore reported to the TNAA's regional director for the Pacific Region (Japan, Australia, New Zealand, and Southeast Asia), based in Tokyo. The regional director, in turn, reported to McCann's world headquarters in New York City. Major policies were set by McCann headquarters or by its parent, the Interpublic Group of Companies, also based in New York City.

Another TNAA that uses Singapore as its regional base is Kenyon & Eckhardt. It has emphasized the special regional importance of its Singapore office:

> One of its roles is to channel additional creative help, generally on a task force basis, as and when required by any office in the Region. Additional input will usually derive from Singapore, where continuing success and a comparatively pragmatic expatriate employment policy allow us to employ a large pool of first class creative talent.[19]

Through a TNAA like Kenyon & Eckhardt, advertising that has "worked," or been developed, in Singapore can easily be transferred "down" to neighboring Malaysia or Indonesia.

The counsel and software provided by the TNAAs' regional offices to their sister agencies elsewhere in the region understandably reflect the values, symbols, images, ideas, and vested interests of Center-nation creators or the bridgeheads that process materials within the region itself. Many of the TNAAs' messages are created, produced, and tested in affluent industrialized societies with large, homogeneous, affluent markets, and then transmitted—sometimes intact or adapted at little cost—to *very* different markets in Malaysia, Singapore, or Indonesia. Many local admen complained to me that not enough creative work was being done indigenously and that some of the TNAAs' advertisements were inappropriate because they emphasized situations and images, particularly using sex, that were alien to local consumers.

Part of the problem has to do with language since the master copy of

TNAAs is often prepared in English and then translated into local languages. The TNAAs' expatriates, like those in top positions with TNC advertisers, usually do not speak local languages well, so they have to either rely on trusted local staff or have everything translated and run the risk of losing some of the meaning in the process. Given the diversities of language, religion, culture, and life-styles within the region, the TNAAs' expatriates can easily become frustrated with local situations. As one Malaysian government official explained:

> The longer the foreign creative writer works in this region, the more taboos he is bound to run into. By the time the creative writer learns to skirt the more commonplace taboos, he has finished his tour. Out comes another creative man from the Madison Avenue environment. And he goes through the same frustration, exasperation and gnashing of teeth until he discovers that often his norms and values have very little validity with his target audience.[20]

Because of their go-between status, Singapore and Hong Kong provide the TNAAs with a less frustrating working environment than either Malaysia or Indonesia. In the eyes of the TNAAs, Singapore's official "open door" policies give that nation a clear psychological advantage over Malaysia. Center nations perceive Singapore as more sophisticated, advanced, better-governed, more honest, and generally more receptive to foreigners in advertising or anything else. Whether such a positive image in foreign investors' eyes can continue, or whether Singapore will ever change its laissez-fair policies remains to be seen. Ultimately, Singapore's small population will be a disadvantage since it leaves little room for the growth that TNCs need. And the nation's small land mass also will be a problem since Singapore is rapidly becoming advertising-saturated and pressures to limit "visual pollution" in outdoor advertising are already strong. Some day the TNAAs might well need to bypass Singapore's small advertising "cake" and concentrate their efforts on penetrating the much larger but far more complex and nationalistic markets in Malaysia and Indonesia.

Despite the fact that Singapore is a different type of Periphery nation from either Malaysia or Indonesia, the intranational centers of each of these nations are internationalized and coupled together in the same transnational power structure controlled by a few Center nations. The mere presence of so many TNAAs in these nations is evidence that the commercial and political establishment believes that, overall, the presence of the TNAAs is a positive factor in their nations' (or at least in their elite groups') development efforts. Advertising dependence continues within each of these nations because policies and procedures—official and unofficial— exist that presume that the "goods" provided by the TNAAs are indispensable and cannot be obtained elsewhere. Advertising Centers, particularly the United States but with some considerable assistance from less powerful advertising Center nations like Japan, Britain and Australia, rule over these nations' advertising industries. As power senders, the Centers' advertising ideas penetrate the power recipients and help shape culture and other aspects of the Periphery's daily life. A small local elite—frequently Chinese, sometimes indigenous groups—serves as a bridgehead.

To facilitate the smooth transfer of transnational advertising influences to the Periphery, the TNAAs hire and train English speaking, bright, enthusiastic local elites who are able to master TNAA techniques and emulate foreign models. Occasionally, the best of these students become involved in a "brain drain," as they are sent to the Center for more orientation, training, and experience. While outside their home-nations at TNAA facilities in London, Sydney, Chicago, New York, and Tokyo, these elites can uncritically pick up many of the Western values and interests shared by other TNAA admen and the Center generally. In this manner, harmonies of interest are developed as bridgeheads become somewhat denationalized or internationalized through exposure to the Center and identification with the TNAA organization and its "mother" nation.

The international division of labor and the allocation of resources (including human) facilitated by the TNAAs help transfer Center culture to Malaysia, Singapore, and Indonesia. The result, as Galtung's model argues, is that the Periphery, by accepting such cultural transmission, implicitly "validates for the Center the culture developed in the center, whether that center is intra- or international" and "serves to reinforce the Center as a Center, for it will then continue to develop culture along with transmitting it, thus creating lasting demand for the latest innovations."[21]

Advertising influences, then, are often developed (most often in English, of course) in TNAA Center nation offices, in glamorous, stimulating, and innovative places like London, New York, and Tokyo, which are widely perceived by both Center and Periphery societies as having the best brains in the advertising business and as centers of ideas, fashions, music, art, media techniques, and professionalism. All of these pieces of the advertising process have a built-in life cycle, and new "models" and advertising campaigns using them are constantly being developed under a TNAA policy of planned obsolescence. Campaigns considered out-of-date in the Center can simply be passed down to the Periphery and recycled. In Southeast Asia, such a recycling process often begins in Hong Kong or in Singapore, where TNAA materials have no problems entering, and then spreads to other nations. Through this asymmetric pattern of exchange and interaction, the culture of the Center has become the culture of the world.

Advertising patterns of exchange and interaction in Malaysia, Singapore, and Indonesia illustrate only a few aspects of a dynamic phenomenon that I have described as the transnational power structure. Compared to Malaysia and Indonesia, Singapore is more internationalized and better integrated into this structure of dominance. The Singapore government believes that the very existence of the vulnerable island republic would be threatened should it try to alter the dominance relation between itself and the Center nations. By establishing horizontal interaction with its neighbors and adopting development strategies that would lead to advertising-related and other types of defeudalization, the government fears Singapore's foundation as a pro-TNC, global city would be weakened. Center nations, of course, are content with the status quo and with the Singapore government's general position that it has no alternative but to continue to pursue integrative and associative strategies. These act to keep Singapore's borders open to such foreign influences as Western advertising services, foreign investment, tourists, and nonindigenous, English-based culture generally. Although certainly dependent on Center nations, Malaysia and Indonesia are at somewhat different stages of integration into the Center-dominated global system. The governments of Malaysia and Indonesia recognize the evils that the general structure of dominance can bring to their efforts toward greater self-respect, self-sufficiency, and independence. Compared to Singapore, neither of these governments feels that the TNAAs are absolutely indispensable, and each has a degree of consciousness that has motivated the government to take modest "immunization" steps to counteract external advertising power and to try to make certain that TNAA services are supplied somewhat on their terms. In Malaysia, for example, TNAAs and local agencies must inject "Malaysian identity" into their TV commercials, and in Indonesia TNAAs are not to have equity in any ad agency. In China, of course, all foreigners must work through state-run advertising and trading corporations.

Like Singapore, however, neither Malaysia nor Indonesia has had sufficient strength or power-over-itself to withstand the intense, transnational pressures (including those from TNCs who want TNAA services) that are exerted on nations. Neither Malaysia nor Indonesia has been very successful at controlling the TNAAs through regulatory policies and dissociative strategies. This 1978 observation from a Malaysian government officer illustrates how extremely difficult it is for Peripheries to make the TNAAs more accountable:

> They have been in the country for more than 15 years and they continue to dominate the advertising scene. To a fairly large degree they also continue to be the main arbiters of Malaysian advertising trends. Nearly all the TNCEs [transnational communication enterprises] have undergone a process known in local parlance as "Malaysianization." And that is, the gradual phasing out of foreign experts and replacing them with Malaysian advertising men. This process of Malaysianization was scheduled to have been completed in 1975, when only the heads of the TNCEs would continue to be foreign. All the other personnel would be local. Only one TNCE has met this target date. The agency is Ogilvy & Mather which completed the Malaysianization process about three years ago. Nearly all the other TNCEs pleaded inability due to varying reasons.

One TNCE even went to the extent of forming "ghost" companies and applying to the authorities for expatriate quota to serve as heads of these paper companies. By means of this ploy, it was able to have on its staff more expatriates than any of the other TNCEs.[22]

Through foot dragging and other ploys, the TNAAs in Malaysia and Indonesia have been able to get around various policies designed to transfer power from expatriates to indigenous admen. The basic reason such practices have been tolerated is that Malaysia and Indonesia, as well as Singapore, essentially pursue development models largely defined by the West. Indigenous businessmen, admen, and politicians have vested interests in cooperating with foreign admen and other investors from advertising-rich nations and maintaining the existing transnational power structure. One consequence of such an alliance has been that advertising in each of these societies is largely influenced by foreign rather than local interests. The major advertising agencies generally are not autonomous indigenous businesses. Both their ownership and their decision making processes are largely in the hands of foreigners, and these nations and their elites are unable or unwilling to resist the advertising power pressure to which they are exposed every day. In a sentence, they are unable to be anything other than go-betweens and advertising power receivers.

5. *Periphery nations that had to struggle to gain their political independence from a "mother" Center nation are more likely to pursue dissociative policies toward TNAAs than are those nations which gained independence more peacefully.*

The advertising agency in Malaysia and Singapore is very much an Anglo-American organization that evolved historically from the area's relatively cordial colonial ties with the West. As "mother" nation, Britain's political and economic influence declined after these colonies gained independence; formal power was transferred to anti-Communist, Western-educated, multiracial elites. Also, America moved in after World War II and filled the British economic, political, and cultural vacuum. This transition process was relatively painless at first because American corporate structures, media influences, and culture (language and values) were not very different from the British influences long familiar to the area. American ideas of law and order, democracy, economic growth, media, and other ingredients of development differed little from those of the British. Unlike Indonesia, the nation building process in both Malaysia and Singapore had relatively little socialist or Communist content. It exhibited politics of moderation, of economic growth, and of consumerism, and generally was influenced more by relatively conservative Center-generated plans than by change-oriented and Periphery-generated strategies.

In Indonesia, the situation was substantially different. Dutch colonial policies had been harsher, and the colonial rulers did not provide many opportunities for indigenous Indonesians to acquire power—political or economic. These circumstantial factors led to xenophobia, liberation from colonialism, some anti-capitalism, and a strong sense of Indonesian national identity. While Singapore and Malaysia allowed an essentially colonial economy to continue after independence, restless Indonesia wanted a sharp break with the past. Sukarno wanted to sever most Western links and lead Indonesia into maturity through autonomy. After years of anticolonialism and general political and economic turmoil, Indonesia's "New Order" began without Sukarno in 1965. As the nation took a sharp turn to the right, the Anglo-American advertising agency, as a modern Western business organization previously largely unknown to Indonesians, was imported as part of a larger package of Western and Japanese influences. Unlike the British or the Americans, the Dutch had had no TNAAs. Indonesians, therefore, had had little firsthand experience with colonial-style advertising. More important, they had little experience withstanding power directed from non-Dutch Western sources using such relatively new and sophisticated means as the TNCs and mass communications. Indonesia's bitter experiences with colonial submission and its severe poverty have contributed to a situation in which many Indonesians are highly suspicious of foreigners. At the same time, however, Indonesia is too weak to effectively mobilize itself as a unified nation to oppose foreign power, particularly TNC exploitation. Various obstacles, including weak administrative organizations and "restrictive participation,"[23] found in many Third World nations are evident in Indonesia, and they combine to make policies of justice and strategies for structural change unrealistic. Even policies that gradually reduce the tensions that inevitably accompany the presence of the TNCs are difficult to implement in "soft-states" like Indonesia.[24] A major factor in these difficulties is that the powerful transnational power structure, of which the TNAAs are one component, provides incentives to elites in Indonesia and elsewhere who choose not to work for structural change or to curb TNCs' power.

In such an atmosphere, dependence, fear, and corruption are common, and the TNCs (including the TNAAs) can easily become centers of resentment and political attention. Occasionally, as with Indonesia's anti-Japanese riots in 1974, the realization that the nation or particular groups lack important resources and occupy low positions in the structure, results in mounting mass demands and sometimes violence. The Indonesian government often finds itself forced to respond expediently to mass antigovernment or antiforeign views by implementing what appear to be dissociative policies toward foreign investors and by finding scapegoats such as the local Chinese. Such a volatile environment—in which political nationalism accompanies economic nationalism—can have direct consequences on advertising. For example, after the 1974 disturbances, the Suharto government had to be seen to take firm action forbidding the advertising of luxury goods, particularly cars, on television, and de-emphasizing Japanese investment. The government at the same time had fostered a more authoritarian political climate by pursuing law and order in the name of political stability. The latter was exactly what the TNCs needed in Indonesia, as well as Malaysia and Singapore, to continue to aggressively pursue growth and profits.

Compared to Indonesia, antiforeign sentiments seldom erupt openly in Singapore or Malaysia. In the case of Singapore, anyone advocating a tough stance against the TNCs and dissociative policies generally would be considered antinational, and the government's firm control of political activity and mass media content ensures that the status quo is preserved. In Malaysia, the plural nature of the society has made communalism *the* overriding problem, and the Malays, Chinese, and Indians have been so physically, economically, and culturally isolated from each other since colonial days that any genuine multiracial alliance other than among the English-educated elites has not been feasible. Until the various groups are truly united as Malaysians along lines other than ethnicity, Malaysia's tradition of conservative, pro-Western, associative policies in terms of foreign investment are likely to continue. These policies tend to maintain the status quo in advertising and everything else. Changes are particularly difficult in the Malaysian context because of their close connection to sensitive communal issues. Malaysia's advertising—like the economic system generally—is divided along racial lines (Caucasians and Chinese are the "top dogs"), and any public effort to redress various intra-and international imbalances carries considerable domestic security risks.

In short, while there are differences in how Malaysia, Singapore, and Indonesia regulate advertising and the TNAAs, such differences are relatively insignificant. What *is* important is that each of these nations pursues a capitalistic type of development that favors associative policies and a status quo that allows Center nations to continue to exercise considerable advertising control.

Dynamic Propositions

1. *In advertising there is growing Center coordination, particularly among the capitalist powers.*

My data show that with advertising, as with other types of exchange, the various capitalist Centers are *not* fighting against one another but rather are cooperating to oppose those who would weaken the basic system that permits Western-style development—and advertising—to function. A classic example of this trend developed in 1981 when Dentsu and Young & Rubicam joined forces to establish a joint venture in Tokyo. That same year, IPG's SSC&B:Lintas system was establishing an active association with another Japanese agency, Hakuhodo. My data also show that the Peripheries of Malaysia, Singapore, and Indonesia are increasingly moving away from a wider range of partners for their advertising interaction and toward a one-Center world of American advertising.

The Centers of Japan, Britain, and the European Economic Community seem content to maintain the status quo in which the United States is clearly still the strongest advertising power, and its super-Center advertising status is virtually unchallenged by *any* Center—either capitalist or socialist.

A closer look at my findings from these three Peripheries illustrates the trend among the TNAAs toward greater coordination and centralization. In large measure, this trend has been facilitated globally by the Center nations' use of instant communication to coordinate their actions. Major improvements in global communications and transportation speed and capacity explain why TNAAs might voluntarily—rather than under Periphery elite or mass political pressures—change the ways and means through which they work in the Periphery and generally operate transnationally.

I believe that transnational advertising in these particular Southeast Asian nations functions no differently than it does in most Third World nations. As part of the world market system, Malaysia, Singapore, and Indonesia have all been affected by near-global trends toward not only more standardized, homogeneous advertising at the local consumer level, but also toward more highly centralized TNAA decision making. The TNAAs themselves argue that advertising is becoming more highly differentiated structurally, with centers assuming different roles as advertising takes new forms. For example, a JWT executive has predicted greater TNAA coordination and centralization of decision making:

> In ten, twenty years' time an international agency might be able to concentrate its creative resources into, say, ten centers—let us say, New York, London, Paris, Sao Paulo, Buenos Aires, Sydney, one to cover the important area from Japan to the Indian subcontinent, one in Black Africa, one in Moscow and, perhaps, hopefully, one in Peking. Some of these may be the wrong centers and others may more usefully take their places. But I can foresee such concentration of main offices, with smaller service stations in other countries completing the network.[25]

The trend toward more TNAA-controlled, transnational advertising appears irreversible. A McCann International vice president has predicted that competition among the TNAAs will continue to be intense but will be limited to only about twenty giant agencies, which will have their decision making centers in those nations already powerful in advertising:

> Multinational agencies will have to set up major centers, which I shall call "key agencies." They will have one, two, or even three of them per continent; the actual number will depend on the stage of development of advertising in the continent concerned. In countries other than those

where key agencies are established, multinational agencies will have "contact offices" which will adapt multinational campaigns created by the key agencies and will also handle certain national accounts completely. No multinational agency will be able to avoid adopting this structure in the coming ten years.[26]

The SSC&B:Lintas, McCann-Erickson, Needham, Harper & Steers, Dentsu, Compton, Hakuhodo, and Kenyon & Eckhardt offices in Singapore seem to clearly be evolving into key agencies for Southeast Asia. The Ogilvy & Mather and Burnett offices in Kuala Lumpur show somewhat similar patterns of emerging as key agencies for the region. JWT's key agency in the region has always been Manila, and Y&R prefers Hong Kong, but both of these prestigious agencies have new offices in Singapore. In terms of relations with China, the Hong Kong offices of all of these TNAAs are becoming increasingly important.

Under advertising imperialism, present and future political control in terms of advertising decision making is firmly in the hands of a relatively few TNAAs. In Indonesia SSC&B:Lintas is, and always has been, the premiere agency, although O&M is a close competitor. In Malaysia, O&M and Burnett stand out. In Singapore, O&M, Kenyon & Eckhardt, and Leo Burnett top the TNAA field. In China, McCann-Erickson and Dentsu are the pioneers. All of these giants within the Malaysian, Singaporean, and Indonesian context are from one Center—the United States—and only Japan seems to be competing with American TNAAs in China. As advertising develops more rapidly throughout all of Asia, local agencies and medium-sized TNAAs that lack a strong multinational footing are not likely to have much influence. This is because the TNAAs deliberately do not develop "creative resources centers" or key agencies in the Periphery. Time will tell whether Singapore or other Asian cities other than Tokyo can achieve key agency status. As global instant communications improve and the trend toward greater centralization of TNAA decision making in Europe and elsewhere continues, it is conceivable that the need for even "contact offices" in some Periphery nations will disappear. Standardized near-global advertising campaigns could be created, produced, and disseminated by a handful of efficient key agencies, thus bypassing many nations completely. Future patterns of advertising imperialism could emerge in which the Center can interact with its bridgeheads in the Periphery via international communication rather than having to be frozen into more permanent institutional networks.[27] Under such new arrangements, the United States would continue to coordinate transnational advertising, but the need for extensive TNAA field operations in many Periphery nations would diminish and the TNAAs would take on new forms.

Significant improvements in global communications and transportation are very important factors in explaining why at least some of the TNAAs in Southeast Asia have "voluntarily" implemented "localization" efforts. A

TNAA like O&M, which has been in the region for years, no longer needs many expatriates actually in the field in Malaysia, Singapore, and Indonesia to oversee its investment. A few reliable experienced expatriates in field offices, plus frequent exchange of advertising materials, electronic and mail communications, and regular visits from regional coordinators and other parent corporation executives are sufficient to insure that offices function smoothly and that major international clients are professionally serviced, even in small markets that might not be especially profitable. When problems arise in Kuala Lumpur, Singapore, or Jakarta over anything important (from creativity and foreign exchange to career development and performance goals), O&M's executive director international, based in Sydney, is only an eight-hour flight away. Also, whenever particularly large campaigns are underway or emergencies develop, various mobile "creative commando" or "flying squad" teams from elsewhere in a TNAA's network can be tapped.

Agencies that are relative newcomers to these three particular nations seem to want (and need) their own people directly in the field. JWT, for example, entered the Malaysia-Singapore market directly for the first time in 1975 with a joint-venture in Kuala Lumpur. Although the TNAA could have handled its Singapore business relatively easily from Malaysia, it was decided to establish a wholly owned, autonomous office in Singapore.

During the 1970s, several TNAAs gained greater control over their Southeast Asian offices. For example, the Singapore office of Hakuhodo began in 1973 with the Japanese agency owning 60 percent share and a local Chinese 40 percent. This partnership was unsuccessful and in about a year Hakuhodo had full ownership.[28] In 1978, Compton of New York, ended a deliberately low-key policy toward the area. It completed a major reorganization of Lash-Compton, which since 1975 had been half owned by Compton and half by Guthrie, the pioneer trading agency. The American TNAA gained majority control of the Singapore operation; renamed it Compton Advertising (S) Pte. Ltd, and sent its own expatriate to upgrade the office and serve on its board of directors.

While local agencies have been struggling to get off the ground and various foreign agencies have been moving into the region and consolidating their operations, a far more important development has been underway globally and within Southeast Asia: the unmistakable transnationalization of American advertising. In Malaysia, Singapore, and Indonesia, American advertising power has been increasing as British advertising power has been declining. This has even been the situation in Britain's Hong Kong.

In terms of advertising Centers, these societies historically have only been penetrated for any length of time by Britain, Japan, Australia, and the United States. TNAAs from other nations simply are not active in Malaysia, Singapore, Indonesia, and China.

Among the Center nations active in contemporary Asia, the United States clearly predominates, and its influence—most visibly through direct ownership patterns—is increasing. America's TNAA gains have largely been at the expense of Britain, whose advertising influence clearly has declined since the end of formal colonialism. American agencies in the 1960s and 1970s gradually acquired London-based TNAAs, particularly S. H. Benson and the London Press Exchange, that had far-flung operations in the colonial areas and elsewhere. This Americanization was repeated in Australia when American agencies moved into that nation in a big way. For example, Leo Burnett took over Jackson Wain, and Ted Bates acquired George Patterson and Cathay. Table 40 summarizes how major TNAAs in Southeast Asia have moved from Commonwealth control to total American control over a fifteen-year period. Britain and Australia continue to have influence as major sources of expatriate personnel to head the Periphery operations of the TNAAs in Malaysia, Singapore, and Indonesia, but their influence in terms of ownership and parent corporate decision making is minimal compared to that of Americans. Japanese advertising is significant in the ASEAN region, but Japan's direct influence through its advertising agencies is not sizable, particularly in Malaysia and Singapore.

2. *The TNAAs' power in Periphery nations is changing in form but not decreasing relative to the indigenous non-TNAA enterprises.*

The gap between the advertising-rich and the advertising-poor nations

Table 40

Major Transnational Advertising Agency Ownership Changes in Southeast Asia

Agency Name	Nationality	American Agency Name	Percent American Share	Year of American Acquisition
Cathay and George Patterson	Australian	Ted Bates	100%	1963
Jackson Wain	Australian	Leo Burnett	100%	1971
London Press Exchange	British	Leo Burnett	100%	1971
S. H. Benson	British	Ogilvy & Mather	100%	1971
Lintas	British/Dutch	SSC&B	49%	1970
SSC&B:Lintas	British/Dutch/American	Interpublic Group	100%	1978
Grant International	Canadian	Kenyon & Eckhardt	100%	1975

NOTE: This table shows that much of America's dominance of Southeast Asian agencies has been built on a British Commonwealth foundation. Grant Advertising was originally a Chicago-based TNAA that operated a very successful transnational network, particularly in the 1950s and 1960s. In 1972, it was sold to a Toronto corporation called Comcore Communications Ltd. In 1975, K&E, New York City, bought the Asian Region of Grant International and made it part of the worldwide K&E Group. By 1980, Interpublic had acquired SSC&B, Inc. and its 49 percent interest in the SSC&B:Lintas International agency system. By 1982, the remaining 51 percent should be in Interpublic's hands.

SOURCES: Based on personal interviews with these agencies' executives in Southeast Asia and on background materials supplied by the TNAAs' headquarters.

always has been—and continues to be—enormous, and Galtung's theory has maintained that structural change is necessary to decrease the gap. My data from Malaysia, Singapore, and Indonesia illustrate how difficult it is to change the structure of advertising. Despite years of independence, these Peripheries' resource and structural power remains comparatively weak. A closer examination of trends within these nations will suggest reasons for this advertising dominance relation.

Since about 1970, Malaysia, Singapore, and Indonesia have acquired some advertising resources that have enabled advertising agencies to locally plan, create, and implement relatively sophisticated advertising campaigns that only a few years earlier were beyond indigenous capabilities. In Malaysia, for example, four film production houses were operating in 1972, and about 176 commercials were produced locally. By 1978, the number of production companies had grown to sixteen and they were producing about 450 commercials annually.[29]

Much of the credit for the rapid modernization and professionalization of advertising in these nations must go to the TNAAs. They have not only invested capital but also have brought in expatriate managers, creative personnel, and other specialists (and their Western techniques, skills, and values). The presence of the TNAAs also has resulted in such spin-offs as film production houses, public relations firms, and survey and market research organizations to supplement TNAA services. All of these "goods," however, have not been distributed very equitably in any of these nations, and the overall impact has been that the TNAAs occupy a position of high power potential within each nations' advertising industry. Compared to the indigenous agencies, which come and go, the TNAAs have come and stayed. Rarely do they go out of business, particularly compared to indigenous agencies. A reason for their stability is that relative to local businesses, the TNAAs have far more weaponry. Their power is greater because they have more of virtually all the essential resources—particularly human—that make an agency relatively strong economically, creatively, and politically. Also, the TNAAs' structural, or relation, power is greater because they are linked not only *organizationally* to commanding, commercially successful transnational corporations that are centrally located in the world power structure, but also *politically* to a few industrialized nations that are powerful by virtue of their economic, military, cultural, and communications patterns.

Despite the rapid growth in the sheer number of indigenous agencies and the number of local personnel in advertising in the three nations, the power of the TNAAs relative to indigenous agencies has not diminished. The nature of the TNAAs' presence, however, has changed. Most significantly, far more advertising is being produced locally rather than being imported. This has meant that the TNAAs have invested in large full-service operations in these nations. The Leo Burnett office in Kuala

Lumpur is but one example. It began in 1966 with a staff of two and billings of about $32,000. By 1977, the TNAA claimed to have a staff of eighty-five and billings of more than $7 million. Its services are virtually a small replica of everything that a full-service Center agency could offer in creativity, accounting servicing, media, production, and financial strength.[30]

In addition to the TNAA's improved facilities, the TNAAs have given greater responsibility to local personnel. In 1977, for example, Ted Bates in Singapore allowed a Singaporean to sit on its local board for the first time, and other agencies also have given a degree of formal control to trusted indigenous people.[31] Local personnel in nonmanagerial positions also were becoming more involved in the advertising cycle, even though it is still highly standardized. Table 41 shows how the number of expatriates in major TNAAs has generally declined in recent years while the number of local staff has generally increased. An agency like O&M, for example, has reduced its expatriates in Malaysia from nine to one and in Singapore from five to two. Nearly all TNAAs boast that they are creating advertising locally for the unique conditions of the local environment.

Since most expatriates do not have much knowledge of local languages, they cannot be too actively involved in the copywriting of advertisements. Theoretically then, as a TNAA moves toward greater use of non-English campaigns, its needs for English speaking creative people should decline. In part, this explains why table 41 reflects such a sharp drop in the number of expatriates employed by a group of major TNAAs. Several other factors, however, also account for the reduction. Costs of maintaining a highly paid expatriate have greatly increased in recent years, and the TNAAs find it cheaper and better—as a long-term investment—to hire local personnel and train them as professionals. The agencies increasingly seem to realize that local elites, particularly if Center-trained and then carefully supervised by expatriates, can create more effective (and, therefore, more profitable) advertising than expatriates, who do not know the local language and culture very well and seldom stay in one place more than a few years.

By using local personnel, the TNAAs—particularly in Indonesia, but also in Malaysia—not only avoid the problems of getting government approval on work permits but they also win favor with government officials who are under growing pressure to promote localization in all job fields. While consciously thinking they "have it made," many local TNAA employees seem to be unconsciously contributing to the maintenance of the status quo within the industry. Under expatriates, the TNAAs generally were "top dogs" in the local advertising industry. Today, under fewer expatriates and more local elites, the TNAAs generally continue to dominate local advertising. This is because the TNAAs are able to buy the best indigenous skills *and* conduct their own costly on-the-job training programs *and* send promising local elites (at even greater expense) to TNAA offices

Table 41

Trends in Transnational Advertising Agency Staffing in

Malaysia, Singapore and Indonesia, 1973-77

Agency	Location	Number of Expatriate Staff		Number of Local Staff	
		1973	1977	1973	1977
Grant, Kenyon & Eckhardt	Kuala Lumpur	4	2	31	32
Hakuhodo	Kuala Lumpur	2	1	12	19
Ogilvy & Mather	Kuala Lumpur	9	1	. .	. .
SSC&B:Lintas	Kuala Lumpur	2	1	30	50
Ted Bates	Singapore	3	1	49	32
Grant, Kenyon & Eckhardt	Singapore	11	6	86	60
Hakuhodo	Singapore	1	2	9	11
Ogilvy & Mather	Singapore	5	2	. .	. .
Chuo Senko	Jakarta	3*/	3	10*/	15
Fortune	Jakarta	5	1	39	23
McCann-Erickson	Jakarta	1	2	25	27
Ogilvy & Mather	Jakarta	3	3	25	39
	TOTALS	49	25	316	308

*/ = 1976 figures

NOTE: This table includes only major TNAAs for which comparable data comparing local versus nonlocal hiring totals were available.

SOURCE: Above information was provided directly by the agencies in the form of verbal information given during visits to the agencies or in written response to my request for such information from the agency's managing director.

in the Center. Abroad, as well as at home, these young bridgeheads are socialized by the TNAA organization and taught to "do advertising" through Center eyes. Training, therefore, reinforces organizational, cultural, and other patterns developed in advertising-rich nations when, usually under their own terms, they transmit advertising skills to the Periphery. Training, nearly always conducted by expatriates, is like other transnational patterns and processes: it appears to discourage any serious rethinking of how advertising should function in the Third World. Also, it seems to contribute to a situation in which Periphery nations such as Indonesia remain relatively advertising-poor and psychologically dependent on a few Center nations that are almost automatically assumed to have higher professional standards. While integrated into the world advertising system, Periphery nations like Indonesia tend to be isolated from meaningful interaction with other Periphery nations experiencing similar advertising problems and concerns. For example, although Malaysia shares a common national language and a similar cultural heritage with Indonesia, it is not doing much to assist its less affluent neighbor to develop indigenous advertising resources. A major reason for continuation of the status quo in advertising is that the industry in Malaysia (and Singapore) is controlled by a coalition of expatriates and local Chinese who understandably are reluctant to redistribute their various benefits. Neither of these politically vulnerable groups wants to give up any economic advantage.

In short, the power level of indigenous agencies has remained relatively low in each of the three nations, and the TNAAs have been able to keep control over local advertising. Local personnel have been particularly useful in maintaining the TNAAs' near monopoly on advertising. Nationals have become the backbone of the TNAA's operations, but they are largely restricted to lower- and middle-level positions. Top positions are almost inevitably occupied by expatriates who not only carry out the parent corporation's policies, but also train and supervise the locals. There is no evidence that local personnel have much of a chance, if any, to transfer from a Periphery office into a Center office. The TNAAs train local personnel to *remain* in local positions where their knowledge of the local situation can be fully tapped. The chances of, say, an O&M local executive in Jakarta being promoted to head the Singapore office or being moved on more than a short-term basis to a Center office are neglible. Such a situation reinforces Galtung's argument about division of labor. In advertising, the Center nations have the power to determine what processing is to be conducted where and by whom. In the case of local TNAA staff, the Center clearly has decided that indigenous personnel are most productive in their Periphery nations carrying out routines assigned by the Center. Such a decision can lead to tensions and role-conflict for the talented local who may want greater freedom and has aspirations that cannot be fulfilled locally.

3. *In plural Periphery nations, the presence of the TNAAs has a destabilizing effect on ethnic relationships and is exacerbating social and political tensions between different ethnic groups through influences on negative, intra-actor effects.*

It is difficult to generalize about the impact of TNAAs on the complex nagging political and social tensions (often with racial overtones) in Malaysia, Singapore, and Indonesia. It is safe, however, to conclude that advertising is a relatively conservative industry that is tightly connected to foreign investors and that the possibilities of conflict surrounding distribution of the "pie" are great in these societies where one group is more economically active, urbanized, or Westernized than another.

The TNAAs in plural Malaysia, Singapore, and Indonesia—like their big TNC clients—want stability coupled with economic growth. Therefore, they and other foreign investors have an interest, along with the government and business elites generally, in maintaining capitalist development policies and plans and restricting local participation in areas such as advertising. They want to discourage, or at least slow down, the transfer of an important economic and communication activity like advertising to indigenous hands. In the case of Malaysia, the status quo means inequality within and between the major ethnic groups, and especially lack of much real economic (and, therefore, advertising) power for most Malays. In cosmopolitan Singapore, the status quo means continued foreign domination of the economy (and, therefore, advertising) through a system imposed by the colonial powers and sustained through a lack of organized political opposition. In Indonesia, the status quo means continued widespread poverty and enormous gaps between a few elites, heavily concentrated in Jakarta and making conspicuous material progress, and the majority of the nation's population in relatively isolated, tradition-bound rural areas.

The TNAAs tend to aggravate these status quo-related problems because they are in a highly visible, labor-intensive service industry that is an integral factor in mass communications and cultural process and in continuation of Western-style development patterns. Some of the TNAAs talk about being culturally sensitive. Leo Burnett, for example, has consciously down-played its "American-ness":

> Leo Burnett's International network has preserved intact a vast rich complex of talents and of ethnic attitudes, experience and reputation, British, European, Latin American. The International Board itself is multi-racial and representative of these groups. The Group principles, to which we all subscribe, are certainly not American. They are universal truths for the advertising industry, wherever it is located. All of us have benefited by the interaction of points of view of people far removed from ourselves in custom, creed and color.[32]

At the same time, however, the TNAA cannot help but reflect the values and the products of its headquarters and Center nation. In 1977, for example, Leo Burnett in Singapore tried to recruit a visualizer with an advertisement that emphasized:

> At Leo Burnett there are some really exciting happenings afoot. Happenings that require the services of a top-flight visualizer. This guy must think Internationally. Must be fast on the board. And turn out stuff that will make the world sit up and look, not just Singapore. We're part of the 3rd biggest ad agency in the world. So we're not thinking small. If the guy's good, so's the money.[33]

The mere presence of the TNAAs, coupled with their business methods and aggressiveness, hurts local advertising entrepreneurs who, like indigenous businessmen generally, are struggling to develop themselves by becoming "modern" while at the same time maintaining a degree of loyalty to their traditions. The widespread TNAA use of bridgeheads, including visualizers, can aggravate already existing class distinctions and create an enclave of Western-oriented, well-paid elites whose values and life-styles are far more oriented toward the happenings of New York, London, Sydney, or Tokyo elites than toward the majority of their own people. An observation from a TNAA expatriate manager about the Malaysian situation seems equally appropriate to Singapore and Indonesia:

> I really do believe that the people creating advertising in Malaysia are a-typical. They normally come from the upper strata of society, and because our trade pays an awful lot of money to people, they are not typical consumers. It's an elite trying to communicate with an enormous mass of people who are very different.[34]

Detailed information about the racial composition of these elites, including the TNAA bridgeheads, is unavailable. It obviously is also a sensitive topic, particularly in Malaysia where communal balance is the political reality: foreigners have the advertising power, Malays have the political power, and the Chinese have the economic power. In 1970, for example, 7 percent of the "professional and managerial" group in Malaysia's manufacturing sector were Malays; 68 percent Chinese; 18 percent foreigners; and 4 percent Indians.[35] My conclusion is that in a relatively sophisticated, Westernized service industry like advertising the racial imbalances are also great. The sketchy information available suggests that most of the locals in prestigious TNAA positions are Malaysian Chinese. Such evidence supports the view within and outside of Malaysia that the Chinese somehow are "more progressive" or "better" than the indigenous peoples in commercial activities—including advertising, which is such an urban-oriented and highly competitive business. My impression from interviewing Malaysian advertising personnel and observing the characteristics of those in advertising is that Malays certainly are greatly underrepresented, particularly in the more senior positions and in jobs other than artist and translator, compared to Chinese and foreigners. In 1977, for example, O&M in Kuala Lumpur had only one expatriate on its staff (the managing director) but the local Malaysian staff was predominantly Chinese. Eleven of the TNAA's thirteen account executives were Chinese, and only two were Malays. Of the agency's local board, four members were Chinese, one expatriate, and one Malay.[36] Historically, the Chinese seem to have benefited more from the government's industrialization and foreign investment policies than have the Malays, and such patterns seem to persist today.

An argument can be made that the TNAAs that continue to rely upon expatriate and Chinese talent are at least indirectly contributing to the major socioeconomic imbalances that are reflected throughout Malaysian society. Through the existing structure, relatively little TNAA know-how—especially in managerial and financial areas—seems to be rubbing off on the Malays.

Continued reliance on expatriates and English-educated Chinese has resulted in continued emphasis on English rather than Bahasa Malaysia, which the government has been trying to promote as a means toward greater national integration, or other vernacular tongues, which must be used to reach many older Malaysians. It also has encouraged the continued use (or "transplantation") of Western themes and images, which the government has been trying to discourage through its "Malaysian identity" efforts.

In addition to the intra-Malaysian group unrest and the competition between Malays and non-Malays, there also exists in Malaysia (and in Singapore, Indonesia, and in many other developing nations) tension between indigenous admen and foreigners. The fact that local advertising agencies are so weak in all three nations and that top positions in most major agencies are held by expatriates creates resentment on the part of the locals—regardless of their ethnicity—who feel they should have more power over their own national industry. Advertising resources, however, are scarce, and in interethnic competition a disproportionate number of Chinese seem to come out on top in all three nations. This situation contributes to tensions and conflicts in which the indigenous admen perceive themselves as losing out to Chinese and expatriates. In both Malaysia and Indonesia, it also tends to isolate the Chinese and make them highly vulnerable to various pressures at the hands of the non-Chinese majority. The 1969 riots in Kuala Lumpur and various anti-Chinese outbreaks in Indonesian cities in recent years dramatically showed how the Chinese can become scapegoats. The Chinese minority in Malaysia and Indonesia seems to fit

Galtung's description of the center in the Periphery as a group that is resistant to change:

> In fact, from a purely human point of view this group is perhaps the most exposed group in the whole international system, on the one hand the pawn and instrument of the center in the Center and on the other hand the exploiters of the periphery in the Periphery. In such a cross-pressure it seems reasonable to expect that the group will sooner or later have to choose sides. Either it will have to relocate and join the center in the Center, or it will have to stand in solidarity with the periphery in the Periphery.[37]

The Chinese majority in Singapore has gone along with the government and joined the Center in mutual efforts to take advantage of Singapore's position midway between two Malay hinterlands. In both Malaysia and Indonesia, the Chinese are very exposed to political cross-pressures, but they have managed to maintain their economic (and advertising) power through various alliances with foreigners and with indigenous ruling elites. Despite these unstable partnerships, particularly between Indonesia's bureaucracy and the Chinese, in neither nation has the level of disharmony within the periphery and within the centers reached the stage where the government would want to either sever its ties with the transnational power structure or seriously redistribute the benefits and the costs of maintaining such relations.

I have shown how the governments in all of these nations have either been unwilling or unable to restructure the way advertising agencies are organized. In Malaysia, for example, rather than cut ties to the transnationals, the government itself has publicly gone out of its way to establish them. The Pernas decision to establish a joint-venture with JWT and operate PTM Thompson on a commercial basis—rather than primarily for social benefits such as providing needed entrepreneurial help to potential middle-class Malays—is an indicator that the government itself wants the TNAAs. In this unique "special relationship" between a prominent American TNAA and three prominent public organizations, the Malaysian government itself serves as a bridgehead. Without the backing of senior government officials affiliated with Pernas, the national airline, and the national tourism organization, JWT probably would not have risked entering the already crowded Malaysian market.

PTM Thompson *is* a commercial success, but it is still too early to say whether it is a social or political success. More time is needed to assess what long-term spinoff effects the venture will have, particularly in terms of more jobs and better training opportunities for Malays or progress toward development of an indigenous Malaysian style of advertising. The ultimate test of the agency's success will be whether the government can eventually transfer ownership of PTM Thompson from government enterprises *and* the TNAA's parent corporation to private Malaysian individuals such as those employed by PTM Thompson or to those without political connections. If the venture only provides a government-sanctioned means by which another TNAA can do business in Malaysia, *or* concentrates nominal Malay equity in large government organizations, *or* serves the private interests of a handful of Malay elites rather than poor Malays (or non-elites generally), then it will not have contributed to any basic changes in Malaysian advertising. It will have only contributed to a reinforcement of existing imbalances and communal tensions, and this may well be unacceptable to the Malay masses who have had such high expectations since the New Economic Policy was implemented after the 1969 disturbances.

Finally, it must be emphasized that in plural societies the institution of advertising—even if in indigenous hands—tends to frustrate efforts to achieve national unity. This is because advertising, by its very nature, is geared toward the interests of the affluent, and it fosters a new consumption society. In the context of Malaysia, Singapore, and Indonesia, advertising is heavily influenced by transnational forces and seems to better serve the needs of Chinese and expatriates rather than indigenous groups. In each of these plural societies, the Chinese and expatriates tend to be concentrated in a few urban centers. They have more discretionary income (and therefore greater buying power) as well as more access to media and to advertised products. The rural-based, poorer, indigenous peoples then might develop desires for consumer goods through their increasing contact with the media (such as Indonesia's new satellite-disseminated television system), and yet such desires—stimulated in part by budget-strong TNC advertising—cannot easily be satisfied for any number of economic and political reasons. The end product of the pursuit of Western consumer patterns can be a feeling of deprivation on the part of people, who may feel influenced not only by foreigners but also by a small foreign-oriented elite from within their own nation.

More research is needed in this area. For example, a breakdown over time of use by various ethnic groups of heavily advertised TNC and non-TNC products would be helpful. If such trend data were available, they probably would show that Chinese and expatriates are generally the best consumers since they are better integrated into the so-called mainstream of modern economic activity than are the poorer, more rural indigenous groups. Advertising messages are understandably geared toward urban dwellers and others who can afford to buy goods and services, and this tends to exclude the poor, who can meet only subsistence needs. Continuing improvement in the dissemination of media and growing sophistication of advertisers and their agencies, however, mean that everyone in the Periphery is being increasingly subjected to persuasive messages (from government, as well as from the private sector).

Throughout Asia, the poor and the parochial *are* coming into continuous, daily contact with diverse kinds of advertising. Their long-run passivity and their ability to withstand such pervasive commercial pressures and to fend off feelings of deprivation *and* antielite resentment remain an open question.

In developing societies like Malaysia, Singapore, and Indonesia, then, goals such as the eradication of poverty, unemployment, and inequality need to be given higher priority. If this is not done, the centers in these and other Peripheries might someday find themselves confronting disorder and mass frustration far more serious than the "routine" tensions and conflicts that they have become adept an containing.

Notes

1. Wherever they operate, the TNAAs tend to use Western research techniques. In Singapore, for example, O&M in 1978 began "Listening Post," a consumer research study conducted exclusively for the agency on a regular basis by a market research firm. The study monitors consumer attitudes and life-styles and is an effort by the agency to make advertising based on scientific knowledge.

2. John Elliott, "How They manage Ogilvy & Mather." (Speech prepared for 4As' Regional Conference, 17 February 1978, pp. 7–8.

3. Ibid., p. 9.

4. Ibid., p. 13. For an overview of TNAAs' expatriate life overseas, see "Lifestyles of Admen Abroad," *Marketing/Communications* 297, no. 9 (September 1969), pp. 51–73.

5. Elliott, "Dear Stockholder," *Ogilvy & Mather International, Inc., Advertising Annual Report,* p. 3.

6. Tom Sutton, "All Advertising is Local; So Why are the Multinational Agencies Peeing in Our Garden?" (Paper prepared for Tenth Asian Advertising Congress, Sydney, 3 November 1976), p. 1.

7. These "common creative denominators" might include the concept, the copy, the visual, and the unique packaging. These aspects of TNAAs' creative strategy are discussed in Jean-Max Lenormand, "What Will Happen to Multi-National Advertising in the Seventies?" *IPA Forum,* no. 33 (January 1971), pp. 26–28.

8. Kenyon & Eckhardt, for example, has a worldwide policy of some local ownership by key executives. In Singapore, for example, the New York-based parent corporation owns 60 percent and in Kuala Lumpur 75 percent.

9. I interviewed Henry Chia in Singapore on 4 November 1977.

10. For example, the old Marklin regional network suddenly collapsed in Malaysia and Singapore. Also, an agency grouping called Circle 5—one agency in each ASEAN capital city—has failed, and the MANA regional network, established in 1976 by seven local agencies from Philippines, Indonesia, Thailand, Malaysia, Japan, Singapore, and Hong Kong, has had its regional problems. For background on MANA, see "An Asian Look for Admen," *Asiaweek,* no. 23 (4 June 1976). The member agency in Malaysia is Idris Lim; in Singapore Pace; and in Jakarta Antara. The latter was closely associated with ANTARA, the government's national news agency. The president was the news agency's secretary-general.

11. For example, while in Jakarta in 1977 I noted that TVRI was using an American-made Coca-Cola commercial rather than, say, a Made-In-Malaysia Coke commercial that might be more culturally relevant to Indonesians. The head of Perwanal Utama, Coke's McCann-Erickson agency in Indonesia, told me that the Malaysian film was not used because Malaysians and Indonesians were different and because Indonesians were more interested in seeing young Americans than Malaysians! The commercial used in Jakarta has an Indonesian sound track but the "international 'real thing' series" theme.

12. The Federation was established at the 11th Asian Advertising Congress, which was held in Manila, November 15–18, 1978. The major force behind the Federation was Antonio R. de

Joya, head of Advertising & Marketing Associates, a major local agency in Manila. De Joya is also a major force behind the MANA network, to which his agency belongs. For several reports on the Manila meetings, see "Special Report," *Media*, December 1978, pp. 17–23.

13. Galtung, "A Structural Theory of Imperialism," *Journal of Peace Research* 8, no. 2, p. 89.

14. Galtung, *The European Community: A Superpower in the Making* (London: Allen & Unwin Ltd., 1973), p. 43.

15. Tunstall, *The Media Are America: Anglo-American Media in the World* (New York: Columbia Univ. Press, 1977), p. 95.

16. Elliott, "How They Manage Ogilvy & Mather," p. 6.

17. Personal correspondence with O&M's Ball, Sydney, 4 April 1978.

18. Personal correspondence with David Bell, managing director, P. T. Perwanal Utama, Jakarta, no date. I also interviewed Bell in Jakarta on 20 July and 12 October 1977. Shortly thereafter, he was transferred to Kuala Lumpur as head of McCann's Malaysian operations.

19. "Grant, Kenyon & Eckhardt Malaysia" (Kuala Lumpur: Grant, Kenyon & Eckhardt Sdn. Berhad, no date), p. 13.

20. Kum, "Madison Avenue to Change Alley: A Route Full of Misconceptions," *Media*, January 1977, p. 28.

21. Galtung, "A Structural Theory of Imperialism," p. 86.

22. Kum, "The Malaysian Case History" (Paper prepared for the Advanced Summer Seminar, on Transnational Communication Enterprises and National Communication Policies, East-West Communication Institute, Honolulu, August 6–19, 1978), pp. 7–8.

23. "Restrictive participation"—economic, political, and social—is discussed as a feature of dependent capitalism in Benicio Viero Schmidt, "Dependency and the Multinational Corporation," in Frank Bonilla and Robert Girling, eds., *Structures of Dependency* (Stanford, Calif.: Bonilla and Girling, 1973), especially pp. 18–19 and 30.

24. See Gunnar Myrdal's use of this concept in his *The Challenge of World Poverty* (Harmondsworth, Britain: Penguin Books, 1970).

25. Sutton, "A Profits' Prophet," *The International Advertiser* 10, no. 2 (2 November 1969), p. 7.

26. Lenormand, "What Will Happen to Multi-National Advertising in the Seventies?" p. 28.

27. Galtung recognizes that the transnational corporations will increasingly be exposed to growing criticism and maintains that "instant communication" will make it possible for the Centers to continue to coordinate their action in the Periphery. See his discussion of the future phase of imperialism in "A Structural Theory of Imperialism," p. 95.

28. Personal interview with Ryuichi Ishino, managing director, Hakuhodo (S) Pte. Ltd., Singapore, 15 November 1977.

29. Kum, "The Malaysian Case History," p. 25. Although more advertisements *were* being made locally, a number only substituted Malaysian models and settings for foreign ones and continued to reflect alien situations.

30. See "The Leo Burnett Organization" (Kuala Lumpur: Leo Burnett Sdn. Bhd., 31 October 1977), p. 7.

31. "Choo Wins Bates' Director Seat," *Media*, May 1977, p. 28.

32. "An Outline of Services" (Singapore: Leo Burnett Pte. Ltd., no date), p. 4.

33. "If You Reckon You're the Pick of This Town's Visualizers . . . Maybe We Could Tempt You with an Apple," *Straits Times*, 25 October 1977, p. 29.

34. Managing Director, Lintas Ltd., Kuala Lumpur, quoted in Bonney, *Patterns of Advertising in Malaysia Today*. (Master of Arts thesis, University of Malaya, Kuala Lumpur, May 1974), p. 164.

35. *Mid-Term Review of the Second Malaysia Plan 1971–75* (Kuala Lumpur: Government Press, 1973), p. 10.

36. This information on O&M, Kuala Lumpur, provided in a personal interview with Stephen Bong, O&M senior account executive, Kuala Lumpur, 28 March 1977.

37. Galtung, "A Structural Theory of Imperialism," p. 108.

11
Shaping the Future

The possibility that societies may be organized in small units
with limited power seems implausible. Adam Smith's model
of a world with little firms and Karl Marx's model of a
society of benign utopian proletariats both seem to me gro-
tesquely implausible. The challenge in social organization is
to ensure that the large units on which our future societies
are likely to be based act as countervailing political powers,
not as mutually reinforcing ones.
—Raymond Vernon, *Sovereignty at Bay*[1]

The question implicitly raised throughout this book has been whether
TNAAs, as a subset of TNCs, are in the business of development or exploitation. Obviously, there is no simple answer, but the subsequent data and
analysis from the advertising boom in Malaysia, Singapore, and Indonesia
have addressed this inherently political question by suggesting that the
TNAAs help maintain advertising inequality and dependence and contribute to a style of development that might not necessarily be in the interest of
the majority of people in a developing society.

The TNAAs in these three Southeast Asian nations, or in China, or
anywhere else are in the business of making money—not nations. They do
help produce political relations within their host nations, and they can be at
least partially understood as part of the "development" problem. The
TNAAs are very successful at making both advertisements and profits and
at fostering economic growth. But the cumulative effects of their commercial activity on nation building sometimes impede national, needs-oriented
development plans, influence governmental actions, and overpower competition from local entrepreneurs.

This analysis of the "Madison Avenue connection" and the structure of
advertising in four Asian nations has suggested that the TNAAs have
power over value-forming institutions within each of these societies except
China, where the evidence is not in yet, and that the overall picture of
advertising remains characteristic of colonialism, with ex-colonies at a disadvantage.

If such an analysis is correct, several broader generalizations about contemporary world politics can be made. First, we live in an age of both increasing mass communications and mass consumerism. We live in an age of large, powerful transnational corporations. We still live in an age of great inequality within and between groups of individuals and nations. We still live in an age of dominance in which old, as well as new, forms of exploitation, fragmentation, and penetration operate to maintain essentially an "old" order. And, perhaps most significantly, we live in an age of emerging mass consciousness in which growing numbers of people realize that things need to be altered if the world is to move toward greater peace and development.

If my analysis of transnational advertising in Asia is valid, it is easy to see how some host nations might consider even responsible TNAAs as part of the problem.

In poor, weak nations—individually and collectively—the large, vertically integrated TNAAs exercise power that gives rise to, or at a minimum indirectly helps maintain, intrasocietal tensions and conflicts. These and other problems certainly would *not* disappear if the TNAAs disappeared, but their high visibility and political salience would diminish if the influence of the TNAAs were reduced. Especially in plural Third World nations, the potential for advertising—dominated by nonindigenous forces—to "do bad," particularly by exacerbating differences between classes and ethnic groups, is greater than in more affluent, homogeneous societies. Like other transnational corporations, the TNAAs are important in their own right as political and media actors and, at one and the same time, are "devils" and "angels." But their major effect on poor societies' internal development processes is maintenance of an uneasy status quo.

As long as the status quo is maintained, the chances of the emergence of a stronger, expanded national communication capacity and of redressing various advertising-related imbalances are slim. In short, as the situation now stands in many developing nations, the possibility of anything resembling an independent, indigenously controlled, national advertising industry or, more comprehensively, a "new communication order" emerging is unlikely. In political terms, this means national development within these societies will likely suffer because old structures fostering such mutually reinforcing problems as poverty and urban-rural gaps remain.

The combination of these factors has made it important that nations in Asia and elsewhere deliberately determine their own advertising directions if genuine development is to be achieved. In such a process, the TNAAs are but one external factor linked to the larger transnational power structure and the economic growth-based Western development package, which needs to be carefully considered through explicit national policies and communication planning. The reasons any nation might want to adequately control the TNAAs can be summarised in two ways:

1. The TNAAs, like other private TNCs and businesses, are *social enterprises* whose existence in the First or the Third Worlds can be justified only insofar as they serve public or social purposes. TNAAs exist in poor nations because someone allows them to do so in the hope that they will benefit someone in some way. Foreign advertising specialists have no right per se to work in another nation.
2. The TNAAs, like other TNCs and businesses generally, are *political systems* whose leaders exercise power, influence, and control. The decisions of the TNAAs have an impact on large numbers of the people reached by their advertising messages and, more indirectly, on national development processes affecting the welfare of society generally.[2]

In the developing world, advertisers—particularly the big TNCs—obviously recognize the power of the TNAAs because they are willing to spend millions annually on their services. Also, political leaders recognise such power. Imelda Marcos, addressing the 1978 Asian Advertising Congress in Manila, undoubtedly spoke for many Third World leaders when she exclaimed:

Like God, advertising and advertisements are everywhere. They literally grow on trees, they light up the sky, they line the streets, they decorate the buildings. They are in everything that people see, read, hear, and wear. One out of three words spoken are advertisements. Here is power indeed!

As if that were not enough, this pervading presence of advertisements is propelled on wings of the most modern vehicles, the megawatts of radio-tv stations, the billions of reams pouring out of printing presses, flown by jet planes, transmitted by satellites.

And what more susceptible audiences, more sweetly credulous viewers are there than the mass consumer markets? They lap up every word, devour every picture and comic strip, absorb every musical note, ready to believe every extravagant claim made on advertisements.

What a formidable, awesome, truly overwhelming power yours is![3]

Mrs. Marcos's comments suggest the significance of advertising power and the need for those in political control to control its use within their borders and for those who wield advertising skills to use them responsibly. When advertising power is largely in the hands of foreigners working for a few large TNAAs and their large TNC clients, it can take on special importance and have unmistakable consequences for national development. In many Third World societies, foreign ownership and control of most major ad agencies is firmly entrenched, and the roots can be traced to colonial communication and trading patterns. The structure of advertising in these nations is highly resistant to change because of a combination of external and internal constraints.

The case of transnational advertising in developing nations like Malaysia, Singapore, and Indonesia is a revealing one because it suggests how nations can almost drift into acceptance of Madison Avenue–style advertising. The lure of TNC advertising, media influences, and other forms of external conditioning is almost irresistible. Ideally, therefore, nations need to carefully deliberate over an organization like the TNAA before it is allowed into a society. In much of the Third World, however, commercial communication influences were present long before political independence. With the important exception of China, few developing nations have had the luxury of being able to operate in a society free of foreign advertising influences.

Given the inter- and intranational aspects of the present order, and recognizing that advertising dependency is a question of degree, what can developing nations do to move along the continuum from perfect dependence to perfect independence in a critical area like advertising?

Toward a New Order?

The deceptively simple route to a new order lies with a clearly articulated national advertising policy. Such a policy would be part of a national communication policy, a concept that L. R. Beltran has defined as a "sufficiently *integrated, explicit* and *durable* set of partial policies organized into a consistent body of behavioural principles and norms for a country's communication activities or processes."[4] In turn, a national communication policy is an integral part of a nation's overall national development policy.

A national advertising policy would deliberately address the planning of the future of advertising generally and of the TNAAs specifically. It would be based on a deliberate assessment of the individual society's advertising *and* development problems and prospects. China could be an exception but few societies have yet been able to systematically develop such an explicit policy on advertising within the broad context of the nation's particular needs, aspirations, and resources. This fact is hardly surprising given the advertising industry's traditional resistance to any government efforts to oversee its activities and many governments' unclear ideas about the preferred kind of advertising (or development).

Developing nations, of course, all have a number of government agencies that get involved in planning activities that affect the TNAAs and broader issues of communication or foreign investment but few seem to have a visible, democratic, formal, and unambiguous national advertising policy that provides a basis for local control over advertising activities. Because of other priorities and the complex, dynamic and interdependent nature of TNAA-related issues, most nations seem content to muddle through with ad hoc policies or policy interpretations. These often emerge on a disjointed, crisis management basis from such diverse, often competing government offices as those responsible for economic planning, trade, foreign investment, information, culture, internal security, health, and immigration. Few policymakers have stopped long enough to ask themselves how advertising purposively and ideally should be organized to complement national development, and advertising seems to have "just happened" in much of the Third World. The result of such an evolutionary process is that coherence and public participation and consultation in national policymaking efforts have often been nonexistent.

Despite these circumstances and the unlikelihood that any Third World nation could become truly autonomous in an area that historically is as transnationally influenced as advertising, even if local elites wanted it to, societies *do* have some unilateral options. All require better planning and more effective national administrative structures, and all need utmost study before adoption. All, too, involve various costs and benefits.

One extreme option is complete *dissociation,* in which a nation deliberately chooses to decouple itself and keep apart from the developed nations as a means of gaining independence and building up its own advertising institutions. Through various "xenophobic," "secessionist," "isolationist" or "noncooperative" actions and policies such as nationalization of the TNAAs, expulsion of all expatriate admen, bans on imported ads, and so forth, a society conceivably could unilaterally produce changes in how it relates to the developed world and the TNAAs. But the nation itself would have to raise the capital and other advertising-related resources domestically, develop its own advertising and related communication know-how, train its own people, and do without foreign talent and imported software. These steps would be difficult, especially if governments are interested in a "favorable" world investment image and are trying to be responsive to TNC advertisers' demands for Western-style advertising services and facilities.

Given contemporary political and economic realities, few nations (or more accurately perhaps, their ruling elites) are willing to tolerate the enormous costs of isolation and inefficiency that such a self-directed advertising order would bring. The more realistic option is an integrative and *associative* strategy, in which the developing nation would, perhaps after an initial phase of dissociation and getting its own house in order, implement policies that would bring it together in cooperative relations with other nations. Such advertising exchange would foster reasonably nonexploitative ties and reflect nationalism.

Carefully conceived and administered by governments that presumably would not be "soft" when it comes to corruption or bureaucratic policy implementation, associative policies do seem to have the potential to foster greater advertising independence and other forms of autonomy and to address the TNAA not as an evil but more as an entity whose relatively great power has led to imbalances that need correcting. Such imbalances include an uneven flow of foreign ownership, foreign managerial influence, foreign cultural values, and overall foreign development patterns. Judicious associative policies and hard bargaining can be used to correct these imbalances and generally give indigenous people a fairer chance at running their own advertising and related industries and services.

Associative policies call for developing nations to be innovative and selective in their associations with the TNAAs and the developed world generally. If a Third World nation is serious about a new internal advertising order for itself, it would need to take some steps to break the hold that foreigners have on local advertising. This is needed to ensure that all ad agencies operating in the nation are "thinking nationally" and are formally controlled by indigenous rather than foreign interests.

An ideal, indigenously generated, national advertising policy might require that only autonomous advertising agencies should be given the privilege to conduct business as a national *service* entity (not only a *sales* entity) with the dual functions of serving client *and* nation. To be truly "autonomous," for example, every ad agency in practice might have to meet broad but straightforward criteria within a policy framework of "corporate citizenship" and national development. Such criteria, which would amount to a corporate social and political code of development conduct, might include these requirements for an agency:

1. It has a majority of its ownership in the hands of people from the Third World host nation.
2. It has its administrative *and* creative decision making processes in the hands of managers who are citizens of the host nation.
3. It may employ noncitizens but only for short terms, only when engaged in formal training capacities, and only after authority for such employment has been expressly granted jointly by both the government *and* the national professional advertising organization.
4. It has explicit corporate goals that reflect creativity, and employment and training schemes designed to accelerate the removal of any imbalances within the society, whether inherited or modern.

If carefully and fairly implemented, such criteria obviously would require *both* foreign and local agencies in many nations to change their outlook and their practice somewhat. TNAAs would be allowed to own up to 49 percent of an agency, and such a requirement would force the nonnational TNAAs into joint ventures with local businessmen or public enterprises. It would also require all foreign admen to serve as advisors and trainers under explicit educational assistance contracts, designed along the lines of existing management contracts but jointly approved by both government and advertising industry representatives. A dialogue then would be established between government and local businessmen. Most significant, compliance with the criteria should serve at a minimum to transfer formal control of agency decision making from foreigners to locals. It should widen the capacity of advertising to define reality and reflect *national* identity (rather than foreign or parochial interests) and to take into account basic indigenous needs and local cultural realities. The vertical division of labor would be abolished since all foreigners in the national advertising industry would be in the Third World not to "do advertising" *on* indigenous peoples but specifically to work *with* and *under* indigenous management in conducting training to help the host nation gain greater advertising power-over-itself. In short, the advertising industry in these developing societies would be forced to learn—perhaps painfully and slowly—to stand on its own feet without being propped up and unduly influenced by the TNAAs. At the same time, the TNAAs would have to act in ways that the host nation would perceive as less antinational. Their goals of profits, growth and consumerism would need to be tailored to fit the developing nation's particular national development needs.

Without incentives from these kinds of national, self-protection criteria, the TNAAs—like other TNCs—could not be expected to conduct their business with the interests of only the Third World in mind rather than the interests of parent corporation and nation. Provided these criteria are applied across the board to all agencies and the developed nations show restraint and do not intervene, the Third World—individually and collectively—might be able to reconstruct advertising so that the institution fosters social, as well as economic, development.

Conclusion

It is hoped that the preceding research and policy-oriented discussion of advertising in Third World Asia will stimulate new areas of interaction and provide more insight into the present and the future of the transnational power structure. It should help First World forces, including ad agencies, to better understand the impact they are making in developing societies. Also, it should assist Third World nations in becoming more conscious of how and why modern advertising virtually began as an American phenomenon, still is one today, and most probably will remain so in the future despite greater talk about the need for a basic reformulation of the role advertising can play for indigenous development.

Without this global perspective on the transnationalization of American advertising and without details about how advertising actually functions in individual Third World societies, those questioning the old advertising order are unlikely to be anything but frustrated in their efforts to quickly bring about changes.

Consciousness formation will not be an easy challenge to meet during this time of uncertainty and difficulty for both world and national economies. The interrelated forces of new life-styles, new technologies, big power politics, and Third World nationalism and regionalism will require time and a greater base of alienation before the deficiencies of advertising at all levels are redressed through alternatives that better satisfy human needs. In the interim, a few large TNAAs will continue to go about their global business as usual promoting the Madison Avenue "model" of advertising and development, and many of their Third World hosts will continue to take political risks by maintaining the status quo and containing tensions in the name of economic development.

Notes

1. Vernon, *Sovereignty at Bay: The Multinational Spread of U.S. Enterprises* (New York: Basic Books, 1971), p. 273.

2. These two axioms are adapted from the work of Robert A. Dahl, "Governing the Giant Corporation", in Ralph Nader and Mark J. Green, eds., *Corporate Power in America* (New York: Grossman Publishers, 1973), pp. 10–11.

3. Imelda Marcos, "A Timeless Gift." (Speech delivered at the 11th Asian Advertising Congress, Manila, 18 November 1978), p. 4. In honor of the regional conference, President Marcos declared 1978 as "The Year of Developmental Advertising and Communications."

4. L. R. Beltran, "National Communication Policies in Latin America." (Working paper for the Meetings of Experts Communication Policies and Planning in Latin America to be held in Bogota in 1974. Paris: UNESCO 14 December 1973), p. 3.

Selected Bibliography

In addition to the materials cited in the notes at the end of each chapter, these citations are helpful in understanding advertising, Asia, international communication, and development issues:

Academy for Educational Development. *The United States and the Debate on the World "Information Order."* Washington, D.C.: Academy for Educational Development, 1978.

American Association of Advertising Agencies (4As). "What Advertising Agencies Are, What They Do, and How They Do It." New York: 4As, 1976.

Anderson, Michael H. "Transnational Advertising and the 'New World Information Order.'" Working Paper no. 7, Transnational Corporations Research Project. Sydney: University of Sydney, April 1980.

Asian Federation of Advertising Associations. *Asian Advertising: 1980.* Manila: Asian Federation of Advertising Associations in cooperation with Philippine Board of Advertising and De Joya Management and Development Corporation, 1980.

Asian Federation of Advertising Associations. *Development Communication and the Asian Imperatives.* Manila: Asian Federation of Advertising Associations in cooperation with Philippine Board of Advertising and De Joya Management and Development Corporation, 1980.

Barnouw, Erik. *The Sponsor: Notes on a Modern Potentate.* New York: Oxford University Press, 1978.

Burnett Company, Leo. "Introduction to Advertising in China." Hong Kong: Leo Burnett Ltd., 1980.

Casmir, Fred L., ed. *Intercultural and International Communication.* Washington, D.C.: University Press of America, 1978.

Cherry, Colin. *World Communication: Threat or Promise?* New York: John Wiley & Sons, 1978.

Fejes, Fred. "The Growth of Multinational Advertising Agencies in Latin America." *Journal of Communication,* Autumn 1980, pp. 36–49.

Fisher, Glen. *American Communication in a Global Society.* Norwood, N.J.: Ablex, 1979.

Gerbner, George, ed. *Mass Media Policies in Changing Cultures.* New York: John Wiley & Sons, 1977.

International Advertising Association (IAA). *Multinationals in Confrontation. How Can Better Communication Help to Meet This Crisis?* Report on the IAA Symposium, Geneva, September 23–26, 1975.

Katz, Elihu and George Wedell. *Broadcasting in the Third World: Promise Performance.* Cambridge, Mass.: Harvard University Press, 1977.

Keegan, Warren J. *Multinational Marketing.* Englewood Cliffs, N.J.: Prentice-Hall, 1974.

Keohane, Robert O. and Joseph S. Nye, Jr., eds. *Transnational Relations in World Politics.* Cambridge, Mass.: Harvard University Press, 1972.

Legum, Colin. *A Free and Balanced Flow: Report of the Twentieth Century Fund Task Force on the International Flow of News.* Lexington, Mass.: Lexington Books, 1978.

Lent, John, ed. *Broadcasting in Asia and the Pacific.* Philadelphia: Temple University Press, 1978.

Mankekar, D. R. *One-Way Flow: Neo-Colonialism via News Media.* New Delhi: Clarion Books, 1978.

Neelankavil, James P. and Albert B. Stridsberg. *Advertising Self-Regulation: A Global Perspective.* New York: Hastings House Publishers, Inc., 1980.

Packard, Vance, *The Hidden Persuaders.* New York: David McKay, 1957.

Rahim, Syed A., ed. *Communication Policy and Planning for Development: A Selected Bibliography.* Honolulu: East-West Communication Institute, 1976.

Read, William. *Rethinking International Communication.* Cambridge: Harvard University Press, 1980.

Richstad, Jim and Michael H. Anderson. *Crisis in International News: Policies and Prospects.* New York: Columbia University Press. 1981.

Righter, Rosemary. *Whose News? Politics, the Press and the Third World.* London: Burnett Books, 1978.

Schramm, Wilbur and L. Erwin Atwood. *Circulation of Third World News: A Study of Asia.* Hong Kong: Press of Chinese University of Hong Kong, 1981.

Smith, Anthony. *Geopolitics of Information: How Western Culture Dominates the World.* London: Faber & Faber, 1980.

Smith, Anthony. *The Politics of Information: Problems of Policy in Modern Media.* London: Macmillan, 1978.

Tiffen, Rodney. *The News from Southeast Asia: The Sociology of Newsmaking.* Singapore: Institute of Southeast Asian Studies, 1978.

Index

Abdullah, Tunku, 226
ACE, 165
Adforce, 170
Advertising, 22, 23, 43, 44, 49–53, 59, 64, 71, 75, 81, 93–96, 190; and alcohol, 174, 194, 196, 221, 276; in Asia, 22, 129–49; in Brazil, 102–3; bridgeheads, 51–52, 302; in China, People's Republic of, 269–93; and colonialism, 50, 80, 130, 132, 143–46, 202, 338; dependence (or dominance), 14, 39–42, 61, 66–67, 138, 143, 261, 297–335, 336, 339; and development, 39–58; and expatriates, 5, 66, 75, 77, 144, 259–62; in France, 113; in Germany, West, 112; in Great Britain, 88; in Indonesia, 153–97; in India, 123–24, 126; and Islam, 180, 194; in Japan, 96–97, 101, 102–3, 108, 113, 132–33, 134, 139; of infant formula, 21, 60, 197; in Malaysia, 198–229; organizations (*see* Advertising agencies; Advertising associations); origins of, 59, 87–89; in the Pacific, 132; and pharmaceuticals, 180, 194, 276, 284; and power, 14, 70–84, 338; public service, 191, 192, 240; in Singapore, 238–63; and social effects, 173–74; 193; in socialist societies, 48–49, 81, 132, 269–94, 318; in Southeast Asia, 113, 129, 132–46, 297, 309; and tobacco, 60, 125, 174, 243, 276, 284, 293; and training, 261; and Third World concerns, 59–69; in the United States, 20, 28, 59, 70, 71, 87–93, 96–100, 103
Advertising, Marketing, and Communications (AMC), 165, 226
Advertising Age, 70, 110, 121, 270
Advertising agencies, 22–23, 71, 75–77, 297; American, 87–113, 133–38; autonomous, 75; Brazilian, 102–3; European, 102–3; French, 102–3, 108, 134; German, West, 102; groupings of, 107–8, 154; in Indonesia (biro reklame), 153, 155; Japanese, 102, 108, 134; nondependent, 75–76; in

the Pacific, 132; in Southeast Asia, 132–46; Swiss, 102; world's largest, 104, 111
Advertising associations, 305
Advertising expenditures, 72; global, 26, 96, 98–100, 107; Indonesian, 160–61; Japanese, 96–100; Malaysian, 204; Singaporean, 245–246; Southeast Asian, 130–31; Third World, 95, 100–101; tobacco, 60; United States, 26, 96–100
Advertising imperialism. *See* Imperialism: advertising
Advertising Media Owners Association of Singapore, 245
Advertising Standards Authority of Malaysia, 214
Advertising Standards Authority of Singapore, 291
Afghanistan, 132
Ajinomoto, 158
"Ali Baba" arrangements, 175
American Express, 90, 163, 211, 270
American Industrial Report, 273
Amoy Canning, 205
ASEAN. *See* Association of Southeast Asian Nations
Asian Advertising Congress, 157, 306, 338
Asian Federation of Advertising Associations, 306
Asian Wall Street Journal, 127
Association of Accredited Advertising Agents (4 A's): in Malaysia, 199, 214, 305; in Singapore, 199, 248, 261, 305
Association of Southeast Asian Nations (ASEAN), 132, 133, 193, 242, 245
Astra Group, 170, 172–73
Australia, 72, 73, 109, 112, 134, 154, 172, 248, 297, 300, 306, 307, 316, 323
Austria, 112
Avon, 112
Ayer, N. W., 281

346